WHAT
CAN WE LEARN
FROM
THE GREAT
DEPRESSION?

*The Long Honduran Night: Resistance, Terror, and
the United States in the Aftermath of the Coup*

*Local Girl Makes History: Exploring Northern
California's Kitsch Monuments*

*Bananeras: Women Transforming the
Banana Unions of Latin America*

*Three Strikes: Miners, Musicians, Salesgirls,
and the Fighting Spirit of Labor's Last Century*
(with Robin D. G. Kelley and Howard Zinn)

*Buy American: The Untold Story
of Economic Nationalism*

*Purchasing Power: Consumer Organizing, Gender,
and the Seattle Labor Movement, 1919–1929*

WHAT CAN WE LEARN FROM THE GREAT DEPRESSION?

STORIES OF ORDINARY PEOPLE & COLLECTIVE ACTION IN HARD TIMES

Dana Frank

Beacon Press
BOSTON

BEACON PRESS
Boston, Massachusetts
www.beacon.org

Beacon Press books
are published under the auspices of
the Unitarian Universalist Association of Congregations.

27 26 25 24   8 7 6 5 4 3 2 1

This book is printed on acid-free paper that meets the uncoated paper
ANSI/NISO specifications for permanence as revised in 1992.

Text design and composition by Kim Arney

*Library of Congress Cataloguing-in-Publication
Data is available for this title.*
Hardcover ISBN: 978-0-8070-4690-6
E-book ISBN: 978-0-8070-4694-4
Audiobook: 978-0-8070-1714-2

To Hamsa Heinrich,
With All My Gratitude

CONTENTS

Introduction ix

CHAPTER ONE
A New Social Order: From Mutual
Aid to Mass Relief Protests 1

CHAPTER TWO
A Tale of Two Caravans: Mexican
Repatriados and "Dust Bowl" Migrants 65

CHAPTER THREE
Whose Labor Movement? The 1937
Chicago Wet Nurses' Strike 113

CHAPTER FOUR
A Nest of Fascists:
The Black Legion in Lima, Ohio 165

Epilogue 229
Acknowledgments 233
Notes 239
Index 297

INTRODUCTION

In a crisis, people lie awake at night trying to imagine a way forward for themselves and their families. They talk to their neighbors; they talk to their loved ones; they listen to the news, to the gossip, to the streets. They read notices pasted to telephone poles or, in more recent times, posted online. And sometimes—sometimes—they hear about a path forward with other people and choose to join them.

During the Great Depression of the 1930s, the US economy almost completely collapsed. By 1933 a third of all those who'd had jobs were unemployed; another third were scraping by with lesser work. Racism, far from collapsing, festered and metastasized as insecurity rippled through the country, pushing people of color even further downward.

I offer here four little-known stories of how ordinary working people, facing the enormous crisis of the Great Depression, responded by taking up creative, powerful, and often visionary collective action. I follow their paths from panicked impoverishment to shining hopes for a better future, through the joys and achievements of their collective projects to the barriers and challenges they faced along the way (including the often unromantic world of actually organizing with other people). As we face our own crises today—a precarious economy, outrageous inequality and poverty, growing racism, climate change—and lie awake at night, facing our own fears, these stories from the Great Depression offer us new and often surprising insights into our own time, our own choices.

Two chapters focus on inspiring, often audacious militance, especially by women. One of them tells the story of seven African American women who worked as wet nurses selling their breast milk to the City of Chicago Board of Health, who daringly staged a sit-down strike at city hall to demand better pay and an end to racial discrimination. It follows their path from hyper-exploitation to empowerment, tracing the sources of their militance deep within South Chicago, in Black women's labor activism, and in the larger labor uprising of the 1930s.

The other one looks at the ways people sought to meet their basic needs nationwide through mutual aid, cooperatives, eviction protests, and demands for government relief—some by building institutions of horizontal reciprocity among themselves, independent of state control; others by making immediate demands on the state—in the process often imagining alternative societies that over and over again looked like socialism, even if they didn't always call it that. In these movements, as in the wet nurses' strike, women's militance lay at the center of working-class activism. Yet both the labor and unemployed movements marginalized women, including their work in the home.

In another chapter, I look at the forcible expulsion—known as "repatriation"—of a million Mexicans and Mexican Americans during the Great Depression. I explore its roots, in part, in farmworkers' successful multiracial union activism, and follow the ways in which Mexican *repatriados* and their allies organized collectively and proudly to survive racist hostility and removal. I contrast their story—which has received extensive scholarly attention but remains largely ignored in mainstream histories of the 1930s—with the exalted, in many ways fictional, narrative of white so-called "Dust Bowl" migrants, who stepped into the jobs vacated by Mexicans.

In the final chapter, I look closely at the Black Legion, a white supremacist fascist group in the Upper Midwest organized by working-class white men (and a few women), whose hundreds of thousands of members believed that racism, antisemitism, anti-Catholicism, and a fascist seizure of the state were the answer to the Great Depression. I zero in on the city of Lima, Ohio, where the legion was founded, and trace its appeal, its activities, and the forces that brought it down—and its chilling legacy today.

I am looking squarely at the hard parts here, as well as the beautiful stories. Collective action during the Great Depression at times meant protest against inequality and racism, or it meant new strategies to simply survive such hostilities. Or it meant finding new ways to blame and oppress others. At its best, it meant powerful new forms of horizontal reciprocity and solidarity through which ordinary women and men, by working together, sought to provide the bread, beans, and comradeship of daily life, drawing on long traditions and new ideas alike. In acting collectively, they built carefully from below, interlocking their lives and visions, planting seeds for the next generation, and laying roots for struggles in our own time. They weren't always successful. But history doesn't move forward that simply: One seemingly obscure, invisible struggle can have enormous impact that's hard to trace. Or it can reappear decades later to offer new inspiration or warn us of sleeping threats.

Together, these stories paint a moving portrait of the Great Depression at the grass roots, deep in the hearts and dreams of working people and their abilities, over and over, to organize themselves and try to improve their lives and their communities. The people who step forward here—poor Black and white people who occupied relief offices demanding food and jobs; Mexican tenant farmers who traveled together to the border with family and friends in caravans of thousands of vehicles; white pipefitters who dressed up in black robes and pirate hats to burn down restaurants owned by Catholic immigrants—contrast sharply with the usual mainstream depiction of poor people during the Great Depression, with its familiar images of passive, hopeless, suffering white men in breadlines or of desperate white farmworkers in rags. Nor do they fit with heroic, progressive images of masses of white male industrial workers who staged sit-down strikes at automobile plants.

The people here are far away, too, from the story of President Franklin Delano Roosevelt and the white elites who designed the New Deal, the enormous package of programs that transformed the federal government beginning in 1933. In my chapters, I trace the uneven fruits of what the New Deal offered each group of working people depending on their gender and race, as it brought enormous and unprecedented gains to some working people—but not all. In some contexts, the New Deal actually produced or exacerbated people's problems, or erected barriers to their aspirations.

At its core, this book is about point of view: both our own viewpoint in understanding US history and the viewpoints of working people during the 1930s. What did the world look like to them? Where did they think the answers to their problems lay? What did the striking wet nurses have to say, for example, when reporters interviewed them? What did cooperative activists dream of? What did Mexican share-croppers in Texas proclaim, as they stepped over the border?

I want to underscore that in writing these stories, I am indebted to the research of hundreds of other researchers and scholars who have provided so many building blocks that made the book possible. Mexican repatriation and the Dust Bowl migration, in particular, have been powerfully analyzed, if separately, as have the unemployed movement, South Side Chicago, and individual ethnic groups' mutual benefit societies. I am also indebted to social scientists who have analyzed the race and gender politics of the New Deal welfare state and labor relations systems. Finally, I am deeply grateful to the hundreds who recounted their experiences in oral histories, and those who interviewed them, making it possible for me to bring forward here the voices of ordinary people and build my writing on the vivid bedrock of their anecdotes, detailed life histories, and frank opinions.

During the 1970s, when historical scholarship on the Great Depression boomed, its authors looked to the 1930s for models of how to build powerful social movements in their own time. I do the same today. But I am also conscious that this book has been written in a darker time, in which racism is viciously resurgent, democratic systems are under attack, and real fascism looms once again. The limitations of the New Deal are also clearer to us now. New themes resonate; new lessons can be learned.

While the four chapters here overlap in theme, each is autonomous from the others. They can be read in any sequence, although they follow a rough chronological order and narrative arc. (I leave it to the reader to discover the three figures who make repeated cameo appearances.) Each chapter begins with a specific focused story, then gradually pulls out to larger comparisons, dynamics, and ripple effects, following stories within stories, by chapter's end carrying us briefly and reflectively to the present.

Together, these stories help us address the challenges of our own time. They help us imagine and construct movements that do not themselves replicate racism and patriarchy. They help us imagine a labor movement, for example, that serves all working people and puts the work and activism of women, especially women of color, front and center. They help us look squarely at the origins of working-class white supremacist fascism and its tentacular politics, in order to combat it. They help us learn from people who fought and survived racist immigration politics in the past. And finally, they help us imagine what our own transformation of the state might look like, in service to the common good.

These are just four case studies, of millions. I offer them as a contribution to our ongoing collective project of learning about the past in order to build a future based on social justice, constructed from the wisdom of working people. I hope we can be inspired by the joyous creativity and militant determination recounted here, through which hundreds of thousands of ordinary people took up collective action and by doing so became part of something larger than themselves, as can we.

CHAPTER ONE

A NEW SOCIAL ORDER

From Mutual Aid
to Mass Relief Protests

I n the fall of 1931, as the nationwide tide of unemployment continued to rise inexorably, fifty men started an encampment along the
docks near downtown Seattle. They chose a sandy lot owned by the
city's Port Commission, where the waters of Puget Sound lapped on
two sides. "We immediately set out to construct a relief system of our
own" in which the residents could "take care of themselves," recalled
a leader. Twice the police burned down all their houses; twice the men
rebuilt. Finally, in June 1932, the city gave them permission to stay.
Word got out, and the encampment's population swelled.[1]

The residents named their community "Hooverville," as did similar
camps throughout the country in the early 1930s, mocking President
Herbert Hoover's ineffectiveness in the face of the Depression. A
researcher in 1934 reported that 455 of its residents were white,
120 Filipino, 29 "Negroes," 25 Mexican, 2 Japanese, 2 "Eskimos,"
2 "American Indian," 3 Costa Rican, and 1 Chilean. Two-thirds of
those he categorized as white were immigrants, overwhelmingly from
Sweden, Norway, and Finland.[2]

Using cardboard, canvas, and discarded construction materials,
much of it donated by sympathetic local businesses, the residents
built little houses for themselves ranging from tiny, leaky shacks that
might smell of fish to an elaborate multiroom home with a flower
box hanging outside. "We discovered that gas tanks from automobiles
made good stoves to cook on when set upon legs and a pipe was fitted

to take care of the smoke," one resident recalled.[3] They covered their interior walls with magazine covers, bits of wallpaper, postcards, and sometimes lingerie ads.[4]

During the day, the men fanned out into the city to make a living, finding odd jobs selling newspapers, working on boats, or fixing shoes. A few built or salvaged tiny rowboats and caught salmon and trout to sell. Some made two-wheeled pushcarts to collect and sell paper that had accumulated in downtown alleyways, or to carry home wood and donations from grocers.[5] Otherwise, the men, mostly older, spent their days tinkering on their houses or hanging out and talking, while drinking a lot. One observer reported "an almost universal geniality, friendliness, and hopefulness."[6] Formerly seamen, cannery workers, lumberjacks, domestic servants, day laborers, and miners, "all that they have ever known have been camps and jungles," one resident emphasized. "The men apparently like to live here."[7]

Donald Roy, a young white graduate student who lived in the camp for a month in 1934, described its race relations as he saw them: "A spirit of camaraderie is carried over racial barriers," he said. "Mutual adversity has brought animosity to a minimum, and white and colored are tolerant if not actually friendly." He wrote that "although spatial and social segregation of the Filipinos and Mexicans is a general rule throughout the village, this sorting may be the result of acquaintance ties and preferences and difficulty of expression in English."[8] In Roy's account, "only rarely would a white be heard to express antipathy toward the colored races, although some believed the depression [was] due to the influx of Filipino labor to the U.S."[9]

Roy also reported that sexual relations between men were "rampant," in his phrase, including same-sex partnerships in which two men shared a household. "Several made no pretense of concealing their 'marital' status" during conversations, Roy said. He himself was regularly "sounded out" about his views on sex with other men by those interested in him, and was propositioned three times. One man offered: "If you live with me I'll treat you fine and get you a good job later on when I get mine back." Another, whom Roy identified as African American, proposed: "Stay with me and I'll hustle you all the food you can eat. I'll bring you chickens, pork chops, oranges or anything you want." Roy counted eleven interracial relationships between men living together. Four of them involved a Mexican man and a white man;

three were Filipino-white, two Black-white, one Black-Filipino, and one "Filipino-Eskimo." He reported: "On many occasions the writer strolled arm in arm up [the camp's] streets with Negroes and Filipinos; his gestures of friendliness were taken for granted."[10] But other residents, Roy reported, "stigmatized" gay sex. One camp leader glared at him, "insinuated that the investigator's interest in his fellow Hooverites was sexual," and threatened, "We're going to run all the punks out of here!"[11]

Although the city barred women from living in the camp, several did anyway; all were described as "elderly," and all but one accompanied husbands.[12] Other women, some of them apparently Native American, visited the camp to work as prostitutes.[13] "I never heard of anybody mistreating any woman who came down here," one resident reported, "but it is not a safe place for them."[14]

Overall, Seattle's Hooverville offered its male residents a remarkably independent experiment in collective life. They were clear that their encampment was a vast improvement over what the do-gooders at the Salvation Army or other agencies had to offer. In a 1938 memoir, Jesse Jackson, a white former logger originally from Texas who had helped found the community, denounced the treatment he and others had experienced at a city shelter, where dinner "resembled pig swill more than it did human food. . . . One week of this kind of abuse was enough."[15] Hooverville, by contrast, offered the space for self-government. The residents chose a six-person committee to manage themselves, composed of two Filipinos, two African Americans, and two whites. Jackson, one of the two white members, was soon identified as the informal "Mayor of Hooverville" and spent his days adjudicating disputes, interfacing with authorities, and bringing in doctors when needed.[16]

Hooverville certainly wasn't perfect. The homes could have rats and bedbugs and were uniformly damp; there was nowhere to bathe. Alcoholism was pervasive. The men shared only four outhouses, perched over the water on pilings reached by rickety wooden walkways, below which raw sewage plopped directly into the Sound or rotted on the beach intermixed with garbage, dead fish, and kelp. Crime was widespread. The residents had their own ways of addressing it internally—in some cases they asked men to leave, then dismantled their houses entirely. But police, fire, and welfare authorities entered regularly to enforce safety codes and arrest people for theft, stabbings, and "drunken brawls." For all Hooverville's successful self-government, Jackson underscored, "most laws are not laid down by us, but for us, by city authorities."[17]

S eattle's Hooverville offers us a vivid example of the ways in which ordinary people, faced with a nonfunctioning economy, a federal government that was utterly failing to address the crisis, and few prospects for a viable economic future, chose the path of collectively managing their needs from below. They chose to "take care of themselves," as the men in Hooverville put it, especially during the earlier years of the Depression before the New Deal stepped in.

A close look at three paths, different but overlapping, through which working people ran their own grassroots organizations takes us deep into that world, into the day-to-day ways in which ordinary people, often without paying jobs or other forms of cash income, found ways to nonetheless provide themselves food, housing, funerals, and haircuts. We look first at mutual benefit societies, organized by an astonishingly wide spectrum of ethnicities—including Mexicans, Jews, Cubans, African Americans, and native-born white people—which delivered burial insurance, health care, ethnic solidarity, and cultural sustenance. A second path lay with consumer and labor exchange cooperatives, which sprang up by the thousands—such as the Young Negroes' Cooperative League in Harlem, directed by future civil rights leader Ella Baker, or a multiethnic network of cooperatives in Los Angeles that embraced ninety-two thousand people in 139 branches, and delivered everything from firewood to shoe repair to cabbages. In both mutual benefit societies and these cooperatives, people constructed vibrant networks "among themselves," and invented new ways to come together in outpourings of creative solidarity, while in many cases building on organizational structures they had shared for decades. They offered dignified alternatives to the hierarchical condescension of charity.

These activists believed they were modeling a future ideal society based on reciprocity and caring. They dreamed of a different way of organizing human life. Over and over, they remarked that their projects brought out the best in people. What did that mean, though, in a larger society rife with racism? How did women fit in—if they were allowed in at all?

A third, enormous wave of organizing during the early 1930s, led by Communists, Socialists, and other leftists, chose a more militant collective path to providing aid. They organized eviction protests, relief protests, and mass marches of the unemployed to demand that the government itself, especially the federal government, deliver relief for working people. They built on the idea of working people's self-management and then expanded it to overtly and militantly challenge the state itself, demanding a transformation of its class politics and using their protests to try to bring about long-term structural social change. Eventually, they flowed toward Washington, DC, to demand a state that didn't just act like an organizing committee of big business but actually served its people. The Communists placed fighting racism front and center in their politics and built thriving and respectful interracial communities at the grass roots. But when it came to fully modeling equality—including between women and men—well, their story is thick too.

In many ways, the unemployed movement was fantastically successful. It helped millions reject the shame of private charity and stop blaming themselves, and instead feel entitled to aid from the government. When Franklin D. Roosevelt finally took office in 1933, the federal government responded to the unemployed movement's pressure and that of additional mass movements of the elderly, veterans, and others, and through the New Deal created the bedrock of the US welfare state.

But those benefits were mostly—if not entirely—designed for white men. The new programs built in racial exclusions that echo powerfully and destructively to this day. And when the New Deal's prizes were handed out, there wasn't much in the bag for women, especially those who worked in the home, and least of all for women of color.

All these grassroots organizations, as they faced the poverty and fears of the Great Depression, struggled with the tension between modeling reciprocity and mutual aid in the present, on the one hand, and on the other hand, using their organizing power to transform the larger system of capitalist rapacity in which they were trapped, as they tried to build a long-term future for themselves and their children. They grappled with the tension between autonomous "self-help" from below, and the powers and potentials of the official government from above. And they lived with the tension between their sincere ideal of harmony among human beings, and the unromantic, messy, often conflictual reality of actually working together.

CULTURES OF ASSISTANCE

The Great Depression generated unemployment and economic fear on a vast scale, worsening year after year. Even before the stock market crashed in October 1929, three million people (around 3 percent of the labor force) had been unemployed. By the spring of 1931 that number shot up to eight million, and by 1933, the worst point of the Depression, fifteen million people, or one-third of previous wage earners, were considered "unemployed." Another third were "under-employed," which meant working for pay at jobs paying well below what they'd received before, or with fewer hours. The ripple effects of unemployment in turn devastated small businesses, farmers, and small landlords. Banks started to fail, five thousand of them by 1933.[18]

African Americans were especially hard hit, as the Depression made their already terrible economic options even worse. "The Negro was born in depression," reflected Clifford Burke, a Black community activist in Chicago interviewed by white radio host and historian Studs Terkel in the late 1960s. "The Great American Depression, as you call it. There was no such thing. The best he could be is a janitor or a porter or a shoeshine boy. It only became official when it hit the white man."[19] A 1931 study of ten US cities reported that 40.5 percent of Black men were unemployed, compared with 27.2 percent of white men.[20] Tens of thousands of those white men were laid off from well-paying jobs in manufacturing, construction, and other sectors. Black men, though, hadn't been allowed into those jobs in the first place; they could only work as porters, janitors, day laborers. Skilled white men who did remain employed were sometimes able to use their unions to fight employers' wage cuts and stop further layoffs. But those same unions usually didn't admit Black workers (or any women), and their white members used union power to keep Black people out of skilled jobs in the first place.

Among women, racial disparities were even higher. In that same study, white women's unemployment rate was 16.8 percent, Black women's 43.4 percent.[21] White women actually suffered fewer layoffs overall than did white men, because some of the sectors in which they worked—garment manufacturing, for example—were less hard hit.[22] Historian Lois Rita Helmbold has shown how white women, themselves restricted to a very narrow range of occupations, began the decade with better jobs than Black women, and then during the Depression bumped Black women down the hierarchy of female jobs—from clerical work to factories to domestic service—and in some cases out of the labor market altogether.[23]

How were working people supposed to survive, without jobs, without cash?

Across diverse cultures, the family was usually the first source of support. One strategy was to combine households across two or three generations. Another was for women to take up the slack by performing more unwaged work at home—canning more food, sewing and patching more clothes, strategizing how to switch from meat to chicken to beans, all while managing the complexities of living with other impoverished relatives in ever-smaller housing units, and performing the emotional labor of trying to hold together their families. Multiple studies found that unemployed men, although they now had more spare time at home, didn't do more housework.[24]

Thousands of families fractured under the pressure. Many men, their wages gone along with their sense of pride as head of the household, left town in search of work—some planning to return, but others fleeing responsibilities, abandoning wives. Shame tore men apart inside. "I used to see men cry because they didn't have a job where they could bring home the food for the children," recalled Adela Navarro, a social worker in San Antonio, Texas. "They were belittled before the eyes of their families and they couldn't take it. And you know that's lowering the pride of manhood."[25]

As the Depression advanced, the marriage rate plummeted. "I was going with someone when the Depression hit," recalled one woman who never married. "We probably would have gotten married. . . . Suddenly he was laid off. It hit him like a ton of bricks. And he just disappeared."[26] The birth rate dropped dramatically, too, as young people felt they couldn't afford to start new households.

The definition of "family" varied widely, as poor people drew on diverse cultural traditions to survive. Chinese men in San Francisco, for example, practiced creative cultures of sharing. Because US immigration policy barred the entrance of almost all Chinese women, the community was overwhelmingly male. Most of them had immigrated to the western United States in the late nineteenth century to take jobs in railroads, mining, and agriculture, and then been driven out of their communities by white mobs. Taking refuge in San Francisco's Chinatown, those who remained after the Chinese Exclusion Acts of 1882 and 1892 were only allowed to live in a few square blocks. Landlords then exploited the situation by jacking up rents. When the Depression hit, many Chinese workers lost their precarious incomes as laundry workers, cooks and waiters, and hotel employees, or could only pick up occasional work.[27]

"During the Depression I was so broke, quite often I was with no money in my pocket," recalled a man named Fong, interviewed by Victor G. Nee and Bret de Bary Nee in the early 1970s. "You wonder how I lived?. . . . We got a room, there's five or six of us and sometimes we pay the rent, sometimes we don't. We got a sack of rice for a coupla dollars and we all cook every day and we eat there. Sometime one night you see forty or fifty guys come in and out, the old guys go to each other's place, sit down, talk all night long before they go to sleep the next day."[28] Their strategy drew on district and village associations carried from China. Wei Bat Liu recalled that in San Francisco, "all the cousins from the Liu family in my village had one big room so all the members could fit in it, and we slept in that room, cooked in that room, one room. Anyone who had a job had to sleep outside the room, because he could afford to rent space and get a bed for himself. Anybody who couldn't find work slept in the beds in this room. At the end of the year, all the members would get together and figure out all the expenses."[29]

Working-class African American people in Harlem organized what were known as "rent parties." Like Chinese immigrants in San Francisco, African Americans who had migrated from the South to New York City in previous decades were segregated into a narrow strip of substandard brownstones and apartment buildings, where landlords charged exorbitant rents. Beginning in the 1920s (by some accounts drawing on an earlier tradition in the South), working-class people who lived in those Harlem apartments started inviting neighbors, friends, and strangers into their homes for informal music and dance parties, usually on Saturday nights, and charging a small fee to make their rent.[30]

A party's hosts would push the furniture back to the walls or move it to another apartment. Women would fry up chitlins, chicken, and fish, make potato salad, pigs' feet, and other side dishes, then place it all on display in the kitchen or on a table to the side. Guests were expected to buy both food and homemade alcohol (it was during Prohibition). A band would show up, and it was time to dance.[31]

Harlem's rent parties were spectacular fun, and soon famous. Women who worked six days a week as domestic servants let loose on Saturday nights and until dawn on Sunday morning.[32] Wallace Thurman, the Harlem novelist, described one couple "doing the 'fish tail' dipping to the floor and slowly shimmying into an upright position then madly whirling for a minute before settling into a methodical slow drag one-step."[33] Jazz pianist Willie (The Lion) Smith recalled: "During these hours close to dawn the dancers would grab each other tightly and do the monkey hunch or bo-hog. . . . The lights would be dimmed down and the people would call out to the piano player, 'Play it, oh, play it.'"[34]

Rent parties also became safe spaces for women and men of wide-ranging sexual identities and interests to express themselves and explore new possibilities. The singer and performer Mabel Hampton recalled of her visits: "Some man over there was kissing another one. A woman over there was kissing another one. Boy—everybody was kissing. Seen the rest of them do it, what the hell, I'll do it too." She described all kinds of play. "The bulldykes would come and bring their women with them. And you wasn't supposed to jive with them, you know. They danced up a breeze. . . . I just had a ball."[35]

As Harlem's rent parties exploded in the early 1930s, they became famous incubators of jazz, blues, and other musical styles, where performers practiced their crafts, learned from each other and from interactions with partygoers, and augmented their incomes. Fats Waller, Bessie Smith, Jackie "Moms" Mabley, and Duke Ellington all played the parties. "They used to hire me to play when I was very young," recalled jazz pianist and composer Thelonious Monk. "They'd pay you about three dollars and you'd play all night for them. And they'd charge admission to people who would come in and drink. That's the way some people used to get their rent together, like that."[36] During an otherwise terrible time, rent parties were a key way for poor Black people to pool their wealth, transform domestic labor into cash, and seize life.

Finally, churches and other faith-based institutions remained an essential source of spiritual as well as material sustenance throughout the decade. In Black Protestant churches, for example, women's committees visited struggling families in their homes, carrying neighborly concern, faith in the power of God, and baskets filled with food. Catholics, Jews, and Protestants donated to national-level organizations such as the National Catholic Social Welfare Council, the Central Committee of American Rabbis, and the Federal Council of Churches.[37] But in larger congregations, faith-based assistance could often take the form of charity that, in its hierarchal framework of benevolent grantor and grateful recipient, was something quite different from grassroots mutual aid among equals.

INSTITUTIONALIZED RECIPROCITY

Wei Bat Liu was careful to point out that he and his cousins in San Francisco had survived because of the village association they brought with them from China. As millions of working-class people confronted the Great Depression, they turned to a resource that provides our first, large-scale example of collective provision of basic needs from below: mutual benefit associations, also known as voluntary or mutual aid associations. Usually organized on the basis of racial/ethnic identity, mutual benefit societies delivered concrete services to their members in exchange for dues payments, augmented by fundraising. In many cases, their original and most basic function was to provide for funeral and burial expenses. Some also provided cash or loans to unemployed members, advice and succor in hard times, or health care—even hospitals. Many were dedicated to preserving beloved cultures and languages. All provided a deeply rewarding sense of community in action.

The scale of mutual aid associations, carried to the US by peoples from Asia, Europe, and Africa beginning in the eighteenth century, was immense. In 1930, they counted 124,000 different groups with 10.8 million total members. In a 1920 survey, one in three men in the entire country belonged to a mutual benefit society; the percentage was even higher among working-class men. Lithuanian immigrants in Springfield, Massachusetts, alone, for example, formed sixty benefit associations by 1910.[38]

It's easy to dismiss these mutual aid associations as old-fashioned or even boring—as more staid, somehow, and less potentially transformational than other forms of political action. But to their founders and to the ordinary people who sustained them for decades and decades, they were thriving cultural and social spaces that modeled the good society, in which community members took care of each other on an intensely local scale, outside the sphere of profit-making. Some of the largest were in fact self-consciously devoted to getting rid of capitalism and replacing it with socialism or anarchism.

Take the Italians. As millions of people, overwhelmingly poor, migrated from Italy to the US in the late nineteenth and early twentieth centuries, they brought traditions of what they called *società di mutuo soccorso* (mutual assistance societies) from their home villages, fusing material aid with religious practices that drew on pre-Christian imagery as well as Catholicism. They commissioned sculptures of the patron saints of their hometowns, carried the figures across the sea to the US with great devotion, and placed them carefully on display in meeting places that ranged from kitchens to basements to storefronts to saloons and, eventually, their own halls, where they danced, sang, drank, told stories, and ate luscious food produced by the womenfolk, who cleaned up afterward.

For these Italian immigrants, mutual aid societies were a conscious extension of the family. "These urban clubs absorbed certain functions which the family had performed in the Old World," writes historian Virginia Yans-McLaughlin in her 1971 study of Italians in Buffalo, New York, "especially when death, sickness, or unemployment occurred."[39] When the Depression hit, Italian mutual benefit societies continued to provide essential services, loans, and cash payouts to their members.[40]

Throughout the US Southwest, and soon spreading north and westward, Mexican immigrants and people of Spanish and Mexican origin formed mutual aid societies, too, drawing on traditions developed by artisans' guilds and village associations in Mexico, and before that in Spain. Known as *mutualistas*, these societies provided burial insurance, short-term loans, payments for the disabled, and help for those looking for work. At the same time, they built community cohesion in the face of the poverty and racism that surrounded them. As historian Emilio

Zamora notes, "Mutualista organizations . . . gave their members and communities a sense of belonging and refuge from an often alien and inhospitable environment."[41] Their members, he writes, viewed the organizations' financial benefits as the embodiment of their larger ideals of altruism, harmony, and reciprocity.[42]

Mexican and Mexican American mutualistas became thriving centers sustaining Mexican culture. They sponsored dances, guest speakers, and celebrated Mexican national holidays; built their own libraries and schools; taught their children about Mexican history and fostered pride in being Mexican. Men largely dominated the mutualistas' top leadership. But women played key roles, not only cooking and decorating for all those celebrations and cleaning up after them, but as journalists, editors, and guest speakers.

Many, if not all, mutualistas were composed of working-class people who self-consciously understood themselves as workers and used their organizations to support strikes. By the late 1920s, the mutualistas were functioning as proto-labor unions throughout the Southwest, their orators consciously fusing the family, the fraternal society, and the workers' movement. Sara Estela Ramírez, a Laredo teacher, poet, and writer originally from Saltillo, in the Mexican state of Coahuila, speaking at a local society's anniversary, called on members to tap into their "spiritually innate altruism"; to remember that "their arms maintain the wealth and growth of industry"; and to draw on "something grand, something divine, that will make us sociable, that will ennoble us as human beings."[43]

Similarly, tobacco workers from Spain, Italy, and Cuba formed associations in late nineteenth-century Tampa and Ybor City, Florida, that were thriving when the Depression began. These groups started out as social clubs organized on the basis of specific national identities, promoting internationalist visions of anarchism and socialism, then came to share both resources and revolutionary ideas across lines of national origin and language. Visiting speakers included Luisa Capetillo, the famous Puerto Rican anarchist labor leader, and top leaders of the Industrial Workers of the World (Wobblies) such as Irish American Elizabeth Gurley Flynn and Italian immigrant Carlo Tresca. By the 1930s, the associations owned a magnificent 1,200-person theater with velvet seats that offered opera performances, a bar, and a library. They had a bowling alley, a gym, and dance halls, and provided fully developed mutual aid services including cemeteries and two hospitals, one with sixty beds.[44] These societies, though, "protected and promoted the idea of the supreme Latin male," historians Gary Mormino and George Pozzetta concluded. "Women's auxiliaries existed to serve the male members."[45]

The most highly developed mutual aid system among left-wing immigrants was the Arbeiter Ring (known in English as the Workmen's Circle), organized by working-class immigrant Jews. A closer look reveals its impressive ability to deliver for its members, its gender politics, and its members' efforts to square the circle of simultaneously constructing a beautiful socialist future and modeling socialist practices in the here and now.

The emotional power of the Workmen's Circle shines through in a booklet celebrating its thirty-fifth annual convention: "On Sunday May 5, 1935, the sidewalks of New York were thronged with Workmen's Circle members, all bound for Madison Square Garden, to attend the opening of the Thirty-fifth Jubilee Convention of their organization," exulted the booklet's author, Maximilian Hurwitz. "They filled the vast auditorium to the rafters, . . . a happy holiday-attired crowd, more than twenty thousand strong. . . . Suddenly the air was rent by the roll of drums, the call of trumpets, and the crashing of cymbals; and to the heroic strains of the *Internationale*," as almost a thousand official delegates—from Appalachia, California, Florida, the Gulf of Mexico, Louisiana, Maine, Manitoba, Oregon, Pittsburgh, Quebec, Texas— marched into the hall "bearing banners, crimson, gold-embroidered, glorious; and the vast multitude, waving little pennants, greeted them with salvo after salvo of applause and cheers." The Women's Club Branch then marched in, followed by teachers and students from the Circle's Yiddish schools, then the children who belonged to its English-speaking clubs. "And now all the links in the three-ply chain of gold which binds the member, his wife, and his children to their organization were in their places," rejoiced Hurwitz.[46]

Founded in New York in 1892, the Workmen's Circle had grown by the 1920s to eighty-five thousand members in 750 different branches. It was strongest in the New York area but spread all over the US and Canada among immigrant working-class Jews, who founded the Circle as an explicitly socialist body. "Our idea was not only to look after a sick man with a dollar a week," one early member wrote. "Our aim was a much higher, deeper, and broader one . . . a more beautiful world with a better society, a society where people would be secure in their lives, but cared for in life."[47] Its first general secretary, Benyomen Faygnboym, expounded in 1901 that the Circle's members were dedicated to "freedom of thought and aspiration, workers' solidarity, and faithfulness to the interests of their class and its struggle against oppression and exploitation."[48]

In practice, achieving socialism with the help of the Arbeiter Ring in part meant the classic practices of mutual aid, on a grand scale. It offered its members death benefits, health care, medical clinics staffed with two dozen doctors, and a tuberculosis sanatorium in Liberty, New York. It had its own bank and its own cooperative apartment buildings. On the eve of the Depression, its life insurance fund held $5.5 million in reserves. By 1934, the Arbeiter Ring had paid out nearly $9.6 million in debt and disability relief. Between 1929 and 1935, it paid out $250,000 to unemployed members.[49]

In the Circle's earlier years, though, some in the Jewish immigrant community had objected that providing such material benefits would undermine the more important long-term struggle for socialism. As historian Judah Shapiro writes, these critics believed that "the social revolution . . . would dissolve the very problems that lodges and mutual aid societies were dealing with, and the formation of such a new organization among the workers was seen as a dissipation of energy and a distraction from the larger goals."[50]

By the 1930s, the members of the Workmen's Circle had settled comfortably into self-consciously left-wing secular Judaism. Its branches celebrated the Jewish holidays of Passover, Chanukah, Purim, and Succoth, and also May Day (International Workers' Day), the Fourth of July, Lincoln's Birthday (marking, they said, the "Emancipation of the Negroes"), the anniversary of the founding of the Paris Commune, and the anniversary of the Russian Revolution (for which they allowed a local option of celebrating in either February or November). The Circle remained inseparable from the Jewish labor movement, which counted millions of members in this period, especially in the garment industry of New York. (Members of the Circle could be expelled for strikebreaking.)[51] Hurwitz estimated in 1936 that "its contributions to strike funds have been known to run into sums of five figures."[52] The Circle also generously funded the Socialist Party (with which its membership overlapped), Jewish refugees in Europe, and *The Messenger*, edited by African American labor leader A. Philip Randolph.[53]

Worried, by the 1920s, about keeping their children in the fold, the Workmen's Circle set up 104 schools teaching Yiddish and Yiddish culture after school and on the weekends. According to their 1919 Pedagogical Principles, the schools would "acquaint them with the life of the worker and the Jewish masses in America and other countries," and "cultivate in them a feeling for justice, love for the oppressed and for freedom, and respect for fighting for freedom."[54]

The Workmen's Circle wasn't all one big equal socialist family, however. As with all these immigrant mutual aid associations, the original membership was for men only; female affiliates were subsumed under their husbands. (The organization didn't change its name to the "Workers Circle" until 2019.) When women did participate in meetings, their voices were ignored; meanwhile, their responsibilities in the home made it difficult to carve out time to attend at all. Perhaps most egregiously, women didn't receive most benefits, even through their husbands. When women did eventually receive medical care, male leaders excluded what they deemed "women's diseases" and left out pregnancy and childbirth altogether. In the Workmen's Circle, as in other immigrants' mutual aid societies, the family as metaphor implied a patriarchal family, in which women were subordinate to men.[55]

Jewish women nonetheless fought hard for a place inside the Circle, historian Mary McCune has shown, and gradually expanded their own independent spaces whether in subordinated women's auxiliaries, as prescribed by their menfolk, or through their own independent Women's Clubs. They raised money for health-care facilities, for strikers, and for Jewish refugees in Europe. Within their female branches they organized lectures, dance lessons, singing groups, and drama clubs. In Rochester, New York, they organized "herring and potato dinners" to raise funds for a lecture series.[56] On the eve of the Depression, they founded and ran a new Social Services Department, which offered legal aid, mental health services, advice on childcare, and other services that helped two thousand people a year during the Depression.[57]

Native-born white people of Northern European descent also organized mutual benefit societies. Here is where the really big numbers come in: in 1930, the six biggest all-male fraternal orders in the US together counted 7.5 million members (out of a total US male population of 55 million, including children), including the Loyal Order of Moose, International Order of Odd Fellows, and the Knights of Pythias. These organizations, like other ethnic groups' aid societies, offered burial insurance, life insurance, and in some cases, medical care or loans during hard times, as well as the opportunity to enjoy community-building through secret rituals of male bonding, uniforms, and marching in parades.[58]

They also gave men who identified as white a way to draw a circle around themselves and keep out those who they identified as nonwhite. Consciously and assiduously, almost none of the white native-born men's associations admitted people of color.[59] They also would have excluded many immigrants from Southern and Eastern Europe considered nonwhite at the time, such as Italians and Greeks.[60] "Theirs was an egalitarianism made possible by the exclusion of women, blacks, and ethnic minorities from the relevant social universe, a universe whose boundaries fraternal institutions helped to demarcate and guard," writes Mary Ann Clawson in *Constructing Brotherhood*.[61] Most mutual benefit associations in the United States were organized on the basis of a specific ethnic/racial identity. But the exclusions constructed by white native-born men carried serious power that those of other groups did not: white men's membership in fraternal orders overlapped with membership in labor unions, local businessmen's organizations, and informal social networks that enforced job exclusions, housing discrimination, segregation in transportation, and a host of other forms of racism, both personal and institutionalized. White native-born men had access to far greater economic resources, both as individuals who could get better jobs and housing, and as a group. White women, for their part, responded to white men's gender exclusions by forming their own parallel organizations like the Ladies of the Maccabees, which had two hundred thousand members in 1920 and fought for the rights of women while glorifying the home.[62] But white women, too, were quick to turn around and themselves exclude women of color.

Mutual aid societies among African Americans boomed in the late nineteenth century and early twentieth centuries, too, drawing on African collectivist traditions as well as the example of European fraternal orders. Black mutual aid societies started with burials and health care and then expanded into banks, stores, newspapers, and homes for the elderly, widows, and children, as did other ethnic groups.

But African American mutual aid societies, like Black churches, also provided crucial independent spaces away from white domination, as did the Mexicans' mutualistas.[63]

The largest Black associations audaciously matched the names of the white ones from which they had long been excluded. Their own, independent Odd Fellows, for example, in 1910 counted three hundred thousand members, or over 11 percent of all Black men in the United States. Each of these male groups in turn worked closely with affiliated women's organizations founded jointly, such as the Order of Calanthe, the female partner to the African American Knights of Pythias. The largest independent organizations were the United Brothers of Friendship, based in Louisville, and its partner, the Sisters of the Mysterious Ten, which at one point had 250,000 members.[64] A surviving photo of one Sister shows a middle-aged woman, Dinnie Thompson, wearing a long-skirted uniform with curlicues embroidered on it, a military cap, white gloves, and a long sword hanging at her side.[65]

Maggie Lena Walker, the most powerful female leader in the Black mutual aid societies, directed the woman-led Independent Order of St. Luke, which grew to one hundred thousand members in twenty-six states, and founded the prominent St. Luke Penny Savings Bank in Richmond, Virginia. She promoted a "womanist consciousness," historian Elsa Barkley Brown has written in a classic 1989 essay, that both empowered Black women and challenged Black men to join with them as equals in struggle and in economic life, in order to lift up the whole Black community. "The Saint Luke women challenged notions in the black community about the proper role of women; they challenged notions in the white community about the proper place of blacks."[66]

The Depression fundamentally tested all these societies, heightening demands on their resources. They needed to deliver benefits at higher and higher levels, right when members increasingly had problems making the weekly or monthly dues payments on which the associations' collective financial edifices depended. Immigrant parents felt their children drifting away from their language and culture, and toward the new mass culture attractions of radio, the movies, and other commercial entertainments. Some mutual aid associations were in fact a bit stodgy by the 1930s. The printed programs of the annual banquets organized by local branches of the Workmen's Circle in New York, for example, show photos entirely of older men in suits, who bought display ads for their small businesses.[67] The big threat, though, was the rise of for-profit commercial life and burial insurance in the 1920s, peddled door-to-door by salesmen throughout the country, which undercut the bedrock benefit offered by mutual aid societies. Beginning in early 1933, moreover, massive government relief from the Roosevelt administration supplanted many of the functions of mutual aid.[68]

None of that diminishes the impressive power and scope of mutual aid societies in their prime during the early Great Depression—not just those surveyed here, but the societies built and sustained by Swedish, Puerto Rican, Japanese, Slovak, and Filipino people, and hundreds of other ethnic groups. We're taught that US history and culture are all about individualism—bootstraps, rugged men, the pioneer with his axe. But over and over again, members of mutual benefit societies dedicated themselves to the opposite: to horizontal reciprocity institutionalized from below by ordinary people through organizations they managed themselves. Over and over again, they invoked the same values of fraternalism, of sharing, of mutuality. The similarities across diverse peoples are remarkable—including male dominance, and women's challenges to it. And yet at the same time, these associations were extremely culturally specific; indeed, they were usually dedicated to preserving and expanding their specific culture. Their meeting halls dot our landscapes today, still providing spaces for weddings, quinceañeras, graduation parties, visiting speakers, and grassroots activism for social justice.

BUILDING A NEW COOPERATIVE ORDER

The Great Depression very quickly ignited another nationwide push for collectively provided aid from below, in which tens of thousands of diverse people turned to consumer and barter cooperatives—both as a way to feed themselves, and, for many (but certainly not all), as a way to transform the economy. The cooperative movement takes us deeper into the Depression itself, and into the messy, unromantic world of actually figuring out how to run grassroots organizations. Here, too, the impulse for socialism emerged, if often by other names. But the more powerful that impulse grew, the more it served as a red flag to the powers that be, threatening a surprising cast of characters who soon sought to restrain, capture, and destroy the cooperatives.

Today the cooperative movement isn't usually associated with revolutionary Black liberation, but during the Great Depression it was. In New York City in 1930, George S. Schuyler, a famous African American journalist with a prominent column in the Black-owned *Pittsburgh Courier*, launched an organization he called the Young Negroes' Cooperative League, and hired as its executive director twenty-seven-year-old Ella Baker, who would later become a famous leader of the Civil Rights Movement. Baker had by that point been living in Harlem for six years, thriving in its exploding and visionary sea of African American radicals—Socialists, Communists, followers of Marcus Garvey, and diverse Black nationalists—while remaining herself independent, her biographer Barbara Ransby has shown.[69]

Both Schuyler and Baker, Ransby underscores, viewed consumers' cooperation as an immediate way to address Black poverty during the Great Depression, and more deeply as a path to fundamental social transformation and the empowerment of African Americans, especially young people. "We are called upon to be in the vanguard of the great world movement toward a new order," Baker exhorted in September 1921.[70] A year later, in a letter to the League's membership, she argued that through cooperatives, "the Negro can and will save himself from economic death."[71] Schuyler, in a widely distributed pamphlet called *An Appeal to Young Negroes*, argued that "co-operative democracy" meant that the "means of production, distribution and exchange would be owned cooperatively by those who produce, operate, and use them."[72] In his view, the Young Negroes' Cooperative League promised to be "the most truly revolutionary the Negro race has launched in its entire history."[73] Black activists like Schuyler and Baker drew on a long tradition of Black cooperatives that pioneering sociologist W. E. B. Du Bois, in a book-length 1907 report, *Economic Co-operation Among Negroes*, understood as part of the same larger project of collective empowerment as Black-controlled mutual benefit associations, churches, schools, and banks.[74]

In practice, it was Ella Baker, not Schuyler, who took up the painstaking work of building a full-fledged organization. She set up educational programs, outreach projects, and helped found twenty-two branches of the League extending to the New York cities of Albany, Buffalo, and Elmira, as well as Detroit, Kansas City, Cleveland, Cincinnati, Philadelphia, Pittsburgh, Baltimore, Santa Barbara, Washington,

DC, and small towns in Pennsylvania and Ohio, counting four hundred members by 1932. Groups affiliated with the League soon included a grocery cooperative and a milk cooperative in Harlem, buying clubs in Philadelphia and Cincinnati, and plans for a grocery store in Columbia, South Carolina, a "fresh egg club" in New York City, and in Washington, DC, a "combination shoe-shine parlor and cleaning [and] pressing establishment."[75] It's largely unclear, unfortunately, how exactly these cooperatives functioned.

Deploying the skills she would later employ in the NAACP and the Student Nonviolent Coordinating Committee, Baker encouraged members to build careful alliances with already-existing organizations in the Black community, including the Brotherhood of Sleeping Car Porters, Urban League, National Federation of Colored Women's Clubs, Black sororities and fraternities, the NAACP, the Housewives' League, and Domestic Workers' Union of New York, drawing on networks of both African American women and white women. To keep the larger organization cohesive, she planned travel to chapters in far-flung states to provide advice and support.[76]

But for all of Baker's sophisticated organizational skills, she remained hemmed in by the movement's men. In theory, the League was committed to gender equality. "There shall be no distinction between males and females," its bylaws declared.[77] Delegates to its first convention, in October 1931 in New York City, passed a resolution affirming that "we seek to bring women into the League on equal basis with men"[78] Those statements, though, may have been promulgated (by Baker, we can guess) in response to growing gender discrimination. One early list of nationwide members shows two-thirds were men and one-third women, who were largely listed as "Miss."[79] But at that October 1931 convention, twenty-seven of thirty delegates were men, only three were women; the twelve-member newly elected Executive Board of the League counted eleven men, plus Baker.[80] At the local level women did appear in prominent roles; at an event presented by the League's New York branch, for example, men provided the "Welcome" and served as the master of ceremonies, while Schuyler, Baker, and another woman gave speeches.[81] The program of a Columbia, South Carolina, event, though, listed twelve all-male officers and only male speakers.[82]

Despite Baker's deep commitment to alliance-building, however, her boss George Schuyler was trouble. He enjoyed being confrontational and was overtly hostile to the Black church, the YMCA, the Black middle class, and almost all extant organizations in the African American community. He forbade the Young Negroes' Cooperative League from seeking or accepting endorsements, funds, or even meeting space from "any other organization or institution."[83] As a result, in part, there was never enough money in the League's coffers—for an office, for Baker's salary, for her travel. There are hints, too, within individual co-ops of a tension between democratic, grassroots enthusiasm and the technical challenges of financial management. One undated letter to the League's board of directors from "Harlem's Own Cooperative" concluded: "I feel like we have been too co-operative practically to the point of being unbusinesslike and that until we throw sentiments out of our affairs we cannot hope to approach the goal we are hoping for."[84] Running on Baker's volunteer labor, with no funds to launch cooperatives or even to sustain internal communications, the League collapsed by 1933, although a few of the individual co-ops with which it was associated apparently survived for some time.[85]

Meanwhile, Black cooperative enthusiasts in the East looked to a successful cooperative in Gary, Indiana, as their model. In 1932, an African American high school teacher named Jacob L. Reddix happened upon a classic 1921 book in the Gary public library entitled *Consumers' Co-operative Societies*, in which a Frenchman named Charles Gide extolled cooperative grocery stores, farmers' cooperatives, credit unions, and other forms of cooperation that had flourished throughout Europe. The book transformed Reddix's life. He threw himself into studying economics and started visiting cooperative leaders all throughout the Midwest. "I concluded from my studies that a cooperative system might well be a way out for black people who were entrapped by unemployment, poor wages, and economic exploitation in the United States," Reddix wrote in a 1974 memoir. "If the black workers could pool their purchasing and productive power they might lift themselves by their own boot straps."[86]

Reddix started a study group that met at Roosevelt High School every week for eighteen months, "for the purpose of finding a solution to the serious plight of the Negro population which resulted from the depression," wrote economist John Hope II in 1940. Soon calling themselves the Consumers' Cooperative Trading Company of Gary, the group formed a buying club and then a retail cooperative. A Women's

Guild offered two extremely popular adult classes at the high school, "History and Philosophy of Education" and "Organization and Management of Cooperatives." By 1934, the co-op included over four hundred members, employed seven people at its store, and had launched a gas station and credit union as well. Working-class African Americans who'd been laid off from the local steel mills formed its core. Reddix later wrote that in 1936 the Gary cooperative "was said to be the largest grocery business operated by Negroes in the United States."[87]

Other small cooperatives popped up all over the Upper Midwest. In Chicago, a group of African American postal workers and professionals who all lived in the same apartment building started discussing alternatives to the local chain grocery store, which was using its monopoly power to overcharge those who lacked transportation to shop elsewhere. Advised by Jacob Reddix from Gary, they launched a cooperative buying club in October 1936, starting with "eleven pounds of bacon which was enthusiastically divided among ten members. Each person received one pound, and all drew straws for the privilege of buying the extra pounds." Run by the part-time labor of two women, the co-op functioned for eight months out of the basement of their apartment complex. By decade's end, the group had 191 members and was running a store in a converted garage.[88] "There was no need for a leader," wrote one member in 1939. "Mutual confidence and respect for our group techniques has [sic] been the life of our society."[89]

RECIPROCAL ECONOMY

These organizations formed by African Americans—and there were dozens more—were just the tip of an iceberg of enthusiasm for consumer cooperatives nationwide during the 1930s, especially in the decade's earlier years. Producer cooperatives, especially among farmers, grew on an immense scale as well, their story unfortunately beyond our scope here. Those who founded consumer cooperatives often understood their projects as immediate mutual aid; outsiders spoke of them as "self-help," in which people came together to ensure basic necessities, especially food. But as with the mutual benefit societies, many of the founders also saw their projects as the seeds of a deeper transformation of the nation's economic life, through which they were building "a new order," as Ella Baker put it.

The cooperative movement in the US dates back to the 1840s, when a group of English textile weavers known as the "Rochdale Pioneers" developed a codified model for how to democratically manage cooperatives, using a system in which every member had one vote, and no one made a profit. The Rochdale model spread worldwide into a loosely affiliated federation of Rochdale cooperatives that by World War I counted over four million members in the US, and influenced far more.[90] Jacob Reddix's cooperative in Gary, Indiana, for example, modeled its bylaws on the Rochdale principles, as did the Young Negroes' Cooperative League.[91] During the 1860s–1880s, industrial workers and other workers in the northeastern and midwestern US formed cooperatives on a huge scale, especially through the Knights of Labor, which organized hundreds of cooperatives in thirty-five states.[92] Adherents of these cooperatives overlapped with a broad range of other political movements of the time, from trade unions to farmers' associations to anarchists and socialists. In Western Europe, the workers' cooperative movement boomed so powerfully that by the 1910s in France it became understood as one of the "three pillars" of the socialist movement, along with the labor movement and the political party.[93]

Our most comprehensive source on the US cooperative movement that flourished in the 1930s remains Clark Kerr's 1939 dissertation, entitled "Productive Enterprises of the Unemployed, 1931–1938." Kerr would go on to become the chancellor of the University of California, Berkeley, during the 1950s and then president of the University of California until 1967. White, self-assured, an assiduous overachiever (his dissertation numbered 1,296 pages), Kerr meticulously documented consumer and producer cooperatives throughout the country during the Great Depression, excluding the agricultural sector. He was especially interested in organizations during the early years of the decade that used barter-and-scrip systems—involving donated labor, gleaned agricultural products, and a system of internal currency—to provide food and other necessities. Kerr counted over four hundred such organizations in the US by 1934, involving half a million people.[94]

One of the largest projects of the barter-and-scrip variety was the Unemployed Exchange Association (known as the UXA) in Oakland, California. It began in 1932 when an unemployed white electrical engineer and orchestra conductor named Carl Rhodehamel visited an encampment by the waterfront in East Oakland where hundreds of unemployed people were living in sections of abandoned sewer pipe. Rhodehamel convinced a group of its residents to go door-to-door in the neighborhood with gunnysacks and offer their labor repairing homes, in exchange for whatever junk people might want to get rid of from their garages. By 1933, the project had expanded to 1,500 members and provided food, clothes, firewood, auto repair, day care, barber services, health and dental care, and sometimes housing. It also ran a foundry and machine shop, a soap factory, and a food canning operation.[95] Its members appear to have been all white, its elected officers middle class—an accountant, a stock and bond salesman, a laundry manager, and a publicist for Pacific Gas & Electric. The appointed officers, though, included a machinist, an aviator, an auto mechanic, a painter, a draftsman, two housewives, a former bookkeeper, and a truck driver. Rank-and-file members were all over the map in terms of class and included many of the long-term poor.[96]

Together they managed it all through an elaborate system they called "Reciprocal Economy," in which members gained credit for labor hours and then exchanged those credits for goods and services. Eventually, the UXA sprouted affiliated branches all over the Bay Area and to the east and drew in agricultural products from the far hinterland—peaches from Turlock, raisins from Fresno, wood from Prather. An additional array of smaller, unaffiliated food-distribution co-ops sprouted up all over the region, organized by San Jose cannery workers, Palo Alto white-collar workers, Atascadero poultry farmers, and many others.[97]

Oakland's UXA committed itself to internal management based on egalitarian democracy and mutual respect. Achieving that ideal, however, was formidable. The association officially governed itself through a series of committees that met weeknights, which in turn answered to the weekly meeting of a General Assembly. "Picture a large, oval table twelve to fifteen feet in diameter with all the way from twelve or fifteen to twenty-five or thirty persons gathered around, men and women, . . . old and young, . . . smoking pipes and cigarettes until the air was thick, but none the less deeply engrossed in the discussions taking place," one observer reported. Outside the circle sat additional members, he said, "eagerly listening to the various problems discussed." Often, "a newcomer or participant became so interested that he or she would venture a suggestion at which he or she would be invited to 'sit up to the table' and take part."[98]

Other evidence makes clear that the internal politics of the association weren't all so lovely. The wrong types "always want to put in for leadership, for themselves," complained a member in April 1933, for example.[99] An undated pamphlet produced by the Oakland cooperatives' education department admitted: "MORE FAULTS EXIST IN UXA THAN DO FLEAS ON THE BACK OF YOUR OLD PET CAT."[100] George Knox Roth, who in 1934 conducted a detailed study of a cooperative covering Compton and the Los Angeles area, reported that meetings were thick with vitriol, resentment, off-the-wall speechifying, and self-aggrandizement.[101] One leader told him: "There is as much destruction as construction in these meetings, and we don't want to hold meetings anymore for *that* reason."[102]

As the co-ops expanded through the Bay Area and Southern California, so did tension between rank-and-file poor members and middle-class members who moved into management roles. A December 1935 article in *Monthly Labor Review* analyzing self-help projects throughout California noted "the difficulty of reconciling democratic methods with efficiency."[103] Part of the problem was that cooperative members didn't always share promoters' uplifting visions of collective democracy managed by the middle class. Kerr, in the sections of his dissertation focused on California, observed that "almost every unit had its share of 'deadwood,' members who sat around the warehouse or playing cards as they formerly did around the corner barber shop or grocery store." Without what he described as "the whip" of hiring and firing power, "there was little individual incentive to increase efficiency since all received equal pay regardless of work performed." Kerr's California sources regularly expressed anger and disgust with their fellow members.[104] At an April 1933 meeting, for example, a member groused that "a lot of men come up to eat and talk and not to work, if you give them a saw, and they spoil the saw [i.e., damage it]."[105] In another co-op, according to Kerr, "all members bitterly complain that there is no co-operation."[106]

Again, the challenge was not only managing an increasingly complex business enterprise, but also bridging the gap between those who saw cooperation as a path to a beautiful social transformation, and those who saw it as a path to dinner. In 1935, a man named

E. L. Osborn interviewed cooperative members in the Oakland area and typed up "An Opinion on the Causes for Cooperative Failures." "Perhaps the largest amount of trouble comes from a lack of interested participation by the members who are, in many cases, only there for what they can get today," he wrote. "Things will pick up again so there is no use in trying to build this set-up, just take what you can get and let it slide when you can do better." Osborn concluded that a "definite basic difficulty" was a failure to grasp the role that cooperatives could play in "solving our every problem, poverty, periodic unemployment, crime and war."[107] A field representative from the American Friends Service Committee who worked with the unemployed in Los Angeles–area cooperatives told Roth: "There was a perennial desire of everyone to be freed from the necessity of co-operation . . . as soon as they could, hoping from day to day to 'get a pay job.'" They lacked the impulse, he said, to build "a new social order. . . . Without moral indignation to develop into radicals, or moral courage to be liberal reformers, they languish in the stupor of relief."[108]

A NEW SOCIAL ORDER FOR MEN

The cooperatives' gender politics limited the beautiful dream still further. Although women expressed interest in co-ops, over and over male cooperators blocked them from membership or only allowed them to perform subordinate roles, dramatically limiting the co-ops' ability to grow, let alone to enact democratic practices that would model a new society. Or perhaps the men *were* modeling their ideal society, and it was patriarchal.

In the African American–run co-ops, women do appear in top positions: Myrtle Cook, in Kansas City, led her cooperative's educational program; Ella Baker served as the executive director of the Young Negroes' Cooperative League, backed up by the League's official commitment in its bylaws to gender equality.[109] But, as noted, women were swiftly excluded from its executive board. The white-run co-ops were even weaker. Among the members of Oakland's Unemployed Exchange Association, only three women appeared on a 1933 list of twenty-five elected and appointed officials; one was in charge of the Handicraft Section, one ran the commissary, and the third, a former payroll clerk at Shell Oil, was in charge of the records.

A group of white men who formed a big cooperative in Compton, near Los Angeles, initially excluded women altogether. "They thought the organization was no place for women," one female member told Roth, although they let women work in the office. But the men changed their minds when they realized women could be useful to them, Roth reported, and let them join.[110] Women who joined appear to have been largely working-class, but not entirely. One 1934 list of the former occupations of women members included three laundry workers, twelve seamstresses and dressmakers, four waitresses, six office workers, eighteen domestic workers, and seventy-seven housewives.[111] Women began to manage the clothing department and work in the kitchens of the Compton co-op, and on their own founded a social service department that provided health care, medications, and milk for babies. But a woman who'd been head of that department reported: "The women never played a very large part in the organization. The men didn't want them to."[112]

Some women in Los Angeles–area cooperatives spoke positively of the aid that co-ops provided. "We could always eat while I worked here, and we could 'get by,'" one young woman, whose husband had lost his job and become disabled and then had lost her own job as a secretary, told an interviewer.[113] "It is much better than charity . . . because we felt we were supporting ourselves, and we were, too."[114] Another woman, "Mrs. R," in Oakland, told Kerr: "I am very thankful to the UXA because we are able to give my little daughter dancing lessons and have her eyes corrected," but the most important benefit from the association was "a re-born husband. . . . He has a future of security for himself and family."[115]

Other women were overtly hostile to the co-ops. One longtime Oakland member, a man, told Kerr that "at first women were almost unanimously against the movement"; they wanted their menfolk to keep looking for jobs. "I've listened to hundreds of women . . . voice their resentment towards 'their man' 'wasting his time' with this UXA Club," he recounted.[116]

> Perhaps occasionally, the boss would phone, on short notice, for "Bill" to work a day or two. The wife would come in frantic search for him, and I'd have to tell her that "Bill" was way up in the woods, or out past Hayward picking peas and that we would not see him

until night. The wife's opinion of me, the UXA, and "Bill" would be expressed in an extremely unflattering manner, and I would be commanded not to give "Bill" any more work.[117]

We have to read this evidence backward, trying to see past the viewpoints of both Kerr and the man he interviewed, and guess at the viewpoints of the women themselves. What was or wasn't "Bill" telling his wife, for example, that would make her hostile to the whole enterprise?

Another incident illustrates men's exclusion of women from internal governance, and at least one woman's willingness to challenge men's power. A male informant told Roth the story of a secretary who'd been fired from an unnamed Los Angeles cooperative because she allegedly obtained outside work, who had then tried to address a meeting to request reinstatement. But the chair wouldn't let her speak, because, he said, she wasn't a member anymore. So she climbed up "on one of the tables of the rear of the room and shout[ed] at the top of her voice, 'Injustice!'" the informant recounted. The chair told her to sit down. "I won't sit down," she retorted, "and I will stay here as long as I want and speak as long as I want to, and no five men of you can throw me out, either," then started yelling, "Point of order, point of order!" at the top of her lungs. Finally, after fifteen minutes of the officials ignoring her, she climbed down off the table and walked out.[118]

One final story offers us a tantalizing glimpse of how women organized cooperatives on their own terms. On May 28, 1935, a researcher named W. Hicks, who was investigating cooperatives in the San Fernando Valley northwest of Los Angeles, reported: "I found no Cooperative Unit in Canoga Park, except the unorganized, unknown, and unsung efforts of a little group of women headed by Mrs. Bertha Marmo." The women lived with their families in a settlement of migrants from the Midwest, who'd hoped to make a living growing fruit and poultry. "The little homes are picturesque and all of them beautiful in their natural setting of trees, vines, and flowers," wrote Hicks, but "inside they are tragic." Almost all the families had "eaten up their flocks and abandoned their larger gardens," unable to sell at a profit because prices had plummeted so low. "The men are mostly too old to work hard."[119]

"Into this situation, with the men sitting around daming [*sic*] the government and everything therein, the women, under Mrs. Marmo's leadership have bonded together for mutual help," reported Hicks. Bertha, her four children, and "the women of the neighborhood" had set up a laundry collective. One of the girls played the organ, and while the women worked they all prayed, sang church songs, and improvised their own church services. Mrs. Marmo told Hicks they hadn't considered joining the regional network of cooperatives; they figured "hard times will disappear some day as quickly as they come. . . . We will feel prouder if we pull through mostly on our own hook."[120]

Overall, these voices from rank-and-file members, both female and male, give us pause in assessing the larger political objectives of those involved in the cooperative movement of the 1930s. Clearly, many of its leaders were self-consciously socialists: Ella Baker in New York, most obviously; and the founders of a large cooperative network in Seattle, the Unemployed Citizens League. Other cooperators never used the term "socialism" nor were evidently associated with the socialist movement, but promoted values of equality and horizontal reciprocity, while explicitly rejecting capitalism's creation of vast wealth and vast poverty. Many proponents used the phrase "a new social order," which might have been a code word for socialism or might have been an alternative to it.

In Utah, for example, a cooperative network built among members of the Church of Jesus Christ of Latter-day Saints (Mormons) in 1931, called the National Development Association, promoted an ideal of "Natural Government" that included the Golden Rule, beauty, cooperation, "love of all creation," and unselfishness. They contrasted Natural Government with "Unnatural Government," which included mortgage loans and interests, profits, competition, rents and insurance, and stocks and bonds.[121] An observer at the time reported: "One gets the feeling that these people are all inspired with . . . a sense of creating a new order." Its members were apparently white, given that Kerr never described them otherwise, and ranged from carpenters and cleaners to barbers, shoemakers, and "professional people." There was no discernible use of the S-word here, but we can identify many of the same underlying principles as those of the socialist movement and a wide range of nineteenth-century utopian movements. By 1934, the association, using a combination of scrip and cash, had spread from Utah into six other states, counted thirty thousand members, and was operating a store, barbershop, health-care center, laundry, dry cleaners, a furniture repair shop, and a restaurant serving two hundred people a day.[122]

Still other cooperators, as we've seen, spoke of cooperation as simply a way for people to take care of each other collectively, eschewing charity and government alike. Bertha Marmo in Canoga Park, for example, explained that "we will feel prouder if we pull through mostly on our own hook." Jacob Reddix, from Gary, proposed: "If the black workers could pool their purchasing and productive power they might lift themselves by their own boot straps."[123]

Others, though, especially among the rank and file, were simply using cooperatives as one of many tools and strategies to get by in very hard times. They weren't particularly committed to using co-ops to bring about long-term structural change or even to build a loving collective bubble through which to make it through the Depression. If a better option were available on a given day, they'd take it. They were exhausted and downtrodden from decades of hard labor working for brutal and exploitative bosses, who discarded them at will. Those "deadbeats" might have been freeloading jerks, or maybe they were just tired. Or they were women, tired of their men disappearing or sitting around while they themselves tried to create dinner out of five beans, night after night.

TAMING THE COOPERATIVE THREAT

The more the cooperators' dream of a "new social order" grew, though, the more of a threat they indeed became to the old social order. By 1933, broader political-economic interests at both the local and national level were stepping in to try to control the cooperative movement. In Los Angeles, the biggest cooperative network in the country became a political football lobbed back and forth by Left and Right, its history shedding sobering light on the relationship between the cooperative movement, big business, and the emerging New Deal—with race politics, at times, flaming in the middle.

Los Angeles–area co-ops began in Compton, where a group of white veterans offered their labor to local Japanese truck gardeners in exchange for produce. By 1934, that branch had grown to a federation of

139 cooperatives in Los Angeles County and its environs calling itself the Unemployed Cooperative Relief Association, which spread north to Tujunga and Roscoe, east to Pomona, and south to Long Beach, involving as many as ninety-two thousand people. Together, its affiliates counted 45 percent of all self-help cooperatives in the United States.[124] They obtained and exchanged a vast range of goods and services, from food to haircuts to shoe repair. During the second week of January 1933, the founding cooperative in Compton alone distributed 6,325 parsnips, 5,000 carrots, 2,640 cabbages, 10,020 oranges, 5,450 "lettuces," 2,858 loaves of bread, 24 bacon rinds, 1,852 soup bones, and 425 fish.[125]

In sharp contrast to cooperatives in the Bay Area and Seattle, many of these cooperatives in the Los Angeles area were sustained by people of color, especially Mexicans and African Americans. Kerr and his dissertation adviser, Paul Schuster Taylor, counted a total of twenty co-ops in the area with people of color as members.[126] In his PhD dissertation, Kerr identified several co-ops composed entirely of African Americans and some composed of both African Americans and Mexicans, in which, he said, "the Negroes provided the leadership."[127] Kerr and Taylor also reported a co-op in Santa Monica that included "whites, Negroes, Chinese, Japanese, and Mexican members," and another in Westminster composed of Mexican farmworkers who "resort to self-help in the fall and winter when harvests of oranges, beans, walnuts, and sugar beets are over."[128] Constantine Panunzio, in his own study, counted eighty-two Mexican cooperators in the Los Angeles region, representing 4.9 percent of the total members he surveyed.[129] That same year, an investigator in Emeryville, north of Oakland, reported "a Mexican grocery store, in connection with the cooperative movement."[130] The only statewide survey we have, from 1935, counted six "cooperative groups composed wholly of Mexicans and about 10 groups wholly of Negroes."[131]

But the majority of Los Angeles–area co-ops, Kerr and Taylor reported, were "composed entirely of white Americans," including the founding branch in Compton, and another that explicitly barred Mexicans from joining. "Several cooperatives segregated white and Mexican women workers," Kerr found (the only indication of Mexican women's involvement in the cooperatives). Yet, in their official statements, all but one of the whites-only units claimed they "adhered to the slogan of 'no race or color lines,'" he reported.[132]

Beyond that, the researchers who studied the California cooperative movement at the time, all of whom were white men, tell us little
more. What were the exact mechanisms through which white members
practiced racial exclusion? What did cooperation mean to people of
color who formed or joined co-ops? Did they prefer to "take care of
themselves" on their own? Clark Kerr reported that African Americans'
cooperatives in Los Angeles "had more difficulty securing food and
making contacts than did the others, partly because they were in the
City of Los Angeles."[133]

It seems safe to presume that white racism was one of the difficulties
they faced. Black cooperators in the Midwest faced formidable opposition, too: in Chicago, white owners of empty stores wouldn't rent to
the cooperative; in Gary, white merchants and the white school board
threatened teachers who considered joining Jacob Reddix's cooperative.[134] White cooperators, by contrast, had the privilege of not having
to deal with racism. White farmers, small businesspeople, and local
officials were regularly sympathetic to them and provided concrete aid.

Into this landscape stepped the Communist Party, itself embracing
a wide range of racial/ethnic groups including African Americans,
Japanese and Japanese Americans, and Mexicans and Mexican Americans, albeit under largely white leadership. Here another approach
to the decade's challenges begins to enter our broader picture. In the
fall of 1932, Communist activists began to deliberately join LA-area
cooperatives and challenge them to take a more militant stance in
relation to the government. They mocked the limits of "self-help" and
demanded relief instead. "Your stomachs are getting emptier all the
time. This is a self-starvation movement," local Communists charged.[135]
A national-level Communist pamphlet argued that "instead of struggle to force the bosses and government, who control the wealth, to
provide adequate relief and unemployment insurance, they [the coop-
erators] advocate that we, workers, shall help each other by sharing
our poverty."[136]

By 1932, Communist members of the downtown branch of the
Los Angeles–area Unemployed Cooperative Relief Association started
foregrounding militant, direct demands for relief from the government.
They launched eviction protests, through which they forcibly stopped
police from tossing out furniture.[137] When co-op members had their
electricity or gas shut off for nonpayment, activists turned it back on.[138]

An undated statement entitled "Conscious Left Wing in Action in Co-ops," signed by "Left Wing, Unemployed Co-op Relief Society of L.A. County," outlined what was apparently a Communist Party program for influencing cooperatives. It began by charging that the movement was impaired by "the backward ideology of the workers," which included "Faith in State government" and "policies of class collaboration rather than of class struggle," but concluded that the cooperative movement was nonetheless a powerful potential threat to entrenched elite power. "The State government looks upon this movement with fear, hatred and distrust. It knows . . . that the efforts to placate, control and bribe a growing organization of the workers is like playing with a pet lion. It may turn its claws upon them at any time."[139]

As historian Laura Renata Martin has shown, relations between the cooperative movement, Communists, and business interests who indeed feared the lion's claws climaxed at a January 1933 convention of the Unemployed Cooperative Relief Association in Los Angeles.[140] Communist activists introduced resolutions demanding free gas, water, and electricity from the city; an end to all evictions; and $50,000 a month from the community chest for the unemployed.[141] But now new, powerful conservative forces showed up as well: John Porter, the Republican mayor of Los Angeles, and the city's chief of police, who led its viciously anti-Left Red Squad.[142]

As the conference opened, copies of an anonymous leaflet, entitled "California's Unemployed Feed Themselves," materialized throughout the meeting space. It insisted that the unemployed, by helping themselves through cooperatives, were "able and willing to work, in fact overwhelmingly averse to becoming forced to accept charity in any form."[143] This brand of what Martin calls "conservatism cooperativism" rippled through the convention, emphasizing individual responsibility, "respect for private property," and "a rejection of state-managed redistribution of wealth." With it, business elites were attempting to turn the cooperative movement's mutualistic, democratic thrust toward self-help into a weapon against state support for the poor and the unemployed, and more broadly against anything redolent of the Left.[144]

The Right's intervention into the conference climaxed during a dramatic speech by Colonel Huntington (his first name was never identified), who had been sent as the official representative of Republican

governor James Rolph. Huntington first riled up the crowd by denouncing forty-five thousand "itinerants"—the so-called Dust Bowl
migrants—who, he charged, were taking jobs away from "California citizens." He then attacked "foreign products": "Buy American
goods made by Americans and for Americans," he commanded, deliberately evoking a nationwide anti-Japanese, anti-immigrant campaign launched that winter by newspaper mogul William Randolph
Hearst.[145] Then Huntington turned on Asians living in the United
States, denouncing "cheap living Filipinos and dirty Chinamen doing
Americans' work. . . . Foreigners are here leeching you, taking food
out of your mouths and clothes off your backs—we are not ready to
give the country to foreigners."

The cooperative movement, Huntington concluded triumphantly
with an added anti-Communist jab, was "American the whole way
through"; it wasn't "going to Russia for advice."[146] The conference's
closing speaker, from the business community, warned: "We want to
help you to help yourselves as long as you are Americans and are not
hunger marchers or do not go into politics or try rioting."[147] Ernie
Krueger, director of the Unemployed Cooperative Relief Association,
merely fell in line, insisting that "we are behind Old Glory—we do
not ask for aid or relief."[148]

Martin concludes that the convention, taking place in the interreg-
num between Roosevelt's November 1932 election and his March 1933
inauguration, "represented a moment when conservatives still hoped
to control the Depression independently, to deal with it 'in-house,' so
to speak."[149] They were looking for a way to manage social unrest
without resorting to an activist state or disrupting current power
structures—in part by framing the issues around nationalist white
supremacy, allegedly threatened by a racial enemy within. They would
have been closely watching the interracial alliances emerging within
both the cooperative federation and its new Communist activists.

The conference's impact on the Los Angeles cooperative movement
thereafter is unclear. But other powerful interests nationwide were
also carefully watching the movement's growth by that point, and
consciously looking to repress its potential radical thrust. Perhaps
surprisingly, they included adherents and managers of the New Deal.

Clark Kerr himself was high on the list. In a series of articles in
social science and government publications he published with Taylor

in 1934 and 1935, and throughout his 1939 dissertation, Kerr consciously promoted cooperatives as a counter to the Left.* In a summary of his dissertation, he underscored, for example: "The effect of participation in self-help production of the unemployed was to concentrate their interest in a productive action rather than in protest for higher relief payments."[150] In a 1934 article in the journal *Survey Graphic*, Kerr and Taylor cautioned: "Cooperatives face continually the hazard of penetration from the left, which feeds on political activities and upon doubt that business and government will give an opportunity for effective economic activities."[151] They quoted approvingly one "self-help leader" who asked his members: "You have a brick in your hands; are you going to throw it, or are you going to place it, and build?"[152]

In June of 1933, Roosevelt's nascent New Deal launched an initiative called the Division of Self-Help Cooperatives, under the aegis of the new Federal Emergency Relief Administration (FERA). Clark Kerr served as its Southern California field supervisor.[153] Jacob Reddix, the founder of the Gary, Indiana, cooperative, moved to Washington, DC, to serve as the division's second-in-command, becoming one of the highest-ranking African American administrators in the new administration.[154] Paul Taylor went to work for the New Deal, too, in the California office of the Farm Security Administration.[155]

The new Division of Self-Help Cooperatives, zealously committed to the idea that producer cooperatives were the answer to the nation's plight, paid out $3.2 million between 1933 and '38, mostly during 1934 and 1935, in local grants designed to deliberately direct the cooperative movement away from consumer-based barter-and-scrip projects, and into wage-paying producer cooperatives instead.[156] By mid-1934, FERA stopped funding self-help projects based on the barter-and-scrip model that included non-currency exchanges, consumer goods, and volunteer labor, and instead directed enormous funds to straightforward producer cooperatives. It "began to insist on production by cooperatives and

---

*Leftists in the LA cooperative movement were on to Kerr. He recounted in a letter to his father that at one meeting in August 1934, leftist leaders denounced Kerr and a colleague as "liars, crooks, thieves, lizards living with Hollywood actresses, robbers who have kept food from the starved bellies of women and children and clothes from the backs of the poor." Clark Kerr to Dear Dad, August 4, 1934, in BANC MSS CU-302, Box 70, Folder 15, Bancroft Library, University of California, Berkeley, Berkeley, CA.

made funds more liberally available," reported Kerr and Taylor.[157] The Division of Self-Help Cooperatives also sent out fleets of experts who insisted that every cooperative adhere to a codified model for internal management and bookkeeping, centered on a single, highly qualified manager. There was no place in this framework for the earlier co-ops' creative experimentation with grassroots democratic self-management, however challenging; no place for the Chicago bacon-buying club whose member reported, "We have no need for a leader."[158]

Meanwhile, the supply of surplus goods and agriculture that the barter exchanges had relied upon started to dry up. More powerfully, in 1933 the New Deal launched generous, broad-scale federal relief programs that put white men, and in fewer cases Black men, to work on public projects, undercutting the demand for cooperatives. By 1935 the Works Progress Administration (WPA), which offered federally funded jobs on a huge scale, forbade all its recipients from participating in self-help projects. The famous writer Upton Sinclair—who ran for governor of California in 1934 on a platform supporting mass-scale cooperatives—in a 1936 book entitled *Co-op: A Novel of Working Together* referred to the Works Progress Administration as "that arch-enemy of self-help."[159]

The New Deal's support for *producer* cooperatives and government-funded work relief reflected a deep belief that men should be put to work in jobs that paid cash. It wouldn't do for them to get by with scavenging and bartering and a few odd jobs, then spending their days, like the men of Seattle's Hooverville, amiably tinkering with their houses while schmoozing with their neighbors. That would undermine the much-touted "work ethic." Men needed to fulfill their roles as household patriarchs and be ready to return to work in the private sector once the economy rebounded, implicitly keeping its profits flowing. Kerr and Taylor even titled one of their articles, "Putting the Unemployed at Productive Labor."[160]

Within two swift years, the self-help cooperatives embracing scrip-and-barter had mostly collapsed. In Oakland, notes historian John Curl, the new federal relief jobs produced "sudden labor shortages" at the Unemployed Exchange Association. "It now had difficulty delivering on work promised, and fell deeper and deeper into a hole."[161] In Los Angeles, "higher relief budgets, the Works Progress Administration, and the upturn of business during 1935 and 1936 [drew] many members from the self-help ranks"—decimating their membership, reported Constantine Panunzio in his 1939 study of cooperatives in Los Angeles.[162] The total number of units plummeted as well. Kerr and a research assistant concluded in 1939 that "barter activity declined after 1933. Surplus commodities were not so easily available, and federal and state assistance, as well as increased private employment, drew many members out of the cooperatives."[163] The impact of the federal Division of Self-Help Cooperatives was clear: "When the emphasis was shifted to governmental support of production units, the number of labor-exchange units dropped rapidly."[164]

In the 1930s, it wasn't just the cooperators' dream, and practice, of a "new social order" that was so threatening to the powers that be, though. It was what lay over their left shoulder, the militant specter with the claws, marching through the streets in the hundreds of thousands demanding relief.

"RED RIOTS" OF THE UNEMPLOYED

On Friday, September 25, 1936, Mrs. Ruby Lucas was evicted from her bungalow on the South Side of Chicago because she had failed to pay her mortgage for three years. But Mrs. Lucas refused to go away. For four days she sat on a mattress on her front stoop while heavy rain drenched her furniture and household goods, which had been dumped onto the sidewalk in front of the house. "She drew a squirrel coat up about her neck, readjusted her bedroom slippers, and sipped coffee from a milk bottle and declared: 'I'll stay here until I get my home back or die,'" reported the Associated Press. "'I'm warring on the millionaire bankers whose greed has turned widows and orphans and destitute into slaves.'" Lucas told the press that she and her husband, from whom she was separated, had bought the house for $7,000 and made their payments regularly for nine years. "Then I figured I had paid all the place would bring if I sold it and refused to pay any more."[165]

Ruby Lucas was one of thousands of people who staged eviction protests during the 1930s, most of which were successful, if sometimes only temporarily. She was part of a national protest movement of the unemployed that between 1930 and 1933 involved an estimated two million people, offering a third, dramatically different model in which ordinary people sought to meet their basic needs collectively.

The unemployed movement wasn't trying to slowly build things up brick by brick. It drew whole neighborhoods into the streets, usually placed fighting racism front and center, targeted the rich, and took on the government directly. It was organized by the Left, in most cases a multiracial Left. But the organized Left didn't completely control it, as ordinary people at the grass roots took the movement's ideas and ran with them.

The core organizing thrust behind the unemployed movement came from the Communist Party. Even before the stock market crashed in October 1929, its leadership had chosen to emphasize unemployed organizing as one of its top strategic objectives, and by the first few months of 1930, it was instructing members to organize new Unemployed Councils on a very local level. The leadership envisioned that unemployed activism would highlight the failures of capitalism, mobilize unemployed people into a militant fighting force, and thus promote the class struggle.[166] As an undated "Program of Unemployed Work," preserved in the archives of a New York Communist activist, instructed: "First and foremost, it is necessary to develop struggles on the minutest and most concrete issues facing the workers in the neighborhoods and around these struggles build the organization."[167]

The basic unit of the Unemployed Councils, in theory, was the block committee, through which party members were instructed to investigate local issues and be ready to "rally all the workers at a moments [sic] notice."[168] In practice, rank-and-file members improvised. They hung out wherever unemployed people were passing their time—breadlines, pool halls, factory gates, relief offices, saloons, and around the neighborhoods—talked to them about their grievances, then helped people address them. DeWitt Gilpin, a white Communist involved in Chicago's Unemployed Councils union, recalled in a 1970 interview with Studs Terkel that the councils attracted organizers "who were youthful in character and ideas. . . . They sort of threw away the rule book and just organized people to get something to eat."[169]

Very quickly, the Unemployed Councils were able to mobilize tens of thousands of people all over the country, not only in the Northeast and Midwest but in the Deep South, California, and San Antonio, where a young Mexican American Communist named Emma Tenayuca helped lead an Unemployed Council, most of whose members were Mexican.[170]

On March 6, 1930, only a few months into the Depression, the
Communist Party pulled off immense demonstrations by the unemployed and their allies in cities all over the country, calling for federal
unemployment relief. In Detroit, for example, a hundred thousand
protesters marched peacefully up Woodward Avenue. But as soon as
they held up their signs reading "work or wages," police swept in to
club and arrest them, including "girls" who, according to the Associated Press, played "hide and seek" with the cops while trying to raise
signs. Seven women and twenty-four men were arrested; fourteen
people were hospitalized.[171]

In Washington, DC, a hundred "men, women and girls" began
to peacefully walk back and forth on Pennsylvania Avenue in front
of the White House, according to the *Washington Post*. But when a
man climbed up onto a lamppost and was about to speak, "before
scarcely a word came from his mouth he was dragged to the pavement.
Police launched tear gas into the crowd, which dispersed," the *Post*
reported. "A large proportion of the rioters," it said, "were Negroes
and a number were young white girls."[172] Newsreel footage shows
Black and white demonstrators, mostly but not all men, marching
peacefully in a line three people or so wide, carrying picket signs that
read, "We Demand Work or Wages," and "Fight or Starve," with by-
standers and authorities thick on either side.[173] In Cleveland, police on
horseback charged into and shut down a demonstration of eighteen
thousand people. In Boston, where five thousand demonstrated, police
"mounted, on foot, and carrying ropes, charged the crowd, swept the
streets, and restored order," according to the Associated Press. The
police turned the Los Angeles protest into an "an eight-hour clubbing
party," a presidential commission later concluded.[174]

The most vicious and dramatic scene was in New York, where at
least thirty-five thousand demonstrators gathered in Union Square.
"The mob was led by a group of women and children holding aloft
placards and singing the Internationale," according to the *New York
Times*. When William Z. Foster, the general secretary of the Communist
Party USA, gave a call to march, authorities launched an army of a
thousand police and soldiers—on foot, on horses, on "armed motorcy-
cles"—who "barred the advance of the mob and in fifteen minutes of
spectacular fighting scattered it in all directions," reported the *Times*.
"A police emergency wagon . . . swung with its siren screaming into

the centre of the square, breaking up the huge crowd into a chaotic mass of individuals running for cover." "From all parts of the scene of battle came the screams of women and cries of men with bloody heads and faces," as "hundreds of policemen swinging nightsticks, blackjacks, and bare fists rushed into the crowd, hitting out at all with whom they came in contact."[175] A few demonstrators did fight back. "One woman swung wildly at a patrolman," the *Times* reported, and then bit and kicked a detective arresting her. The *Times* reported that twenty people were arrested, most of whom "had been severely punished before they were booked."[176]

These "Red Riots," as they were called, splayed across front pages throughout the country.[177] The nation's elites quivered in their silken sheets; here, seemingly was the real threat of revolution, tightly organized, interracial, militant, and affiliated with Moscow. It had only been thirteen years, after all, since the Russian Revolution shook their world. In the US, no one knew what the suddenly crashed economy would produce next. That specter would remain throughout the Depression—haunting the rich, haunting the Republicans, haunting Clark Kerr, haunting the architects of the New Deal.

The Communist Party USA, with approximately ten thousand to fifteen thousand members in the early 1930s, was founded in the aftermath of the 1917 Russian Revolution, and tightly allied with the Communist International (Comintern) in Moscow. The Comintern promulgated an evolving "party line" that members worldwide were expected to carry out—in theory, at least. Internally, the Party was organized on a strict hierarchical basis, with a commitment to "party discipline." Members were expected to obey top-down orders or be potentially expelled.[178]

Today it's hard to understand the prestige Soviet Communists enjoyed at that historical moment. Worldwide, many believed that the Russians had actually pulled off the much-dreamt-of workers' revolution, and that the Soviet Union should therefore be defended at all costs and deferred to in order to spread communism globally. In practice, members' commitment to a Moscow-emitted party line and to party discipline within the United States meant that thousands of Communists were deployed simultaneously as part of a united project with aligned, focused goals, giving them power far beyond their numbers.[179] In contrast to the mutual benefit societies or the cooperatives, though, there was no vision here of ordinary people deciding for themselves how to run things from below, no grassroots democratic management—despite a bit of rhetoric to the contrary. Rather, an elite group, the Communist Party, was in charge of the working-class struggle, its own policies determined from high above. In the Communists' Marxist-Leninist model of the "vanguard party," a dedicated cadre, presumed to be politically superior to "the masses," would lead the masses to the Revolution, and beyond that to the workers' state, which it would run.

The Communist party line in the 1930s included a deep, sincere, and militant commitment to fighting racism. While its very top leadership in the US was almost all white, Black men held many key positions. In Birmingham, for example, an African American former sharecropper and steelworker named Hosea Hudson was director of the city's Unemployed Councils.[180] The Party placed fighting racism front and center in both its policies and its projects. Most prominently, it chose to foreground the case of the "Scottsboro Boys," nine teenagers in Scottsboro, Alabama, who in 1931 were falsely accused of rape by two white girls. At the local level, Party members together fought police brutality, evictions, and housing discrimination, and called for equal relief payments for people of color.[181] In Birmingham, historian Robin D. G. Kelley found, the local Unemployed Councils demanded "free utilities for all unemployed and underemployed workers, provisions for opening all schools and free lunch for school children, and the right to vote without restrictions and irrespective of race."[182]

Thousands of people of color joined the Party during the 1930s because they understood it as a pathway, however flawed, to some measure of justice and a better future; they included Mexicans, Mexican Americans, Puerto Ricans, Cubans, and Filipinos, joining tens of thousands of Jews, Finns, and other immigrants from Europe and their children.[183] To attract Asians, the Party also organized affiliated groups such as the Chinese Unemployed Alliance of Greater New York, the San Francisco Chinese Unemployed Alliance, and the Japanese Section of the Los Angeles Unemployed Council.[184] It even put out two different Japanese-language newspapers in California.[185]

African Americans, especially, respected the Communists for their commitment to the Scottsboro Boys, for their struggles to meet Black peoples' quotidian demands for housing and food, and for their willingness, on occasion, to discipline members judged guilty of "white chauvinism," the Party's phrase at the time. Black people made up around 9 percent of the Party's total membership by the mid-1930s, although their turnover rate was even higher than that of whites.[186] Like white members, African Americans who joined or worked with the Party didn't necessarily subscribe to the full party program or feel fealty to Moscow; but they were seizing opportunities for alliances with white militants who were welcoming and willing to fight hard together, if also often condescending or patronizing.[187]

The Communist Party "unquestionably used Negroes," observes Nell Painter, who conducted and edited a book-length oral history of Hosea Hudson, the Birmingham leader. "What is important here is that blacks like Hudson were able to use the Communist Party in their turn." The Party, she writes, provided "a satisfying explanation for the oppression of Blacks in America"; it expanded Hudson's worldview and educational opportunities. "Most important, the CP gave Hudson self-confidence."[188] As Hudson put it, "The Party made me know that I was somebody."[189]

Despite the substantial and militant presence of women in the Party—making up almost a fifth of its membership in these years, or about five thousand people, including hundreds of African American women who were deeply committed—men didn't elevate women of any racial/ethnic group very far into its middle or upper leadership ranks.[190] Moreover, the Party didn't really have an understanding of housework or of women's endless responsibilities for performing it, or imagine a place for housewives in the revolutionary struggle— women were supposed to get paid jobs, like men, and organize militant unions.[191] But like men of color, thousands of women members of the Communist Party were nonetheless transformed individually by their experience in it, and carried themselves thereafter with a deep sense of self-worth and a lifelong, daily commitment to social justice. They became the kind of people who went to meetings every night.[192]

"SO A HANDFUL OF US MARCHED UP TO THIS HOUSE . . ."

Communists' grassroots work in the unemployed movement laid the basis for thousands of eviction protests that exploded all over the country during the early 1930s, with enormous success.[193] In Detroit, for example, activists "practically stopped evictions," reported Edmund Wilson in the *New Republic* in 1931.[194]

Katherine Hyndman, a white Communist who grew up poor in the coal fields of southern Iowa, recounted a Chicago eviction protest in vivid detail in a 1970 oral history collected by Staughton Lynd and again in Julia Reichart's classic documentary, *Union Maids*. Hyndman recalled how she and her allies heard about an attempted eviction near Ashland and Thirteenth Street on the South Side, during which protesters were repeatedly carrying the family's ejected furniture right back into the house: "Police had been arresting people all day long, just taking them by the wagonfuls all day long." Hyndman and her friends rushed to the neighborhood just as it was getting dark, but not a soul was on the street—which normally would be alive and crowded. She could see the evicted woman and her children at their house, with the furniture in front.[195]

"So a handful of us marched up to this house. . . . As soon as we got there the police [who] had been hiding around different buildings," immediately rushed out to surround her group. A detective "jump[ed] up on the steps with a sawed-off machine gun," waving it back and forth. "He was so big and so mean, and he says, 'The first son of a bitch that sets foot on these steps is going to have his head chopped off.'" Hyndman started up the steps anyway, "and a young white fellow came along with me. And then suddenly I see a young Negro man and his wife on each side of us." Together they marched past the detective, put their backs to the door, and started kicking it open with their heels. The detective, meanwhile, was "threatening he is going to chop us up. He's going to kill us."[196]

Suddenly, as more police cars sped in, "the people came out of their houses. They came swarming out and they surrounded the police." Finally, the policeman in charge of the operation announced: "Damn it! I'm tired of this. Let's call it quits. To hell with it." He called to the landlord, who was hiding among the police. "I'll tell you what we're going to do. . . . I'm going to pass my hat for a collection. And every policeman has to put some money in this hat." When he was done, he handed the hat to the landlord. "Now here's your damn rent, and I don't want to hear another damn word. Now go and open up that door." The mean detective, though, hauled Hyndman and her three comrades off to the police station. "He was so mad he was literally frothing at the mouth. . . . 'You sons of bitches. . . . Just one word, just one peep . . . and I'll kill all four of you.'" They held hands in the back seat and "didn't say one blessed word."[197]

Hosea Hudson recounted a story from Birmingham of an unemployed older African American man who'd worked for the railroad and was about to be evicted by a real estate company. Hudson and three other Black men visited its office. "We told them that we was sent down by the people from the community. . . . We always said the neighbors is anxious to know." Hudson and his comrades craftily pointed out to the agent that empty houses got burnt up, and they couldn't stop it. The agent agreed to let the man stay as long as he came in every month and confirmed that he was still unemployed. Eventually the railroad took the man back, and "he stayed in his house until he died."[198]

The Communists' Unemployed Councils soon expanded to extensive grassroots struggles helping individuals obtain government relief. Activists would accompany poor people into government offices, joined by anywhere from a handful to hundreds of other people, and cajole, demand, or implicitly threaten welfare officials to provide aid. "We were fighting for an old lady that had died," recalled Black Chicagoan Willye Jeffries in an interview with Studs Terkel. "They didn't want to give 'em that hundred dollars toward the burial. We got a crowd of about fifty people and went to the station. We gonna stay until we get this hundred dollars for this old lady." After two or three days, they got it.[199] Historian Mark Naison unearthed multiple stories of this kind of successful relief protest in Harlem. One woman recounted: "I stood in the rain for three days and the Home Relief Bureau paid no attention to me. . . . Then I found out about the Unemployed Council. . . . We went in there as a body and they came across right quick."[200]

Jeffries recounted a case in which organizers were trying to shake loose a burial payment from the Chicago welfare office. "We had a white lady, weighed about two, three hundred. We called her Ma Kuntz. She looked out. We were marching up and down, you know, picketing the place, because they wouldn't bury this old man. So we just took the corpse over there—not the man, but something resembling the corpse—and just sent it in there. Where the workers was." The social workers fled upstairs, so the protesters occupied the downstairs, singing "We Shall Not Be Moved." When lunchtime arrived, the social workers collected five dollars and sent it down to the protesters "and told us to get something to eat."[201]

Then the police arrived and saw Ma Kuntz out in front. "She had that old stick, and she's just marching, keeping time with that stick, see?" They stood by the door for a while staring at the protesters and then "got back in that patrol [sic] and went about their business." The protesters stayed camped out at the relief office for two weeks. "We had blankets, we moved a piano and we had a big time." Then they won.[202]

These stories offer moving evidence of people in authority choosing to side with protesters in shared solidarity—the social workers providing lunch, for example, or the policemen taking up offerings to pay the rent. Eviction and relief protests in fact depended for their success on a popular moral economy, in which poor people decided for themselves, individually and collectively, what was just. Think about Ruby Lucas, on her stoop in the rain, with her crystalline analysis of what she did and didn't owe the mortgage holder, and how the bankers were turning widows and orphans into "slaves." Communist activists, in initiating and supporting these protests, were encouraging ordinary people's own political conclusions while also seeking to expand them with their own critiques of capitalism and its agents.[203]

The responses of those in authority could also, though, have been about real fear of what protesters might do next. Did that cop pass the hat because he sympathized, or because he didn't want a crowd to beat him up? Hosea Hudson, for his part, knew what he was up to when he pointed out to the Birmingham real estate agent that empty houses frequently burned up. Sociologists Frances Fox Piven and Richard Cloward concluded: "Relief officials, who were accustomed to discretionary giving to a meek clientele and were not much governed by any fixed set of regulations, usually acquiesced in the face of aggressive protests."[204]

But in many, perhaps most cases, authorities met relief protesters, especially people of color, not with sympathy but with vicious repression. DeWitt Gilpin, the white Communist in Chicago, emphasized in his interview with Terkel "the brutality in the jails, the treatment of the unemployed, especially Negroes."[205] Police in Los Angeles were disproportionately brutal to Japanese and African American activists in the unemployed movement, historian Mark Wild has found.[206] On

August 3, 1931, Chicago city authorities, responding to pressure from big landlords, decided to crack down on Communist leadership of eviction protests. That morning, police arrested a top Unemployed Council leader at an eviction site. In response, activists from the local council marched from Washington Park on the South Side to Fifty-First and South Dearborn Streets, where a seventy-two-year-old Black woman named Diana Gross had just been evicted. As the marchers arrived, police shot and killed Abe Grey, a leading Communist organizer in the city. Outraged by the killing, John O'Neil took up a gun and was shot and killed too. A friend of Grey's was later found dead in Washington Park, shot in the head and mutilated. All three of the men who were killed were Black.[207]

Five days later, the Party organized an immense funeral march for the men, in which sixty thousand people participated, an estimated 60 percent of them Black, 40 percent white.[208] "State Street was covered with thousands of people from wall to wall, from one end of State to the other," recalled Katherine Hyndman. "It was just a mass of people. Young people with a sheet went along the sidewalk, and they would throw money into the sheet. The streetcars could just barely crawl along through the crowd."[209]

In New York City, Party members escalated individual eviction protests into enormous collective rent strikes by Jewish immigrants from Eastern Europe, targeting apartment buildings that seethed with labor and left activists of all stripes. "In the Bronx you could get two hundred people together if you just looked up at the sky," recalled Kim Chernin, a young Jewish Communist at the time. By late 1932 and early 1933, Communists and their allies had launched as many as two hundred rent strikes in New York City. At demonstrations ranging in size from one to five thousand people, pitched battles erupted between police and tenants. Women were at the forefront. "On the day of the eviction we would tell all the men to leave the building. We knew the police were rough and would beat them up," Chernin recalled. "It was the women who remained in the apartments, in order to resist." When police arrived, the protesters roped off the street outside, and people gathered. "The police put machine guns on the roofs, and they pointed them down at the people in the street."[210]

Sometimes the women would start haranguing the workers sent to carry out the evictions. "You, too, are unemployed men who have had to take this job in order to eat. . . . Come up here without the police and without the marshal and we will pay you off," they offered. They could see the marshals hesitate. "The water is hot in our kettles," the women hissed. "The doors are locked. We're not letting you in." The marshals would sometimes depart; other times, they would enter, take the money and leave, or knock down the doors and fight the women over pieces of furniture. "Sometimes we poured the hot water on the men. Sometimes they would hit us," recalled Chernin. If they did, the women would run onto the fire escape, "grab a bullhorn and shout to the crowd: 'They're hitting us. They're big men and they're hitting us.'" She said that sometimes the police got the furniture as far as the street, but the women moved it right back in and changed the locks.[211]

In other protests in the Bronx, women also scratched, kicked, and bit police, tearing their uniforms. Mark Naison notes that in these rent protests, women "constituted the majority of the crowd, the arrestees, and those engaged in physical conflict with the police." Soon, though, the landlords mobilized court injunctions, blacklists, further evictions, and other tactics against the rent strikes, and largely shut them down.[212]

What's remarkable here, and elsewhere, is how often protesters fought back against police and got away with it. Listen to this story Hudson told Painter in riveting detail: In Birmingham, on May Day, 1933, Communists held a "mass meeting" of the unemployed. The protesters, Black and white, gathered quietly, but police wouldn't allow any speeches. When Jane Spear, a white woman, finally climbed up on the bumper of a truck to speak anyway, the police told her to get down. "The unemployed people, mostly black women, began to cry out, 'Let her speak! Let her speak.' Some of those women wanted to tear up the police," recalled Hudson.[213]

As their protest escalated, "Uncle Ned Goodman he walked up with a stick," joined the chant, and "just hauled off and hit the police upside of the head with the stick," Hudson recounted. Other policemen wrenched the stick away from Goodman and were about to hit him in the head, but then Hudson grabbed the stick, at which point another cop hit Hudson in the forehead with a blackjack. At that point, Hudson recalled, "some of them little Negro women went to wailing at him, 'Turn him aloose, turn him aloose,' and come up here and there with their parasols." Just as a policeman was about to whack Hudson on the head with his pistol, "Uncle John Beard . . . hauled off with his

fist and hit the police in the eye and knocked him down." Hudson
himself continued attacking policemen: "One guy I throwed as far as
that door had a nickel-plate automatic."²¹⁴

The story has a startling ending. "He [the policeman] aimed at
me, and just as he did that, the sergeant hollers, 'Put them guns up,
use them sticks,'" Hudson recounted. "The police said, 'We can't do
nothing with these damn n-----s with these sticks!'" In a meeting at
city hall that night, the police were told "they could not use their guns
on the Reds if the Reds did not use guns," Hudson and his colleagues
later learned. "When the police was told that fifteen of them walked
up and turned in their guns and badges, saying they were not going up
against those Negroes with their sticks." After that, the Birmingham
police switched from short billy clubs to long sticks.²¹⁵

Over and over again in these protests, Black and white women as
well as men dished it right back at authorities or threatened to (and
Black women would have suffered even more brutality than white
women in response). Notice Ma Kuntz, outside the welfare office,
standing guard with her stick; or the woman in the 1930 march in
New York who "swung wildly at a patrolman" and then bit and kicked
the detective trying to arrest her. In Cleveland, hundreds of militant
Black women filled the ranks of the Unemployed Council, LaShawn
Harris and Melissa Ford have shown. In October 1931, six hundred
activists marched into its city hall to demand more relief, and when
police blocked their way, women "screamed, scratched, hissed at the
policemen as they fought their way through."²¹⁶

Here's a remarkable story: Max Naiman, a white lawyer for the
poor in Chicago, told Terkel about a bailiff who, trying to evict a
Black family, "shoved his foot in the door and yanked out his pistol
to command attention. . . . A struggle developed between the bailiff
and the lady of the house." A plank came off the edge of the door. "So
the woman picks up the plank and . . . socked him across the wrist
and forced him to drop his gun." The bailiff and his men gave up;
the plank-wielder was arrested and charged but found not guilty by
a jury.²¹⁷ (There's the popular moral economy, again.) Willye Jeffries
recalled that in the Chicago unemployed movement, "there were a lot
of Polish women in this organization, too. They had cayenne pepper,
and they threw it in those policemen's eyes, and nobody knew who
done it, but they went blind." Men, she said, would get knocked down,

and "get right up and fight again." But "the women, they played the biggest roles."[218]

For all the Communist Party's official top-down rigidity and white male hierarchy, at the grass roots, its activists proved flexible, creative, and attuned to the day-to-day realities of the poor. The Communists didn't define their project as building a new social order in the present, as did the cooperatives and the mutual benefit societies. They were in it for the big haul. But in their own way, they nonetheless modeled the best of human relations: concrete solidarity among the downtrodden, a refusal to accede to racism, and a great joy in struggle, even in the face of brutal repression.

THE WHITE CITIZEN UNEMPLOYED

By 1933, the Communists' work had snowballed into a larger wave of unemployed activism taken up by Socialist activists as well, adding to the movement's power and its potential threat to entrenched power—and highlighting the choices made by different white leftists.

The Socialist Party built its own organizations among the unemployed during the 1930s, but at that point was a pale creature in comparison to the Communist Party, much diminished from its heyday in the 1910s when it had elected two members of Congress and the mayors of 182 cities, including Berkeley, Buffalo, Butte, Cleveland, Eureka, Grand Junction, Milwaukee, Minneapolis, and Schenectady.[219] In 1934, the Socialist Party counted only twenty thousand members, in two cohorts: aging European immigrants, and US-born, middle-class, white twentysomethings. By that year, the Party had built sixty neighborhood-based "Workers Committees" of the unemployed, mostly in the Midwest and East, that drew in twenty-five thousand people, and helped individual poor people obtain coal, rent relief, and other forms of assistance. The Socialists were deliberately much less confrontational with relief authorities than were the Communists. They did pull off one big march in Chicago in the fall of 1931 when the city announced it was going to cut relief payments. Its members, almost all white, evinced almost no interest in fighting racism.[220]

A different group of independent socialists influenced by A. J. Muste, a Protestant minister and labor educator, organized unemployed activism through an organization called the Conference for

Progressive Political Action. Its activists—highly educated, white, formally dressed, known popularly as "Musteites"—deliberately emphasized what they called an "American Approach," featuring, for example, the rattlesnake flag from the American Revolution and its slogan, "Don't Tread on Me." In 1932, they quickly organized one hundred thousand people, especially native-born whites, into unemployed groups in Ohio, plus another forty thousand in Pennsylvania, that merged collective self-help projects with educational work, entertainment, and pressure for more generous relief provisions. In August 1933, the Musteites organized a mass march to the Ohio state capital in Columbus demanding relief, and that same year mounted a convention that drew delegates from thirteen different states.[221]

In stressing "Americanism," the Musteites were playing with fire. In the Midwest in the 1930s, "American" functioned as a code phrase for "not immigrant," "not Jewish," "not Catholic," and "not Black." Ohio was thick at the time with current and former members of what became known as the "Second Klan," which had exploded during the 1920s, fusing antisemitism and anti-Catholicism with its traditional hatred of Black people. Two different sources reported that attendees at the Musteites' Ohio convention included members of the Ku Klux Klan.[222]

We can see similar politics play out more subtly in a final example, in Seattle. In 1931, two middle-class white men with decades of experience in the city's progressive movement and its Socialist Party, and who had been influenced by A. J. Muste, founded the Seattle Unemployed Citizens League, which spread like wildfire to include a total of twenty-two branches across the city. It was admired, studied, and emulated by cooperative advocates nationwide, including Clark Kerr.[223] Its founders put out a small newspaper, *The Vanguard*, that promulgated a forthright class analysis of the Great Depression. "Capitalism Is Bankrupt—Build a Profit-Less System," ran a banner across its front page in February 1932.[224]

The Unemployed Citizens League merged cooperative self-help, local relief demands, eviction protests, and militant demands on the state. Through the League's cooperative "commissaries," members solicited donations, harvested crops, and distributed agricultural products and firewood on a scale even larger than that of the Los Angeles–area cooperatives. It members found empty homes for the poor, successfully used protests to stop evictions, and sometimes did a bit of private rewiring on the side to steal electricity.[225] At the same time, the League pressed for city and state authorities for unemployment insurance, a minimum wage, school lunches for children, free bus fares for the jobless, a million-dollar city public works fund dedicated to job creation, a stay on evictions and the tax payments of those who couldn't pay, and increased taxes on high-end properties.[226] "Unemployed men and women of Seattle, don't look for a saviour," its newspaper urged. "Depend upon yourselves. Organize yourselves in your own communities to demand relief through work at fair wages without the stigma of charity. Demand Federal and State unemployment insurance through taxation of super-wealth." Notice how seamlessly the author moved from self-esteem to self-help to larger, class-based demands on the government.

Its members overwhelmingly, perhaps entirely white, the Seattle Unemployed Citizens League did not include racism among the problems it identified facing working people. The League's newspaper on occasion expressed racist views, such as the idea that Asians were able to "live on a bowl of rice."[227] Its founders consciously chose the name Unemployed *Citizens* League because they wanted to emphasize that the organization's members were voters who would be ready to mobilize in local elections.[228] But their use of "citizen" cut off noncitizen immigrants from the larger body of "workers" and the poor people for whom the movement was ostensibly intended. In the context of 1930s Seattle, that meant excluding Japanese, Chinese, and Filipino residents, who were ineligible for citizenship at the time, as well as a wide range of other immigrants, especially the city's large population of Scandinavian immigrants, who would not necessarily have become US citizens—and who had a robust, recent tradition of cooperative enterprise in Seattle.[229]

By 1932 the Unemployed Citizens League nonetheless numbered forty to fifty thousand members and had amassed real power. That spring it elected one of its key activists as mayor and two other supporters to the city council. But the Communist Party, jealous of the League's success, organized its own, separate Unemployed Councils in Seattle and began to move in on the League's branches, infiltrating and sometimes deliberately disrupting them. In July 1932, both groups tried to march to the state capital in Olympia to demand a system of state and federal unemployment insurance but were forcibly blocked by police from entering the city. Meanwhile, the new Seattle mayor and city council betrayed the League, cutting city workers' wages and siding with business elites. By the time the Roosevelt administration began to implement extensive federal relief in the spring of 1933, the Seattle unemployed movement had largely dissipated.[230]

Soon the Communist Party itself largely abandoned grassroots work among the unemployed nationwide. In 1932 it moved resources into promoting a federal unemployment insurance bill instead, and in its work on unemployment issues increasingly began to function as a pressure group in Washington. In 1933 the New Deal began to unleash millions in relief funding, which took much of the steam out of grassroots demands by the poor. By 1935 the Communists had merged their Unemployed Councils with the Socialists' and Muste-ites' unemployed organizations to form a new nationwide Workers Alliance, based in Washington, DC, which became a proto-union advocating for workers employed by the new federal Works Progress Administration (WPA).[231]

All this organizing, whether Communist, Socialist, or Musteite, was built around the category of the "unemployed." But who did that mean, exactly? The concept of "the unemployed" assumed that all poor people had once been employed, and now weren't—and therefore needed to make demands from landlords or the government to obtain food, housing, and other needs, since they didn't have access to cash from jobs anymore. But the majority of women hadn't been employed for pay in the first place. In 1930, less than one in four white women and half of all Black women had been in the labor force; among married women, only one in ten white women and one in three Black women held a job.[232] Most women survived instead through dependent relations on men within families, whether husbands, fathers, boyfriends, or extended family members.

In the self-definition of the unemployed movement, the unemployed were implicitly male, as were the much-exalted "workers." Women's unpaid work in the home putting food on the table, raising children, and tending to the old, the sick, and the disabled didn't qualify as work. Nor did housewives get to qualify as workers. Yet in the movement of the "unemployed," especially that of the Communists, women were literally at the forefront, over and over, fighting hard, even "protecting" their menfolk.[233]

ENTITLEMENT

By the time Roosevelt took office in March 1933, the cumulative power of the unemployed movement was immense. It had transformed the way millions of poor people and much of the mainstream press understood charity, the nation's relief system (or, rather, its lack thereof), and the obligations of the federal government.

For President Hoover and many others, private charity was supposed to have been the answer, but its providers had fallen far short of the task during the early years of the Depression. The big faith-based organizations hit a limit of their willingness and ability to pay out. Mutual benefit societies and local churches depleted their wells. City and county governments paid out hundreds of thousands in aid, then teetered on the edge of bankruptcy, often unable to pay teachers or police; some went under. By the beginning of 1933, at least a thousand local governments had defaulted on their loans.[234] Even if cities did continue to pay out relief, the amounts were tiny—$3.60 a week in 1932 in Detroit, for example (the equivalent of $73 today), 80 cents in Baltimore.[235] Congressmember George Huddleston of Birmingham testified in 1932 that his city "decided as a measure of relief to dig a little canal from some funds they had left from another improvement." When the city advertised for 750 workers to build it, 12,000 people applied.[236]

At the federal level, President Hoover continued to insist that the economy was sound and blame the Depression on European trade policies. In February 1932 Congress passed a bill authorizing funding for work relief, but Hoover vetoed it. That year he did release $300 million in loans to the banks and big business through the Reconstruction Finance Corporation, and reluctantly authorized over $600 million in relief. But deep down he believed that responsibility fell to individuals and local communities, not the federal government. In February 1931, writes historian Irving Bernstein, he insisted that federal relief "would destroy 'character' and strike at 'the roots of self-government.'"[237]

Even if mass relief had been available, a powerful stigma discouraged impoverished people from accepting, let alone demanding, government relief. Sociologists Frances Fox Piven and Richard Cloward, in their classic studies *Regulating the Poor* (1971) and *Poor People's Movements* (1977), have described how the stigma of the "dole" had long been deployed to keep people from seeking or accepting relief, so that working people would be forced into the labor market on any terms. "The more important function of the relief system was accomplished, not by refusing relief, but by degrading and making outcasts of those few who did get aid."[238] Moreover, even though headlines during the earlier years of the Depression screamed every day with statistics showing that the larger economy had collapsed and a third of the country was unemployed, sociologists and other observers reported that white men continued to blame themselves for their poverty.[239] If their value depended on providing for a family, but they couldn't, a deep sense of shame often tore apart their sense of self-worth, paralyzing them. For women, though, the stigma was less severe, and two decades of state-level relief programs known as "mothers' pensions" had cast some white women as worthy recipients of aid.[240]

People who did swallow their pride and apply for relief had to run a gauntlet enforced by social workers, government officials, and even other recipients—a process that could involve powerful shaming, enhanced by racism. Alice Walker captured it powerfully in her 1973 short story "The Revenge of Hannah Kemhuff," based on an incident her mother experienced. Kemhuff, an impoverished Southern Black woman, decides reluctantly to finally go down to the relief office and apply for aid when her children are nearing starvation. Trying to look presentable, she carefully dresses herself and her four children in nice clothes that have just arrived from a relative up north. In the line at the relief office, though, she sees that the other African American applicants have all deliberately dressed "in tatters," in order to appear properly desperate and deserving of aid. When Kemhuff arrives at the head of the line, the white social worker pronounces: "You don't need nothing to eat from the way you all dressed up. . . . Move along now." Kemhuff flees in shame, as others that she knows in the line laugh at her. (In Walker's story, Kemhuff enlists an African American root doctor decades later and gets revenge on the white lady.)[241]

The left-wing unemployed people's movement of the early 1930s helped shatter that publicly deployed, privately internalized shame associated with relief. As hundreds of thousands joined eviction protests, sat down at the local relief office, and marched in the streets alongside others demanding "work or wages"; as the press covered their activism prominently and sometimes approvingly; and as even cops took up collections to support them, ordinary people's understanding of the economy, of themselves, and of the responsibilities of the federal government changed altogether. "Each victory over relief officials added morale and momentum to the movement of the unemployed and further weakened the doctrine that being 'on the county' represented a public confession of failure," write Piven and Cloward.[242] The movement produced two seismic shifts, they argue: first, many men stopped blaming themselves, and second, people came to believe they were entitled to aid from the government—that the government in fact *owed* them relief, whether through direct cash payments or through government-created jobs.[243]

Popular understanding of the right to government relief, of the legitimacy of organized protest demanding it, and of the failures of the Hoover administration climaxed in flames during the summer of 1932, in an encampment that mirrors the one with which we opened this chapter. In May and June of that year, twenty thousand despairing, impoverished veterans of World War I, largely white but also Black, accompanied by a thousand wives and children, flowed into Washington, DC, from throughout the country to demand early payment of a "bonus" they'd been promised after the war. They called themselves the Bonus Army and were careful to insist that they were loyal Americans, not interested in the Left. Once they arrived, a sympathetic chief of police arranged for some of them to occupy four buildings owned by the Treasury Department, with permission of its secretary, in the area now known as the Federal Triangle; the rest camped out in Anacostia, near the river, where they governed themselves in remarkable peace, American flags flying everywhere from their tents and shacks.[244]

In June, the House of Representatives passed a bill authorizing early payment of their bonuses; but the Senate voted it down.[245] Exhausted and despairing, most of the veterans stayed in Washington anyway. On July 28, following orders from President Hoover, General Douglas MacArthur, chief of staff of the US Army, led two hundred cavalry troops, four hundred infantrymen, tanks, and other armed vehicles right up Pennsylvania Avenue from the White House to the Treasury buildings. Without warning they launched tear gas and charged into the buildings with bayonets, then burned the buildings down altogether. The troops then turned on the peaceful crowd of ten thousand or more watching outside in the streets. "Men and women were ridden down indiscriminately," one reporter recounted in horror. By the end of the

day the US Army had killed two veterans, stabbed another, shot a by-
stander in the shoulder, and "a veteran's ear [was] severed by a calvary
sword." Two policemen's skulls were fractured. A twelve-month-old
baby died from tear gas.[246]

Then MacArthur marched his troops to the big camp in Anacostia
and burned it to the ground—tents, American flags, and all—in a giant
conflagration. Eleven thousand residents fled into the night carrying
babies, clothes, and what was left of any hope for the future. President
Hoover watched out a White House window as the whole DC sky
burned red to the southeast, then turned away for the night.[247]

The next morning, much of the nation woke up shocked when they
read the news. The United States Army had marched upon, tear-gassed,
bayoneted, and killed Americans, most of them white male veterans
who'd themselves fought for their country in Europe just a few years
before. Hoover's already-diminished status plummeted. It was a mere
three months before the presidential election, and the path was open
for the November victory of his Democratic opponent, Franklin Delano Roosevelt.[248]

When Roosevelt took office on March 3, 1933, he was under enormous pressure to address the Depression. Striking a tone of au-
thoritative confidence in his inaugural speech and with a Democratic
majority in Congress at his back, he moved quickly to enact a set of
measures known as the First New Deal, designed, above all, to stabilize
the economy and create the modern regulatory state that would remain
largely in place until the 1980s. The Glass-Steagall Banking Act of 1933
created a firewall between commercial and investment banking and
allowed the Federal Reserve Board to regulate interest rates through
loans. The Federal Deposit Insurance Corporation (1933) guaranteed
that the federal government would back up accounts. The Securities
and Exchange Commission (1934) mandated disclosure of ownership
and licensing of traders and banned insider trading. During his campaign, Roosevelt had condemned "greedy bankers," but once in office
he used federal powers to strengthen them, so the whole capitalist
system wouldn't collapse, as many feared it might.[249]

The relief question loomed, urgently. Right off, Roosevelt authorized huge-scale federal programs creating work relief for the

unemployed. The Federal Emergency Relief Administration (FERA), launched in May 1933, expended $500 million in relief funds, largely disbursed through the states. By January 1934, its subsidiary, the Civil Works Administration, had created 4.3 million temporary jobs. In 1935, the more famous Works Progress Administration (WPA) replaced the FERA and would employ about three million people each year through the rest of the decade.[250]

The focus of all these programs was "work relief," which meant creating jobs for the unemployed so they would engage in what was viewed as "productive labor" in exchange for cash—as opposed to what was known as "direct relief," straightforward payments of cash or food to the poor. In designing its relief programs, the government was taking pains to ensure that the unemployed didn't develop long-term habits of not working for pay.[251]

Let's pause to acknowledge that these programs were a huge achievement, in large part brought about by the unemployed movement. Their creation is one of the most powerful examples in US history that grassroots organizing works. The nation's elites were afraid of a revolution from below, afraid of the Left and its mass demands for relief. Liberal policymakers who designed and authorized the programs also sincerely wanted to help people in the face of mass crisis.

But which people? Surprisingly, African American men were in many cases able to receive work relief under these programs, especially the WPA. In fact, in proportion to their percentage of the population, more Black people than white people received work relief. But Black people were vastly more impoverished to begin with, and relief allotments didn't begin to close that gap. It was certainly unprecedented for them to receive any aid at all from the government, let alone on a large scale. If and when African Americans did get aid, though, racism dramatically restricted how much they received relative to whites. Because federal relief programs delegated funding to the states, local white economic and political interests controlled its dispersal. During planting and harvest seasons, agricultural employers forced Black workers off relief rolls, for example. If employed, African Americans received lower pay than whites for the same jobs and were only dispatched to the worst jobs. Most relief jobs were in construction, but even highly skilled Black construction workers were only allowed to work in unskilled jobs, for the lowest wages.[252]

The pattern was similar for Mexicans and Mexican Americans: men could qualify for relief in some cases, but only through work assignments to the worst jobs, and only when the big agricultural employers didn't want their labor. More insidiously, a million Mexicans and their US-born children were forcibly "repatriated" to Mexico in the early 1930s, many of them put on trains by social workers when they applied for relief.[253]

Women of all racial/ethnic categories constituted 25 percent of the labor force, but when the WPA jobs were handed out, they only got 12 percent of the jobs. Here, too, the mechanisms of exclusion were multiple. Within a given household, only one member was allowed to receive a WPA job, and men came first. If women did qualify, they could only work in jobs considered appropriate to their gender and race, which paid far less than the wide range of jobs available to white men. The majority of relief jobs were in construction, for example, which excluded women.[254] In so sharply restricting relief to women, the New Deal programs were drawing on growing hostility during the Depression to the employment of married women. By 1940, only 13 percent of school districts would hire married women; only 30 percent did not fire women who married while already employed.[255]

When the Democratic Party gained an even greater majority in Congress in the 1934 midterm elections, including a two-thirds majority in the Senate, voters handed a much stronger mandate to FDR, already immensely popular. Beginning in 1935, he led the enactment of deeper, class-based programs designed to both redistribute wealth and place a platform under working people, in what is known as the Second New Deal. The 1935 National Labor Relations Act (Wagner Act) created a system regulating union elections, guaranteeing labor rights, and adjudicating their violations. The 1938 Fair Labor Standards Act abolished child labor and established the first federally mandated minimum wage. The Social Security Act of 1935 created an unemployment insurance program, in which a federal payroll tax was administered by the states. It created a new system of old-age pensions based on payroll deductions, and a new relief program, Aid to Dependent Children, or ADC—later known as Aid to Families with Dependent Children (AFDC), or simply "welfare"—echoing earlier state-level programs that provided what were known as "mothers' pensions." It also set up a new program delivering direct aid to the indigent elderly. Together, these were in many ways the crowning achievements of the New Deal—empowering the labor movement, creating federal pensions for the first time, and providing some workers with a cushion so that they couldn't be forced into the labor market.

But severe restrictions also limited these programs. Only a little more than half of the labor force was covered by the original 1935 Social Security pension system, the National Labor Relations Act, and the federal minimum wage. Government workers, retail workers, workers at nonprofits, including those in health care and education, agricultural field-workers, and domestic workers were all excluded, along with many others. Women worked disproportionately in these sectors. During the 1930s, 90 percent of all African American women who worked for pay and two-thirds of African American people overall worked in domestic service or agriculture. Thus only a small fraction of Black Americans qualified.[256]

Women who worked in the home were excluded as well. Those who had never been in the labor force, or who had left it while raising children, caring for elders, performing housework, or otherwise tending to their assigned roles in the patriarchal family, weren't considered the unemployed, so they didn't deserve relief. The exception was widows with young children, who qualified through ADC. But women's relief payments through that program were only half what men received through their own relief programs. Moreover, the federal system handed the authority to determine individual women's eligibility to the states, which implemented insidious morality tests including what would become known as the "man in the house" rule, in which social workers invaded women's homes randomly to see if there was a man present—whether he was financially supporting the woman or not—and policing her intimate life, setting up long-term stereotypes of Black women relief recipients as immoral and lazy cheaters. Overall, relief programs directed at men, through Social Security and unemployment insurance—and, later, veterans' benefits—were understood as appropriate, based on entitlement flowing from their gender. By contrast, the program directed at women, ADC, was government charity, "welfare."[257]

Finally, the new old-age pension system established by the Social Security Act, for its part, only paid out to heads of households, based on payroll deductions contributed from employment for wages. That meant that when wives working in the home got old, they only received Social Security indirectly through their husbands—as dependents, not as individuals. Some women did receive Social Security from their own wages. But most women's labor force participation was not continuous, given their responsibilities for childcare, housework, and elder care, and if they did work for pay, they were restricted to a narrow range of jobs that paid far less than men's, dramatically diminishing the amount they paid into the Social Security system and therefore later received as pensions. And again, Black women, although they were more likely to remain in the labor force their whole lives, worked in sectors that were originally not covered by Social Security at all. [258]

Ruby Lucas, camped out on her stoop, Ma Kuntz at the welfare office with her stick, Bertha Marmo with her laundry cooperative—none of them would probably have received a relief job or Social Security as individuals. They would only get ADC relief if they were widowed with young children. For all their militance in the "unemployed" movement, all their perseverance, all their invisible domestic labor keeping it all going both in their families and in their organizations, housewives were largely locked out of the gates of the new welfare state. The New Deal thus used federal power to implement many of the same gender politics that were playing out in the grassroots organizations we've examined: men mattered first, women were by nature inferior, dependent, and subordinate, and domestic labor in the home, whether paid or unpaid, was largely invisible and not to be valued.

All the limitations of the New Deal should not, though, diminish our understanding of the enormous, unprecedented gains it brought, based on the idea that the federal government should deliver for ordinary people on a grand and permanent scale. The New Deal didn't end with the Great Depression, moreover; it grew and grew. By the 1970s the Social Security old-age pension system would finally include most wage earners. The broader New Deal package in later decades would expand dramatically to include Medicare and Medicaid (1965), the Great Society programs of the 1960s, and, in one last act, the Americans with Disabilities Act (1990).[259]

WE MAKE THE ROAD BY WALKING

In the late 2010s and early 2020s, mutual aid has had a creative and enthusiastic resurgence, especially among young people. Through new horizontal networks built on democratic practices, they are consciously modeling a future society based on neighborliness and solidarity. Local groups have provided food, medical care, housing, and transportation to neighbors and those in need. In Oakland in 2017, for example, as wildfire smoke descended onto the city, LGBTQI activists formed a collective to distribute masks to the homeless. In New York, new mutual aid groups raised money to help out sex workers, street vendors, and other service workers.[260] In Chicago, African American activists in the prison abolition movement formed a group, called People's Grab-n-Go, that in the summer of 2020 delivered food and household goods to over five thousand families on the South Side, combining mutual aid with militant protests in the streets that demanded defunding of the police and other criminal justice reforms.[261]

The COVID pandemic brought even more enthusiasm for mutual aid at the grass roots.[262] Rebecca Solnit and others have documented a long history of disaster engendering mutual assistance. In *A Paradise Built in Hell*, Solnit traces flourishing communities that emerged in the aftermath of Hurricane Katrina in New Orleans, after earthquakes in Mexico City and San Francisco, and after September 11 in New York, through which people rushed to aid loved ones and strangers alike, especially at the neighborhood level, with a heightened commitment to altruism—in the process discovering a new sense of self and of community.[263] The Great Depression, too, was a disaster, to which ordinary people, over and over, responded with beautiful practices of solidarity.

But there's a missing piece here. During the 1930s, as mutual benefit societies, consumer co-ops, and unemployed protesters rushed to provide basic necessities, the question of private-sector jobs—and their disappearance—still loomed like a dark shadow over all their endeavors. Then and now, the question remains of who creates those jobs, who gets them, who doesn't, how people are compensated, and who reaps profits from the often brutal, degrading, or mind-numbing labors of others—and what a "job" is, anyway. In the Great Depression, the real disaster was capitalism, which turns some labors into commodities to be bought and sold in a market for profit, and renders other labors invisible or suddenly superfluous, while deploying racism to do its work. Capitalism remains the root disaster today, racial to its core, whether during a "crisis" or in its smooth, day-to-day, exploitative functioning.

The question also remains of the relationship between, on the one hand, modeling the good society on a very local level in the here and now, and, on the other, working for long-term structural social change. In a 1997 essay entitled "Looking Backward: The Limits of Self-Help Ideology," historian Robin D. G. Kelley cautioned against an over-celebration of "self-help" in the Black struggle: "I am convinced that we need to get [a] sense of entitlement back," he wrote. "Opposing strong government supports in favor of some romantic notion of self-reliance is tantamount to relinquishing our citizenship." But in 2022, in a new introduction to his collection *Freedom Dreams*, Kelley qualifies that stance: he writes that his daughter, Elleza Kelley, "schooled me on the importance of mutual aid as a potentially radical practice of prefiguring the future we want to build." Responding to his original critique of self-help, Kelley reflects: "Ten years ago, I encouraged grassroots organizations to make greater demands on the state," but "contemporary grassroots movements have compelled me to soften my position and to re-evaluate the power of organizational independence, the radical traditions of autonomy and 'self-help,' if you will." Today, he concludes, he "would encourage readers to pay more attention to the Zapatistas and Autonomista movements in Argentina—movements more concerned with creating spaces for prefiguring or modeling the world they want to create than with taking state power."[264]

It's not a choice of just one or the other, of course, as Kelley well knows. During the 1930s, Chinese men in San Francisco may have shared tiny apartments on an informal basis and drawn on resources from their village associations, but they also joined the Communists' Chinese-language Unemployed Councils to demand relief. In New York, African American people who joined a march demanding large-scale government assistance might have understood doing so as simply an extension of the programs and collective virtue they also sought through mutual benefit societies or cooperation. Still others, in

Seattle, might have just wanted to camp out by the docks and gossip all day without government interference, but also wanted access to city-funded soup kitchens and, through barter exchanges, free fish.

"We make the road by walking," wrote Spanish poet Antonio Machado ("Se hace camino al andar").[265] Today, as we walk together, we can draw strength from ordinary people's paths during the Great Depression, and ask each other, how do we want to manage our lives together with love, respect, and reciprocity, now and in the future? Slipping into the well-worn seats and onto the wooden stages of our local meeting halls, originally built by Portuguese or Mexican or Lithuanian mutual aid societies, we can listen to their walls, and add our own voices and visions to those who spoke before.

In 2022 the *New York Times* ran a prominent story about a campaign to save the Brooklyn meetinghouse of an African American women's secret society called the United Order of Tents, founded in 1848 and linked to the Underground Railroad. The Tents, as members called themselves, once spread from the South all the way up to Massachusetts and provided burial services, care for old people, and aid to the needy, always rooting their work in a deep understanding of Black women's sisterhood.

By 2022 the Brooklyn Tents were the last remaining chapter in the Northeast and numbered a diminished total of twenty-four women, only a handful of them young. Their headquarters, a two-story nineteenth-century mansion, was in danger of crumbling to the ground and being repossessed for back taxes.[266] One of its younger members, Erica Buddington, put out a desperate call for donations to save the building, and in an online campaign raised $210,000, much of it in small amounts of ten or twenty dollars. "That building is a symbol of a legacy," another Tent, Akosua Levine, seventy-one, told the *Times*. We can only begin to imagine how much those walls, like the Tents, have to teach us.[267]

CHAPTER TWO

A TALE OF TWO CARAVANS

Mexican *Repatriados* and "Dust Bowl" Migrants

Two caravans of migrants moved across the Southwest during the Great Depression. In the first, between 1929 and 1935, as many as one million Mexicans and US citizens of Mexican descent were "re-patriated" across the United States border into Mexico. Sixty percent of them were children. In long lines of cars and trucks, they streamed down from the Upper Midwest and across Texas; flowed from California, Arizona, and New Mexico to the southern border; and even drove east from California all the way to the official crossing at El Paso. They filled trains, month after month, from St. Louis, from Detroit, from Los Angeles. Some even left on ships from San Diego.[1] In 1930, Pablo Baiza, who'd lived for fifteen years in Texas, simply crossed the Rio Grande at Johnson's trading post in what is now Big Bend National Park, in a wagon full of his family's belongings, pulled by four burros.[2]

In late September 1931, two thousand starving farmworkers and tenant farmers from the area around Karnes City, Texas (population: 1,141), decided to travel with their families to Mexico together in a caravan. Many of them were so poor they planned to walk the entire 150 miles to the closest border crossing in Laredo. In response, the Mexican and Mexican American communities of nearby San Antonio and Laredo loaned dozens of cars and trucks for their passage, do-nating medications, canned food, vegetables, and meat. "Mr. Matilde Elizondo, owner of the gas stations of this city that carry his name, together with his two brothers, carried 28 *repatriados* in their cars," reported *La Prensa*, San Antonio's Spanish-language paper. Mr. Carlos Palacios and Mr. Baldomeron Puig "each gave a cow." The paper reported that Miss Julia García Naranjo de Faría at the Droguería del Refugio was handling further donations.[3]

On October 17, a first group of 250 Karnes City migrants waited in a vacant lot "with varying degrees of patience" for their caravan to leave. "Hundreds of children run about and play among the heaps of personal belongings ranging from rolls of bedding to crates of poultry," reported the English-language *San Antonio Express*. "The women sit stolidly by their belongings while the men pace the ground or gather in groups to discuss the trip."[4] When their caravan reached San Antonio, "cars and trucks loaded with furniture, bundles of clothing, kitchen utensils, and agricultural implements" passed through the city. "Hundreds of persons gathered at the corners where the caravan passed to greet and bid farewell."[5] The next day, in Laredo, "all afternoon trucks . . . rolled into the city," where more well-wishers waved in support.[6] "Clinging to meager personal belongings the refugees disembarked . . . for their short trip across the border into Mexico," reported the *Express*. "All appeared weary and exhausted from their 250-mile trip."[7] Five babies were born along the way, including three in the patio of the Laredo customs house.[8]

For all the moving community support mobilized for these Karnes City migrants, the caravan was full of "scenes of sadness and of pain," in the words of the *Laredo Times*. "On one of the smaller trucks was a family of four and an aged couple bent by the burden of years. The woman was palsied and emaciated, and the old man too weak to sit up."[9] Some of the migrants crossed into Mexico full of powerful pride in the original homeland where they had been born. One "elderly Mexican," leaving on horseback after twenty-five years in the US, threw his hat down as he crossed the border and shouted "Viva Mexico!"[10]

These people weren't being deported, exactly—they are referred to as *"repatriados"*—those repatriated, distinct from the eighty-two thousand Mexicans the US government formally deported during the 1930s.[11] Officially, they left voluntarily, but it's more accurate to describe their departure as coerced removal. They were made to feel unwelcome and unsafe in the US during the Great Depression, as hostile employers, local authorities, relief officials, and the press turned on them with racist and increasingly vitriolic blame for the economic crisis. Faced with enormous economic challenges, just as were millions of others during the Depression, they chose to make their way southward.

In the mid-1930s, a second large wave of 315,000 people traveled from Arkansas, Kansas, Missouri, Oklahoma, and Texas into California. These migrants were overwhelmingly white (5 percent were African American), fleeing failed farms, lost jobs, and the nation's ever-deepening agricultural crisis, exacerbated by drought and, in some parts of the region, devastating dust storms that engulfed entire towns. Once in California, many of them worked in the fields; throughout the state, they were derided as "Okies" and "Arkies."[12] "Dad bought a truck to bring what we could. There were fifteen people to ride out in this truck in addition to what we could haul," Boyd Morgan recalled of his family's 1934 passage from their farm in Council Hill, eastern Oklahoma, to picking cotton in Tulare, California. "That wash pot sitting right there was one thing that came, also sewing machines. The kitchen table with the legs taken off was nailed across the bed across the top of it. Things were packed underneath like bedding." On the back of the truck hung two five-gallon cans full of cookies his stepmother had baked. At night "we just camped by the side of the road." The truck broke an axle. It took eleven days.[13]

Sociologists quickly rushed to document the living and working conditions of white migrants who began to work in California agriculture. Dorothea Lange, the famous documentary photographer working for the New Deal's Farm Security Administration, called attention to their plight in arresting photographs of women and children in rags.[14] By 1939 John Steinbeck had thrust them onto the national stage with his blockbuster novel *The Grapes of Wrath*, about a white Oklahoma family that loses its farm in the Dust Bowl, makes a tragic trek westward along Route 66, and ends up picking crops in California in dire poverty.[15] Hollywood director John Ford made the story into a successful film the next year.[16] Together, Lange, Steinbeck, and Ford exalted the plight of the poor, noble, white farmworker in Depression America, in what became the great iconic images of the "Common Man" during the Great Depression.

The two migrations, each described as an "exodus," appear strikingly parallel in many ways: displaced people reluctantly leaving their homes, sundering their extended families; old trucks and cars moving across the landscape with mattresses piled atop them and pots and pans hanging outside, precious sewing machines inside next to exhausted, fearful family members.[17] All were hoping to build a new, more economically viable future. Within California, the two migrations were in fact intertwined: as Mexicans and Mexican Americans vacated farm labor in California, white and Black migrants from the Midwest and Southwest moved in to take their places. In labor camps and union campaigns, they at times overlapped in uneasy solidarity.

But one migration was largely white, the other wasn't. One has been enshrined in official US historical memory as a tale of noble poverty, of survivors who triumphed over adversity. The other has been pushed off the map of "US history," almost never taught in schools or universities, although it was an atrocity on a grand scale in which a million people were driven out of their homes, their livelihoods, and their communities, in wrenching separations that tore parents from their children. Most people in the US don't even know that the 1930s repatriation of Mexicans, along with their deportations, ever happened—although Americans of Mexican descent, and the descendants of the repatriados in both countries, carry its memory today in oral traditions and in multigenerational trauma.

Together, the two migrations tell us a lot about the politics of poverty and welfare during the 1930s and about how the governments of two nations addressed the crises of the Great Depression. They tell us about how farm labor fared in California both before and during the New Deal; how racism sliced through the nation, cutting out residents of Mexican descent; and how borders sliced apart families. Last, but by no means least, their histories are also, once again, tales of collective survival, vibrant organizing, and the power of families to reframe their own lives in the most challenging of circumstances.

PASSAGEWAYS

For decades, people of Mexican descent had knit together livelihoods and communities in the US, while often remaining connected to Mexico. It's important to underscore that tens of thousands of Mexicans who lived in the US were never immigrants—they first became part of the country in the 1830s and '40s when the US government conquered the parts of Mexico that became Texas, California, Arizona, New

Mexico, Nevada, and Utah. In 1930, the US census counted 1,422,533 "Mexicans," including foreign and native-born people, living in the US. The actual number was probably far higher.[18] By that point, people of Mexican descent who lived in the US included those who had been in the country for multiple generations, as well as many who had migrated north in a small, steady stream during the late nineteenth century. After 1900, increasing poverty in Mexico, exacerbated by the disruptions and violence of the Mexican Revolution (1910–20), convinced hundreds of thousands more to move northward in search of work, often following railroad lines.[19] "I abandoned Zacatecas at the first outbreak of the revolution when the Villistas [followers of Pancho Villa] came into the towns robbing and burning houses," recalled one Karnes City repatriado.[20]

In a March 1927 editorial entitled "A Caravan of Sorrows," the Mexico City newspaper *El Universal* lamented: "Day by day the procession of laborers emigrating to the United States grows larger. . . . Every day trains leave for the neighboring republic, crowded with workers seeking employment on the ranches of Texas and California, and on the railways of the great West." This caravan flowed northward, carrying its own sorrows. "These unhappy exiles go against their will. They are driven abroad by the imperative quest for food."[21] In the first three decades of the twentieth century, 10 percent of the entire Mexican population chose to travel north.[22]

Mexican immigrants worked most often in farm labor, traveling in many cases as families in annual circuits—one of which moved up through California from lettuce in the Imperial Valley to peaches in the Sacramento Valley to hops in the Pacific Northwest; another, from cotton in Texas to tomatoes in Ohio and sugar beets in Michigan. Gradually, some migrant families settled into more permanent work as wage laborers, sharecroppers, or tenants on farms in the US Southwest, especially growing cotton in Texas, where nearly half of all Mexicans in the US lived in 1930; another quarter lived in California. Urban populations grew—in El Paso, San Antonio, Detroit, Chicago, and in smaller cities and towns. By 1930 the Mexican-descent community in Los Angeles counted a hundred thousand people. Working people in turn spent their money at small businesses run by their compatriots—butchers, bakers, auto mechanics, drug stores—forming a tiny Mexican American middle class. Most men still worked in unskilled labor; some began to move into skilled occupations, like installing irrigation pipes or laying bricks. In Texas, three-quarters of construction workers were Mexican American. But women mostly found paid work only as domestic servants.[23]

During all this time, migration to and from Mexico stayed fluid. In the wintertime, after the season was over, many farmworkers returned home to their villages in Mexico, returning to the US when it warmed up to plant the next year's crops. Others made trips to Mexico to celebrate weddings or see their parents and grandparents one last time before they passed. But by the 1910s and especially 1920s, crossing the border into the US was getting harder and harder. In 1924 the US increased the number of border patrol agents from 64 to 450, who worked more and more with local and state law enforcement to harass, round up, and deport those deemed undesirable. At border crossings, agents increasingly humiliated Mexicans. Lines extended for hours. In El Paso, authorities forced prospective entrants from Mexico into narrow rooms and fumigated them with toxic "gas baths" of kerosene and other substances. At the same time, informal, sometimes hidden border crossings still proliferated—like Johnson's Crossing, where Pablo Baiza took his burros across the river.[24]

Through all these years, Mexican immigrants, as did most immigrants to the US, continued to identify with their country of origin, their ties reinforced by the proximity and permeability of the border. In the West, Southwest, and Upper Midwest during the 1870s onward, they formed mutual benefit societies—mutualistas—that originated as collective insurance funds for burials and medical emergencies and, sustained by the work of women, also provided cultural and educational programs celebrating key dates in Mexican history like September 16, Independence Day, and, in many cases, traditions of rebellion. The societies chose names that deliberately evoked prominent figures from Mexican history—such as La Sociedad Mutual Protectora Benito Juárez in Laredo and La Sociedad Mexicana Miguel Hidalgo in Pasadena.[25] In addition to attending to the "immediate and pressing material interests of their largely working-class membership," notes historian Emilio Zamora, the mutualistas "also reinforced a collectivist spirit with resolute statements of purpose in support of nationalist principles and moral values, an active civic role, and strict rules that disciplined their members into conscious Mexicanist proponents of the ethic of mutuality."[26]

Some immigrants chose to become US citizens. Others very consciously chose not to (dual citizenship was not allowed in these years), bound by patriotic ties to their homeland that aggressive Mexican nationalism in the aftermath of the Revolution actively reinforced. In a 1971 interview, Emilia Castañeda de Valenciana recalled that her immigrant father, a repatriado, "said that he would never become an American citizen. He wasn't going to step on his flag. I think this is the way he used to say it: 'Yo nunca voy a pisar mi bandera.' ('I am never going to piss on my flag.')."[27] Like Japanese immigrants in this period, many immigrants from Mexico were also aware they weren't welcome in the US and hedged their bets, unwilling to sever ties to Mexico should their citizenship status be challenged or degraded in the US.[28]

FORCES OF EXPULSION

Then the Depression hit, unleashing forces that propelled between a third and half of all Mexicans living in the US back to Mexico, taking many of their US-born children with them.

The general economic collapse hit Mexicans especially hard. They were concentrated at the bottom of the economy, especially in agriculture, so when agricultural prices plummeted, farm incomes and wages for farmworkers did too. In Texas, the vast cotton economy collapsed.[29] "Due to the significant drop in the price of cotton in all markets, and a result of that the decrease of agricultural activities in the Karnes County region, a multitude of Mexican workers have been left without employment," La Prensa reported from San Antonio in late September 1931. "Few have been able to continue working in the fields, with a miserable pay rate of 30 cents a day." Only a third of the usual acreage was being seeded for the next year's crop, moreover.[30] By 1931, Texas cotton pickers who in 1929 had been paid $1.11 for a bag of cotton now only received 44 cents.[31] The evaporation of agricultural income rippled, in turn, through Mexican and Mexican American small business communities in the Southwest and California. Cities offered no respite. By 1933, the unemployment rate in Los Angeles was 41.6 percent, for example.[32]

Emilia Castañeda de Valenciana, born in Los Angeles in 1926, remembered how before the Depression, her Mexican father had enjoyed steady and lucrative work as a skilled stonemason and bricklayer. "My dad . . . used to like to dress well and he had quite a bit of jewelry." Her family owned a duplex. Inside, "our house was very well furnished"; outside, they had fruit trees, turkeys, chickens, rabbits. The neighborhood "was a United Nations," she said, with Mexicans, Filipinos, Japanese and Japanese Americans, Chinese and Chinese Americans, African Americans, Greeks, and Jews. But when the Depression arrived, her father couldn't get work. Her mom worked as a domestic servant, and her dad now stayed home with the two kids and let struggling friends, including Castañeda's godparents, stay in the other half of the duplex. "Since times were bad, he just let a lot of those people live rent free." But then her parents lost the house, "since my dad had no employment." After that they lived in four different places. In 1934, her mom died of tuberculosis.[33]

While many white people in economic distress could expect some measure of government relief, especially once the New Deal kicked in, Mexicans, along with African Americans and those of Asian descent, could not. Some Mexicans in the US received small amounts of welfare assistance.[34] But most lived in states, especially Texas, where the relief payments paid by conservative state and local governments to anyone were a pittance or nonexistent. Between January and September 1931, Detroit, for example, paid out $6.59 per recipient and Los Angeles, $3.40, but Dallas only paid 49 cents, El Paso 29 cents, and San Antonio 15 cents.[35] Ten thousand Mexican immigrants in Los Angeles did receive aid in 1933–34, less than 1 percent of the city's caseload.[36] "I remember we used to get groceries from a warehouse," as well as clothes, Castañeda recalled. "I guess my dad paid utility bills with the money he got through welfare."[37] More often, though, when Mexicans and Mexican Americans applied for relief, authorities simply turned them down for being Mexican. In Detroit, relief authorities deliberately humiliated Mexicans by forcing them to eat in special cafeterias that served sauerkraut and other unfamiliar foods that sickened people, deliberately trying to lower the city's caseload.[38]

Struggling like so many others, Mexicans confronted an immense tidal wave of racism that accelerated the minute the Depression hit. Widespread racism against those of Mexican descent dated back to the US conquest in the mid-nineteenth century and earlier, and flourished into the twentieth century with longtime stereotypes marking Mexicans as lazy, dirty, criminal "greasers." During the 1920s, broad nativist hostility to almost all immigrants led to the Immigration Act of 1924, which cut off immigration from Asia and sharply restricted entry for Southern and Eastern Europeans, who were deemed racially inferior. Mexicans were allowed to continue to enter to meet the labor demands of big agricultural interests, but were nonetheless cast, along with Asian immigrants, as "aliens" who were "invading" the United States. When the Depression began, anti-Mexican racism erupted into even greater hostility, as Mexicans and Asians were blamed for causing and exacerbating the Depression by their very presence—fueling pressures to leave.[39] Repatriation, underscores historian Erika Lee, "was not just a xenophobic campaign to get rid of foreigners. It was a race-based expulsion of Mexicans."[40]

Severo Márquez, born in Chihuahua, Mexico, fought in the Mexican Revolution and then spent two decades working in Texas, Arizona, and California. In the early 1930s he was living with his wife and kids in Belvedere Gardens in East LA, working as the materials handler for an Italian contractor who employed a road-paving crew of eight other Mexicans. Márquez saved enough to buy a Dodge and a Ford; his wife was going to night school to learn English. "On Sundays, if we weren't working, we'd go to the beaches—to Santa Monica, to Newport, to Long Beach," he recalled, or to a "very pretty waterfall in that canyon in Santa Ana." But when the Depression hit, the contractor fired all the Mexicans on the crew, including Márquez. "There wasn't a lot of work, so they wanted what little there was to go to citizens."[41]

In February 1931, a US-born former sergeant in the Army, of Mexican descent, told the Los Angeles newspaper *La Opinión* that every morning for three months he'd arrived downtown at the construction sites where he was well known and had gotten work before. "Soon the supervisors come out and tell the people that are waiting to get a job to line up on one side, all the white people, and on the other side the ones that are not." He said that because he was "of dark complexion I stay [sic] with the people of my race and of course, do not get hired because the supervisor has the order to hire only the 'white people.'"[42]

Informal job discrimination like this coalesced into laws explicitly banning the employment of noncitizens, especially Mexicans. In August 1931, the City of Los Angeles made it illegal for any employer who received public funds to hire "aliens." That same month, the passage of the Alien Labor Act prohibited anyone in the state of California who received public funds from employing noncitizens.[43] Colorado and Arizona passed similar laws, as did El Paso. In January 1932, a man who identified himself as "Six Shooter Bill" wrote to the mayor of El Paso, threatening to blow up city hall if jobs were not provided for unemployed white Texans. "Brother we passed the court house the other day. Look who was a clerk, a Mexican. A Mexican, can you beat that? In a white man's place."[44] Much of this pressure came from exclusionary labor unions of white workers, especially in construction. In San Antonio, for example, the bricklayer's union complained to the US Department of Labor and the Department of War, protesting the hiring of Mexicans on military bases.[45] By 1937, the federal Works Progress Administration had instituted a national ban on employing noncitizens on any of its projects.[46]

Other aggressive government initiatives sought to terrify Mexicans into leaving altogether, in concerted campaigns designed to target those in the country without proper papers, and implicitly those with legal status as well. In December 1930, Hoover's new secretary of labor, William Doak, announced that there were four hundred thousand "illegal aliens" in the US that should be deported to create work for Americans. Doak then launched deportation raids nationwide. The City of Los Angeles mounted an especially aggressive campaign directed largely against Mexicans. Charles P. Visel, newly appointed chair of the Los Angeles Citizens Committee on Coordination of Unemployment Relief, telegraphed in January to federal authorities in charge of emergency employment that of the four hundred thousand Doak had enumerated, "estimate five per cent in this district. We can pick them all up through police and sheriff channels. Local United States Department of Emigration [sic] not sufficient to handle. You advise please as to method of getting rid. We need their jobs for needy citizens."[47] On January 26, Visel and his allies unleashed a citywide publicity campaign in which they announced on the radio and in English- and Spanish-language newspapers, all on the same day, that aliens were going to be deported—deliberately trying to scare those with and without papers.[48]

Visel called in immigration officials from Nogales, Arizona, San Francisco, and San Diego, who started raiding neighborhoods in El Monte, Pacoima, and elsewhere. On February 26 at 3 p.m., authorities suddenly moved in on La Placita, a public park in central Los Angeles, surrounded and detained four hundred people, demanded their documentation on the spot, and took sixteen of them into custody—four of them Chinese, one Japanese, eleven Mexican. The raid was splayed across the Spanish-language media, its deeply terrifying message rippling throughout the region. Similar campaigns of state-sponsored terror designed to evict Mexicans erupted in Denver, Detroit, Chicago, Gary, San Antonio, and throughout the Southwest in the early 1930s.[49]

Officials arrived in San Fernando the afternoon of March 5, Ash Wednesday, and "rode around the neighborhood with their sirens wailing and advising people to surrender themselves to the authorities," described María Luna in the Spanish-language *La Opinión*. "They barricaded all the entrances to the colonia so no one could escape," and began arresting men as they returned home from work in the local lemon groves. "We the women cried, the children screamed, others ran hither and yon with the deputies in hot pursuit yelling at them that their time had come to surrender."[50]

Through these campaigns and other mechanisms, an estimated eighty-two thousand Mexican nationals were legally deported or "forcibly removed" by the US government during the 1930s, in addition to the hundreds of thousands who purportedly repatriated voluntarily.[51] Los Angeles received the most publicity, but the deportations accelerated nationwide. In February 1931, the chief US immigration officer in Houston wrote to his superiors that since 1927 his workload had increased fourfold.[52] In 1929 a new federal law, directed at Mexicans, made it a crime to enter the US without documentation.[53]

White relief workers, swimming in this same racist sea and working for agencies embedded in the same local governments that pursued deportations and repatriation, not only turned down Mexicans for welfare or sharply restricted what they received, but actively and aggressively pushed them to leave the country. Social workers handed Mexican applicants free or subsidized train tickets and told them they weren't welcome.[54] In Detroit, a case worker noted that an applicant, "Mr. M," was a US citizen but nonetheless "demanded that he repatriate himself in view of the dependency of his family." Another applicant, "Mary Lou (age fifteen)," was born in Wayne, Michigan but was recommended for repatriation even though she "did not wish to return to Mexico."[55]

Dennis Nodín Valdés tells the story of Pedro González, who initially received relief in 1931 after Ford laid him off in Dearborn, Michigan.

Officials pushed him to repatriate; he said no. "Welfare officials requested assistance from the police, who first forced him to appear before immigration authorities to prove legal residence." When he still wouldn't leave, police dragged him out of his house and off to the railroad station. He still refused to go.[56] In Los Angeles, county welfare authorities took Mexicans out of hospitals and mental institutions and put them onto trains, along with orphaned children, many of them US citizens.[57] "It cost the County of Los Angeles $77,249.29 to repatriate one trainload," reported journalist Carey McWilliams, "but the savings in relief amounted to $347,468.41 for this one trainload."[58]

In a complex counterpoint between different forces, Mexican workers' own powerful organizing further provoked repatriations and deportations. In California, large agricultural employers had opposed immigration restriction vigorously up through the late 1920s. They wanted to make sure they kept their labor supply so their crops would be picked, their fields hoed. Mexicans counted half to three-quarters of the entire California farm labor workforce in 1930, along with Filipinos and smaller numbers of African American, Japanese, and white workers.[59] Beginning in the late 1920s, these workers began to launch small, isolated strikes in the Imperial Valley, organizing by ethnic group. In 1930, five thousand Mexican, Japanese, and Filipino lettuce workers in the valley then joined across ethnic lines in a single strike. By 1932, small, united strikes were erupting all over the agricultural zones of California. In Half Moon Bay, for example, when growers decided to cut piece rates, Mexican, Filipino, and Puerto Rican pea pickers walked out together. Filipino and Mexican workers increasingly began to coordinate their efforts, aided by individual white, Japanese, and Mexican Communists in the Cannery and Agricultural Workers' International Union.[60]

In 1933, their efforts climaxed in a massive strike wave throughout California agriculture. A total of 140,000 workers walked out in 140 different strikes, from berry pickers in El Monte to pea pickers in Santa Clara County. The climax was a cotton strike in the San Joaquin Valley in which twelve thousand workers—around three-quarters of them Mexican and one-quarter white, joined by African Americans and Filipinos—all quit. The strike was led by savvy Mexican organizers, their skills honed during a decade building horizontal networks with deep roots in the migrant circuit. The strikers succeeded in raising cotton wages by 25 percent, right at the very lowest point, economically, of the entire Depression.[61]

In response, the California growers swept down viciously on militant farmworkers and their allies throughout the state, in what journalist McWilliams called "the rise of farm fascism."[62] They organized Citizens' Committees that launched spies, blacklists, brutal beatings, and shootings in a reign of fascist rural terror. Agricultural interests soon coalesced into the Associated Farmers, backed by the Bank of America (which held mortgages on half of all California farmland), Pacific Gas & Electric, chambers of commerce, the California Highway Patrol, and local police, who by 1935 were conducting "preventive arrests" of union organizers. Mexican workers who'd organized the big cotton strike were swiftly seized and deported.[63] Smaller strikes did continue—in 1934, Filipino and Mexican lettuce workers struck once again in the Imperial Valley. But the repression was immense.[64]

In Salinas in 1934, for example, seven hundred Filipino workers were marched out of the city at gunpoint, their camp "burned to the ground."[65] Filipino immigrants had been welcomed for a decade as a new source of seemingly exploitable farm labor. But once they starting striking, they, too, were suddenly unwelcome. In 1934, Congress passed the Tydings-McDuffie Act, which cut off almost all immigration from the Philippines and revoked the special status Filipino immigrants had held as US "nationals."[66]

Perhaps surprisingly, the final key factor driving repatriation was the Mexican government. As hostility to Mexicans in the US mounted, the country's leaders, still consolidating their power and legitimacy in the aftermath of the Revolution (1910–1920), used the issue of repatriation to simultaneously fan the flames of nationalism at home and demonstrate their commitment to the broader flock of Mexican citizens abroad. "Repatriation was a political football made to order for extolling the virtues of Mexican nationalism," Francisco E. Balderrama and Raymond Rodríguez underscore in their classic study, *Decade of Betrayal: Mexican Repatriation in the 1930s*. "Rather than deal with the nation's problems, politicians diverted public attention by pointing the finger at the transgressions of the Colossus of the North."[67]

In practice, it was local Mexican consulates, usually acting on their own, who provided the most help to Mexicans in the US, often through aid to individuals seeking to return. Throughout the

Midwest, Southwest, and Southern California, consuls organized Comités Pro-Repatriados (Pro-repatriate Committees, sometimes called "Comités Pro-Repatriación") that mobilized Mexican and Mexican American small business communities to provide food, clothes, and even cash to those leaving. The central Mexican government, for its part, paid for train tickets from the US border to the Mexican interior and waived duties for repatriates' imported goods. Most famously, it promised agricultural land to those who returned. Word traveled fast among those in the US that the Mexican government would give you farmland if you went back, convincing many they'd be taken care of if they returned. Within the US, consuls and their allies deliberately pulled on nationalist heartstrings. Writing in *La Prensa* about the 1931 Karnes City caravan, for example, José Rojas Jr. exulted: "They had never stopped being Mexicans and because of that they return to their land happy." The Zacatecas migrant he interviewed, quoted earlier, told him: "I trust that the Government of my country will help me."[68]

"Central to the concept of México de Afuera [Mexico Abroad, or Mexico Outside] was the belief that people would return to Mexico one day," notes historian Daniel Morales, in a study of *La Prensa*, mutualistas, and the Mexican consulate in San Antonio. "The Great Depression put this to the test," he underscores, "and led nearly every Mexican organization in Texas to support and organize repatriation." Ultimately, Morales concludes, "México de Afuera ultimately hindered the creation of a forceful defense of Mexican migrants as members of the US polity."[69]

As the Karnes City caravan formed in September 1931, the Mexican consul in San Antonio, Eduardo Hernández Cházaro, launched a support network that spread throughout the region's tiny towns as well as its cities. In Laredo, he solicited the help of three women described as "of good society" to form a Comité Pro-Repatriado—Arnulfa Guerra de Casso, Virginia Sánchez de Garza Lozano, and Julia García Naranjo de Farías. They met in Garza Lozano's home on Matamoras Street and organized a Comité that reached out to the presidents of local clubs and societies, visited car rental agencies, and invited supporters to a big meeting in the auditorium of San Agustín Catholic church, three blocks from the border crossing. Men who worked with the consulate, meanwhile, lined up a hundred cars and trucks to transport the migrants.

Many of the donors to the migrants were small businesspeople. In Laredo, for example, the Tarin Market and other meat markets donated five rams, which El Fenix restaurant offered to cook, donating bread to go with it. Other middle-class donors included professionals and white-collar workers, such as the Sociedad de Damas Profesionistas en Obstetricia (Society of Women Obstetrics Professionals), which donated five dollars. Alberto W. Saldaña, a bank teller at the First National Bank, organized a support committee in the little town of Hebbronville. In Laredo, "the young ladies employed at the Woolworth's store" donated two hundred glasses of milk.[70] Still more funds flowed in from mutualistas in tiny towns like Kerrville, Realitos, or Eagle Lake, where forty to fifty members of El Campamento de Hacheros "Vicente Guerrero" (Encampment of the Modern Order of Woodmen "Vicente Guerrero"), a mutual benefit society, donated a total of $17.40.

La Prensa listed every donation in meticulous detail, the well-wishing sacrifices of ordinary people who in some cases contributed a nickel, a dime, or a quarter. In Laredo, Julián Orozco gave twenty-five cents, Delfina Morales gave fifteen, Niña Josefina Garza one cent. Some of the well-off donors, though, never came through with their promised aid, the San Antonio consul complained. "The occasion only served to display them . . . in order that their names would appear in the papers," so that people would think they were "palatines of the most pure nationalism."[71]

Residents of Nuevo Laredo, over the border, jumped in to help as well. Apolonio Ortíz, secretary of the newly formed carpenters' union, personally crossed into the United States to deliver 25 Mexican pesos to the Comité Pro-Repatriados. Almost fifty individuals and businesses contributed milk, bread, tortillas, meat, and funds collected at a baseball game. Others donated items to a fundraising raffle, including Sr. Miguel Mesquita, who gave a manicure case; Sr. Dr. Gutiérrez de Lara, a crystal fruit bowl; Sr. Fidencio Rendón and his brothers, six tins with patches for tires; Sr. Mauro Alcaraz, a shirt; Botica Central, six jars of brilliantine hair cream; and Sra. Alicia Z. Vda. de Theroit, who donated "several artistic objects."[72]

CROSSING OVER

For individual Mexicans and their families making decisions about their futures, the logic of leaving increasingly added up. Asked forty years later why he had left, Severo Márquez replied that it was the Depression and the loss of his job on the roads that had produced his decision, but added: "I don't know, it made me want to return to my land, and so that my children would get to know their grandparents, their aunts and uncle, their people."[73] Emilia Castañeda de Valenciana, when asked, recounted her father's inability to find work as a bricklayer, her mother's passing, and the humiliations of the meager welfare they received, then also reflected: "I'm sure [my father] was looking forward to going back to his country at some time."[74]

Rachel Tamayo, born in Houston in 1922, told an interviewer that her father hadn't lost his office job with the railroads in Houston, but "he got panicked. He said there were a lot of people committing suicide because they were losing their jobs." She recalled: "My dad asked the county to send him back to Mexico. . . . He knew he could get work there." He "said that things were looking bad here. He didn't want anything to happen to any of us." The family sold their house and left.[75] Pablo Baiza, interviewed as he crossed the Rio Grande with his burro wagon, said that he was sick of being harassed by US authorities.[76]

The stories that returnees told at the time reverberated with loss and resignation. "I've lived away from Mexico for twenty years. . . . I've left my youth and my energy in the fields of Texas. My children were born in this country," the unnamed day laborer from Zacatecas who joined the Karnes City caravan told Rojas. "I had a little bit of money saved; but I spent it in the time I was without work and now with a bundle of junk I'm returning with my children to Mexico."[77]

Many repatriating families had to make excruciating choices about leaving children behind. Teenagers and young adults often didn't want to leave, and refused to go with their parents, Balderrama and Rodríguez found. Brothers and sisters might make different choices and be torn apart for decades.[78] Other repatriados were returning to their loved ones, with a measure of hope. A twenty-one-year-old mother of six from Houston told a reporter as she was about to cross the border: "My husband gets no work here, and we have no people. What we eat is given to us. In Mexico, we have our mamma and papa, brothers and sisters. We will plant a garden, and make our own living among our own."[79]

By the end of the decade, a quarter of all Mexicans in California, and almost one-half of all those in Texas, had left.[80] Richard F. Boyce, the US consul in Laredo, reported that in the second half of 1930, the repatriates leaving through his city came from "forty-two states and the District of Columbia."[81] In Los Angeles an estimated 30 percent of the entire Mexican population returned.[82] "Once bustling colonias took on the eerie look of abandoned ghost towns," write Balderrama and Rodríguez. In Belvedere Gardens, where Severo Márquez's family had lived, "discarded furniture littered the yards." Weeds took over.[83]

Márquez and his family traveled to Mexico in their car in a little caravan with two other families he'd grown up with in Chihuahua. They left their houses behind completely full of furniture. "There was nobody to buy anything." They could only bring "the most essential," he remembered, "the clothes and what we could bring in the cars, a mattress up on top of the car, of each car." It took them three days to get to El Paso and enter Mexico.[84] Others left by ship from San Diego, New Orleans and elsewhere, especially those who were returning to Gulf states like Veracruz and Tamaulipas, since oil companies and the big banana companies offered cheap passage. Hundreds of thousands took trains using free tickets provided by relief authorities, local Mexican organizations, employers, or the railroad companies.[85] "Since my father used to work for the railroad, he didn't have to pay for moving his furniture because we took part of the furniture and dishes and things like that," recalled Rachel Tamayo of her family's exit from Houston. They brought a Victrola and her brother's little pool table.[86]

In Los Angeles, Valenciana's family packed up a single truckful "with maybe a few dishes, our blankets, and a few of our clothes," and left on a train from Union Station.[87] Carey McWilliams, the journalist who would later write the classic *Factories in the Field*, reported: "I watched the first shipment of 'repatriated' Mexicans leave Los Angeles in February, 1931. . . . *Repatriados* arrived by the truckload,—men, women, and children,—with dogs, cats, and goats; half-open suitcases, rolls of bedding, and lunchbaskets."[88] Allan Hunter, a white Congregational minister, witnessed entire trainloads full of departing Mexicans. "All I remember is gettin a feelin of mass exodus," he recalled.

His church offered food and other help, but the scene was grim. "We thought it was utterly unjust what was being done."[89]

Conditions at the main border crossings in El Paso and Laredo were grim too. Throughout 1930, '31, and '32, as tens of thousands reached the checkpoints in waves, trains south into Mexico were not always immediately available. Cars had to wait to get across the border. Márquez's family waited with their car in El Paso for five days.[90] There often wasn't enough food or water for those waiting to cross. In an article for *Survey* magazine, Robert N. McLean described the scene in early January 1931 at the El Paso customhouse: "There is a large corral, where early in January more than two thousand *repatriados* camped and starved, huddled together, waiting for a kind government to provide them with transportation so they can move on." During freezing cold nights, in thin clothes, they cooked beans and tortillas on "little charcoal burners." Some food was provided, but "there was much suffering. Women swarmed about the warehouses picking up one by one the beans which spilled through holes in the sacks." Eventually, after three weeks, they were able to leave in thirty-three boxcars arranged by the Mexican government.[91]

The moment of actual crossing was filled with emotion. Lucas Lucio, a neighborhood leader from Southern California, recalled in an interview with Balderrama the "terrible cry among the repatriates upon reaching the border." Some "did not want to cross the border because they had daughters or sons who had stayed behind."[92]

And yet the repatriados were carried in the hearts of their families, their communities, and by the Mexican government, all of whose efforts transformed the meaning of their departure. Alejandro V. Martínez, the Mexican consul in Laredo, reflected about the Karnes City caravan: "Even when the coming of the compatriots was a reason for sadness, it would be converted into a beautiful spectacle, through the generosity of our women, who know of suffering."[93] As the caravans passed through San Antonio, hundreds gathered on the street corners to support them. "A smile, a movement of the hand, and an adiós, countryman, was the farewell; but that farewell meant a last tribute of admiration and affection," reported *La Prensa*.[94] One photo from Laredo showed a fifteen-foot-high pile of giant bags of provisions about to be handed to the repatriados. Another photo captured a downtown street with a long line of cars and open-backed trucks full of Mexicans moving through on one side, and rows of well-wishers and observers standing five deep on the other. Similar scenes were enacted all along the border.[95] In May 1932, Houston's Comité shepherded three groups of fifty returnees each to the border 350 miles away. A photo of them in the *Houston Chronicle* showed men, women, and children standing and waving atop their luggage in the committee's flatbed truck, with "Comité Mexicano Pro-Repatriación" painted in bright letters on its door.[96] Like the Karnes City migrants, the Houston repatriados were embraced in their community's energetic love.

The story of repatriation is indeed an atrocity, but not a simple one of passive, individualized victims. Yes, examples of overt resistance to repatriation and deportation are hard to find. Any protest would have carried enormous risk, given the dangerous, racist climate of the 1930s United States. But we do have a few examples. Balderrama found that at a 1932 meeting organized by the Chamber of Commerce in Los Angeles, the Confederación de Sociedades Mexicanos supported repatriation by those who chose to leave, but protested the job discrimination against Mexican workers that helped produce it.[97] In Detroit, the Mexican consul helped arrange support for repatriados, historian Dennis Valdés found, but also protested against abuses by welfare authorities and the police—objecting, for example, to the treatment of Pedro Gonzáles, who, as noted earlier, refused to be loaded onto a departing train. Valdés concluded that the limited numbers who chose to accept free transportation to Mexico during a 1925 local repatriation drive "indicated that there was still widespread resistance to repatriation." Catholic priests pushed back, too: "Although the church took no official stand on repatriation, individual priests discouraged their parishioners from leaving." The International Labor Defense, a legal arm of the Communist Party, opposed repatriation as part of a broader policy protesting deportation and repatriation of any immigrants.[98]

But overt resistance to repatriation was by no means the only form of collective action by Mexicans and Mexican Americans during these years, as we've seen. Individual families linked together with family, friends, and neighbors to form caravans for traveling safely. Their allies in the Mexican community responded collectively to repatriation on a grand scale through the mutualistas, clubs, and Comités Pro-Repatriados in Los Angeles, Detroit, and nationwide. California

cotton workers and thousands of other farmworkers organized successful strikes against the growers, and won big. Elsewhere in the United
States, Mexican factory and other workers organized and joined unions
that often struck and won. Middle-class Mexicans in 1929 formed the
League of United Latin American Citizens (LULAC) and used it to fight
for voting rights, equal education, and other civil rights.[99]

In 1938, seven years after the people of San Antonio gathered on
the city's street corners to cheer goodbye to the Karnes City caravan,
six thousand to eight thousand pecan shellers walked off their jobs in
an immense citywide strike, and won a wage increase. Ninety percent
of them were women, largely Mexican or Mexican American, led by
the famous Mexican American organizer Emma Tenayuca and other
Mexican American Communists.[100] Some of those strikers, we can
surely imagine, would have been among the crowd waving to the
repatriados.[101]

WHITE FLIGHT

If the repatriation and deportation of Mexicans was erased from mainstream US history, another migration through the Southwest during the
Great Depression was burned into public memory as a heroic tale of
suffering victims, proud and white. While the story of the Mexicans has
largely disappeared, this other migration, about a third as large, is so
romanticized that it's impossible to discuss without clearing past thick
webs of distorted images, myths, and racism. In this second migration,
between 315,000 and 400,000 people, overwhelmingly white, but also
including a small percentage of African Americans, plus Indigenous people and others, moved to California from Arkansas, Kansas, Oklahoma,
Texas, Missouri, Nevada, and Utah during the Great Depression.[102]
They have been enshrined ever since in a codified tale of poor white
farmers who were driven westward by the Dust Bowl and ended up
as impoverished migrant farm laborers living in California ditches,
nobly surviving. But the reality of their migration is far different. The
"prevailing image of the Dust Bowl migrants . . . is extreme," cautions
historian James Gregory in his classic study, *American Exodus: The
Dust Bowl Migration and Okie Culture in California*. The migrants
should not be viewed as refugees, he cautions. "The Dust Bowl migration was a tragedy in the rather privileged white American sense of the

term." It was "mass internal migration," he writes, driven by economic factors, like many migrations before it.[103]

The terms used to describe this second wave of migrants are themselves subject to debate. Those who migrated from the Midwest and Southwest to California during the 1930s are usually referred to as "Dust Bowl migrants," but only 6 percent of them actually experienced the Dust Bowl. They are widely described as "Okies" but most weren't, in fact, from Oklahoma. Whichever their state of origin, migrants who were called "Okie" after they arrived in California experienced the term as a deliberate insult, a pejorative term. Gregory prefers the more respectful "Southwesterners." The Southwesterners themselves, in their oral histories, often referred to their fellow migrants from the region as "people from the east."

What can we learn about this second migration, then, without getting sucked into the vortex of its myth?

Before they left their sending communities, 43 percent of the Southwestern migrants did work in agriculture, growing wheat, corn, livestock, and especially cotton. Whether they owned their farms, farmed as tenants or sharecroppers, or worked as farm laborers, the Depression's plummet in agricultural prices wiped out their livelihoods, just as it had devastated Mexican farming communities. "You couldn't hardly sell what you raised because nobody had money to buy it," remembered Boyd Morgan of his family's farm in Oklahoma. "I remember one time my dad took eight hogs to market and brought them back home."[104] A series of terrible drought years, especially 1934 and 1936 when it didn't rain at all in some regions, made things even worse. Wells dried up altogether. "At the place where we lived the water was just down to a little mud so we had to go over to the next farm and get drinking water and laundry water and haul it back," recalled Juanita Everly Price, whose family fled Oklahoma in 1936. "That was terrible."[105] Unemployment tore through their communities. Lois Smith Barnes, who had lived in Madison County, Arkansas, told an interviewer, "There was no work at all around there. . . . One time all we had to eat was turnips." For "a month or two. Nothing but turnips." White-collar workers lost their jobs too. Robert Kessler's dad lost his as a Caterpillar tractor salesman, for example.[106] But "many of the 1930s migrants were neither destitute nor the dirt farmers of popular paradigm," Gregory underscores.[107] They were people experiencing the hard times of the Depression who chose to look elsewhere for livelihoods, as did so many others.

In addition to drought, dust, and dropping prices, federal policy itself helped force people off their farms. In 1933, the Agricultural Adjustment Act, one of the first and largest programs of the early New Deal, paid big farmers to take crops out of production in order to raise prices by restricting supply. The big farm owners then took the payments, kicked their tenants off their land, and used the money to buy tractors to mechanize production, further diminishing their need for farm labor and making it nearly impossible for small farmers to compete. As a result, hundreds of thousands of sharecroppers, tenant farmers, and farmworkers throughout the South, Southwest, and Midwest lost their livelihoods—white people, Black people, Native Americans, Mexican Americans, and Mexicans—directly leading to migration to both Mexico and California.[108]

Fifty-six percent of the migrants from the Southwest hadn't worked in agriculture at all, though. Two-thirds of them had lived in cities and towns. One in six was a white-collar worker, professional, or small business owner.[109]

Like Boyd Morgan's family with their tins of chocolate chip cookies tied to the outside of their truck, some Southwestern migrants to California did leave in cars and trucks loaded up with mattresses on top, just like in the iconic imagery—although, as Morgan took pains to point out, his own family's vehicle "wasn't a jalopy. It was a good truck. It was only a five-year-old truck" with new tires.[110] Others, though, took trains, hitchhiked on boxcars, or traveled in nice new Studebakers or other "classy cars," migrants recall. Juanita Price and her family took the Greyhound bus. It took anywhere from three days—driving all day and night straight through—to a couple of weeks to arrive in California, sometimes because the vehicles broke down, but also because people chose to visit relatives along the way. Usually, they traveled as single vehicles. At night they stayed in privately owned car camps or just put out their mattresses by the side of the road. Some stayed in motels.

When they reached California, the migrants did face a border crossing. The State of California maintained agricultural inspection stations at all sixteen of its entry points, at which officials rifled through vehicles demanding disclosure and destruction of forbidden fruits and vegetables that might be carrying pests. "I remember my folks . . . had heard others talking about how rough it had been," Lois Barnes recalled. Her family set up camp right next to the inspection station and boiled their burlap sacks over a fire right in front of border authorities, to prove the bags weren't carrying disease.[111] Some also pulled off elaborate subterfuges. Barnes recalled that her parents, expecting trouble, "put their canned goods right up behind the truck seat. They built a false wall there," and the inspectors didn't see it.[112] Most Southwestern migrants, both Black and white, remembered the officials as generally friendly—smiling and treating them with respect.[113] But Hattye Shields, whose family was white, told an interviewer years later that "this was quite a shock, this inspection at the border." She said that their car moved through the lines quickly, "but it was just the manner in which they conducted the inspection. We'd never had that kind of situation before with people in command." Her dad had once been a county sheriff in Oklahoma, and "Mother was a very proud woman. To be treated like that in that situation with those border guards . . . was very, very demeaning to them. They just didn't get over that for a long time."[114]

California border authorities could in fact be deliberately hostile. Shields concluded correctly that the inspectors "were trying their best—[to find] everything they could find to turn people back."[115] Although state border officials were legally charged only with inspecting for agricultural purposes, in February 1936 the Los Angeles Police Department, escalating campaigns against "transients" entering the state, dispatched 150 officers to staff the border stations, in what was known as the "Bum Blockade," directed largely at Mexican and Asian entrants. When the ACLU protested loudly, the LAPD pulled back within two months. But a year later, the state passed what was known as the "Okie Law," making it a crime to bring an indigent person into the state. It was eventually overthrown by the US Supreme Court in 1941 in *Edwards v. California*.[116]

Certainly, the state border was nothing compared with the bureaucratized, armed, and hostile US border that Mexicans had to negotiate. And the daring subterfuges that white migrants later boasted about were presumably undertaken on the assumption that, if caught, one could simply relinquish the banned produce. Mexicans who were caught playing the same tricks, by contrast, might have been subject to deportation. The prideful sense of having been humiliated that Shields's father experienced could have been shaped, in part, by the privileges he had enjoyed so far in his life as a white man, and a deputy sheriff, to boot. By contrast, an African American man from Oklahoma or Arkansas, passing through the inspection, would have experienced it in the context of a lifetime of demeaning harassment, much of it wrought by law enforcement officials such as Shields's father.

Once in California, tens of thousands of the three hundred thousand Southwestern migrants did end up working in farm labor, as whole families merged into the seasonal migrant cycle. "They'd go to Modesto and pick peaches when peaches were in season and when cotton picking started they'd go to Bakersfield where they'd start first and then go north as it progressed," Morgan recalled."[117] Many were already familiar with picking cotton and highly skilled at it.

Even after the strike wave of 1933 led to higher wages, the pay remained terrible and housing limited, dangerously unsanitary, and often not available at all.[118] Juanita Price's family settled in the Bakersfield area but "lived in half a dozen places," she recalled. Billie H. Pate's family went to live in Firebaugh, where his mother had two half sisters. "We got here in the fall of 1935 and we were out on this one ranch and we picked cotton that fall . . . and then the winter months came on and they were terribly bad." He remembered "living in the camp with no running water and no inside plumbing which we had never had though [sic] but the mud."[119] The next year, his family moved to live at the Lyon Hoag Ranch, which "had a few houses, cabins, where people lived the year-round."[120] Many farm laborers, like Pate's and Price's families, settled for a time on ranches where the grower provided land and minimal facilities, sometimes a basic little house. Even on these ranches, though, the conditions could be chilling. "At Tranquility on the west side of the San Joaquin Valley on the Russell Giffen Ranch," Boyd Morgan remembered, "there must have been at least 400 to 500 people in that tent city. It was out in the gumbo-mud in the wintertime." Tents were pitched four or five feet apart in rows that "covered at least five acres." Some families living in those tents did have kerosene heaters, but his family didn't.[121]

Many sympathetic descriptions at the time depicted horrific "brush camps," where the poorest of the migrant poor set up. Shields, though, in her oral history described her family's brush camp in loving detail:

one farmer couldn't offer her family employment, she said, "but he did allow Dad to move in and at this place we set up our tent and built a brush arbor and it was a beautiful little camp." A brush arbor was "a patio with brush around it," she explained. "Of course, there's no cement. It's just hard dirt. You sweep it clean and then you take leaves or branches off the trees and you put it along the side to keep the sun out and make yourself a little lean-to."[122] What to children like Hattye was a great adventure, though, would have been something else to her parents, who would have had to cook and stay clean in the dirt, as insects plopped down from the brush overhead.

Some white migrant families remained mired in the migrant cycle for the rest of the decade and beyond, dealing with the same labor exploitation and conditions that farmworkers of color had experienced for decades. But in many cases, white migrants could get better wages and jobs.[123] If we pay close attention to their oral histories, we can notice advantages and privileges that positioned them above people of color already working in the fields or arriving alongside them, and that provided the white migrants stepping stones to move up—and even enabled them to migrate in the first place. When Billie Pate arrived in Firebaugh, for example, his uncle already had a store serving the labor camp where they stayed, and through him Pate's dad got a job driving a tractor and could escape the backbreaking work of picking and hoeing. Pate's dad had recently inherited thirty-six dollars when his own father died, and they were able to use that to rent a house in King City, where they had an aunt.[124] Lois Barnes's father sold a life insurance policy back home to pay for the trip. Boyd Morgan's father had owned farms back home, so once in California he was able to obtain bank credit and buy a 160-acre farm and then a new tractor.[125]

More than half of all the Southwestern migrants hadn't worked as farmers or farmworkers at all back in their home states. And they didn't when they got to California.[126] After Robert Kessler's father lost his job in Oklahoma as a tractor salesman, he got a new job nearby as a pressman at a newspaper. But lead poisoning from the type was killing him, so the family moved to the West—where he got a job within two weeks selling tractors again.[127] In California, many Southwestern migrants worked in construction, especially, or in the oil fields.[128] In the cities, studies have shown, they actually fared as well as previous residents, on average, and sometimes better, getting jobs in construction but also in white-collar work.[129] But wherever you lived, whatever your racial/ethnic background, you couldn't get that kind of well-paying job if you were a woman.

Southwestern migrants were also able to get access to welfare. Overall, the California state government was far more well-funded than the states that the migrants had left. The same California welfare offices that turned down Mexicans or handed them train tickets provided regular relief to Southwestern migrants. In one 1939 study, two-thirds of Southwesterners had received some kind of aid during the year before. "More than anything else, relief checks made it possible for most Southwestern migrants to establish a settled existence," Gregory found. "Between picking seasons, if no other work was available, eligible families could often count on either a job with the WPA or help from the State Relief Administration [SRA]."[130] Mexican farmworkers, by contrast, if they remained in the state, remained stuck in the migrant stream, without access to welfare in rural areas.[131] And, as Christina Heatherton notes, beginning in 1933 the big growers worked hand-in-glove with state relief officials to push Mexican workers off relief and into the fields during the harvest season, and even forced recipients to scab in exchange for aid.[132]

African American migrants to California do tell of receiving government aid. "They had what they called commissaries," Christina Veola Williams McClanahan recounted. "You got an order blank and . . . actually ordered the stuff." Her family would get a crate of oranges, often. "We'd have new dresses and the boys would have new jeans and new underwear"; the girls might get pink seersucker bloomers. During the farming off-season, her father worked for the WPA clearing riverbanks or performing other manual labor. "He would be on the WPA or the SRA and together he got $48," using that money to finally buy a car.[133] Juanita Price's family, too, got groceries from the welfare office; her husband got WPA work.[134]

Accustomed to white privilege, struggling in many cases in the new, brutal world of farm labor, using every strategy they could to pull themselves out of the ditches, Southwestern migrants of Northern European descent—those understood at the time as being of "Anglo-Saxon stock"—were all the more shocked by their treatment, throughout California, as a despised category of people known as "Okies," regardless of which state they'd come from. "Okies" were widely viewed to be lazy, drunk, "shiftless," untrustworthy, and dumb—many of the same stereotypes ascribed to African Americans, Native Americans, and Mexicans. "Okie" was almost a racial category, but not quite. Its usage nonetheless challenged the whiteness of Southwestern migrants of European descent, who were often equated with those marked as inferior people of color. In the San Joaquin Valley especially, signs in front of stores read "No Mexicans or Okies" or, at a theater, "Negroes and Okies Upstairs."[135]

In their oral histories, white migrants such as Boyd Morgan remembered being bullied or beaten up at school by other kids because they were "Okies." ("About the time they'd say, 'Okie,' I'd put my fist in their mouth," he recalled.)[136] Pate recalled, "Our teacher resented [sic] and made it known that she didn't like the Okies and the Arkies and the Texans." She "made it very difficult for us. . . . She was abusive towards us . . . calling us trash," he said. "We were just Okies to her and Okies were inferior."[137]

Working through their own new status as members of a maligned group, white migrants at the same time had to process the experience of laboring and in some cases living alongside groups of racially marked people they'd never encountered in their home states, including Mexicans, Japanese, Chinese, Koreans, Filipinos, and Italians. Back home, the white migrants had lived in regions that usually included African Americans and, in some cases, Indigenous people. But other groups were new to them. "Everything back there was white people," Kessler told his interviewer in 1981. "You didn't know what a Mexican was. You didn't know what an Oriental was. You never even saw anyone from Asia, a Chinese. . . . There were just plain white people." In their Southwestern homes, if whites did live near African Americans, segregation kept them apart. Where Kessler came from, "the colored people lived in the elbow in Guthrie," down by the bottomlands of the Cottonwood River, he said. "I never did see a colored guy in town. They all stayed in their own place." When his family got to California, "we'd see a dark complected guy or an Oriental guy and just look at that fellow. He wasn't a white man!" Kessler insisted that he had no "animosity toward them or anything." But "it just seemed like I was in a foreign country almost. I couldn't get used to guys not being white."[138]

Billie Pate said that his new school at a labor camp "had many Mexican-Americans, and we were not accustomed to these people. We had never been around them and so my mother wasn't comfortable with it at that time."[139] Jessie De La Cruz, a Chicana farmworker who would become an organizer for the United Farm Workers in the 1960s and '70s, recalled: "Anglos didn't want anything to do with the Mexicans [and] tried to stay away from the Mexican people. . . . They wanted their own labor camps, they didn't want to be mixed in with the Chicanos, the Mexicans."[140]

If we listen to the oral histories of African American migrants from the Southwest, the privileges that white people enjoyed—and enforced—emerge even more clearly. Christina McClanahan grew up in an all-Black town in Oklahoma; Blacks weren't allowed in the nearby white town after the sun went down. When she was seven, her family decided to move to California. "It was a combination of bad crops one year, the animals dying the next and then the dust bowl and the Depression. Prices were down and so my mother thought that a move anywhere would do us good."[141] Her mother and six children, along with an aunt and uncle, drove west in a 1929 Chevy with a trailer behind it. "Did you stay in tourist camps or did you camp out as you were coming?" her interviewer asked. "Are you kidding?" replied McClanahan. "You know they don't allow blacks to go in anyplace. The only thing we could do was stop on the side of the road." The family eventually came to live in a Black settlement near Buttonwillow, west of Bakersfield, and largely stayed in fieldwork—never becoming foremen, buying tractors, or selling them as whites did. Her family came to California with no inheritance, no nest egg.

Juanita Price, also Black, migrated with her family from Payne County, Oklahoma. "When the Depression came my father lost all of his things that we owned—all the livestock and everything. Then we became just sharecroppers."[142] They decided to go to California after a dust storm "devastated all the crops. Everything was gone." She was sixteen at the time, married, and had already lost a son and given birth to a second baby. In September 1936 the family arrived near Bakersfield. "We had a lot of relatives here," she recalled, including her husband's sisters and brothers and her father's four brothers.[143] Price and her husband "started right in on picking cotton. I used to carry my baby into the fields."[144] The family moved constantly around the area, living on various ranches, sometimes in houses provided by the owner. On one ranch, in 1937, it was just a tent. A big storm blew away "our washtub and almost everything else and tore up the tent. It was just terrible." Once, her family's employer gave them a little house; but even there, "it was a problem to carry water to drink, water to bathe, water to do your laundry, water to do everything."

Price remembered that Black families lived near each other in all-Black groupings on the ranches. Asked about working alongside other groups that were "considered minorities," she answered that "they were never a problem. But there were problems with the white people. . . . They were taught that they were better than blacks. So they had to wear that off, and some of them haven't worn if off yet."[145]

The question was whether white migrants would organize collectively and strike to improve their conditions—and whether they would do so together with their multiethnic coworkers. During the immense 1933 cotton strike in the San Joaquin Valley, the workers had been 75 percent Mexican and 20 percent white, plus African Americans and Filipinos; the strike leaders were Mexican leftists with long histories in labor struggles. But by 1935, in the wake of continued repatriation and deportation of Mexicans and their children, the ethnic balance in the California cotton fields had shifted dramatically: now more than half of the valley's farmworkers were white. By 1937, they counted 90 percent.[146]

Despite repeated, concerted efforts to organize them, white Southwestern migrants for the most part resisted unionization and other forms of collective labor action during the 1930s. Historians have noted that unlike Mexicans and Filipinos, white migrants didn't have a decade or more of experiencing migrant labor and learning how to organize and fight back collectively. They thought of themselves as individualistic entrepreneurs about to build a new life as farmers, with help, perhaps, from relatives. "The myth of upward mobility and the perceived value of citizenship and white skin kept alive the hope that they could leave the ranks of farm labor," concludes historian Devra Weber in her study of California cotton workers during the 1930s. "Even though they were called 'Okies' and treated not much better than their non-white co-workers, racism and a desire to be accepted members of the white community made it hard to establish common ground with the Mexicans."[147] They "identified with white growers as Mexicans never had."[148] White migrants' lack of commitment to unions, in turn, exacerbated the challenges that nonwhite farmworkers

faced after 1933, as the growers' anti-union strategies became exponentially more sophisticated, aggressive, violent—and effective.[149]

To understand the migration of whites from the Southwest, it's
important to get the nuances right, overall. These were people who
suffered great heartbreak and economic distress, both in their sending
states and, in many cases, once in California. They'd lost their jobs,
farms, crops, and secure futures for their families. In California, tens
of thousands out of the total 315,000 migrants ended up working
under the burning sun, living in filthy tents or shacks for their first
year, or longer. They were marked by hostile stereotypes as a despised
group, and accused of being lazy, stupid thieves simply because of their
accents or alleged states of origin.

But unlike Mexicans and Mexican Americans, they weren't forced
out by a hostile government—although the New Deal's Agricultural
Adjustment Act contributed to the economic devastation of many. In
the communities they had moved from, they didn't have to get out of
town by sunset, as did African Americans. On the road to California,
they could stay in roadside camps. They got the better housing on
the ranches; they got paid more; they had uncles who owned stores;
they had an aunt they could stay with in San Jose. Most found work
in the cities and did as well as those already in place, on average. If
they needed help, they weren't turned down for welfare because they
were "foreigners" or from the wrong ethnic group. In later interviews,
white former migrants, unlike Mexican repatriados, didn't speak of
traumatic child separation—they spoke of moving by choice to join
uncles, aunts, brothers, sisters, or older children who had already
migrated to California the decade before.

Just at the moment when Mexicans were forced out of California
farm labor on a grand scale—and out of jobs throughout the state—
white Southwesterners rushed in to fill the vacuum. And the vacuum
was there because government policy—on multiple levels, from the
Immigration and Naturalization Service to city governments—had created it. If we put the pieces together, it's clear that white Southwestern
migrants were precisely the "Americans" in the vicious anti-immigrant
campaigns of the 1930s that demanded "Jobs for Americans." As individuals, as families, and collectively, they benefited from private vigilante activism, from social workers who forced impoverished people
onto trains, from contractors who fired Mexican workers and other

workers of color in order to hire whites, from union demands to the government that no Mexicans work on military bases. They moved into the houses, the jobs, the business opportunities that Mexicans had just been forced to vacate. The racism here wasn't merely a question of white migrants' personal distaste for Mexicans or Chinese or Japanese, or even individual discriminatory acts by employers. It was also deeply institutionalized racism on the part of the government, designed, in the face of economic crisis, to take care of white people.

"THEIR BLOOD IS STRONG"

How, then, did the invented tale of the noble Dust Bowl migrants become so central to the national narrative about the Great Depression, so ingrained in public memory ever since?

The answer begins, in part, with the New Deal. In 1935, the federal government created the Resettlement Administration, which was initially designed to find bits of land for displaced Southern farmers to begin new lives. By 1937 it was renamed the Farm Security Administration (FSA), placed under the Department of Agriculture, and its mandate broadened to include farmworkers. In 1935 the agency hired a well-known economist at the University of California, Berkeley, named Paul Schuster Taylor to document the situation of California farmworkers; Taylor, in turn, hired photographer Dorothea Lange.[150] Within months of working together, they were deeply in love and preparing to get married. Lange's stunningly evocative photographs of impoverished farmworkers in their shacks, their tents, their broken-down cars—"the handsome homeless," as her biographer Linda Gordon calls them—moved quickly into the national media, shaping the visual narrative of California agriculture.[151]

Lange took pictures of a wide range of farmworkers, including those of Japanese, Mexican, Filipino, and African American descent, but two-thirds of her photos were of white migrants.[152] Her employer, the Farm Security Administration, which owned and controlled the images, used almost entirely those she took of white people. It was Lange's white migrants whose images quickly seared into the popular imagination, calling attention to the terrible poverty of white migrant farmworkers just as they became the numerically dominant labor force. Most famously, her *Migrant Mother*, first published in the

San Francisco News in 1936, became the ultimate image of the poor during the Great Depression. Lange shot the photo in a migrant camp of pea pickers near Nipomo, north of Santa Barbara. She set it up as a Madonna and Child: a poor, ostensibly white woman with a baby in her lap, along with two young children clinging to her, with one of her hands raised up to her worried-looking face.[153]

In *Migrant Mother*, as in other photos, Dorothea Lange's farmworkers were pure, suffering victims, not militant strikers nor former tractor salesmen with an uncle in town or a bit of money back in an Arkansas bank. Deeply moving, her images were designed to make the viewer feel that the migrants' situation was terrible, in order to elicit support for New Deal programs on their behalf. "Lange ennobled, monumentalized, even exalted working people. Her poor people are virtuous and resilient, rarely resentful, never lazy or violent," notes Gordon.[154] "Their whiteness made their suffering more shocking to the elite."[155] As historian Lawrence Levine observes, they were "perfect victims."[156] Lange was from a well-off white family (her father, a lawyer, served in the state legislature), although her parents' divorce complicated that. She traveled in culturally elite circles and pitched her photographs to people like herself who would, hopefully, be moved by the images she staged.[157]

Lange's white farmworkers appear to be of Northern European descent—the "Anglo Saxons" exalted by white racists. They were not recent immigrants from Southern or Eastern Europe, the Italians or Jews or Greeks whose ascendance into whiteness was still marginal and contested at the time. Lange's "white" subjects could tap into sympathy among middle-class white viewers that would not have been available for other workers. Decades later, journalist Geoffrey Dunn and others tracked down Lange's famous *Migrant Mother* herself, Florence Owens Thompson. She turned out to have been born in a teepee on a Cherokee reservation in Oklahoma, to Cherokee parents; her stepfather, with whom she and her mother moved to California, was Choctaw. Gordon recounts that in 1958, Thompson learned that her image had been published in *Look* magazine as part of the Family of Man photo exhibit and demanded that *U.S. Camera* magazine, the publication where she saw it, "recall all the un-sold Magazines," because her image had been used without her permission. She threatened to sue.[158] "I wish she hadn't of taken my picture," Thompson told the *Los Angeles Times* in 1978.[159] She never got a cent from the worldwide usage of her image. Her daughter, Norma Rydlewski, later told Dunn that *Migrant Mother* misrepresented the family's experience. They hadn't, in fact, sold their car's four tires for food, as Lange reported after taking the photo. "Rydlewski noted that while the Depression was hard on the family, it was not all suffering. 'Mama and daddy would take us to the movies a lot. We'd go to the carnival whenever it was in town. . . . We listened to the radio.'" They'd get ice cream; relatives visited.[160] Thompson and her family, moreover, had migrated from Oklahoma to California in 1926, not during the Great Depression.[161]

Many of the migrants who did arrive in the 1930s were from the section of Oklahoma that had been designated by the federal government in the nineteenth century as semi-independent "Indian Territory," which, beginning in 1889, was opened to settlement by non-Indians and later incorporated into the state of Oklahoma. "My father came out to Indian territory in 1893 when he was 13 years old," recalled Boyd Morgan.[162] Robert Kessler told his interviewer that his father's parents "came down from Iowa in the 1889 run for the land when Oklahoma was a territory. They got a place southwest of Guthrie with 160 acres."[163] Juanita Price said the ranch where she and her mother were both born "was called Indian territory at the time."[164] In other words, the romanticized "Dust Bowl" farmers, depicted as displaced from the farms they'd lived on for generations, were themselves quite recent invaders and appropriators of Native lands. Many of the Native people living in "Indian Territory" by the early twentieth century, for their part, including Florence Thompson's Cherokee and Choctaw people, were themselves in Oklahoma because they had previously been driven out of southern Appalachia and the Southeast during the brutal Trail of Tears during the 1830s, forced to walk all the way to Oklahoma.[165] Even some Southwestern migrants to California who identified as Black or white descended in part from this much earlier migration that thousands didn't survive. Lois Barnes, for example, who identified as white, recounted that her father's mother was half Native American. "His grandmother had seen her parents killed when the U.S. troops made the Indians leave Tennessee. The white people came in and killed all the Indians in the village. She and her brother ran in to the woods and escaped from it."[166]

T hree years after Lange's photographs established the visual imagery of the "Common Man," John Steinbeck, in his novel *The Grapes of Wrath* (1939), took the image of white suffering and thrust it onto the national stage as an epic narrative. The book shot to the top of the bestseller lists, sold 430,000 copies by the end of 1939, and won Steinbeck the Pulitzer Prize, the National Book Award, and eventually, the 1962 Nobel Prize in literature. Since its publication it has sold at least 14 million copies.[167] At 850 pages, the book tells the story of the fictional Joads, a white extended family that lost its farm to the Dust Bowl in Arkansas and ended up in migrant labor in California. A third of the book follows their arduous journey along Route 66 in a converted sedan; two grandparents die along the way. Once in California, the Joads remain mired in deep poverty as they follow the migrant labor cycle and live in ditch camps and boxcars. Steinbeck ends the novel with a deliberately mythic image of the family's daughter, who's just lost her baby, breastfeeding a starving man who is lying in her lap in the corner of a barn—another Madonna and Child. Steinbeck consciously casts their experience as an exodus story, employing a biblical tone at times: "And it came about that the owners no longer worked their farms," he intoned in a description of California agriculture, for example.[168]

Steinbeck, like Dorothea Lange, was pulled into writing about farmworkers by the New Deal's Farm Security Administration, which consciously shaped his viewpoint. In 1936, Eric Thomsen, a regional FSA manager, and Tom Collins, the manager of a migrant workers' camp it operated near Arvin, a small town near Bakersfield, took Steinbeck on a tour of farm labor camps in the southern San Joaquin Valley, to help him conduct research for a series of essays he'd been encouraged to write for the *San Francisco News*. Collins provided him with reports, talked his ear off, and even lodged him in the FSA camp Collins was managing.[169] Two years later Steinbeck, sincerely moved by what he'd seen on that tour, obsessively ambitious, and looking for a "big story" about which to write a famous novel that could take on mythic themes of grand proportions, wrote *The Grapes of Wrath*.[170] Hollywood producer Darryl Zanuck and director John Ford then snatched it up and turned it into a 1940 hit film starring Henry Fonda as Tom Joad, further codifying the visual image of suffering white migrants.[171] At the exact moment when California farm

Rent strikers and police in the Bronx, New York, February 26, 1932. NEW YORK DAILY NEWS ARCHIVE VIA GETTY IMAGES

Jesse Jackson (L), the "Mayor" of Seattle's Hooverville encampment, and fellow resident. *THE SEATTLE TIMES*

Relatives and well-wishers waving goodbye to 1,500 *repatriados* leaving on trains to Mexico from Union Station, Los Angeles, August 20, 1931. WIKIMEDIA COMMONS/NEW YORK DAILY NEWS ARCHIVE VIA GETTY IMAGES

Repatriados atop freight train and waiting to board passenger trains, in the copper-mining town of Miami, Arizona, on their way to Mexico, 1932. CHRISTINE MARIN PHOTOGRAPH COLLECTION, CHICANO RESEARCH COLLECTION, ARIZONA STATE UNIVERSITY LIBRARY

Striking wet nurses (with registered nurse in uniform in back) occupying the front office of Dr. Herman Bundesen, president of the Chicago Board of Health, Chicago City Hall, March 15, 1937.

WILLIAM VANDIVERT/*LIFE*/SHUTTERSTOCK

Registered nurse bottling wet nurses' milk at Chicago Board of Health milk in 1947. FROM *CHICAGO'S REPORT TO THE PEOPLE,* 1947 PUBLICATION BY THE CITY OF CHICAGO

Detroit police officers modeling seized Black Legion uniforms and weapons, May 1936. WALTER P.
REUTHER LIBRARY, ARCHIVES OF LABOR AND URBAN AFFAIRS, WAYNE STATE UNIVERSITY

Virgil F. Effinger, "Major General" and topmost leader of the Black Legion, May 26, 1936. WALTER P. REUTHER LIBRARY, ARCHIVES OF LABOR AND URBAN AFFAIRS, WAYNE STATE UNIVERSITY

labor became overwhelmingly white, much of the nation, through *The Grapes of Wrath*, discovered the terrible plight of the white California farmworker. Farmworkers of color evaporated from the story, appearing only in minor instances.

Steinbeck's writings before *The Grapes of Wrath* anticipated its racial politics and underscore the conscious choices he made in its construction. His first successful novel, *Tortilla Flat* (1935), depicted a group of drunken Mexican Americans he called "paisanos" comically lolling about in Monterey, California, where he'd grown up, in a bizarre amalgam of racist stereotypes about drunken Mexicans and a retelling of the Arthurian legend of the Knights of the Round Table. It's filled with lines like, "'Danny,' he asked sadly, 'how knewest thou I had a bottle of brandy under my coat?'"[172]

In his next novel, *In Dubious Battle* (1936), a short, hardened tale about white union organizers, Steinbeck melded together two actual 1933 strikes, one by peach pickers in the Salinas Valley, and the other the big strike by cotton workers in the San Joaquin Valley. In both of those strikes the workers had been 75 percent Mexican and Filipino. Steinbeck's workers are 100 percent white. He simply disappeared the workers of color—whose leadership as well as rank-and-file militancy had made the strikes successful.[173] In a letter to a friend while he was writing the book, Steinbeck admitted that he didn't even care about labor issues: "I have used a small strike in an orchard valley as a symbol of man's eternal, bitter warfare with himself. . . . I'm not interested in strike as means of raising men's wages and I'm not interested in ranting about justice and oppression."[174]

Steinbeck's nonfiction writings from these years explicitly promoted white superiority and racist concepts about people of Mexican and Asian descent. While he was working on *The Grapes of Wrath* in 1938, the Simon J. Lubin Society, hoping to drum up support for farmworkers, published the essays he'd written two years earlier for the *San Francisco News*. The pamphlet, originally entitled *Their Blood Is Strong* (reissued in 1988 as *The Harvest Gypsies*), featured photos by Dorothea Lange, including a cover shot of a poor, apparently white woman nursing a baby, with her breast and nipple clearly exposed.[175] The essays, about housing and sanitary conditions, the political economy of California agriculture, and the growers' repression, make clear that Steinbeck understood well the logic of hyper-exploitation embedded in the industrial model of California agribusiness. He spoke explicitly about the growers' fascism. He knew about and named the long history of racial discrimination against the series of different ethnic groups who had been brought in to pick the crops, then kicked out when they began to organize.[176] "In recent years the foreign migrants have begun to organize," he wrote, "and at this danger signal they have been deported in great numbers, for there was a new reservoir from which a great quantity of cheap labor could be obtained"—the white migrants.[177]

But Steinbeck distorted that back history. Only white farmworkers, he said, came and worked as families—obliterating the long history of Mexican family labor in the fields. Only white migrants, he said, had formerly owned farms—obliterating the history of Mexican and Filipino immigrants losing their farms in their home countries a decade or more before, off the US stage and often as a result of US imperial incursions.[178] He deployed classic racist stereotypes from the late nineteenth and early twentieth centuries, not only the idea that nonwhite immigrants were "sojourners" who did not want settled lives and were all planning to return home, but the idea that Asian people had "lower standards of living" and were happy to live on a bowl of rice. "The traditional standard of living of the Chinese was so low that white labor could not compete with it," Steinbeck declared, while the Japanese, "almost exactly like" the Chinese, had "a low standard of living which allowed them to accumulate property while at the same time they took the jobs of white labor"—as if Asian workers were yearning to be poorly paid.[179]

When he discussed the Southwestern migrants, Steinbeck explicitly celebrated a racial understanding of the superiority of white farmworkers. "They are resourceful and intelligent Americans," he declared. "They are descendants of men who crossed the middle west, who won their lands by fighting, who cultivated the prairies. . . . And because of their tradition and their training, they are not migrants by nature." Their "one urge" is to own land, he wrote. "This new race is here to stay and . . . heed must be taken of it."[180] "The old methods of intimidation and starvation perfected against the foreign peons are being used against the new white migrant workers. But they will not be successful." California agriculture, he insisted, now needed to take stock and treat its workers differently: "Farm labor in California will be white labor, it will be American labor, and will insist on a standard of living much higher than that which was accorded the foreign 'cheap labor.'"[181] Yet in fact it was workers of color who organized and fought back, not the individualist white workers. Steinbeck's essays were reprinted in a pamphlet entitled *Their Blood is Strong*, with obvious racial implications. White "blood" was strong; the blood of Others wasn't.[182]

The Grapes of Wrath, published three years later, echoes many of the themes from Steinbeck's earlier nonfiction essays, if more subtly. Describing the Gold Rush invasion of California, he writes in the novel: "The Mexicans were weak and fled. They could not resist, because they wanted nothing in the world as frantically as the Americans wanted land."[183] In a climactic passage on California history, which Steinbeck inserted into the text at the dramatic moment when the Joads finally cross into the state, he switches back and forth between third-person declamations and a first-person voice not attached to any particular individual character. "They streamed over the mountains, hungry and restless. . . . Like ants scurrying for work, for food, and most of all for land. We ain't foreign. Seven generations back Americans, and beyond that Irish, Scotch, English, German. One of our folks in the Revolution, an' they was lots of our folks in the Civil War—both sides. Americans."

Ironically, even white migrants on whose behalf *The Grapes of Wrath* was supposedly written and promoted were unhappy with the way it portrayed them. In 1981, oral historians from California State University, Bakersfield, asked migrants themselves what they thought of *The Grapes of Wrath*. Almost all the interviewees didn't like it. Many were offended by the climactic scene of a woman nursing a grown man. Boyd Morgan volunteered that the truck in which his own family had traveled, with its cans full of cookies hanging off the back, "was as near the description of Steinbeck's *The Grapes of Wrath* as anything ever was," but he hated the book: "I think it was degrading to the people. I think it was written to sell. . . . I remember a whole lot of people from Oklahoma were upset about it."[184] "I didn't like the book," said Lois Barnes. "It offended me a little. It just wasn't like my family." Her mom had stressed education, Barnes said; she'd been exact about which other kids Barnes could play with. Her dad most definitely didn't look like someone from *The Grapes of Wrath*. "Every morning he would get his mirror out, his pan of hot water, his shaving mug, and shave," she insisted to the interviewer. "I remember how he would sing a lot . . . when he was out working with his horses."[185]

Juanita Price had read the book and seen the film and had plenty to say. "It was stretched till some of the points were just outrageous"— including the breastfeeding scene and Ma Joad as the "boss over everybody," when in reality "everybody sort of pulled together." She had a crisp sense of Steinbeck as an author creating a narrative. "That was just a writer's theory. That was not the way people really are." Price, who was Black, said, "We lived around a lot of poor white people and I never witnessed that kind of life style ever." Things were just not that terrible. "The book made it sound like the majority of the people were living in that kind of condition but that's a mistake, in fact, it is a lie."[186]

How do we evaluate Steinbeck's racial politics today? We can't excuse him as "a product of his time," the way some still apologize for George Washington or Thomas Jefferson enslaving people. During the 1930s, other white people knew about repatriation, deportations, and the situation of workers of color in California agriculture and were appalled—and helped fight back. They didn't promote white superiority. White Communists Pat Chambers and Dorothy Healey worked as key organizers of farmworkers' strikes up and down California in the '30s. Allan Hunter, the white Congregational minister in Los Angeles who rushed down to Union Station as the trains were leaving for Mexico, brought food down to the repatriates, prompted by white women in his congregation and other churches. The food was "a gesture of friendship," he said. Hunter and the church women smiled and even sang to the passengers. "We thought it was utterly unjust what was being done."[187] In Detroit, the Catholic priests and Communists who opposed repatriation would have been largely white.[188] Most prominently, in 1939—the same year that *The Grapes of Wrath* was published—white journalist Carey McWilliams published *Factories in the Field: The Story of Migratory Farm Labor in California*, in which he explicitly laid out the long history of successive ethnic groups, repression, racism, and rising fascism in California farm labor. He chose that title to call attention to the industrial nature of the state's economy, because he wanted to promote the inclusion of farmworkers in the National Labor Relations Act.[189]

And certainly people of color were writing their own novels about race, the US-Mexican border, and farm labor. In Brownsville, Texas, Mexican American journalist Américo Paredes wrote a novel between 1936 and 1940 titled *George Washington Gómez,* about a Mexican American boy growing up in a fictional city on the Lower Rio Grande that resembles Brownsville. Paredes describes the boy's experience of racism in schools and the terrors wrought by the US border patrol and its private allies.[190] Paredes, who would go on to become a famous folklorist, wrote the book while working as a reporter for the *Brownsville Herald* and publishing poetry in *La Prensa*—the same San Antonio paper that covered the 1931 Karnes City caravan. In 1946, Filipino immigrant Carlos Bulosan published his classic autobiographical novel, *America Is in the Heart,* recounting his family's displacement from their farm in the Philippines and his years of brutal experiences working and organizing in migrant labor on the US West Coast in the 1920s and '30s.[191] Neither book is a victim narrative designed to elicit patronizing sympathy from white people. Paredes weaves a nuanced narrative about internalized oppression; at the novel's end, the main character ends up working as a corporate lawyer in Washington, DC, and buying up land on the Texas-US border, while his nephew secretly works for the US border patrol. Bulosan's characters are fully formed, too, sometimes heroically committed to labor activism and sometimes not; sometimes sexist, sometimes brutal. Neither author eliminated white people from the story.

In *The Grapes of Wrath,* the emotional counterweight to the Joad family's suffering in the ditch camps is the clean and tidy government-owned camp for migrant farmworkers in which the family is able to live for a time. Self-managed by farmworkers under the benevolent arm of the state, the camp gives the Joads a healthy place to live and also protects union organizers from local fascists. For the movie version, director John Ford changed the story so it ends not in the barn with the nursing woman, but at the government camp, leaving viewers with scenes of happy farmworkers sashaying on a government-provided dance platform.

By 1940, the Farm Security Administration had expanded a national network of these new camps for migrant workers to include fifty-three camps, half of them in California, the other half splayed across Texas, Oregon, Washington, Idaho, New Jersey, and Florida.

Although the overall number of people housed in the camps was ultimately small in relation to the total number of migrant farmworkers, the camps were indeed clean, deliberately safe for activists, and managed in part by residents' own committees. But in the novel, in the film, and in real life, they were whites-only. Mexican, Asian, and Black migrants, however desperate, weren't admitted. As Juanita Price remembered about the Arvin camp near where she lived, and where Steinbeck took his notes, "All white people—no blacks."[192] The same Tom Collins who managed the Arvin camp and hosted Steinbeck didn't allow African Americans into it; he later organized segregated, unequal housing units for Black and white workers.[193] It may not have been Collins's preference, though. In designing and countenancing these policies, the white top officials of the FSA in Washington, DC, above him, even when well intentioned, themselves had to answer to multiple political forces, often deeply racist, to their right.

The cultural politics of Dorothea Lange and John Steinbeck, with their compassion, distortions, racism, and immense impact, thus grew directly—if not entirely—out of federal policy in the 1930s, through the FSA's promotional activities in the arts. More broadly, and with much greater impact, the New Deal cut farm labor out of its otherwise monumental programs serving working people, under pressure from Southern white agricultural elites who controlled the Democratic Party and didn't want their workers organizing. Farmworkers were excluded from the all-important National Labor Relations Act (1935), which gave wage workers protections for union organizing. They were excluded from the Social Security Act (1935), which created old-age pensions. They were excluded from federal unemployment insurance. They were excluded from the 1938 Fair Labor Standards Act, which abolished child labor and created the first federal minimum wage. These programs were the crown jewels of the New Deal's programs serving working people. All that was left for farm laborers was relief, which did in some cases reach farmworkers, as we've seen, but largely those who were white or African American.[194]

Once in office in 1933, Roosevelt did help slow the forced departure of Mexicans and Mexican Americans. Deportations continued but were halved to between eight thousand and nine thousand in 1934, down from their 1930–33 high.[195] Repatriation slowed dramatically. George Sánchez, who has looked most closely at its decline, found that repatriation from Los Angeles decreased in mid-1933, and thereafter to a trickle of families. The last train left the city in mid-1934. He tracked a demographic shift within the Mexican and Mexican American community that affected people's propensity to leave: it was now composed of fewer single men, more small business and property owners, more people with residency of a decade or more. The New Deal also made relief somewhat more available than in the earlier years of the decade, as much more money flowed into the state, and federal authorities supplanted—and sometimes challenged—racist local authorities. The Mexican consul, moreover, was no longer supporting repatriation.[196]

And word was filtering back that the situation of those who'd moved to Mexico was dire.

REMAIN IN MEXICO?

The hundreds of thousands of Mexican repatriados, deportees, and their US-citizen children who had crossed the border didn't disappear; they sought to build new lives in Mexico. But it became quickly clear that the great help the Mexican government had allegedly promised wasn't going to materialize. In the border city of Saltillo, in the northern state of Coahuila, for example, locals prepared free food for the newly arrived, but the US consul reported a "very noticeable desire on the part of municipal authorities . . . to hasten their departure from this city"—a response not unlike that of authorities in Mexican border cities in the late 2010s to caravans of Central American asylum seekers.[197] In Monterrey, "a committee of prominent Mexican ladies acting under the supervision of the Monterrey Chamber of Commerce organized some relief for these persons," wrote the US consul there. "It was soon found however that the means at their disposal were far too meager for any effective charity or assistance and their returning fellow countrymen are now being permitted to shift for themselves."[198]

The central government did provide train fare to the interior for many. But its more formal projects of land settlement on a grand scale mostly failed miserably. Elite Mexicans organized a National Committee for the Repatriated that raised 300,000 pesos in 1932–33, to much fanfare, but its actual aid was ineffectual. In its most well-known project, the committee in 1932 transported eight hundred repatriados to a resettlement colony on tropical land in Pinotepa, Oaxaca. Insects, snakes, and tropical diseases plagued the residents, who sickened and died. Supplies and food ran out; dictatorial administrators supervised on horseback, accompanied by armed men. The colonists soon fled. In another large project, the government offered 1,500 repatriados arable land in an already-established irrigation project called Don Martin, in Coahuila, eighty miles west of Laredo, Texas. As many as ten thousand returnees flocked to the area, seeking land or at least farm labor. After some initial success, that project too fell apart within a few years, in the face of severe drought and other challenges. Smaller government-supported enterprises fared no better.[199]

Historian Abraham Hoffman concludes that once in Mexico, "most repatriates simply returned to the area where they had been born and where their friends and family lived."[200] Severo Márquez and his family drove through Mexico for nine days until they arrived in the village of La Capilla, Coahuila, where he'd grown up. "My dad had land there for planting and he gave us some pieces of it," Márquez recalled. "And later the uncles there, first cousins of my dad, landlords and cattle ranchers, also [gave us] . . . a piece of land." He gradually acquired cultivators, plows, horses, and other animals. The prices he could get for his beans and for corn were high, he said, and he was able to buy a nice car.[201] For the next decade, Márquez also worked at local mines, running a winch and supervising work crews, while his family lived on the rancho.

Emilia Castañeda's father took her and her brother back to Gómez Palacio, Durango, "to live with some relatives of my father." They slept outside, even in the rain, because the aunt they were staying with, who had six children of her own already sleeping on floors, said she didn't have room. After a while, her father moved them to live with other relatives in Lerdo, the next town over. There they stayed in two little rooms, with seven-inch-long centipedes crawling across the dirt floors. Her father found seasonal work as a bricklayer, and in the winter worked odd jobs such as selling fruit. Eventually they started living on a series of remote ranchos where her father found construction jobs. "It was nothing but hardships living on the ranches," she recounted. "We had to carry water and walk for miles to get water. . . . We used to carry water on top of our heads."[202] Within two years, Castañeda herself was working full-time as a live-in domestic servant—at age twelve.[203]

Other returnees, especially those with skills or a bit of capital, settled in cities and towns.[204] Rachel Tamayo's father, who had worked for the railroad companies in Houston, took her family back to a small town in Guanajuato, where he'd bought a house before he had moved to the US. He painted houses, and eventually owned a grocery store.[205]

All returnees had to find livelihoods in a precarious Mexican economy itself reeling from the Great Depression. Women returned to a culture with far more conservative gender roles for women than those in the US. They were expected to stay home, stay silent, and obey their mothers-in-law as well as their husbands. Adults, though, knew more or less what they would face once in Mexico. Their US-raised children faced enormous culture shock. Many couldn't speak Spanish. Their new homes often lacked running water, indoor toilets, and electricity, which they'd taken for granted before. "I want to go home! . . . This house is really ugly," Severo Márquez's youngest son protested. "He wanted to leave for Los Angeles," Márquez recounted. But the older children understood, he said.[206]

Castañeda suffered enormously in her new life. "The kids used to make fun of me . . . because I was from the United States." She dropped out of school, for good, and became seriously depressed. "I didn't want to eat. . . . I would cry and cry. . . . I would just sit there on the sidewalk not doing anything." Balderrama and Rodríguez, in *Decade of Betrayal*, found that children who moved to Mexico from the US were relentlessly bullied by local kids and accused of being "*agringados*" (Americanized) for wearing the wrong clothes, speaking the wrong way, wearing too much makeup. Returnee kids were also suddenly cut off from the movies and music that had been central to their lives in the US. Throughout Mexico, adults also faced hostility from locals, who were themselves in precarious circumstances, and who viewed the returnees as competitors for scarce jobs.[207]

Almost immediately, some repatriados decided to return. While exact numbers are difficult to ascertain, a steady stream began migrating back to the US during the remaining years of the Great Depression and during the 1940s. Castañeda came back to Los Angeles in 1944 at the age of eighteen, with the encouragement of her godmother there. "I didn't like the hard life that I had in Mexico. Why would I want to be working as a maid for the rest of my life? . . . Why would I want to wash clothes by hand and carry them on my head?"[208] Legal issues at the border blocked tens of thousands of repatriados from returning, though. Many who were born in the US didn't have birth certificates to prove citizenship; others had failed to obtain necessary documentation when they crossed the border into Mexico; still others lost their papers.[209] Rachel Tamayo did have her birth certificate and was able to return to Houston in 1949, but remembered that "at the time a lot of people didn't register their families," so their children couldn't re-enter the US.[210] Castañeda had papers, but when she tried to bring her father back with her, they couldn't find his birth certificate. Her younger brother wanted to return but eventually "gave up hopes of coming back or of ever being able to afford to come back."[211]

By 1940, the United States they returned to was beginning to change dramatically as well. World War II in Europe was already creating a boom in US manufacturing. With US entry into the war in 1941, federal spending on tanks, airplanes, helicopters, rifles, uniforms, bullets, and food rations quickly pulled white workers out of farm labor and into lucrative, union-protected employment in manufacturing. African Americans, initially barred from the new wartime jobs, after a national protest campaign were eventually able to obtain some of the good factory jobs too. Meanwhile, the draft further siphoned hundreds of thousands of men out of the labor force.[212]

Here the plot twists: If hundreds of thousands of white and African American farmworkers were drafted or left to work in wartime factories, who, then, would pick the crops? White people jumped quickly out of farm labor into the newly booming war jobs and other good jobs that opened up. During the early 1940s, the FSA camps' residents increasingly became people of color, including Mexicans, African Americans, and Filipinos, as the federal government's network of camps for migrant farmworkers expanded, from 53 in 1940 to 110 by 1944, and officials lifted their whites-only policy of the camps' initial years. In *Migrant Citizenship: Race, Rights, and Reform in the U.S. Farm Labor Camp Program,* Verónica Martínez-Matsuda has shown that farmworkers of color who lived in the camps made vigorous collective demands on the FSA's management in these years, and were able to gain improvements in housing, education, and health care, moving from exploitation to collective empowerment. "The FSA's camp program should be considered central to the civil rights movement that emerged in the 1930s," she concludes.[213]

The federal government desperately needed to keep its wartime economy on track, including food production. Its answer was Public Law 45, known as the Bracero Program, which between 1943 and 1947 contracted over two hundred thousand men within Mexico to enter the US temporarily to work in the fields.[214] Just a few short years after kicking Mexicans out, in other words, the US was trying to lure them back in. Some Mexicans who had been repatriated or deported even came back as braceros.[215] But the braceros lacked all citizenship rights. They couldn't organize or join unions. They couldn't object to their living or working conditions or they'd be immediately deported. Often they were never paid. Braceros didn't get to stay in the FSA camps, which were terminated in 1944.[216]

Braceros nonetheless organized and resisted. In the Pacific Northwest, Mario Jimenez Sifuentez has found, they put rocks in the bottom of bags of potatoes they'd picked, in order to increase the weight; they skipped from farm to farm, playing employers against each other and bargaining for higher wages; they struck over two dozen times; or simply disappeared, violating their contracts.[217] Mireya Loza shows that the transnational Alianza de Braceros Nacionales de México en los Estados Unidos organized throughout the program's existence to defend bracero workers, through alliances with unions in both countries, advocacy work on behalf of individual braceros and their families, and pressure on the Mexican and US governments.[218]

Initially enacted as an emergency wartime measure, the Bracero Program was so popular with the growers that it was renewed over and over again after the war. Between 1948 and 1964 the US, in cooperation with the Mexican government, brought in an average of two hundred thousand braceros a year.[219] Through all that time, non-bracero farmworkers had to compete with a labor force that was paid much less, and that couldn't unionize—almost completely quashing farm labor organizing. Only when the program was finally abolished in 1964 were Filipino and Mexican farmworkers able to successfully organize, and soon build the United Farm Workers union.

WHOSE CARAVAN?

Which "caravans" from the Great Depression, then, are remembered today—and by whom? US history textbooks largely ignore repatriation and the deportations. Few people in the country who aren't of Mexican descent know that the expulsions happened at all. *The Grapes of Wrath*, meanwhile, remains widely popular. It's taught in schools and colleges throughout the country, held up as a historically accurate account and a model work of literature. In Steinbeck's hometown of Salinas, thousands of schoolchildren are escorted every year through the privately owned National Steinbeck Center, where no mention is made of the writer's racism.

But collective memory can play tricks on official narratives. Memories can be resurrected, challenged, subverted, or slip sideways, and they certainly don't stop at borders. As quickly as the repatriados crossed into Mexico they began constructing their own narratives. Someone even wrote a "Corrido de Karnes City," a story-song in traditional form, celebrating the work of the Mexican consul in San Antonio in support of the caravan.[220] Former repatriados who remained in Mexico told stories to their grandchildren and great-grandchildren, in some cases. Since then, Mexican scholars have studied repatriation from their own point of view, looking from South to North. Today, repatriation is documented and discussed widely on websites about Mexican American history.

Within the United States, the Chicano movement of the 1960s and '70s prompted new attention to repatriation, and with it new research, especially oral histories of repatriados who'd returned to the United States. Balderrama and Rodríguez, who conducted dozens of interviews, recount the enormous trauma they unearthed. "It had remained a 'hush-hush topic' in the Mexican community."[221] The men and women they spoke to broke down or cried during interviews. Some hadn't ever told their children. "It is such a painful topic," said José López, a repatriado from Detroit. "It is something, personally, I would rather not even think about, much less talk about."[222] Prompted in part by Balderrama and Rodríguez's work, grassroots campaigning produced an official apology from the State of California in 2006, although then-governor Arnold Schwarzenegger voted down a second measure that would have begun to consider reparations.[223]

By the late 1970s and early '80s, oral historians began to also interview former Southwestern migrants, white and Black, who recounted their own difficulties, their own opinions about how they'd been depicted. Well into the early 2000s, they were still telling their children and grandchildren how hurtful it was when they were called "Okies." They, too, pushed back. In the context of the Civil Rights Movement, many in California began to understand "Okie" and "Arkie" as pejorative terms to be eschewed.

Others had fun making connections. Singer-songwriter Larry Hosford, in his 1977 tune "Salinas"—endlessly popular to this day on the local alt-country station KPIG in Watsonville, California—sang about growing up in Salinas among rough-and-tumble people from both Mexico and Oklahoma, who were disparaged in similar ways. If you kicked out both, he quipped, there'd be nothing to eat. After identifying as an "Okie" for most of the song, Hosford declares at its very end that he could be *either* Okie or Mexican.[224]

In 2019, prominent Mexican American playwright Octavio Solis premiered a new play at the Oregon Shakespeare Festival in Ashland entitled *Mother Road*. Its title deliberately riffs on Steinbeck's name for Route 66 in *The Grapes of Wrath*, as well as Ma Joad's name. Solis's play tells of a dying white Oklahoma man, the last living member of the Joad family, who tracks down his grandfather's sole biological heir in order to leave the farm to a blood relative. The only one left turns out to be a Mexican immigrant farmworker living near the Arvin, California, migrant camp—the same one that Steinbeck made famous. Together the two men travel in an old truck named "Cesar" (as in Cesar Chavez) along Route 66 back to the farm, joined along the way by an African American preacher, a Mexican American lesbian, and a Choctaw farmhand who challenges the Joads' claim to Native land. By the play's end, Solis turns *The Grapes of Wrath* upside down and inside out, telling his own, new story that includes racist police, hostility to "Okies," and an embracing vision of multiethnic solidarity.[225]

Lange's *Migrant Mother* lives on today, too, in her own complex ways. You can buy her image printed on a shower curtain, a cell phone cover, a fleece blanket, a face mask, or a yoga mat.[226] She remains the dominant image of the idealized, pitied, and exalted "Common Man" of the 1930s, ready to be deployed in service to those perceived as suffering victims, especially women. In November 2018, a Reuters photographer captured a woman pulling three children in a panic as they fled tear gas launched by US border authorities onto Mexican soil. The woman, Miara Meza, was Honduran and had traveled as part of a caravan of Central American migrants seeking asylum at the

US border. "Migrant Mother Seen Fleeing Tear Gas with Children," headlines announced.[227]

W e can end where our story began, in Karnes City, Texas. On August 8, 2015, forty immigrant women being held by the US Department of Homeland Security at a family detention center in Karnes City began a hunger strike to protest their detention and the conditions under which they and their children were being held, including sexual abuse, contaminated drinking water, and much more—so terrible, they said, that children were considering suicide. In a handwritten letter to Jeh Johnson, then secretary of homeland security, seventy-seven women protested: "Nosotras hemos venido a este pais con nuestros hijos en busca de ayuda de un refugio y se nos esta tratando como delincuentes y no somos eso mucho menos somos un peligro para este país." (We have come to this country with our children in search of help and shelter and are being treated like criminals, which we are not, much less a danger to this country.) "We want our FREEDOM," they demanded. Although some reports in the media couldn't resist referring to them as "migrant mothers" or "vulnerable," the incarcerated women were themselves refusing to be merely suffering victims. They were quite capable of militant protest on their own behalf. They were refusing to be invisible.[228]

CHAPTER THREE

WHOSE LABOR MOVEMENT?

The 1937 Chicago Wet Nurses' Strike

O n a usual day, seven young Black women would show up first thing in the morning at a "milk station" on the South Side to work as wet nurses, selling their breast milk to the City of Chicago. They'd change out of their street clothes into uniforms, seat themselves around a table, and silently express their milk for an hour. But on Monday morning, March 15, 1937, they instead walked into the city hall office of Dr. Herman Bundesen, president of the Chicago Board of Health, sat down in two rows of straight-backed white chairs along the sides of his anteroom, and announced they were on strike. They kept on their coats and their dark, round hats with small feathers tucked into the brims. They kept on their long scarves, with bright stripes or flowers, that wound around and down their necks. Their knees almost touching in the tiny space, they took off their gloves and held them tidily on their laps under their hands, folded atop their purses.[1]

In a photo captured by *Life* magazine, the women's faces are turned to each other, laughing, smiling, full of joyous friendship and audacity. One of them, in the rear of the tiny room, leans forward and to the side a bit, to better catch her fellow striker's words. When a reporter asked the women how long they planned to stay, Mary Hart, age twenty, declared: "We can strike as long as we have to. And we certainly will. We'll be here every day 8:30–4:30."[2]

This extraordinary strike by Chicago wet nurses was just one of thousands of sit-down strikes that erupted throughout the United States in 1936 and '37, especially in the Upper Midwest. Most famously, workers newly organized in the United Auto Workers staged a sit-down strike at General Motors plants in Flint, Michigan, outside Detroit. On February 11, 1937, General Motors, the biggest corporation in the world, agreed to recognize the union and soon negotiated higher wages and improved working conditions. Over the next few weeks, sit-down strikes—or even the threat of one—produced immense union victories for workers in steel and auto plants nationwide and for many other workers as well, especially factory workers. All told, in March 1937 a total of 167,210 workers sat down in 170 different strikes.[3]

But those seven women in Chicago weren't factory workers. Their job was selling part of their bodies. Their work represented one of the most highly exploited form of women's labor imaginable. It falls under the broad category of what feminists understand as "reproductive labor," including domestic work performed in the home, that makes it possible for other working people to leave the home and appear at their jobs daily, while someone else performs the work of cooking and cleaning, taking care of older people, and other similar tasks. Reproductive labor is usually unpaid, largely invisible (except, of course, to those who perform it), and historically, female. When it's done for pay, workers in this sphere have disproportionately been women of color. Under slavery, they were enslaved women of African descent.[4]

What does the heroic labor movement of the 1930s look like if we center our story on Black women's reproductive labor, moving the frame far away from white men working in factories? What can the striking wet nurses tell us about imagining and building a labor movement today that includes all forms of labor, and the labors of all working people? During the 1930s, the New Deal instituted a system of labor rights that is celebrated, rightly, for its gains for working people. But using the wet nurses as our compass, we can ask whether the New Deal labor system's key elements delivered for all workers.

To appreciate the wet nurses and their militant determination, we have to go deep into their world and try to understand the labor they performed, then gradually pull back to understand their daily lives, their city, its cultural and political offerings, and what the broader labor movement and the federal government did and didn't offer them. We can look at the choices they faced as working-class African American women, that made it necessary for them to sell their own babies' milk to anonymous others. We don't have a great deal of evidence about the strike itself. But newspaper reports at the time give us the gift of photographs of the strikers, their names, and, miraculously, their voices. As we follow the women's path from oppression to empowerment, we can trace the resources and the examples of protest available to them in the Black community of South Side Chicago at that exact moment in time, especially among African American women, that made it possible for them to sit down on those white chairs, their hands tidily folded in their laps, with smiles on their faces. Gloves off.

ANCIENT EXTRACTION

The history of "wet nursing," in which a woman nursed another woman's baby at her own breast, is both ancient and deeply chilling, especially when the woman providing the milk was enslaved.

In many human cultures, ancient and modern, throughout the world, lactating women have shared their breasts with other women's babies within families and communities through horizontal, reciprocal relationships—when the mother's own milk didn't flow, she had died, or the baby wasn't thriving. But the occupation of "wet nurse" depends on the existence of one group of women rich and powerful enough to hire or enslave others, and another group of women so poor or oppressed that they have to relinquish their milk to those rich women's babies. Wet nursing has been practiced in hierarchical societies throughout Asia, Europe, and the Mediterranean world, from slaveholders of the Roman Empire to centuries of elites in India to aristocrats in eighteenth-century France.[5]

European immigrants brought the tradition of wet nursing with them when they came to what is now the United States. In the northern colonies, prosperous urban white women who couldn't nurse their babies or, most commonly, didn't want to, often sent their babies out to be nursed by other women in small towns, where health conditions were assumed to be better. In the cities, authorities forced impoverished pregnant or nursing women, often single, into poorhouses and other public institutions, then made them nurse additional babies. Women also hired themselves out as wet nurses into private homes. White, African American, and, in some cases, Native American women all worked as wet nurses in the colonial period.[6]

The cruelties of wet nurses' lives played out most powerfully under slavery. Throughout the colonial period and up until Emancipation, enslaved women were forced to feed the babies of their mistresses and masters, without control over their own bodies. In fact, the classic racist stereotype of the "mammy"—a large, dark-skinned Black woman with a headscarf—refers to literal mothers who nursed slaveholders' babies. Those same babies grew up to whip their former wet nurses, sell them, and sell their enslaved babies at will, all the while nurturing romanticized fantasies of their cherished "mammy."[7]

Under slavery, all enslaved people's bodies were commodities and the property of their masters. That, in turn, meant that the breast milk of enslaved women was a lucrative commodity that could be used or sold by the enslaver. As historian Stephanie Jones-Rogers has shown, slave markets advertised enslaved women as wet nurses in "a niche sector of the slave market."[8] One New Orleans trader offered, for example, "FOR SALE—A Wet Nurse, about nineteen years of age, with her second child, six weeks old, will be sold low for cash, fully guaranteed," along with a seamstress, field hands, and house servants.[9]

In some cases, a master brought an enslaved woman into his house to nurse because his wife or daughter had died during childbirth. But most often, the mistress who'd given birth simply didn't want to be bothered with nursing and its effects on her daily life and body. "White women wouldn't nurse their own babies cause it would make their breast [sic] fall," recalled Betty Curlett, enslaved in Arkansas.[10] Historian Sally McMillen estimates that one in five slaveholding women used enslaved wet nurses.[11] But the practice may have been even more prevalent than that. Jones-Rogers, along with Emily West and Rosie Knight, has culled the interviews with formerly enslaved wet nurses and their daughters that were collected by the Works Progress Administration during the 1930s.* She quotes Rachel Sullivan, of Augusta, Georgia: "All de white ladies had wet musses un dem days."[12] Historian Marcus Wood, who has studied both the US and Brazil, reminds us eloquently, "Black milk, slave mother's milk, was stolen in vast, unknown, incalculable quantities."[13]

---

* As many scholars have noted, the WPA narratives were conducted and transcribed by largely white interviewers, who in many cases transcribed their subjects' words using longtime racist stereotypes of Black English.

The actual work of nursing was exhausting and never-ending. Masters required wet nurses to sleep next to the baby and follow both its whims and those of its parents. On top of the anguish of being enslaved, the nurse had to endure vast emotional pain specific to the task: she was forced to share her breast, all day, all night, with the white child of her enslavers, and separated from her own children. On larger plantations they would be watched over by older enslaved women.[14]

Enslavers needed to maximize enslaved people's labor time in the fields—and any time spent nursing cut into that.[15] After the external slave trade was outlawed in 1807, supply constricted and the price of enslaved people went up, and women became especially valuable commodities: they gave birth themselves to children who were, in turn, commodities to be sold on the market for further profit. So enslaved women were often allowed to bring their own babies with them to work in the Big House, alternating which baby they nursed, or even holding a baby at each breast at the same time. But the master's child always came first. "My mother had been weaned at three months old, that the babe of the mistress might obtain sufficient food," recounted Harriet Jacobs in her classic 1861 narrative of her life as an enslaved woman in North Carolina.[16]

We can only begin to imagine the emotional as well as physical pain of the enslaved wet nurse. She nursed day in, day out, sleep deprived, physically depleted, her nipples perhaps swollen or bitten, her breasts possibly infected, her precious milk coursing into the body of her enslavers' child, strengthening it, while she knew her own baby, like her other children, would continue to live in slavery, possibly sold away from her and never heard of again.[17]

Though brutalized into performing labors of all sorts, enslaved women nonetheless resisted. We don't have evidence of enslaved women's resistance to their specific work as nurses, although West and Knight speculate that wet nurses might have attempted "to sneak away and feed their own baby first."[18] But we know enslaved women everywhere engaged in a great spectrum of activities ranging from small acts of sabotage to feigning illness to complex subterfuges and armed rebellions, all the while sustained by cultures of faith carried from Africa and nurtured in the Americas. We know they ran away, withholding their bodies and labors, whether to hide in a nearby swamp for a week, or for good. Women were less likely than men to try to run away permanently, though, because they were less likely than men to be already separated from their children.[19]

FREE TO SELL

Wet nursing continued during the late nineteenth and early twentieth centuries under free labor. In the wake of the Industrial Revolution, it proliferated in the vast class divide between, on the one hand, prosperous white women—their wealth produced by the new factories, mines, and railroads—who continued to seek escape from breastfeeding, and, on the other hand, a new expanse of urban poor women in the exploding cities, desperate for survival, their poverty created by the same economic engines that produced the employers' riches. When lactating poor women—especially single mothers—sought shelter and aid in foundling hospitals and other public institutions, authorities continued to compel them to nurse other women's babies once inside.[20] More commonly, local officials distributed poor mothers to live in private homes, as a special category of domestic servant. Other mothers found work as wet nurses through their own networks.[21]

As historians Janet Golden and Jacqueline H. Wolf have shown, the men and women doing the hiring were by no means happy about inviting poor mothers into their homes. Wet nurses, unlike other men and women who worked as domestic servants in this period, had special bargaining powers: they were scarce. In contrast to the enslaved, they could quit, and if they did, a baby could sicken or die, quickly. Employers, as a result, had to accept the intimate presence and behavior of poor women in ways they would largely not tolerate with other servants. Native-born, white, of Northern European descent, employers were appalled and felt threatened by the ethnic and class cultures of wet nurses, who were African American or, more commonly in the North, immigrants, especially from Ireland.[22]

The physicians who advised parents on who to hire were horrified too. In an 1899 article in a scholarly journal, Dr. I. N. Love, the vice president of the American Medical Association, referred to wet nurses as "moral lepers" and "moral monsters." He even declared that he would let his own child die before he'd admit a wet nurse into his home. Employers and their doctors were also alarmed that wet nurses, like other servants, might carry tuberculosis or syphilis into their home and, especially, to their infants. As Tera W. Hunter has shown, in the early twentieth century white Southerners hysterically cast tuberculosis as a "Negro disease," "the Servants' Disease," using germ theory to claim that Black people couldn't get sick from TB but were carrying it into white people's homes as servants.[23]

Some white women outside the South were uncomfortable allowing Black women to nurse their babies. But historians have found that slaveholders, and then white women of the postbellum South, for all their deeply racialized projections onto bodies of African descent, and all their repulsion at the idea of interracial marriage, did not object to having Black women nurse their babies, because they were accustomed to the deeply intimate dynamics of dependency on and domination over Black people in which every inch of their lives was embedded.[24]

Working conditions for wet nurses were dangerous and repressive. They themselves could catch TB, syphilis, and other diseases from their charges or from their employers, including through rape. In the late nineteenth century, an estimated 6 to 18 percent of the middle and upper classes had syphilis.[25] Wet nurses' own babies and even their other children could, in turn, contract syphilis or tuberculosis. In 1906 one wet nurse in Baltimore, whose own twin babies had died, contracted syphilis from the baby she was wet nursing, and her nine-year-old daughter caught it too, from kissing the baby. Although wet nurses were paid better than other domestic servants because they were scarce, their working conditions were worse: they had to live next to the baby day and night, and they didn't get a half-day off on Sundays like other servants, who resented and shunned wet nurses because of their higher pay. Employers, moreover, obsessively surveilled wet nurses' eating habits, lest they ingest tea, ice water, alcohol, or other substances believed to be detrimental to their milk.

And what of the wet nurses' own babies? Employers who hired wet nurses for wages had no economic incentive to preserve the health of the nurses' offspring and wouldn't let women bring their babies to live with them. An employer didn't want a baby crying, distracting the nurse, or taking milk that should go to the employer's baby. With almost no options, wet nurses often left their babies in other working-class women's homes, in what were known by the upper classes as scandalous and dangerous "baby farms"—but which in most cases were simply homes where women made a living providing a service to other local women.[26] One source estimated in 1913 that around 90 percent of the wet nurses' own babies died, whether in the nurses' own homes or in those of others.[27] As Golden has observed, "Wet nursing often involved trading the life of a poor baby for that of a rich one."[28]

In the case of those wet nurses who worked for wages, we do have a documented history of individual resistance to their work as nurses, in which they used their considerable bargaining power to push back against employers' demands and improve their own lives. Employers and physicians, in letters and diaries, complained that wet nurses wandered through the kitchen however they liked, eating ice cream, pickles, oysters, and other foods not intended for the servants. They talked back. They "sulked," drank, and slept around. They carried themselves "with airs" considered inappropriate to their class. They disappeared seemingly randomly—often to nurse their own babies. Most powerfully, they often just quit, the classic and most common protest tactic of all domestic servants under free labor. As a result, a constant battle took place between employed and employing mothers. "A wet nurse is one-quarter cow and three-quarters devil," Frank Spooner Churchill, a leading Chicago pediatrician, concluded in 1896.[29] Frustrated employers shared tips and stereotypes in order to better assess prospects. Unmarried women were "more easily controlled," some thought, for example.[30]

In the late nineteenth and early twentieth centuries, doctors increasingly intervened to manage the relationship between birth mothers and wet nurses, anticipating and driving the transition to the "milk stations" at which the Chicago strikers worked in 1937. As part of the larger rise of the medical profession in this period, physicians began advising women about infant care in general and breastfeeding in particular. That advice soon crossed over to inspecting the bodies and babies of potential wet nurses.[31]

The final stage was the bottling of women's milk. Cow's milk had been on the market during the nineteenth century, but it was not a full or healthy replacement for human milk. The dairy industry, moreover, was famously corrupt, and delivered milk that was diluted with water, adulterated with other substances, and carried tuberculosis from the cows. Although vigorous campaigns advocated for pasteurization and other sanitary practices, bottled cow's milk was still not a viable alternative. Meanwhile, public health officials and middle-class white reformers grew alarmed at escalating infant mortality rates at the turn of the century and became concerned that babies were being weaned earlier and earlier.[32]

In response, doctors, child welfare advocates, and hospitals invented in the 1910s what they called "milk stations" at which women expressed their milk, which was in turn pasteurized, bottled, and distributed to other women for their at-risk babies. The first station opened in Boston in 1910; by 1929 they had spread to at least twenty US cities, although the scale remained small, with fifteen or twenty women working at each station.[33]

With the milk stations, health-care professionals achieved the full commodification of breast milk, now a substance isolable from the woman whose breast had created it, in what Golden has called "the separation of the woman and the milk."[34] Thus the long history of wet nursing in the US culminated in an industrialized human milk factory, in which poor women were paid to extract a bodily fluid, and others distributed it to a different mother's child, who the wet nurse would never know.

MILK SYSTEMS

We can now look more closely at the Chicago milk stations where the strikers worked during the 1930s, and their daily lives on the job. The sources are largely from their employers' point of view, although they do offer a few enticing clues about what the wet nurses themselves might have been thinking about their work. When the wet nurses did speak in their own voices, as they explained to the world why they were striking, their own version of the job turned out to be something else altogether.

Chicago's milk stations were embedded in a hierarchical local public health system of infant care stratified by gender, race, and class. At the top were white male doctors. Dr. Julius H. Hess, known nationally as "the father of neonatal medicine," in 1922 established and oversaw a special pavilion for premature infants at Sarah Morris Hospital, a branch of Michael Reese Hospital, located on the South Side at East Twenty-Ninth Street and Ellis Avenue. By the mid-1930s, the pavilion took care of two or three hundred babies a year, in twenty to thirty beds, and employed around a dozen wet nurses. Cook County

Hospital also opened a similar, smaller unit in 1930, which was absorbed into the Sarah Morris facility in 1934. Dr. Herman Bundesen, the flamboyant, publicity-seeking president of the Chicago Board of Health, oversaw both programs. A third, privately owned hospital, Mary Thompson Hospital (known as Women's and Children's Hospital), also employed wet nurses.[35]

In the mid-1930s, the Board of Health, concerned that infant mortality was still skyrocketing in Chicago, set up a new system in which every baby born in the city was registered within twenty-four hours by a visiting nurse, who examined the infant and met with its mother, educating her about best practices. When mortality remained high despite these measures, Dr. Bundesen asked a thirty-one-year-old white registered nurse named Gertrude Plotzke to design a new milk station for wet nurses, which opened between 1935 and 1937 in a storefront at Sixty-Third and Cottage on the South Side. The strikers would have worked at that new facility, or possibly at the older one in Sarah Morris Hospital. Individual women sold or donated breast milk through formal employment at the milk station, or more casually within the hospital. A surviving hand-lettered placard from the Sarah Morris Hospital Premature Station, evidently from the late 1930s, listed among the services it provided: "breast milk obtained from wet nurses and visiting mothers."[36] Another document from the time, delineating care systems for premature babies, listed among Sarah Morris's offerings: "A supply of breast milk to be available, either through a wet-nurse or breast milk station plan."[37]

Native-born white women of European descent managed these milk stations: Plotzke was Polish American; Evelyn Lundeen, who ran the Sarah Morris Hospital program, was Swedish American; Josephine Zuzak Sobolewski, whom Plotzke trained and then in 1944 handed the station over to manage, was also Polish American. (The station was eventually shut down in 1960 after Bundesen died and his successor did not support it.) Additional registered nurses who worked at both stations were all, apparently, white.[38]

Funds for this system came from the City of Chicago, as well as rich white women. When Hortense Schoen Joseph, "a wealthy, young society matron" and the founder of the Infants' Aid Society of Chicago, died suddenly in 1922, she left $65,000 for construction of the new pavilion for premature babies at Sarah Morris Hospital, which was named after her. Encouraged by Dr. Hess, members of the Infants' Aid Society (it had several hundred) then pushed to have the facility built, provided its equipment, and created an endowment, "the income from which may be used only for the employment of the nurses in the station or the procurement of breast milk in necessary instances," Hess wrote. Decades before, in 1865, rich white women had also founded Mary Thompson Hospital for Women and Children, a third site employing wet nurses, to help poor women and to provide white women doctors a place to train and practice.[39]

The money for this philanthropy came in part from profits the donors' husbands and fathers made from the meatpacking plants, steel mills, garment factories, and other mass-scale industries booming in Chicago in the first decades of the twentieth century. The low pay in those factories, in turn, created the poverty that produced the very infant mortality their womenfolk wanted to eradicate. Yet Chicago's factory owners, not unlike slaveholders, had an economic stake in guaranteeing a future supply of workers. They needed babies who, twenty years later, would be healthy enough to endure standing up on an assembly line day after day, hewing apart animal body parts. Meatpacking magnates bankrolled the Board of Health's extensive system of postnatal care by visiting nurses and clinics, through which the wet nurses were hired and their milk distributed. "They were supported by Cudahy, Swift, Armors [sic], see these rich people," Josephine Sobolewski, one of the supervising nurses, recalled. With a sense of noblesse oblige, the donors "felt . . . this is their baby and they'd have a tea for us, once a year and want to meet all the nurses." Swift even donated space in its freezers for the milk station to store extra milk.[40]

Once identified by the visiting nurses, premature babies were whisked in a special heated ambulance to the pavilion at Sarah Morris Hospital, where they received milk from wet nurses, as did other babies whose mothers' milk was not available. Most of the milk from the stations, though, was delivered to premature or ailing babies in their own homes or picked up by family members. No evidence is available of the race ascribed to recipient babies or their mothers. But Evelyn Lundeen, the registered nurse who ran the premature infants' program at Sarah Morris Hospital, wrote in a 1937 article that "there was absolutely no restriction as to color, race, or religion of the prematures. All were most welcome." Her remarks suggest that the babies who received milk in their homes from the city included African Americans.[41] Lundeen recounted that most of the babies treated at Sarah Morris came from poor families; in 1937 Chicago, the poor, especially in the neighborhoods around the hospital and where its feeder clinics were located, would have been overwhelmingly either European immigrants and their children, or African Americans, as well as a small number of Mexican immigrants.[42]

The same system also identified potential mothers who might want to sell their milk and recruited them to work as wet nurses. At prenatal and healthy baby clinics, "nurses in the field watched for mothers that could express," recalled Plotzke. "And when one of them found a mother with a lot of milk they told her first express it in the home and then they brought her into the clinic." Other women came into the stations seeking work through word of mouth.[43]

According to Plotzke, as many as forty-five women worked at her station at any given time (although the exact year she was recalling is unclear). The majority of women working as wet nurses for the city were African American. Of eleven wet nurses working for the city and identified by reporters at the time of the strike, nine were described as African American and two as white; other white women worked at Women's and Children's Hospital.[44] Sobolewski said that when she worked at the South Side station, after 1944, 95–98 percent of wet nurses there were Black. It's possible that Gertrude Plotzke, when she founded the station in 1935, chose its location deep in the South Side in order to be closer to poor Black babies who needed milk delivered to them. But more likely, she knew there would be a supply there of desperate African American women, the poorest of the poor in Chicago.[45] By 1947, the City of Chicago Health Department reported that between 1935 and the end of 1945, "over 794,000 ounces of milk, obtained from 2,296 mothers, were distributed free to infants needing breast milk."[46]

Jacqueline Wolf, a professor of medical history at Ohio University, asked Sobolewski in a 1997 interview if any of the white recipients ever "objected to the fact that most of the donors were black." "No," Sobolewski replied. "You know why? Because that baby meant so much to the mother. She didn't care where the milk came from. And she never saw the mother." Sobolewski said the mother just picked up the milk and took it home. At the hospitals, the distance between milk provider and recipient was even greater. "In the hospital they probably didn't even realize that this milk was being brought in from the city."[47]

A DAY'S WORK AT THE MILK STATION

Wolf's extensive interviews with Sobolewski and Plotzke take us deeper into the specific daily labors of the wet nurses at the station and also offer glimpses into the wet nurses' points of view—albeit always filtered through the white registered nurses' own recollections and biases.

The Chicago milk station operated eight hours a day, seven days a week. Every morning, women who sold their milk—whom the registered nurses referred to as the "mothers"—came into the station and changed into white uniforms with a buttoned-down flap. "We had gowns," Plotzke said. "And they helped design the gowns." After scrubbing their arms and breasts, the wet nurses sat together in silence around a table and gave up their milk. "It was so quiet you could hear a pin drop," Plotzke recalled.[48] Sobolewski told Wolf: "She'd express it into a regular tin cup—pssshhht pssshht—just like that."

"Did they use pumps?" Wolf asked.

"Manually. Manually. Always," she replied. "No breast pumps. Oh they thought that was a sin."

"Why did they think breast pumps were a sin?"

"Well they said they thought it would bruise the tissue," Sobolewski replied. She said the women objected that pumps were painful for their already-sore nipples.[49]

After expressing between 9 and 10 a.m., the women washed up again, changed back into their street clothes, and left. The station's registered nursing staff—in their own uniforms, masks, and close-fitting white caps—then processed the milk. First they carefully poured it into bottles, then pasteurized it in a shining steel machine specially made by a local dairy. In a 1947 report from the Chicago Board of Health, there's a photo of a masked woman in a white cap and uniform, inserting milk from the pasteurizer into glass bottles at a milk station. Across eight decades, we can see the mothers' actual milk in the photo, gleaming through the bottles' clear glass.[50]

Once the milk was pasteurized, a part of it was frozen for future use, but most went out immediately to the babies' homes, via family members, who came in daily to the station to pick up the milk. The babies' names were carefully marked on each bottle. The rest of the milk went to Sarah Morris Hospital to supplement the output of the wet nurses there, or sometimes to other hospitals. A delivery boy would pick up the bottles in a special tin cooler with a tin tray on top for ice. Evelyn Lundeen, the registered nurse who ran the station at Sarah Morris, wrote that beginning in 1934, they "decided to sell any surplus milk which they might have," to help additional babies. "The revenue received from these sales is turned over to the Michael Reese Hospital."[51]

A woman who chose to work as a wet nurse in this system had to accede to tight control over her body. When she arrived at work, she had to not only put on that uniform but also cover her hair with a bandanna, her mouth with a mask. Under the eyes of Plotzke and the other assistant nurse, she had to conduct an exacting process of scrubbing hard with cotton to sanitize her hands, arms, and breasts, in order to prevent bacteria from entering the milk. "You had to scrub your nails really good," Plotzke recalled. While the women were expressing, "a sterile towel lay under their breasts. And they didn't touch anything on the table, or anything." The supervisors also mandated exactly how to express milk to ensure the maximum amount would flow.[52]

In her interview with Wolf, Gertrude Plotzke asserted that the wet nurses internalized these demands for hypervigilant sanitation and took pride in their exacting work of keeping the milk safe for the babies who would receive it. "It was gratifying to see the mothers how they expressed, how careful they were not to contaminate anything. It was really gratifying for the nurses" (here referring to the registered nurses). She said that the mothers even criticized those who transgressed: "They were so interested in doing a good job and they knew when anybody would hit or spill a cup or something if they contaminated [it] and they would say, 'Ooooh, somebody contaminated the cup.'" Plotzke reported that the wet nurses even criticized new nurse-assistants who arrived at the station: "The nurses would come in to scrub, to learn how to scrub you know. They'd be at the sink and after they'd leave the mothers would say, 'They didn't scrub very well did they' [laughs]. Isn't that cute?"[53]

Public health authorities also exercised tight oversight of the wet nurses' health, including a throat culture once a week, blood tests for venereal disease once a month, and regular dental exams. If a mother had dental problems that weren't being attended to, she couldn't work; if she flunked a single test, she couldn't work. "She was very carefully watched," recalled Plotzke. Each wet nurse's milk was sent out for inspection once a week too. "And if they had any bacteria they couldn't sell milk." All these "inspections," which sound like government regulation of the dairy industry, were not designed because the city wanted to improve the health of poor women working as wet nurses. They were instituted to guarantee the quality of the milk delivered to the babies of *other* women—albeit largely poor women as well.[54]

In sharp contrast to the previous history of wet nursing in the US, however, women's own babies were not sacrificed. "The mother had to have enough milk to feed her own baby first," Plotzke recounted. "The baby had to be gaining [weight]." The wet nurses were required to take their babies in regularly for examination at a city clinic. "We never lost a baby," recalled Plotzke proudly.[55] To get to those inspections, though, a mother would have had to expend additional unreimbursed travel time and carfare.

Sobolewski recalled that the milk station would give each woman a quart of cow's milk every day she came in. "And they had to drink half the milk before they left the station because we knew what they would do. They would take it home and give it to their kids." Sobolewski here at least acknowledged the tension between the milk station's objective of harvesting healthy milk, and the wet nurses' objective of raising their own children. "Of course they were very serious those ladies. They'd come in and . . . well they had babies at home and they had children at home you know."[56]

Chicago authorities did not appear to be concerned with the "moral character" or marital status of the wet nurses. Wolf asked Plotzke, "What about their husbands? What did their husbands do?" Plotzke replied, "Well we never made inquiries."[57]

The wet nurses were paid by the ounce, not by the hour. They were not wage workers. They were selling part of their body by piece rate, in a payment system like that used to pay for the number of blouses sewn or boxfuls of peaches picked. According to Sobolewski, the wet nurses "would give us up to 45 ounces an in hour [sic]," providing, in total, two to two-and-a-half gallons a day to the station. She said they were paid five cents an ounce—although that could have been in 1944, when she left, not in 1937, the year of the strike. "With 45 ounces, that's a lot of money." Dr. Bundesen told reporters the wet nurses got free carfare too.[58]

The strikers told an entirely different story. When reporters asked them why they were striking, they replied in a few short quotes full of clarity, force, and a bit of sass. "Starvation wages, that's what it is," declared Carrie Burnish, age sixteen.[59] "Why we never make more than 70 cents (a day) and some days as low as 20 cents," Mary Hart announced. "What they been payin ain't enough for carfare."[60] Another striker exclaimed: "Four cents [an ounce] ain't enough, after we pay someone to watch over our children at home, and buy shoes."[61] After all that, she said, "we haven't realized anything." The strikers also protested racial disparities in payment. Louise Clark noted: "We get 4 cents, but the white mothers at Women's and Children get 10 cents. They shouldn't make any difference between us."[62] And the work of nursing itself, they said, was exhausting: "Burnish shook her head and said, 'This sort o' work is mighty tirin'."[63] Hart agreed: "It is mighty hard work."[64]

To prove their point, the strikers provided exact figures to demonstrate their productivity. "According to the sit down strikers," the Black-owned *Chicago Defender* reported, "they average from 15 to 20 ounces of breast milk a day, which means they earn 60 to 80 cents."[65] A second striker "said her 'high' out put [sic] was 32 ounces in one day, but that her average was fifteen ounces."[66] Theria Foster exclaimed: "Now, the most I ever expressed that is the word the nurses use was 28 ounces a day, and that's just $1.12 for my best day!"[67] They didn't think they were making "a lot of money," as Plotzke claimed. Nor were they expressing 45 ounces a day, as she reported. Note, also, the pressure the women experienced to produce the maximum amount every day, in order to receive the most pay. We can also note that Sarah Morris Hospital, when it sold its excess milk, gave the proceeds back to Michael Reese Hospital, rather than to the mothers who produced the milk in the first place.[68]

Plotzke, though, thought the wet nurses were doing swell. "At that time the mother could buy things for their children that they couldn't afford otherwise. They loved it." She cast wet nursing not as survival but as sort of a lark, producing pin money: "Then they could buy their children little things you know. Because they got paid five cents an ounce. . . . Just normal people who needed a little extra money and they were glad to do it," she told Wolf. "They had a good existence you know. They could keep their families." Her remarks indicate a vast obliviousness to the limited income-generating opportunities and precarious situation of working-class Black families in Chicago—even though her comment that "they could keep their families" indicates that she was quite aware of the ominous alternatives facing Black mothers at every turn.[69]

Plotzke also seemed not to grasp, or at least convey to Wolf, that expressing milk was "hard work," and "mighty tirin'," as the strikers underscored. Stephanie Jones-Rogers, in her examination of wet nursing under slavery, stresses that work as a wet nurse wasn't simply a "natural" process; it took skill and efficiency, of which enslaved mothers, enslaving mothers, and slave traders were all aware.[70]

In Plotzke's descriptions of the mothers, it's almost like she was enchanted by them. She spoke respectfully and enthusiastically of their commitment to sanitary procedures, but her account also carries whiffs of longtime racist US narratives of "happy darkies," still alive and well in Hollywood at the time, in which white observers described enslaved men and women as happily dancing and singing under slavery. "The mothers had a good experience. And they loved coming too," Plotzke insisted. "Isn't that cute?" she concluded her recollection of the wet nurses who had criticized someone who didn't scrub well. The wet nurses' strike, which must have been a clear challenge to her authority and to her vision of contented workers, never comes up in her extensive interview with Wolf sixty years later, although she must have lived through it.[71]

Josephine Sobolewski, for her part, who took over the station in 1944, told Wolf overtly that "Black women are better milkers." "We had a few good milkers that kept coming back," she recounted. "Lydia Hardaway, she was the cream of the crop." Sobolewski said that Hardaway had returned to work at the station regularly over the course of nine years while nursing three or four of her own babies. "She was tall, pendulous breasts," Sobolewski told Wolf. Ninety-six at the time, Sobolewski obsessively returned over and over again during her interview to Hardaway's productivity and the shape and size of her breasts.[72] Historian Jennifer Morgan has traced back this obsession with Black women's breasts to the eighteenth century in Europe and the US, where it was offered as supposed evidence of "savagery" and used to legitimate enslavement.[73]

Physicians reporting at the time to medical journals about milk stations in other US cities spoke in similarly cold and calculating language when they discussed wet nurses and their ability to "produce" like cows. B. Raymond Hoobler, MD, in a 1928 article about Detroit in the *Journal of the American Medical Association* entitled "Human Milk: Its Commercial Production and Distribution," referred to wet nurses as "our producers." Like Plotzke, he claimed the work was "lucrative" and blithely noted, preposterously, that "it does not interfere in any way with their home duties."[74] Similarly, Henry Dwight Chapin, MD, describing in the same journal a system of three New York City milk stations, spoke of wet-nursing mothers as if they were especially productive cows. "It is astonishing how much milk can often be secreted when the breast is properly handled." Handled by whom? "An interesting by-product of the undertaking is the relief of poverty in families in which healthy mothers can easily furnish extra milk and thus aid the family budget," Chapin wrote, as if to give up your milk to strangers was like taking in a little extra sewing. He went so far as to exult that "this plan affords the opportunity of staying at home, looking after her own baby, and at the same time helping another baby in dire straits. It is thus in a broad sense a true community service."[75] It seems safe to presume that his own wife would have chosen other forms of community service—perhaps philanthropy?

Plotzke recalled a parade of out-of-town visitors who came to learn about and observe the South Side Chicago nursing station, as though the nursing mothers were animals on display. "We had so many visitors from out of town," from "big cities," she said. "They couldn't believe it . . . that we could get so much breast milk."[76]

What did the wet nurses get out of the bargain, in exchange for their milk, all that control over their bodies, and all that patronizing racism? They got a tiny income they very much needed, or they wouldn't have come in every morning. They got a limited number of medical tests, whether VD tests, dental exams, throat cultures, or examination of their babies. Inspection wasn't the same thing as treatment, though, and any health assessment they did receive terminated when their breasts were no longer able to produce milk, or if the mother or her milk didn't pass muster. A wet nurse's length of employment was usually six months.[77]

The wet nurses' own values and their opinions of the work do shine through in their supervisors' recollections. As noted, Plotzke said they helped design their uniforms, and said the wet nurses took pride in their new mastery of sanitary techniques. Sobolewski, in her description of Lydia Hardaway, the woman with whose breasts she was obsessed, gives us hints as to Hardaway's perspective: "She got the technique down to a science. And she never did much talking or fooling around." Hardaway was "very serious," Sobolewski said, because she had babies and children at home to feed.[78]

Finally, the interviews show clearly that the wet nurses resisted, in many ways successfully, what their employers wanted them to do: they refused to use breast pumps. If the wet nurses were given a quart of cow's milk for themselves, they tried to take it home to their own kids and got away with drinking only half of it themselves. Over and over again, their commitment to their own babies and children comes forward.

WE HAVE WHAT THEY WANT

At 8:30 a.m. on Monday morning, March 15, 1937, seven wet nurses weren't silent at all. Instead of showing up at the milk station, they walked into Bundesen's office in city hall, sat down on those chairs in his anteroom, so close their knees were touching, and "announced to the white-clad attendants that they were on strike," until their pay was raised from four cents to ten cents an ounce, the *Chicago Tribune* reported.[79] According to the papers, five other women who worked as wet nurses, three of them African American and two white, chose not to join the strike.[80] We have no further information about those women, their reasons for not joining, or of the relations between Black and white wet nurses.

The strikers were quick to convey to reporters an awareness of their own powers, and to affirm their faith that they'd win. "We have what they want and we know sooner or later they will meet our demands," said Ella Gold. "The babies we serve need the milk, and we need the money," she pronounced. "No money, no milk." In classic call-and-response form, the rest of the group seconded, "That's right, no money, no milk."[81] Their milk, they knew, was a perishable commodity that the city needed urgently. They knew the babies who received it were perishable too. According to one news story, the wet nurses' strike cut off four-fifths of the city's usual milk supply.[82] Their choice to sit down in city hall, rather than at their actual workplace, shows they had an analysis of where power lay, and where they would, hopefully, get the best publicity for their sit-down.

The strikers made clear they were going to stay parked on those chairs for a good while. "We can strike as long as we have to," declared Mary Hart. "And we certainly will. We will be here every day from 8:30 to 4:30."[83] As another striker put it, "We're going to sit here until Gabriel blows his horn unless they give us what we want."[84]

At some point in the afternoon, Dr. Bundesen spoke to the strikers and to the press. According to the *Chicago Defender*, he "said he was puzzled as to what steps to take. 'We have about thirteen babies on our list—but since the budget has already been made out for this department, I really don't see how we can raise this money off hand.'"[85] He stressed the supposed impossibility of meeting the strikers' demands. "Of course, we need their milk but we have no way of raising the money offhand. You can't change a municipal budget overnight."[86] In a quote in the *Los Angeles Times*, Bundesen more firmly asserted that alternative sources of milk were available: "The babies will be taken care of. There is an adequate supply in the city so far." He reported that "today's supply of milk for the thirteen children dependent on the wet nurses . . . was obtained from hospitals."[87]

Bundesen sought to distance himself from any control over the program he oversaw, and in a dismissive aside also conceded he would—maybe—bother to request funding from the higher body that he claimed controlled the purse strings: "There is nothing I can do about the strike except refer it to the finance committee. I probably will do that."[88] In none of his many reported comments did he acknowledge the strikers' low pay or its racial differentials, let alone extol the women's sacrifice of their milk. He did try to play the "suffering babies" card, though, to no avail. "Dr. Bundesen conferred with the women but was unable to shake their determination, even with his plea that children might suffer if the strike were prolonged."[89]

"By 2 p.m. two of the mothers had gone home to nurse their own babies," the *Tribune* reported.[90] The other five stayed put until 4:30, when city hall closed up, "but vowed to sit anew" the next day. Tuesday, all seven returned. "Mothers Sit Firm! Seven Insist on 10-Cent Milk," announced the *Chicago Herald and Examiner.* It reported that the Board of Health had on Monday obtained "manufactured preparations"—some kind of baby formula, presumably—to help meet the diminished supply. Bundesen reiterated that "no price increase could be granted unless the city council increased the health budget. 'That might take weeks.'"[91]

In the middle of the nationwide wave of sit-down strikes in the aftermath of the General Motors union victory, the wet nurses' tiny, brave strike made national and even international headlines. Local reporters rushed in to cover it for the major white-owned Chicago papers, and then sent out clips through the syndicated news services, including United Press International and the International News Service. Some of it was frankly celebratory, like the "Mothers Sit Firm!" headline in the *Chicago Herald and Examiner*, emphasizing the strikers' bravery and uniqueness. "Something brand new in sit-down strikes made its debut yesterday."[92] A subhead in the *Los Angeles Times* declared "All Determined."[93] The African American press, with its own syndicated services, especially delighted in the women's courage and was careful to highlight the strikers' protest against racism. "Discrimination About Pay Cause of 'Wet Nurses' Sit-Down Strike," headlined the *New York Amsterdam News.*[94] "Demand an Increase in Milk Wages," read the *Arizona Gleam.*[95]

Most of the white press, by contrast, brought subtle and not-subtle racism and sexism to the story, usually through mockery. "Here are the mothers doing their very best sit-downing at the Board of Health office," captioned a photo in the *Philadelphia Tribune*, for example, which said that the strikers had "plumped themselves down on a bench."[96] Novelty became oddity. The *Kokomo Tribune*, picking up a wire service story, headlined its story "Chicago's Strangest Sit-Down Strike" (and referred to striker Mary Hart as "buxom").[97] In a lengthy description for the *Chicago Tribune*, reporter Marcia Winn was in some ways respectful but also wrote: "There arose one of the most delicate bits of industrial or domestic strife yet encountered in the

Chicago area," as if a serious strike, that entailed loss of pay and possibly loss of future employment, should be equated with a little spat between husband and wife.[98]

A long article sent out by the United Press news service on March 16 included the wet nurses in a summary of small sit-downs erupting all over the country at the time. Picked up by newspapers from Moorhead, Minnesota, to Logansport, Indiana, to Lincoln, Nebraska, with headlines like "Wave of Freak Sit Down Strikes Sweeps Over U.S." or "Hysteria Developes [sic] Ridiculous Angles," the article's main tone was mockery.[99] "America's strikers were sitting down today on everything from logs to city hall benches and demanding almost anything, including higher fees for wet nursing." After telling us about the Belgian consul in Atlanta, who "sat down on his water meter," and then mentioning the wet nurses, the report listed "grade school children, and college students, department store girls and sawmill workers, dog pond employes [sic] and caddies," all sitting down. "Toledo and Huntington, Ind., even blamed peculiar antics of three dogs on 'sit down mania,'" the article continued. It dismissed the striking wet nurses' serious job action, along with strikes by other workers, as infantile, even animal, behavior, in a mocking tone that presumed the author's—and the reader's—superiority.[100]

The racism and sexism could sizzle far more overtly. When the *El Paso Herald-Post* published the same story, it also ran an editorial headlined "Lucky Pickaninnies," commenting: "The news columns inform us that seven Negro women who have been selling mother's milk to the Chicago Health Department have gone on a sit-down strike. They want 10 cents an ounce instead of four. If the mammies will just do their sitting down in rocking chairs it will be a swell break for seven pickaninnies."[101]

But a photo that accompanied many of the same articles told a different story. It was distributed by the Hearst-owned International Press Service, and taken by a white man named William Vandivert, who went on to become famous for his *Life* photographs of World War II concentration camps and ruins. *Life* magazine ran his photo of the strikers two weeks after their sit-down, as part of a glossy multipage photo spread about the national wave of sit-downs.[102] Three different versions of his original photo of the strikers are available in crisp resolution today in the *Life* archives. Vandivert shot them in quick succession; you can see how the women move their heads slightly between takes, react to each other, smile more broadly, or less.[103]

The photographs suggest that the strikers were well aware of the politics of respectability. As women engaged in an occupation involving breasts, providing fodder for titillating innuendo, in a white-dominated world in which Black women were routinely infantilized and stereotyped as "pickaninnies," "mammies," and prostitutes, they would have needed to deflect those images and instead counter them with their own chosen self-presentation. They walked into that office on Monday morning dressed neatly, in coats, hats, sensible dark shoes with square one-inch heels, every hair tucked back, and held their gloves neatly in their hands atop flat purses in their laps. They presented themselves formally, and fully clothed—not as women about to expose their breasts. They sat up straight, knees together.

But the photos also suggest the strikers' playfulness and their joy in dressing up and looking good. One woman is fiddling with her hands a bit, her fingers and thumbs pressed together to make a little rectangle. One of them is wearing a polka-dot dress that peeks out under her coat; another's dress has a large-flowered pattern. Their hats have three-inch-long flat bows sewn into the band; their shoes have long, dark tassels on top. Three of the women have broad fur collars framing their shoulders. In black-and-white photos, we can't see the colors, but the contrast between their dark coats and their much-lighter dresses suggests that the dresses' colors were bright and varying. Two women sported long striped scarves, one perhaps home-knitted, and we can guess those added accents of vibrant color too. Two wore shiny hoop earrings, maybe an inch in diameter.

We can learn about them from their body language too. They are all looking at each other, not at the camera. They are all laughing and smiling. While one woman at the back leans forward sideways to catch what another has just said, a third, next to her, has an open-mouthed smile on her face as if someone has just said something deliciously wicked. Behind them, in a doorway in the back left corner, an older white woman in a registered nurse's uniform, her arms crossed, stands looking down at them, unsmiling.[104]

The photos make clear an enormous and glorious source of the strikers' power—not just their ability to withhold their milk, but the power they drew from each other. They were young, they were strong, they were daring, and they were having a great time.

THE STREETS OF BRONZEVILLE

To fully understand the sources of the strikers' power—their determination, as the *Los Angeles Times* put it—we can step out of that office and leave the milk station; walk away from the white masks, the white uniforms, the white doctors, the white nurses, and the white gaze; and follow the women home to their families, to the bustling neighborhoods that sustained them on the South Side of Chicago at a spectacular moment of exploding African American cultural and political activism.

Miraculously, the *Defender* and the *Tribune* listed the names of all seven strikers and the addresses of six. Tracking those names and addresses, plus tiny bits of information reported by the papers, we can piece together a bit more of who they were, where they lived, and, in two cases, who they lived with:

Ella Gold was the "mother of four children," and lived at 3802 South Park Way.[105]

Mary Hart was twenty years old and lived at 356 West Sixtieth Street.[106]

Willie Morton lived at 3560 Prairie Avenue.[107]

Georgia Lewis lived at 3748 Calumet Avenue.[108]

Carrie Burnish didn't have her address listed but told a reporter she was sixteen.[109]

Theria Foster gave her address as 4001 South Park Way, two blocks away from Ella Gold, and appears in the 1940 US census at 8647 South Calumet Avenue.[110] She was born in Chicago on June 22, 1918, which would have made her eighteen at the time of the strike. In 1940 she lived in a rented apartment with her husband, Frank Foster, age twenty-nine, and a son, Harold, age three, who must have been the baby she was nursing during the strike. Theria had completed three years of high school; Frank, the seventh grade. He was a plumber but in 1940 said he hadn't worked for seventy-three weeks, including all of 1939. No occupation is listed for Theria. Her mother was born in Tennessee, her father in Kentucky.[111]

The seventh striker, Louise Clark, shows up in the 1940 census as well. She gave her age as twenty-five, so she would have been about twenty-two at the time of the strike. The papers reported two different addresses for her: 4641 Evans Avenue and 4805 Evans Avenue; but three years later, she appears in the census at 4559 Evans Avenue.[112] The census listed Louise as head of household, with four children (matching the number listed in the papers): Margaret, age eight; Jean, seven; Randle, five; and Laverne, three, who would have been the baby she was nursing in 1937. So she would have had four children when she went on strike. She had an eighth-grade education. The census-taker listed her occupation as "new worker" and reported that she had not had a job for 117 weeks—over two years.[113]

So much is missing from these reports that we would love to know, but a few patterns do emerge. The women whose ages can be identified were young: sixteen, eighteen, twenty, and twenty-two. Two of them had one child, two of them had four. Theria was born in Chicago, of Southern parents; Louise was born in Georgia. Neither was working for pay in 1940. Neither had had a job for a long time.

The strikers and their families were part of the vast exodus known as the Great Migration, in which 6 million African Americans fled the South during the 1910s and '20s, pouring into the cities of the North, seeking an escape from the near-total system of white oppression that had continued to lock down their lives in the aftermath of Emancipation. Between 1910 and 1930 the Black population of Chicago shot up from 44,000 to 230,000.[114] Arriving in Chicago—sometimes alone, sometimes with kids in tow, sometimes with relatives or friends to take them in, sometimes knowing no one—they hit a wall of fierce housing discrimination. White landlords and homeowners drew strict lines, boxing Black residents and migrants into a constricted zone on the South Side known as Bronzeville. Those African Americans who sought to rent or buy outside it were met with hostility, threats, and often violence.[115]

As migrants continued to stream into the city during the 1930s, the pressure on available housing worsened. Landlords responded by ignoring maintenance and splitting up apartments and houses into smaller and smaller units. African American sociologists Horace Cayton and St. Clair Drake, in their pioneering 845-page study, *Black*

Metropolis: A Study of Negro Life in a Northern City (1945), based on research in the late 1930s, report that three hundred people would be crowded into a building that before had held sixty. Six families would now share a bathroom that had previously served one.[116] More established African Americans were lucky to find flats of three to six rooms, where they lived in extended families augmented by boarders, but recent migrants were forced by the 1930s into minuscule "kitchenettes"—one room with a bed, a gas hot plate, and an icebox—in buildings disintegrating around them. "There was continuous movement from building to building in search of lower rents, more adequate accommodations."[117]

We can try to imagine what the strikers' home lives would have been like, with an infant and maybe one to three other children, crammed into these tiny spaces with multiple others. The challenges of cooking and cleaning and keeping yourself and your babies clean would have been formidable, especially given the shared bathroom down the hall. Cayton and Drake describe one building in which "twenty households, sharing four bathrooms, two common sinks in the hallway, and some dozen stoves and hot-plates between them, were forced into relationships of neighborliness and reciprocity."[118] Intricate relationships of exchange developed: "A girl might 'do the hair' of a neighbor in return for permission to use her pots and pans. Another woman might trade some bread for a glass of milk. There was seldom any money to lend or borrow, but the bartering of services was essential."[119]

When the *Defender* printed the strikers' names, it listed all seven as "Mrs."[120] That could have meant many things: The strikers could have all been legally married and told the reporter they were "Mrs." as they gave out their names. Some of them could have been in common-law marriages, in which they understood themselves as "Mrs." It's possible that the visiting nurses, when they recruited these women to work as wet nurses, selected only those mothers they deemed "married," based on a variety of information or lack thereof—although we can note that Gertrude Plotzke told her interviewer that she never asked if the wet nurses had husbands. Alternately, the strikers, whatever their status or relationships, could have simply chosen to use "Mrs." when they provided their names to the reporter. Or the Black-owned *Defender* could itself have chosen to call them all "Mrs." as a carefully respectful honorific, not wanting to suggest, with "Miss," that any of the nursing mothers were single mothers and therefore not respectable.

Cayton and Drake, in *Black Metropolis*, meticulously depict a rough world of what they called "lower-class" Black heterosexual relationships in Chicago at the time. Their analysis is dripping with class condescension cast as social science, but in their study we can still hear the interviewees' own voices and points of view. According to the two sociologists, working-class Black Chicagoans accepted common-law marriage and single parenthood. Male desertion of women was common during the 1930s, in what Cayton and Drake call "notorious and widespread wandering"—both to other women and to other towns in search of work. Some women described themselves as "widowed" when they were in fact deserted. In the sociologists' depiction, working-class heterosexual relationships were based on negotiation and mistrust. One woman "shouted at an interviewer: 'I ain't never had no husband. Haven't you heard of women having babies without a husband? I don't want to get married.'"[121] What *Black Metropolis* misses, though, is that Black working-class women could also draw love and support from their families, however defined; from other women, including in relationships; and from others they lived with or down the hall from.

Black women's choices for paid work were narrow and grim. The great majority of Black men in 1937 could only work in unskilled and semiskilled jobs—if they could find them—or in their own enterprises in the informal economy. It was even worse for Black women, who couldn't get the jobs in construction, in heavy industry, in coal, lumber, and railroad yards, or in other occupations where some Black men could. The great majority of women worked in domestic service, approximately twenty thousand in Chicago at the time. By the 1930s, most domestic workers didn't have to live in their employers' households anymore, because the balance between supply and demand had tipped in their favor by the 1920s, as immigration restrictions decreased the supply of European women. But they still worked under white women's thumbs, on their hands and knees, often in a degrading uniform they had to keep clean and pressed. Another five thousand Black women worked in commercial laundries—searingly and dangerously hot, under white supervisors, with long, grueling hours and low pay. Other African American women worked as waitresses or cleaning hotels and other commercial establishments.[122]

By the 1930s, a few factory jobs were available—three thousand African American women worked in garment factories—but conditions were miserable there too. Five hundred Black women worked in packinghouses, but only in the worst two job categories. In the casings department, chopped-up animal parts were stuffed into intestines. (One worker described it as "the nastiest, most evil work you can imagine.") But the pay there was higher, well above domestic service, laundry work, and other options available to Black women, on par with that of teachers and nurses.[123]

During the Great Depression, any jobs, even in domestic service, were few and far between, as employers laid off their servants; and working-class white women, facing their own job crisis, bumped Black women down the hierarchy of women's employment and often out of the labor market altogether. The percentage of Black Chicago women who were employed plummeted from 47.5 percent in 1929 to 27.4 percent in 1940.[124]

Another option was prostitution. Cayton and Drake report that negotiations between men and women regularly shaded over into casual prostitution inside those buildings, where it was an acceptable practice involving relatives, lodgers, or acquaintances.[125] The brothels of Chicago's commercial vice district had been officially shut down by authorities in 1912, but "many women worked in teams or small groups that rented and shared furnished rooms and small apartments and coordinated their daily work schedules," writes Cynthia M. Blair in her study of Black women and sex work in Chicago.[126] During the 1930s the percentage of Black women working as prostitutes rapidly increased. One police captain on the South Side told an interviewer for *Black Metropolis*: "There are a lot of women here who are trying to make a dollar and will take a chance and 'turn a trick.' But for the most part these people are just poor women who are out of a job and can't make it any other way."[127] Earnings from prostitution were much higher than from other work available to Black women, and for all its dangers and degradations, it offered an alternative to those of domestic service. One young woman working as a prostitute spat out to her interviewer: "When I see the word *maid*—why, girl, let me tell you, it just runs through me! I'd sooner starve."[128] Other women worked as numbers runners and other jobs in the gambling world; LaShawn Harris notes that such jobs allowed for flexible childcare arrangements, while opening doors for Black women to "radically disrupt" conventional expectations of their behavior."[129]

African American women in Chicago who chose to sell their breast milk to strangers, then, did so in a context of few other options, almost all of them involving the devastation of their bodies, subservience to white people, or most often both. There were no good choices. And they loved their children.

The counter to the oppressions of work and white people was fun. Bronzeville blazed with excitement. "Within Bronzeville Negroes are at home," write Cayton and Drake. "They find rest from white folks as well as from labor, and make the most of it. In their homes, in lodge rooms and clubhouses, pool parlors and taverns, cabarets and movies, they can temporarily shake off the incubus of the white world."[130] For working-class African Americans, "having a good time" offered "escape from the tensions of contact with white people. Absorption in 'pleasure' is, in part at least, a kind of adjustment to their separate, subordinate status in American life."[131]

Before stepping out, first they'd get dressed—dressed up. Clothes weren't just about performing respectability in the face of white dangers or Black middle-class judgments; they were about looking *good*, looking sexy, knowing you were looking sexy, playing with color, style, flow, and a flash of what might be under those clothes. As Tera W. Hunter writes in her classic study of African American domestic servants in the post–Civil War South, *To 'Joy My Freedom*, when the women left work "they shed the sartorial symbols of servility for garments that symbolized style and self-worth," paying "careful attention to their dress style from their hairdos down to their underwear." "Dressing in itself was fun and pleasurable," she underscores.[132] Shane White and Graham White have traced an African American tradition of creative and self-expressive dress back to slavery times and Africa.[133]

The streets of Bronzeville were thronged with women and men enjoying their freedom. Saidiya Hartman, in *Wayward Lives, Beautiful Experiments: Intimate Histories of Riotous Black Girls, Troublesome Women, and Queer Radicals*, interweaves meticulous research with imaginative reconstructions to capture the worlds of African American women claiming their streets and their lives in the early twentieth century Northeast. "Watch her in the alley passing a pitcher of beer back and forth with her friends, brash and lovely in a cut-rate dress and silk ribbons," she writes. Hartman opens with an image of young women lusting after "a pair of fine shoes displayed like jewels."[134]

Chicago's South Side, two decades into the Great Migration, offered enticements and joys on a scale previously unknown in US history. Promenading through its streets, young Black women could see a world of people who mostly looked like themselves, intermixed with immigrants from Europe, Mexico, and a few from Asia. They could peer into and rifle through secondhand clothing shops, watch a movie in a theater, or duck into some of the five hundred "policy shops" tucked into alleys and behind small stores, to play the numbers, which paid out three times a day.[135]

And they could dance. Commercial dance halls and taverns were fun (there were two hundred of them), but cost money. During the Great Depression, people more commonly "simply 'pitched a boogie-woogie' at home, using a radio or a Victrola for music," Cayton and Drake report.[136] As Tera Hunter underscores, in dance settings "blacks could reclaim their bodies from appropriation as instruments of physical toil." She writes, "The blues and dance were created with a fierce sense of irreverence—the will to be unencumbered by any artistic, moral, social obligations, demands or interests external to the community." Black women "could reconstruct notions of womanhood through dance."[137]

Black women in Chicago also stepped out to their own churches—five hundred of them. The Great Migration swelled the grand Protestant churches like Ebenezer Baptist and Olivet Baptist, which had as many as fourteen thousand members. As Wallace D. Best has shown, Southern migrants brought more ecstatic and expressive forms of worship both to the big established churches and to suddenly proliferating new storefront churches, often just a row of chairs and a pulpit, in the process creating "a new sacred order in the city."[138] Like dancing, these churches offered escape, pleasure, and lots of music. Thomas Dorsey and Mahalia Jackson pioneered gospel music in Chicago, with roots in both the rural South and church life in the big city. The world of the dance hall and the world of the church weren't far apart at all. Working-class neighborhoods of Bronzeville were "noisy with the cacophony of both hymns and blues, gospel songs and 'low-down' music," write Cayton and Drake. "It is obvious that some people in Bronzeville take their pleasure by 'making a joyful noise unto the Lord.'"[139]

Male preachers still controlled the upper echelons of the big congregations, but the storefronts were a freer space for women. Overall, two out of every three church members were women.[140] Best tells us about popular charismatic women preachers such as Lucy Smith and Mary G. Evans, who challenged gender conventions on multiple fronts. It seems safe to conclude that the striking wet nurses drew strength from these sacred worlds, whether directly or indirectly, and would have inherited the powerful legacy of Black Christianity. When one of them told a reporter, "We're going to stay here until Gabriel blows his horn," she was drawing on that empowering conceptual vocabulary, and assuming the reporter understood it too.[141]

Finally, Bronzeville was bursting with political movements and ideas. Washington Park, a huge expanse in South Chicago, offered rowboats, a bandstand, flower gardens, a place to promenade, and the South Side's only swimming pool available to African Americans, as well as political speakers atop soapboxes spouting a vast range of information and opinions. By the mid-1930s Marcus Garvey's immensely popular Universal Negro Improvement Association had collapsed after Garvey went to jail for fraud in 1923, but Black nationalism still thrived in the African Legion, the Black Cross, the Nation of Islam, and other groups, alongside more staid, middle-class organizations like the NAACP and the National Urban League. Young Black women in Chicago in the 1930s might also have known about two of the city's powerful role models from an earlier generation: Madam C. J. Walker (1867–1919), who made a fortune selling Black beauty products and spent it supporting the Black freedom struggle, and Ida B. Wells (1862–1931), the unflinching journalist who gave her life to publicizing and fighting lynching.[142]

At the center of the Black political world of 1937 Chicago lay the all-important *Chicago Defender*. With a national circulation of 110,000 in the mid-1930s (down from 250,000 during World War I), the *Defender* was rife with class and color biases, and, through its founder and publisher Robert Abbott, was tied into complex patronage relationships with the city's white-run political machine. But it was an enormous resource and source of pride for the Black community of Chicago and far beyond. Every issue, twice a week during the 1930s, ran detailed news from Black communities throughout the United States, ranging from small cities in downstate Illinois to New York, Georgia, and Colorado. Reporters wrote up national news from Washington and New York through a Black lens, emphasizing civil rights. Within Chicago, the *Defender* had a physical presence not only in newsstands but through hundreds of delivery boys and girls carting bundles and tossing their papers all over town. Once a year the *Defender* sponsored a parade featuring its newsboys and girls, with two hundred floats and thousands lining the streets to cheer.[143]

The *Defender*'s extensive sports section exuded Black pride. It covered not just baseball's Negro Leagues but also basketball, wrestling, track, and much more, nationwide. In the mid-1930s, the big sports news story was heavyweight boxer Joe Louis, the first Black national contender since Jack Johnson two decades before. Much more than a sports star, Louis was a symbol of Black pride and power. In the weeks before the wet nurses went on strike, the *Defender*'s sports page ran dozens of different stories about Joe Louis, next to dramatic display advertisements for a contest that invited readers to write in. "Louis or Johnson? Who Is the Greatest Fighter?" asked one of the ads. "What's Your Answer? Vote! Write! . . . in 25 Words or Less! Hurry! WIN CASH PRIZES!"[144]

Richard Wright, the famous author of *Black Boy* and *Native Son*, moved with his family from the South to Chicago in 1927, when he was nineteen. In 1935 he published his first piece of journalism, entitled "Joe Louis Uncovers Dynamite," for the national Communist Party magazine *New Masses*. Wright described the massive, joyous celebration in the streets of Bronzeville when Louis beat white boxer Max Baer in September 1935: "Two hours after the fight the area between South Parkway and Prairie Avenue on 47th Street was jammed with no less than twenty-five thousand Negroes, joy-mad and moving to they didn't know where. Clasping hands, they formed writhing snake lines and wove in and out of traffic." For the South Side, Louis's power was Black power. "From the symbol of Joe's strength they took strength, and in that moment, all obstacles were wiped out."[145]

The striking wet nurses knew all about Joe Louis. According to a four-sentence article about them entitled "Negress Wet Nurses in Sit-Down Strike," in a newspaper in Adelaide, Australia, "Reporters interviewing them jocularly asked if they acted under instructions of Mr. John [L.] Lewis to form a new union"—referring to the Welsh American who was head of the United Mine Workers union and the Congress of Industrial Unions (CIO), famous as the driving force behind the union upsurge and sit-down strikes of the 1930s. "But they had never heard of the labor organizer," the paper reported. "'You all must mean Joe Louis,' cried one colored girl, who was an admirer of the Negro boxer."[146]

In recounting this interchange, the Adelaide paper, and others that published the same story, cast the striker's response as a joke, implying that readers should laugh at the women's presumed ignorance. But the striker's quick reference to the boxer shows she had her own knowledge, which the reporter didn't necessarily understand. As a Black Chicagoan who admired and, we can imagine, took power from Joe Louis, she might easily have been one of those who poured into the streets to celebrate his victory two years earlier.

FOR THE UNION MAKES US STRONG

But even if the strikers didn't know his name, they drew power from CIO president John L. Lewis, too, and more broadly from the nationwide labor mobilization of which he was the symbolic leader. They chose to strike in the context of a national uprising that was breaking out at precisely that moment. Within Chicago, they were surrounded by a surging wave of multiracial and successful labor activism—including a daring and largely unheralded world of union activity by African American women. All that gave them a new sense of the possible.

At the core of the Black labor movement in Chicago, and nationally, lay the all-important Brotherhood of Sleeping Car Porters, whose members worked for the Pullman Sleeping Car Company as porters and maids. Founded in 1925 by A. Philip Randolph, the most prominent African American trade unionist in the country, the Brotherhood counted 6,500 members by 1938. They were almost all African American, augmented, at times, by small numbers of Filipino men and Chinese women. The Brotherhood, which would eventually force the Pullman Company into an unprecedented contract on April 25, 1937, was a great symbol of Black male dignity. By the early 1930s its grassroots power and militant campaigns, centered in Chicago, forced more cautious and middle-class organizations such as the NAACP, Urban League, and the *Defender* into vigorous support for labor unions. In February 1936, the Brotherhood spearheaded the National Negro Labor Conference in Chicago, attended by five thousand Black labor activists and supporters. Randolph, the conference's keynote speaker, and others spoke forcefully about African American history, evoking famous men such as Frederick Douglass and Denmark Vesey as well as legendary women—Sojourner Truth, Harriet Tubman. The NAACP had already been moving toward more militant forms of direct action through its 1930 "Don't Buy Where You Can't Work" campaigns, in which men and women picketed and boycotted white-owned stores in Black neighborhoods that refused to hire Black workers, successfully demanding that they hire African Americans.[147]

As historians Melinda Chateauvert and Beth Tompkins Bates have shown, the Brotherhood of Sleeping Car Porters drew much of its strength from its women, especially the wives of unionized porters, who were organized in auxiliaries and fanned out to build support for unions throughout Chicago and beyond. In 1927, they formed a special body to advance the labor movement, the Chicago Citizens' Committee.[148]

By 1932 the Citizens' Committee was working closely with another key institution in the Black community, the South Parkway Branch of the Young Women's Christian Association (YWCA), located at Madison Street and La Salle Drive. Its staff member for labor issues was an African American woman named Thelma McWhorter (later Wheaton). Hired in 1931, Wheaton had a master's degree from Case Western Reserve University, a brother-in-law who was a Pullman porter, and a sophisticated dedication to training Black women in labor unionism. At the YWCA and in community outreach programs, working closely with the women of the Sleeping Car Porters, she taught African American women in Chicago how to believe in unions, how to run meetings, how to understand labor law, labor history, and the history of women and work, and—most importantly, she said—how to have the self-confidence to step forward. "We tried to teach the women to learn to speak up," especially since the "trade unions were making 'no effort' to get women to join," she recalled. With funding from the Citizens' Committee and others, Wheaton and the South Parkway YWCA sent Black women workers between the ages of twenty and thirty-five out to attend residential labor education programs that were thriving during the 1930s, at Camp Gray in Northern Michigan, the Bryn Mawr Summer School for Women Workers in Industry in Pennsylvania, and the University of Wisconsin School for Workers.[149]

Bates has traced the fruits of Wheaton's labors in Black women's labor activism throughout the city during the 1930s. Katheryn Williams, sent by Wheaton to Bryn Mawr in 1936, returned to Chicago to work as an organizer for the American Federation of Labor (AFL), where she put her new skills to work. Williams wrote in 1937 that workers would avoid her if she approached them in the street with pamphlets, but they'd talk inside their homes. "Most of our work has been done in our homes. It slows progress but is quite effective." She eventually organized 115 young African American women who worked in an upholstery factory.[150]

Another student of Wheaton's, a former schoolteacher named Neva Ryan, went out into Washington Park to talk to workers and spent years organizing a union of domestic workers. By 1938 it had 150 members, some of whom had themselves been Wheaton's students as well. Its progress was apparently limited, however, by class differences between organizers and organized. A woman described in *Black Metropolis* as "one of the most experienced and energetic organizers"—presumably Neva Ryan—told one of Cayton and Drake's researchers that while she was "primarily interested in union organization," a training program first needed to be created so that "standards" for the workers could be established that would "appeal to employers." A second woman working on the program, by contrast, described by the researcher as "a young colored Communist," was quite critical of the first woman's approach: "We took up the problem of inefficiency and would criticize the girls for untidy appearance, dirty nails, and such things. This antagonized the girls." It was more important, she thought, to talk about "how mean the boss is." "Such problems as long hours should have been talked about more, rather than runs in the girls' stockings."[151]

Throughout the 1930s, Black women affiliated with the Communist Party supported unions of African American women in Chicago, sometimes working within the Citizens' Committee, the National Negro Congress, or the South Parkway YWCA. The Party's largely white national and local leadership followed a strict political line emanating

from the USSR, which included a deep commitment to fighting racism. During the '30s, its prominent national campaigns to free the
nine "Scottsboro Boys" who had been falsely accused of raping two
white women on a train in Alabama, and to free Angelo Herndon, a
Black labor organizer jailed in 1932 for organizing interracial unions
in Atlanta, gradually gained it the trust of many in the Chicago Black
community. In 1932, the Chicago party had 412 Black members, 24.3
percent of the city's total. It's unclear how many of those were women,
but African American women Communists popped up regularly in
labor, anti-eviction, and other activism in Chicago throughout the
decade. In 1938, the Party's local organizer for the South Side nonetheless complained that it had been "almost impossible" to recruit
Black women, "with the exception of old women" (!!). But during a
concerted 1936 campaign, the Party successfully recruited 145 women,
all of them forty-five or younger.[152]

These women were seriously dedicated. One Communist, Eleanor
Rye, served as secretary of the Industrial Committee of the Chicago
Council of the National Negro Congress beginning in 1936, and was
connected to the women of the Brotherhood of Sleeping Car Porters.
She was a member of the executive board of the local union of the
Fur and Leather Workers, and through that role, was active in the
AFL's Chicago Federation of Labor, organizing both Black and white
workers. Rye was no shrinking violet. In the spring of 1937, unorga-
nized workers at the Wilson and Bennett can manufacturing plant,
mostly Black women, occupied their factory to protest low wages.
According to George Schuyler, at the time a prominent writer for the
Black-owned *Pittsburgh Courier*, "The workers hung out a sign 'Go
Get the CIO.' But the organizers who rushed down there couldn't get
past the police who had the factory surrounded." Rye, "undaunted,
slipped through the police lines, scaled a 15-foot fence, got inside the
plant, and signed up everybody." Schuyler added: "Other ace Negro
organizers . . . were the Misses Fanny Brown and Ola Bell Francis."[153]

Beyond all this, we can catch glimpses of still other African American women in Chicago who provided leadership and resources to the
labor movement and might have been in contact with the wet nurses.
Elizabeth Griffin Doty organized a strike of fig and date workers.
Frankie Adams, industrial secretary of the South Parkway YWCA at
the time, gave a speech at the 1930 National Negro Congress about

Black women in industry. Marie Hurston traveled to the USSR and when she came back gave two-hour lectures on Marxist economics in Bronzeville's Washington Park, attended by hundreds. Annie Malone, who had amassed a fortune selling Black beauty products, donated four furnished rooms at her Poro College headquarters for the offices of the National Negro Congress. And at the Communist Party's 1935 May Day March, which drew thirty-five thousand people, listeners could even hear a speech by Lucy Parsons, the famous radical of African, Mexican, and Indigenous descent. Born in 1851, she was the widow of Albert Parsons, one the Haymarket Martyrs hanged in Chicago in 1887.[154]

Well before the wet nurses' strike, this activism helped produce a major, large-scale union victory for Black women garment workers. Fifteen hundred women, mostly African American, worked at the six South Side factories of Ben Sopkins and Sons making aprons and dresses. In 1933 Chicago Communists put a great deal of energy into supporting a strike the women launched through an independent union. One observer wrote that the union was organized "entirely by word of mouth under the leadership of a woman organizer who understood factory conditions and who had been trained in a work-ers' school"—presumably with the support of the YWCA's Thelma Wheaton. When the police brutally attacked the strikers on the third day of the strike, the *Defender* jumped in to support them, joining key Black leaders including a Chicago alderman, US congressmember Oscar De Priest, and James W. Ford, the Communist Party's candidate for vice president. The union won a clear victory that included shorter hours, a 17 percent raise, equal pay for equal work for Black and white workers, and a pledge from the employer that it would not retaliate against the strikers. At the time, the Communists signed up nine hundred of the employees into their unions. But almost all the new members slipped away soon after.[155]

Although we have no evidence connecting any of this to the wet nurses directly, if we add all this activism up it's clear that by the time those seven women walked into city hall in March 1937, South Side Chicago was exploding with ideas about innovative organizing and Black empowerment; with militant, audacious Black women activists (along with other militant women and men); and, most importantly, with examples of ordinary Black women like themselves choosing to unionize, speak out at union meetings, strike, walk picket lines, and even to occupy stores, factories, restaurants, offices—wherever they worked.

Deeper institutional changes in the US labor movement by 1937 offered further potential power to the wet nurses. By the time of their strike, the new CIO had burst to the front of national headlines and was transforming class and race relations in the United States. Formed in 1935 when progressive unions broke out of the racist, conservative parameters of the AFL to form a new national federation, the CIO unleashed organizing energies that swiftly led to dramatic and unprecedented union gains in mass production. John L. Lewis, its president and head of the United Mine Workers, in just one example of solidarity on an enormous scale, donated $960,000 of his union's funds to organize the steelworkers. In 1936, the CIO jumped in to support rubber workers in Ohio who rose up by the tens of thousands at Goodyear and other firms. In December 1936, autoworkers in Flint, Michigan, organized in the CIO's new United Auto Workers (UAW) union, occupied a strategically important plant and shut down the entire General Motors nationwide operation, idling 125,000 workers. On February 11, 1937—a month before the wet nurses' strike—General Motors capitulated.[156]

In Chicago, the CIO launched two immense multiracial organizing drives that spring of 1937. A new Packinghouse Workers Organizing Committee, led by the Communist Party, built on the legacy of earlier organizations to build a militant interracial union with African American as well as white men in leadership positions and a smattering of Mexican male activists. While Black women joined, they were not apparently involved in leadership. A new Steel Workers Organizing Committee (SWOC) launched a campaign in the spring of 1937 to strategically target Black workers on the South Side of Chicago, along with white and Black workers nationwide. An estimated 10–15 percent of Chicago steelworkers were Black, almost all of them apparently men. Eleanor Rye, the Communist fence-climber, pops up again here, serving as the SWOC's liaison to the National Negro Congress.[157]

Perhaps surprisingly, though, far larger numbers of Black women in Chicago were members of AFL unions than CIO ones. The older federation, for all its explicit racism and sexism, was more likely to be present in sectors where Black women worked, and was itself resurgent during the late '30s as a result of both competition with the CIO and broader enthusiasm for the labor movement. Some of these Black women AFL members were in brand-new unions, such as the can-making workers at Wilson and Bennett that Rye organized and the upholstery workers organized by Katheryn Williams. Others were members of older, segregated unions, such as the beauticians' union and the Hotel Employees and Restaurant Employees Union (HERE), whose miscellaneous workers' local in Chicago counted four thousand white members and five thousand Black members, many of them evidently women, by the late 1930s. In addition, African American waitresses belonged to segregated Black HERE Local 444. It's unclear what voice, if any, Black women or men had in these locals. But one white business manager for HERE told researchers working on *Black Metropolis* that "on the whole, the Negro women take an active part, and . . . both Negroes and whites attend the occasional social functions given by the union."[158]

The largest number of organized Black women workers in Chicago belonged to the AFL-affiliated Laundry Workers International Union, which had eight thousand African American members at the time, most of them women, and two thousand white workers. The notes by a staffer for Cayton and Drake taken at a union meeting in the late 1930s make clear that young Black women spoke up loudly and clearly in laundry workers' union meetings. When a top union official presented a new union contract, rank-and-file members weren't happy with it. "What about the curtain stretchers, Mr. Chairman? I notice no mention was made of them," objected a twenty-two-year-old Black woman. "We asked the boss for a raise and when he refused, we struck by ourselves. He gave us thirty cents." She said they'd joined the union because they wanted more. "If the union can't get us more than thirty cents we might just as well get out and fight our battle alone. [She sat down amidst thundering applause.]" Another young Black woman stood up and repeated the same point. "We want more and *we're going to get more! [Applause and cheers.]*" She sat back down, lit a cigarette, "only to rise up two more times and say the same thing in different words," while "the white women sitting around her cheered her on."[159]

BECAUSE EVERYONE IS DOING IT: SIT-DOWN STRIKES

The wet nurses would also have known about the new daring sit-down strikes popping up all around them and involving workers of almost every kind imaginable. During the weeks immediately before and after the wet nurses' strike, the UAW's stunning victory in Flint suddenly inspired workplace occupations all over the Upper Midwest and Northeast, and even worldwide.

Sit-downs, first employed on a large scale in France earlier in the 1930s, offered workers new powers. In an ordinary strike, strikers depended on the moral suasion of picket lines to keep strikebreakers from entering the workplace. In a sit-down, by contrast, strikers occupying their workplace were entrenched inside it. If an employer wanted to break a strike, they would have to call the police to drag workers out, often with tear gas. Although in theory sit-downs threatened the sanctity of private property, public opinion during the depths of the Depression was, as often as not, on the side of the strikers.

Most of the February and March 1937 sit-down strikes in the US were small in scale, lasted only a day or two, and were victorious, as employers swiftly capitulated. The biggest wave was in the Detroit area. In late February, three hundred workers at the Ferry Morse Seed Company, three hundred auto body workers at Briggs Manufacturing, fifty-five charwomen who cleaned the Penobscot Building, sixty high school boys who delivered food to factories, and six workers at the Bon Dee Golf Ball Company all sat down and won, among others. It was a unique historical moment, when suddenly risk-taking became much more plausible and enticing.[160]

Chicago had its own formidable "mushroom growth" of sit-downs, as the *Tribune* put it. During the week before the wet nurses went on strike, two hundred bookbinders, "half of them women," sat down for six hours and won a 12 percent pay increase. Workers at the Fannie May Candy Company sat down for two hours and won their key demand, a forty-hour workweek. Fifteen hundred workers in the warehouse and offices of the Chicago Mail Order Company won a 10 percent wage increase after a three-day occupation. Other sit-downs were launched by typographers, pin setters at most of the city's bowling alleys, and employees at "Wizard, Inc.," where strikers reportedly kept their factory spanking clean "and observed scrupulously the company rules by smoking only in the washrooms." They won a 10 percent raise.[161]

By the end of the week before the wet nurses' strike, there were so many local sit-down strikes underway that the *Chicago Tribune* had instituted a new daily column listing them. Its reports combined awe at the sit-downs' remarkable proliferation, horror at their disruption of economic life, and the *Tribune*'s awareness of the sales value of vivid detail and leering sexism. "Geisha girls" in Japan were sitting down, as were workers at the pyramids in Egypt.[162] On Saturday, March 13, the *Tribune* wrote that the public could peer into the "large plate glass windows of six downtown restaurants of the DeMet's chain," and see for themselves "the comely waitresses passing the time of day with bus boys and fountain men in the locked restaurants." When, after several days on strike, the 450 DeMet's workers, overwhelmingly women and without a union, heard they'd won a 25 percent pay increase, "they played games of ring-around-the-rosy and danced."[163] Most of these multiple sit-downers were apparently white, given that the *Tribune* usually marked African Americans by race but not those deemed white. But it's not entirely clear, in every case.[164]

Perhaps most famous of this wave of smaller sit-downs was the Detroit Woolworth's strike, launched on February 27 by a hundred young white women who occupied their store night and day for a week and won all their demands, including a 25 percent raise, time and a half for overtime, a forty-eight-hour workweek, and even pay for the time they'd been on strike. The strike spread to other stores in the Detroit area and eventually to New York, East St. Louis, and elsewhere. The Woolworth workers' sit-down was splayed across the nation's newspapers, including the *Chicago Tribune*, and even filmed in a newsreel that showed in movie theaters all over. They were later featured in their own glossy multipage photo spread in *Life* magazine.[165]

Finally, we can note that the exact same morning that the seven wet nurses sat down, three hundred other African American women, who sewed aprons and dresses for the Nellie Ann Dress Company, occupied their own workplace on the South Side of Chicago, demanding their wages be doubled. A long sixteen weeks later, with help from the CIO-affiliated International Ladies' Garment Workers' Union to which they belonged, they would eventually win. That spring another four hundred young Black women who made dresses at Sopkins and Sons also struck, organized into the ILGWU by a Black organizer named "Miss Redmond."[166]

When asked by reporters why the wet nurses had struck, Dr. Herman Bundesen replied: "It's just one of those funny things. They want to strike because everyone else is doing it."[167] His answer had a tinge of condescension, implying the strikers were just silly creatures following fashion. But he was also right. The wet nurses would have known about the sit-downs all over the country, all over Chicago. They may have known that the strikes were usually victorious. They could have read about them in the newspapers that we can see sitting on their laps in one photograph. They could have heard about sit-downs from their family members, neighbors in their buildings, pamphleteers in the street, speakers and organizers in Washington Park, at the YWCA, in the Black press, in the white press, or in newsreels at movie theaters. In the months and years before, they might have met any one of those African American women organizers, talked to them in the park, or even taken a class from Thelma Wheaton, the YWCA organizer. When Carrie Burnish declared that they were paid "starvation wages," she was echoing a phrase regularly deployed by Communists during the 1930s, articulating what she already knew to be true.[168] But the wet nurses could equally have been inspired directly by their rank-and-file peers whose names we don't know, who had been organizing, forming their own organizations, striking, and occupying workplaces in Chicago for at least four years.

In contrast to most of these other strikers, though, the wet nurses themselves had no apparent union. Nor is there any evidence of an organizer working with them, whether Communist, AFL, CIO, or independent. The news reports don't mention any allies in the established Black organizations or government. Apparently, no outsiders rushed in to support them or help them negotiate with the City of Chicago. They didn't hang out a sign calling for aid from the CIO. And without a union, the strikers would have lacked key external resources, including media management skills, pay while on strike, advice about negotiating with management, and links to the solidarity of other unions.

In all likelihood, the Chicago labor movement wasn't itself interested in organizing them. Wet nurses weren't workers in industry, which Communist leaders and leftist men in general targeted as strategically important to a hoped-for workers' revolution. They didn't fit any jurisdiction of the established unions organizing Black women, either, whether of garment workers, hotel workers, or beauticians. Nor were wet nurses domestic servants, recently targeted by Black women activists conscious that the occupation employed far more Black working women than any other. The wet nurses were in fact government employees. During the 1930s, unions for public-sector workers, of any job category, were few and far between. The very few organizers who were interested in organizing government employees were white men largely indifferent to any women workers, and who would have viewed wet nurses as a weird anomaly, since the nurses weren't paid wages and instead were paid piece rate, by the drop of milk.[169] From another perspective, though, the wet nurses were in fact factory workers—at a milk factory.

Yet the wet nurses' apparent independence from official union structure may have given them other powers. One news story reported that Mary Hart was "the spokesman."[170] But five different women in fact spoke to the press. It's possible the other two also talked to the reporters too. There is no further indication that Hart was the leader beyond the one reporter's assertion. Instead, the strikers may have drawn collective strength from a horizontal, nonhierarchical structure. Staughton Lynd and other historians, in a collection entitled *"We Are All Leaders": The Alternative Unionism of the Early 1930s*, posit that smaller, more openly structured, nonhierarchical unions were stronger than the CIO's hierarchal, bureaucratized unions with memberships in the hundreds of thousands by World War II.[171] During that sit-down wave in Chicago, the successful DeMet restaurant workers didn't have a union, we can note. The Black women quoted above who worked as curtain stretchers in laundries, who spoke up so forthrightly to their union officials, made clear they had struck on their own before they were in the union, and would do so again if necessary.[172]

Judging by the photos, the wet nurses look like close friends. After all, they spent every morning together changing in and out of uniforms, scrubbing their arms and breasts at a sink, and sitting around a table expressing milk into a tin cup for an hour. What bonds did they form, those mornings in the milk station, and after they had left it? What conversations did they have among themselves, away from their employers' ears, that led them to decide to sit down? Thelma

Wheaton recalled she had been working to build trust among women workers, as well as teaching them about labor law, unions, and labor history.[173] We can only speculate about the trust those seven women had built among themselves, and what, exactly, they whispered or called out encouragingly to each other as they walked down the hall to Dr. Bundesen's office in city hall that Monday morning.

Sitting down firmly, they drew their power from Joe Louis, John L. Lewis, and from each other. They had also, it appears, discovered that militant, dramatic social protest could be a source of powerful joy. Dancing wasn't the only way to feel alive, to claim your body, to push off white domination, and have a great time. You could dress up and sit down in seven white chairs in your boss's office too. The *Tribune*, reporting on the strike wave, observed in horror: "Sitting down, for wages, for working hours—or the joy of sitting—approached a national hysteria."[174]

END GAMES

One of the strikers announced on the first day that they would stay seated "until Gabriel blows his horn." Did they?

Bundesen's statements to the press, noted earlier, suggest he was not about to give the strikers anything. He claimed repeatedly that he couldn't change the budget himself and implied it could take weeks to get anything approved by the city council. "There is nothing I can do about the strike except refer it to the finance committee," he said. That could have been true, and it could have been entirely fictitious. He might have had other sources of funding available that he didn't choose to divulge or draw upon—for example, the endowment to pay wet nurses that the Infants' Aid Society had set up in the 1920s. His laconic answer, "I probably will do that," when asked whether he would forward the strikers' request to the finance committee, suggests a possible unwillingness to address the wet nurses' demands in any way.[175] All of his statements could have been posturing, though. During strikes, employers routinely say they aren't going to budge—until they budge.

We have one additional photograph of the strikers, published on Wednesday, March 17, and presumably taken on Tuesday, the strike's second day. The same uniformed white nurse stands in the corner, watching. The same strikers are still sitting in the chairs, but now they're distributed differently. Instead of tidily held gloves folded over purses and hands, they now have open newspapers across their laps. Most arrestingly, they have completely different looks on their faces than those in the first day's photos. In this one, they're looking at the camera, not at each other, and they are most definitely not laughing and smiling. Their expressions are flat, wary. One of them, sitting up the straightest, has a look of vigilant distrust, her eyes boring right in at the photographer, challenging him. These were Black women who'd spent their lives being harassed and threatened by authorities of every sort. They didn't have the luxury of trusting that the observer was friendly. What had just been said to them, as they looked up to the speaker? What had they been through in the previous twenty-four hours?[176]

In fact, Bundesen or the city government could have called in the police at any moment, and the strikers would have known that. They were trapped in a very small space, with the nurse blocking the rear exit. For all the successful gains of sit-down strikes in Chicago and beyond at the time, in many cases employers were quick to call in force, whether city police or private thugs. On Tuesday, the second day of the strike, the *Chicago Herald and Examiner* reported in an article that appeared just below its story about the wet nurses' strike: "Using night sticks and fists and the threat of guns, forty policemen smashed a sit-down strike of more than 200 men and women maintenance employees in the Jewish Hospital in Brooklyn today."[177] If state violence were deployed against the wet nurses, they apparently had no one to step in to try to stop it, lacking evident allies in the Urban League, NAACP, Communist Party, AFL, or CIO. They were Black, and hence far more vulnerable than the white women who'd occupied Chicago's DeMet restaurants or the Detroit Woolworth's store for a week and hadn't been evicted. Four years earlier, by contrast, police had viciously beaten Black women strikers during the big 1933 strike at Sopkins's Chicago garment factories.[178] Just two months after the wet nurses' strike, the Chicago police would shoot and kill ten striking steelworkers, both Black and white, in the infamous Memorial Day Massacre.[179]

The evidence doesn't tell us when, exactly, the wet nurses ended their strike, or how. As nursing mothers, they needed to be with their own babies, after all, and it definitely would not have been safe to bring them to the sit-down. In contrast to other sit-downs, where strikers camped out in their workplaces all night, all day, the wet nurses went home at night, presumably to be with their babies and other children; two strikers, as noted, even left early on Monday afternoon. Given Bundesen's plea that "children might suffer" if they held out for long, the strikers would also have been conscious that if they stayed out for long, he could easily have manipulated public opinion against them by raising alarms about potentially at-risk infants.

On April 5, two weeks later, the caption to their photo in *Life* reported: "The nurses finally settled for 4c," although they had asked for ten.[180] But four cents is only what they were making all along. It's possible they gained nothing. *Life*'s use of "settled," though, indicates that some kind of formal agreement was reached—that the women didn't just file out, completely defeated. According to reporters, on the strike's first morning, Bundesen "sent word out to the strikers that he would meet with them for collective bargaining," which also suggests that some kind of formal negotiation took place.[181] The reporter's use of "collective bargaining," moreover, indicates that the striking wet nurses, although without a formal union, nonetheless benefited from the labor movement's powerful insistence during the 1930s that employers had to bargain with their workers not just as isolated individuals but as a collectivity.

We are left imagining what happened next. Bundesen must not have called the cops, or it would have made it into the papers. The strikers might have been fired soon afterward, then blacklisted, as happened routinely to workers who sought to unionize in these years. If the strikers stayed working at the milk stations, they might have experienced terrible retaliation, overt or subtle, by any or all of their white overseers, making the wet nurses' lives excruciating in new ways. Personal dynamics between the strikers and the five women who chose not to strike could have been awful too.

Or maybe the strikers got more respect after that. Maybe their employers weren't so condescending. Drs. Hess and Bundesen's well-oiled milk machine didn't run so smoothly after all, it had turned out, and the smug doctors would have been brought up short by both the strike and the national publicity it received. Gertrude Plotzke told Jacqueline Wolf in 1996 that the women were paid five cents an ounce. So at some point they did get a raise from their original four cents—although five cents would still have been insultingly meager.[182]

Whatever the wet nurses gained or lost monetarily from their strike, they were nonetheless part of the enormous labor uprising of hundreds of thousands of US workers during the 1930s that included working people of hundreds of different ethnic groups, all choosing to speak up and take action to demand more of their employers, of the state, and of their lives. The wet nurses were both inspired by that mobilization, and themselves contributed to it.

STATE POWER, UNION POWER

When we pull all the way back to look at the wet nurses' story in national context, the outcome of their strike depended on one final factor: the state, as the New Deal stepped in to dramatically reshape labor relations.

Once Roosevelt took office in March of 1933, the nationwide labor uprising made possible a fundamental transformation of federal labor regulations. First, the National Industrial Recovery Act (NIRA) of 1933 created the National Recovery Administration, the first national system of federal regulation of wages and hours, although it was ruled unconstitutional in 1935. More permanently, the 1935 National Labor Relations Act (NLRA, or Wagner Act) created a system of government-regulated union elections and compelled employers to bargain collectively "in good faith" or face penalties. It protected civil liberties in union campaigns and guaranteed the right to strike and boycott, and paved the way for the stabilization and long-term power of the CIO as well as the AFL.

On another front, the 1935 Social Security Act created the nation's first system of old-age pensions for wage workers and their widows and was eventually expanded to support the disabled. It created an unemployment insurance program, in which a federal payroll tax was administered by the states. The final key measure was the 1938 Fair Labor Standards Act, which abolished child labor and mandated the first national minimum wage. Altogether, this package, known as the New Deal labor system, ushered in a breathtaking transformation of workplace relations, guaranteeing labor rights while providing a safety net under millions of working people for the first time, in turn strengthening many workers' bargaining power with their employers. It was deliberately designed to redistribute wealth by tipping the balance of power between labor and capital toward labor, and it did.[183]

The wet nurses, though, would have benefited directly from none of those laws. The short-lived NIRA only applied to wage workers in certain sectors, largely industrial, and used federal power to explicitly codify unequal wage rates based on race and gender for the first time ever. More bluntly, and with long-term impact, the NLRA, federal unemployment insurance, the Fair Labor Standards Act, and the Social Security retirement system all excluded domestic servants, agricultural field labor, government employees, workers in retail and service, and many other occupations. In 1930, 78 percent of all Black women worked in those first two categories.[184]

Roosevelt and Northern Democrats conceded the exclusion of domestic and farm laborers to Southern Democrats in order to get the bills passed, allowing Southern white agricultural interests to keep their workers exploited in the fields and their maids under their thumbs.[185] The definition of "work" and "workers" under these systems also excluded unwaged work in the home performed by all women. Women in heterosexual marriages and working at home could qualify for benefits as spouses and widows, but only if they were in dependent relationships with wage-earning men working in the sectors that qualified.

Despite their limits, the new federal laws regulating labor relations nonetheless helped fuel the successful resurgence of the US labor movement during the mid-1930s. The NIRA, which created the National Recovery Administration (NRA), included the immediately famous clause 7(a), which stated that "employees shall have the right to organize and bargain collectively through representatives of their own choosing . . . free from the interference, restraint, or coercion of employers." The clause had no enforcement mechanism or real power; but in practice, in its implicit—and unprecedented—endorsement by the federal government of the legal right to organize, it helped inspire an enormous nationwide strike wave in 1933–34, known as the "NRA Strikes." The United Mine Workers grew to three hundred thousand members (three-quarters white, one-quarter Black), struck for three months, and won higher wages, the eight-hour day, the five-day week, and an end to child labor and scrip payment systems. The Amalgamated Clothing Workers and International Ladies' Garment Workers unions gained two hundred thousand new members and, through strikes and other pressures, won union contracts that guaranteed better wages and working conditions. Longshoremen shut down all the ports on the entire West Coast, led a general strike of 130,000 workers in San Francisco, and won union recognition, union-controlled hiring halls, higher pay, and the thirty-hour workweek. In the South, though, a massive strike by three hundred thousand newly organized textile workers was completely defeated by a combination of racism, repression, and employers' control of the National Guard.[186]

The NRA strikes, for all their militance, didn't lead to the broader, permanent gains for labor that activists had hoped for. But they showed what was possible. Only when the CIO broke out of the straitjacket of the AFL after 1935 did labor achieve its huge, long-term advances at a national level, some of which we've noted already. A month after the CIO's auto workers' victory at General Motors, the Chrysler Corporation, fearful of a strike at its own plants, signed an identical agreement with the UAW. The UAW grew to 375,000 members by the end of 1937. Most astonishingly, on March 3, 1937, twelve days before the wet nurses' strike, United States Steel, one of the biggest corporations in the country, totally capitulated and signed a union contract with the CIO's new Steel Workers Organizing Committee without even a strike, because the company was so afraid of what the UAW had just done to General Motors. Workers at a dozen US Steel plants won union recognition, a forty-hour workweek, and a 10 percent raise in pay, swelling the Steel Workers Union to 555,000 members. Hundreds of thousands of packinghouse workers, electrical manufacturing workers, tire makers, and other factory industrial workers gained union recognition and all sorts of improvements in their jobs.[187]

Women's place in the giant new CIO unions, though, was largely limited to those who worked in factories and who fit the model of "industrial workers" to which male organizers were committed—such as auto parts workers in Detroit. The CIO did organize thousands of women, nonetheless, often in interracial unions in packinghouses, rubber plants, auto parts factories, and in the United Cannery, Agricultural, Packinghouse and Allied Workers of America, which organized Japanese and Filipino sugar plantation workers in Hawaii, Mexican and white pecan shellers in Texas, and Mexican and Russian Jewish cannery workers in California.[188] In New York, Black and white women who worked in commercial laundries, who'd been organizing themselves for over a decade, finally gained union contracts through a new CIO-affiliated union.[189]

Soon the older, more conservative AFL affiliates started adding women members as well, as its unions started competing with the CIO, and employers turned to them as more palatable than the militant CIO. The Hotel Employees and Restaurant Employees Union (HERE), for example, organized more and more waitresses.[190] But huge sectors of women workers were almost untouched by the 1930s labor movement, such as the country's two million clerical workers—one in four of all white women who worked for wages—and the vast majority of service workers.[191]

In fact, the closer we get to the wet nurses and domestic labor, the farther away they are from the labor movement, whether CIO or AFL. During the 1930s all kinds of small-scale campaigns organizing domestic workers did emerge nationwide. African American and Finnish women in New York City, for example, formed the Domestic Workers' Union, rented an office in a Finnish mutual benefit association building in Harlem, and in 1936 got a charter from the AFL. By the next year they had between 350 and 1,000 members, mostly African American, historian Vanessa May has found. In Newark, Washington, DC, and San Diego, Black domestics were part of AFL-affiliated unions too. Beyond them lay an array of more informal domestic workers' associations that pushed for increased wages, decreased hours, standard labor conditions, and state-level legislation, aided, at times, by allies from the white-led Women's Trade Union League, the NAACP, and Black churches. But out of three million women who worked in domestic labor in 1930, only two thousand were unionized by the end of the decade. They lacked leadership, funding, and a widespread understanding among workers of the value of unions, Esther V. Cooper concluded in a 1940 master's thesis. All of those resources could have flowed in from the CIO or the AFL, if the federations' top leaders had cared.[192]

The Chicago wet nurses, if they were to build strength through collective labor action, needed a powerful labor movement at their backs, one committed to supporting them with the concrete resources of solidarity. They needed a state that was committed to supporting labor rights for *all* workers. During the 1930s, they got neither.

The New Deal labor system nonetheless set the stage for many benefits that would accrue to Black women over the next decades.

Black men in manufacturing, mining, and other jobs would gain from the continuing empowerment of the CIO during World War II and the decade that followed, benefiting Black families more broadly. Black women who had jobs in industry—in tobacco processing, for example—could gain directly too. The Social Security pension system would eventually be extended to domestic workers, albeit in unwieldy, limited ways. The real change came in the 1950s when African American women finally were able to move out of domestic service and into other occupations, especially clerical and service work. During the 1960s and '70s, affirmative action and the Equal Employment Opportunity Commission (EEOC, created as part of the 1964 Civil Rights Act) would help force open the door to government employment, just as new laws passed beginning in the early '60s made collective bargaining possible in the public sector. By 1983, 22.7 percent of all Black women would be unionized, and they would be among the most militant and committed union members in the country.[193]

SOMETHING LARGER THAN THEMSELVES

It's easy to say, in the end, that the wet nurses "lost their strike," since they didn't apparently gain their demands. But their story, like any story, isn't that simple. Labor history doesn't move forward in a single line of progression in which a single group of workers wins, hangs on to those gains, and then other workers struggle and win for themselves. Rather, workers challenge employers, draw in allies, and make demands that they may or may not win immediately or be able to guarantee for the future through a legally binding collective agreement. They might win all sorts of things but lose them a year later. Yet for every victory that does make demonstrable gains, other workers, sometimes far away or years later, watch carefully, and learn, and themselves experiment with collective action, just as the wet nurses did.

Employers, for their part, watch the disruptions to profit-making that strikes, threatened strikes, or other protests can cause, and in response make concessions even if their own workers haven't themselves formed a union or struck—as the US Steel and Chrysler examples made clear. In the swirling, fast-paced upwelling of the 1930s, farmers, old people, and the unemployed were also engaged in mass protests, helping produce a whole immensely bigger than the sum of its parts.

However their strike ended, the wet nurses were powerful and militant for at least two spectacular days. They were part of something larger than themselves, the great labor uprising of the 1930s, that made possible so much for generations to come. Those seven women refused to be quiet, refused to starve, refused to accept racial disparities in pay. When they placed their bodies and their labors front and center at city hall with such sisterly dignity and demanded that their labor be respected, they refused the invisibility attached to domestic and reproductive labor, whether in nursing babies, cooking dinner, cleaning the toilet, nurturing kids, or lovingly tending to elders—labor so often boxed off into some female zone, yet grueling in its physical and emotional toll, waged or unwaged. The strikers, gazing back at the camera, challenged us to imagine a labor movement that lifts up *all* workers, *all* work, and places women of color at its center.

We can end by wondering what they might have told their daughters, their granddaughters. They did, after all, get to be quite famous—their story and photos were spread all over newspapers throughout the city, the country, all the way to Australia. They smiled away in *Life* on coffee tables nationwide. Carrie Burnish, Louise Clark, Theria Foster, Ella Gold, Mary Hart, Georgia Lewis, and Willie Morton had done at least one great thing in their lives—in addition to everything else they did. Thanks to that surviving photograph in *Life*, their magnificent story can be carried forward for new generations. We can learn from their power and feel it deep inside ourselves, too, as we find our own white chairs, friends to share them, and joy in struggle.

CHAPTER FOUR

A NEST OF FASCISTS

The Black Legion in Lima, Ohio

Typically, a friend or a relative—sometimes it was just a mere acquaintance—invited a potential "Recruit" to a private meeting of an unnamed organization. Its purpose, the friend said, was "protection"; it could help with getting jobs too. At dusk on the appointed night, the friend picked him up at home in a car with maybe three or four other men already inside it, and they drove out to Henry Tapscott's farm three miles east of Lima, Ohio. Once there, the Recruit was suddenly surrounded by thirty, forty, fifty, two hundred armed men—it was hard to see in the pitch-black dark, but some had flashlights—dressed in long black-hooded robes with eye slits, and on top a black pirate hat with a white skull and crossbones. The robes had white trim, a cape with red satin lining, and another white skull and crossbones cut out of felt and safety-pinned to the chest. The Recruit was told to kneel. As a revolver was shoved into his back, two robed men stood on either side of him pointing guns. The Captain of the Guard spat out three questions: "1. Are you a native-born, white, gentile, protestant [sic] citizen? 2. Do you understand that this organization you are about to join is strictly secret and military in character? 3. This organization is classed by our enemies as an outlaw organization; are you willing to join such an organization?"

Once the Recruit replied "yes," he was commanded to swear that he would never reveal anything about the organization or its activities, that he would "accept an order and go to your death, if necessary, to carry it out," and that he would "forget your party and vote for the best man if ordered to do so by your superior officer." A "Chaplain" proclaimed: "We class as our enemies all negroes, Jews, Catholics and anyone owing any allegiance to any foreign potentate. We fight as gorillas [sic] using any weapon that may come to our hand, preferably the ballot, and if necessary, by bearing arms." He made explicit the group's goals: "Our purpose is to tear down, lay waste, destroy and kill our enemies without mercy as long as one enemy remains alive or breath remains." After the Recruit swore to the oaths, he was taught the password—"elect only members to office"—and handed a 38-caliber gun cartridge to keep as a reminder of both his oath and what would befall him should he betray it.[1]

By 1935, around five thousand white men in the town of Lima, Ohio, out of a total population of 42,267, had sworn to those oaths. The organization they joined was known as the Black Legion. It was an offshoot of the Ku Klux Klan, which had boomed and then largely collapsed during the 1920s. By the mid-1930s the Black Legion grew to between a hundred thousand and a million members all over the United States—no one really knows how many—and was especially strong in Ohio, Michigan, Kentucky, and Illinois, as well as West Virginia and Indiana. In Detroit, its members reportedly included the police commissioner, dozens of police, a prosecutor, and the mayor of an adjoining city. It killed at least fifty people, some of them white, some African American, some of them union organizers and leftists.[2] Malcolm X and his family always suspected that the Black Legion had killed his father in east Lansing, Michigan, in 1931 and left him in the street to be run over by a streetcar.[3]

Only when brave police investigators in Detroit got a perpetrator to squeal in May 1936 did national news break about the Black Legion and its activities, and a few prosecutions finally begin. National alarm erupted, driven by daily headlines, as twelve members of the Black Legion were tried in Detroit for killing a white WPA worker named Charles Poole. Hollywood even made two films about the Legion. As the extent, power, and fascist nature of the Black Legion became clearer and clearer (but never entirely clear), as Mussolini and Hitler continued to rise in Europe, and as Senator Huey Long and "radio priest" Charles Coughlin amassed millions of devoted followers in the US, the real possibility of an organized fascist uprising in the United States loomed. Echoing Sinclair Lewis's famous 1935 novel and 1936 play, *It Can't Happen Here*, about a fictional dictator who takes over the United States, A. B. Magil and Henry Stevens, in a 1938 pamphlet entitled *The Peril of Fascism*, observed: "The Black Legion, flinging its shadow across the American scene, jolted the unwary and incredulous into a realization it could happen here."[4]

Reporters soon zeroed in on Lima, a small city an hour south of Toledo in northwestern Ohio, where the headquarters of the Black Legion lay in the home of Virgil "Bert" Effinger, the secret agitator and "Major General" atop the organization. We can follow them into Lima—not just to the Legion's leader, but, more importantly, to its members, its appeal to ordinary white men and women, and the sheer normalcy of white supremacy, nativism, antisemitism, anti-Catholicism, and militarism during the 1930s in the so-called Heartland. "This monstrous organization is not just a grim excrescence on American life," *The Nation* wrote at the time, "but something that has been built into the structure of American business and politics."[5]

The Black Legion fell apart by late 1936 in the face of prosecutions, national outrage, and individuals' decreasing willingness to be publicly associated with it. For every heroic opponent who eventually stepped forward and helped stop it, though, lurked a fully complicit local government official who had joined the Legion or who actively thwarted those who sought to shut it down. They included Robert F. Jones, who in 1934 joined the Black Legion in Lima in exchange for being elected county prosecutor and went on to serve four terms in the US Congress. The story of the Black Legion, from Lima all the way up to the FBI, Department of Justice, and US Senate, raises all-too-familiar questions about law enforcement and political power, who controlled them, and for what ends.

Today, the Black Legion casts a long shadow in Lima. It's deep Trump country. As debate rages over the hearts and minds of white working-class men in the Midwest, the history of the Black Legion in Lima, Ohio, is terrifyingly instructive.

FOUNDING FATHERS

The Black Legion was founded in 1924 by a physician named William Shepard, health commissioner for the small town of Bellaire, Ohio, across the state from Lima on the Ohio River. A reporter for the *Detroit*

News who interviewed Shepard in 1935 described him as "a nervous, active little man with a jet black pompadour and squinting eyes." In an accompanying photo he looks charming; he's smiling as if he's just landed a great joke. Shepard, an established leader in the Ku Klux Klan, decided around 1924 to organize his own semi-independent branch within it he called the Black Guards, using lampblack to change his followers' hoods from white to black. According to Shepard, the Grand Dragon of the Klan then expelled him and his organization because the Grand Dragon was "jealous of the Black Guards' popularity."[6]

When an FBI investigator sniffed around in Bellaire in 1934, his sources told him that Shepard was obsessed with Catholics, immigrants, and violence against them. One interviewee, who said he'd known Shepard for fifteen or twenty years, recalled that "on several occasions while talking with Dr. Shepard the Doctor would state how he hated Catholics and all foreigners and how they should be run out of this country." Some years before, the source said, Shepard had "made the remark that he was going to blow up the First National Bank Building in Bellaire because the president of the bank had been lending money to foreigners." Another source "stated that he had heard Dr. Shepard on several occasions cuss the Catholics" and reported that three weeks before, a group of "gypsies" camping a few miles out of town had been driven out when "someone shot off several loud bombs," and that "he had heard that Dr. Shepard was the instigator of this."[7] Historian Peter Amann, after interviewing Bellaire residents in 1979, concluded that Shepard "was a man of violence and a long time leader of vigilantes who were not just overgrown boy scouts, but men who flogged, tarred and feathered, and ran people out of town." Shepard always carried a .45 in his medical bag. "He was also rumored to be the hometown abortionist who took his fee in sexual favors."[8]

At the time Shepard formed his organization in 1924, the Ku Klux Klan was in its prime. This "Second Klan," as it's known, revived the original Reconstruction-era Klan that had terrorized African Americans in the South. In the 1920s the Klan exploded exponentially to an estimated 4 million members, both men and women, based largely in the Upper Midwest and West but embedded nationwide. It continued to focus its hostilities on African Americans, but it now added Catholics and Jews to its hate list, in a nativist response to rising immigration from Eastern and Southern Europe.[9] Klan members distributed lurid propaganda, for example, insisting that priests were raping and torturing nuns and killing the resultant babies.[10] The vicious hostility of white Protestant Klan members toward African Americans, Catholics, Jews, and "foreigners" was not at all correlated, however, with proximity to or actual competition with them. Indiana, for example, had one of the largest per capita Klan memberships in the country, but its 1920 population was 97 percent white, 95 percent native born, and 97 percent Protestant.[11]

The Second Klan largely fell apart by 1927, increasingly denounced by the public and corroded from within by profit-seeking, internal divisions, and sex scandals. But local chapters hummed along well into the 1930s and beyond, in towns like Bellaire and Lima, Ohio.[12]

The Black Legion, as George Shepard's spin-off group was soon known, followed many of the same patterns as the Ku Klux Klan. Its members wore hooded gowns. They named many of the same enemies. Amann, who researched the Black Legion extensively, argues that the Black Legion had a much higher level of secrecy than the Klan. While KKK members often paraded openly through downtown streets nationwide, hoods off, the Legion thrived on an even more obsessive secrecy, with a clandestine aura and long, elaborate initiation rituals involving chilling oaths to never divulge anything. "You have to have a mystery in a fraternal thing to keep it alive," Dr. Shepard told a *Detroit News* reporter in 1936. "The folks eat it up." Like the Klan, the Black Legion took up night-riding: it kidnapped people late at night and whipped them, burned crosses on hillsides, torched businesses.[13]

In early 1932, Virgil Effinger traveled all the way from Lima across the state to Bellaire to meet with Dr. Shepard. Effinger asked Shepard permission to launch an organizing campaign for Black Legion membership throughout the Upper Midwest. He told Shepard he wanted to call himself the Legion's "Major General"; Shepard would remain the "Commander-in-Chief." Shepard agreed—and that was the end of his control of the Black Legion, as Effinger took it over and swiftly threw Shephard off his own bus, cutting him off from any important role in the organization from then on. "In effect, Dr. Shepard had been kicked upstairs, relegated to the role of an authority figure, to reign but not to rule," concludes Amann.[14]

Virgil Effinger, known as "Bert," was the kind of man locals referred to as a "character." Very tall, very wide, balding, cigar-smoking, glum-looking, with eyes that sagged down at the corners and a mouth that turned down even more, he stood out—and wanted to. "He was a man who liked publicity very much," recalled a Lima attorney.[15] Effinger was born in West Virginia in 1874, which made him around sixty when the Black Legion reached its greatest strength. In 1898 he served in the Spanish-American War and married his wife, Mary; they had two children. Trained as an electrician, he launched an electrical supplies store and repair service in 1926, but by 1934 the store had closed and he was reportedly working for the Ohio State Highway Department.[16]

Effinger's actual source of income during the Black Legion's mid-1930s prime, though, was famously opaque. He was certainly raking in its dues money: ten cents a member per week, although it's not clear how or how efficiently he collected it. George Scheid Sr., an active member of the Lima Black Legion, at the time told his son that Effinger was keeping the dues money—which, if there were 3,500 members by 1935 and 5,000 by 1936, was a lot of money. "My god, if he collected, if he got 100 dollars a week back in those days it was a fortune," reflected George Scheid Jr. in a 1979 interview.[17]

Throughout the 1920s, Effinger regularly shaded over into trouble. In 1929, the Hawisher Motor Company tried to seize a car from him, but he wiggled out of a magistrate's judgment when a jury concluded that Effinger's wife was the rightful owner and awarded her five cents in damages. In the mid-1920s, he signed a $500 bond in support of a crime-prone Prohibition activist charged with forgery. At some point Effinger was kicked out of his union, the International Brotherhood of Electrical Workers, because of his out-of-control political views, and lost jobs as a result.[18]

Effinger did succeed in becoming the head of Lima's Ku Klux Klan. On the Fourth of July, 1925, as the Ku Klux Klan marched openly through the public square in the city's "Defense Day" parade, the *Lima News* reported: "Effinger was walking immediately behind the color bearers in the parade . . . when a Moon automobile" ran him down, breaking one of his ribs. "He was removed to his home and was said to be otherwise uninjured."[19] Of course, the question lingers as to whether the driver deliberately targeted Effinger or his fellow Klan members.

Effinger worked hard, meanwhile, to try to set himself up as a public official, with zero success. In 1921 he ran for city commissioner on the "Labor Ticket."[20] In 1932 and again in 1934, he ran as a Republican for Allen County sheriff.[21] "I will shoot square with everybody, and avoid if possible shooting at anyone," his ad in the *Lima News* promised, rather ominously given his leadership of the Black Legion at the time.[22]

Effinger's politics, like Shepard's, began with sickening hostility toward African Americans, Jews, Catholics, and those he deemed "foreigners." As noted above, the Black Legion's oath, to which he personally swore inductees, declared African Americans, Jews, and Catholics to be enemies, along with "anyone owing any allegiance to any foreign potentate." The category of "foreigners," here, did not in practice include Protestant immigrants from northern and western Europe—it signaled Italians, Eastern Europeans, Russians, Greeks, and other so-called New Immigrants of the first three decades of the twentieth century. In some versions the Legion's password, which Effinger must have written or at least approved, was "place only Americans on guard."[23] In 1936, when he was under public attack, Effinger walked into the office of the *Lima News* and handed the staff a typed statement declaring: "The Black Legion is a strictly American organization. It is a secret society dedicated to the most lofty principles and stands for the highest foray of American progress."[24]

E. J. Penhorwood, a white Methodist minister in Lima, recalled that he had spoken with Effinger regularly and had known him quite well. "If you talked with him privately," Penhorwood said, Effinger would insist that "I'm doing nothing but whats [sic] in keeping with my faith." The reverend believed that Effinger was sincere, "because he was so devoted to the thing that he felt was protecting the American way of life. He was exhalting [sic] in, he was keeping with the basic teachings of Christianity, of exhalting the individuals against institutions that might enslave your religious life."[25] Effinger might have been stringing Penhorwood along, though, since he was attempting to bring the reverend into the Legion's fold.

In July 1936, a man who described himself as an unemployed former apartment manager from Los Angeles, originally from Atlanta, took a Greyhound bus from Cincinnati to Lima at Effinger's invitation. Effinger drove him out into the countryside and swore him into the Black Legion that night, then took him back to his house for a long chat. A month later the inductee, who remained unnamed, recounted their conversation at length to the FBI. "In ancient times" there were societies such as Egypt "that were 100% Caucasian—white," Effinger had expounded, "until they got to importing the black slaves for the white people, until they got to affiliating with them on [a] sexual and social basis and brought about the present conditions of Egypt." Evoking a classic Klan trope, Effinger insisted that in "hospitals all over the country white women [are] giving birth to mulattoes" and that "he had evidence to that effect." Effinger also railed against Communism, the inductee reported. "He stated that this country was swiftly and more or less secretly being overcome by Communism," which was destroying "respect for law," and "making great inroads in the United States." As did many others at the time, Effinger rolled all his targets up into a ball he called the "isms." "The country is once again being threatened by various sorts of ISMS."[26]

For Effinger, the answer was nonetheless yet another "ism," fascism. He promised the new member that the Black Legion would restore "real American traditions as intended by our founding forefathers" that "had been trampled upon." "He told me that . . . according to his idea it would be an [illegible] matter to establish a Fascist . . . dictatorship, he mentioned [the] fact that Mussolini had only about one hundred thousand members who seized the government of Italy and that the present government of Germany under Adolph Hitler was started with two men." Effinger promised that if the Legion seized "strategic points . . . it would be a very easy matter to establish the said dictatorship. . . . It was his idea to have sufficient affiliations with various [illegible] plants and the army and navy."[27] Other accounts confirm Effinger's goals. "The Legion was continually striving to have its members join the National Guard," a different informant told an FBI investigator.[28] Another former member recounted that he'd been asked "to join an organization that could in a very short period of time have thousands of men marching on Washington."[29]

ARMED AND DANGEROUS

By 1935 Virgil Effinger, however glumly odd, however fishy, was able to enlist 3,500 men and women from Lima into the Black Legion, 5,000 by the next year. They met the first Friday of the month at midnight, either in the hall of a fraternal organization called the Order of United

American Mechanics, in the old post office building, in the Ku Klux Klan Hall, in the Old Ford Dance Hall, or at Henry Tapscott's farm to the east of town—where many of the initiations took place—and in the Cridersville Town Hall, to the south. Smaller meetings happened in members' homes. Notification of meetings moved entirely by word of mouth.[30]

Internally, the Legion ran on a strict military structure, with squads, companies, battalions, and regiments and their corresponding privates, corporals, sergeants, lieutenants, captains, majors, and colonels, with graded generals above them. Each general in turn commanded a sector constituting one-thirteenth of the United States, chosen to reflect the nation's original thirteen colonies. Atop them all ruled Virgil Effinger, the major general. The Black Legion also had local subgroups known as "degrees," responsible for specific activities, called the "Foot Legion," "Night Riders," "Black Knights," "Armed Guard," and, at the top, the select "Bullet Club."[31]

Much of this hyper-militarized structure must have emerged out of Effinger's head, as a veteran of the Spanish-American War. The Legion's membership would have included many other veterans, too, especially from World War I. One member, Albert Erfer, was a veteran of US wars in the Philippines and Mexico as well as of World War I.[32] These veterans would have been knowledgeable of and comfortable with the military titles and salutes the Legion employed, and they would have aspired to move up within the ranks and achieve the self-importance, deference, and affirmation that came with being an officer. Informants repeatedly identified individual members by their ranks, suggesting that the Legion's military titles were well known and regularly utilized. In the military culture of the Black Legion, we can see the legacy, by this point well established, of US imperial forays and ambitions in the Philippines, in Cuba, and World War I—and how they helped lay the groundwork for grassroots, domestic fascism.

When we try to put a finger on what the Black Legion actually did, the picture is less precise. Three different Lima informants who spoke to a Cleveland FBI agent in the spring of 1935 said that "they had heard of whipping squads, hanging squads, and killing squads in the order and stated that at the present time there were eight names on the death list, whose death warrants had been signed by General Sloan of Sidney, Ohio, who is an employee of the State Highway Department"—where, we can note, Effinger was reported to be working at the time.[33] But no deaths in the Lima area were ever publicly attributed to the Legion, in contrast to Michigan, where it reportedly killed dozens.

More concrete, if still partial, evidence points to crimes against property. One defector said that Effinger had "ordered him to take 20 men [and] go to the Sigma Theatre in Lima, Ohio, and there destroy a film that was being shown." He said Effinger objected to the film, *White Angel*, "on the grounds that it upheld the Catholic faith." He also said he "heard a discussion in the basement of Effinger's home on the advisability of taking over the Federal Buildings by the Legion." Effinger bragged that the Legion had burned down two roadhouses on the outskirts of town, the Twin Oaks and the Imperial.[34] At 3 a.m. on January 29, 1934, the Twin Oaks roadhouse—a dance hall, club-house, and barbecue stand two or three miles south of Lima—was indeed destroyed, in what the *Lima News* described as a "spectacular fire." An hour later, another fire torched the home of Mr. and Mrs. Charles Reese, west of town. "Other fires in the city kept firemen on the run during the week-end," the *News* reported.[35] The same defector reported that Effinger had ordered him to burn down the Peacock Roadhouse, but he had refused. Multiple sources reported that the Legion was planning to burn down the post office.[36] In May 1935, a committee of the Ohio state legislature received reports that the Legion was responsible for repeated threats against the governor's daughter.[37]

Much of the Black Legion's most well-documented ire, though, was directed at men who refused recruitment, failed to stay active, defected, or squealed. On May 26, 1935, an amiable-looking, fifty-five-year-old white farmer in overalls named William H. Smith told reporters that the previous September 29, after a day spent cutting corn together, a "young relative" had suggested a car ride. They stopped to pick up two other men, then drove fifteen miles out to another farm. "It was raining hard as we tunneled into a long lane" half a mile away from the road, Smith recounted. "Two fellows dressed up like the devil himself walked to the car. Each of them had a flashlight in one hand and a gun in the other." Smith wanted to run away, he told reporters, but it was raining too hard. "The fellow I was with said to one of the fellows, 'two recruits.' . . . I said I'd just as soon sit in the car and wait." Smith saw his relative run into a "little shed," but when Smith entered it, the relative was nowhere to be seen. "I sat down on a box.

They had 12 recruits lined up and a man I knew was filling out cards for them." When Legion members figured out that Smith hadn't filled out a card, they demanded his name. "You know what my name is," retorted Smith. "This is a lot of tom foolishness." The other recruits were clearly too terrified to resist, he told reporters. "Their teeth was crackin' together like a hog eatin' charcoal."

Next, about two hundred Legion members, "all decked out in that paraphernalia," Smith recalled, marched the recruits into a barn, where "the chief gazabo [sic], a great big fellow with a heavy voice"—who must have been Effinger—"was hollering about the Democrats and the Republicans. 'We're going to take over the Government and run it ourselves.'" Effinger told the recruits that if any were Catholic, "you better get out of here real quick." Smith answered that he "was no Catholic but I was ready to leave." When Smith then challenged Effinger directly and protested against initiation, Effinger yelled back, "Why you yellow. . . . . , I'll mash your brains out with this gun." At that point Smith "started shoving to get out," he recounted, and "ran out into the night. But someone grabbed me and I started to fight, but was struck and cut about the head, I think with the butts of guns." He was tied up, carried out into a corn crib, and dumped on the floor. An hour and a half later, around 12:30, "a fellow came up to the crib and asked me if I wanted to reconsider. I said 'hell, no.'" Finally, around 4:30 a.m. they marched him out, while "poking guns in my sides," and told him that he'd die if he ever revealed what had just taken place. The next day Smith told his story to the sheriff. Two days after that, he was threatened by men who informed him, "You told and you're going to die."[38]

The Legion also routinely threatened men who left after having joined. "Those individuals who have dropped out of the order have been approached on numerous occasions and warned that they should not talk," a 1935 FBI investigation reported. One informant recounted that he had been "ordered by Effinger to 'bash in the head' of a man who refused to attend the society's meetings."[39] The Legion's initiation oath included this ferocious—if perhaps difficult to execute—pledge:

Before divulging a single word or implied pledge of this, my solemn oath, and obligation, I will pray to an avenging God and unmerciful Devil that my limbs be broken with stones and cut off by inches; that they may be food for carrion birds; that my body be ripped open and my bowels torn out and fed to the foulest birds of the air; and that my head be split open and my brains scattered over the earth, my heart be torn out and roasted over flames of sulphur.[40]

During initiations, Legion members staged fake hangings off in the dark, in which a Legion member, who appeared to have violated instructions by repeating a phony password, was promptly hung, in partial view of the initiates. One informant, a Mr. Carter, reported that he'd played the role of the victim multiple times.[41]

A year after defecting in 1934, a plumber named George Scheid Sr., who'd been active in the Legion for two or three years and risen to the rank of major, informed on it to J. F. Cordrey, a postal inspector in Lima. After he had left the organization, Scheid reported, a note had appeared on his doorstep "advising him to either commit suicide or leave the country."[42] At one point, "about 50 carloads of men had collected around his house."[43] His son, George Jr., later recalled: "I remember when I was a kid one night that there were a couple of carloads of Legionnaires all dressed up that were gonna take on my father, and they stopped outside the house." Two friends of his father's, who had also defected, were there to help protect him, including army veteran Albert Erfer. "My dad was sitting at his desk loading ammunition" when Erfer told his dad that "he recognized the two cars and he slipped out the back door." The cars stopped, "some men got out," and as Erfer stepped forward, "one of them caught a glimpse of his revolver, and you have never seen people get back in an automobile so fast in your life." After Scheid Sr. defected, he put up security lights around his plumbing shop. "He had weapons at his bed," his son remembered.[44] In a 2000 interview with the *Lima News*, Scheid Jr. recalled that "my dad wouldn't eat dinner unless he had a loaded gun beside him. He carried a gun wherever he went. I can remember him stopping on the sidewalk and reaching for his gun when a car slowed or stopped."[45]

As these accounts illustrate, the Black Legion in Lima was thick with guns and gun culture. Every man at those two-hundred-strong initiation rituals was presumably packing. Initiates were explicitly asked if they owned any firearms. "If they do not own a revolver, shot gun or rifle they are ordered to obtain a revolver and are instructed to carry it at all times," J. F. Cordrey, the postal inspector, reported in February 1935.[46] One informant showed an FBI agent a .45 Colt automatic pistol that he said the Legion had "taken . . . in a raid on some Catholics in another county."[47] In August 1935, an official in Lima reported to the FBI that "on or about September 1, 1934," multiple firearms had been stolen from a display case at the Allen County Historical Society in Lima. They included two German Lugers, a German sharpshooter's pistol, three American-made pistols and revolvers, and sixty-five rounds of ammo for a .45. "It is my understanding that some members of the Black Legion planned to get this equipment," the official reported. "I believe it will be found that one Chas. Hartzog stole this equipment as this man, who is known to be a member of the Black Legion works at Memorial Hall."[48]

More powerful weaponry apparently abounded. According to Scheid Jr., "an ammunition magazine" was stored deep in the woods at Tapscott's farm where initiations took place, containing "explosives, high explosives magazines . . . filled with dynamite and TNT."[49] He recalled that his father was "quite a handloader and . . . collect[ed] arms and ammunitions."[50] One informant told the FBI that "he had overheard Effinger and others discussing the son of D. C. W. Leech . . . who was supposed to own a Thompson submachine gun, and they were planning to pose as Federal men and call upon him and confiscate the gun for the Legion."[51]

It's safe to assume Effinger's own weaponry collection must have been formidable. He vigorously asserted the right to bear arms. In August 1935 he was charged with having brought six hand grenades into a Black Legion meeting in Detroit.[52] According to an FBI informant, Effinger owned "a large yellow map at his home he kept in the rafters of the basement," which showed, Effinger told the informant, "the location of all the secret fortifications in the country." Effinger asserted that "under the Statue of Liberty were concealed several large coast defense guns of the disappearing type."[53] In 1936, a man who said he had been a member of the Black Legion in Lima testified to a Detroit prosecutor that, while visiting Effinger in his home, "he showed me a square mechanism with a metal tube affair and that he claimed was invented by [workers] at the United States Government poisonous gas factory at Firewood, Maryland." Effinger said the device had a timer that could enable it to go off at "a certain time such as a Jewish

National celebration." It would be best to do it in the winter, Effinger pointed out, "when the windows of these Jewish synagogues would be all closed so that the gas could not escape, and you can readily see that we can pretty well exterminate the Jews at one click, it will only take a few hundred loyal me[rest of word unintelligible] . . . and a few of these mechanisms to do it." Effinger then showed him a list of synagogues throughout the United States.[54]

Guns and weapons were everywhere, ever more visible ones, including those arrayed next to children at dinner tables, such as the Scheids'.

Twelve miles east of Lima lay the enormous Scioto Marsh, where a thousand workers picked onions under horrific conditions. In late June 1934, led by a thirty-eight-year-old picker named Okey Odell (sometimes spelled O'Dell), seven hundred of them went on strike. By July, as the strike escalated, fifty-three sheriff's deputies, controlled by the growers, deployed machine guns and tear gas at the picket line; the strikers threw rocks, allegedly stabbed someone, and spread roofing nails onto the highway, puncturing the deputies' tires. One night in early July, "a large group of men, traveling in automobiles," showed up at 2 a.m. at the home of Elijah Odell, Okey's brother, and announced that they belonged to the Black Legion. They said they had gasoline, nitroglycerin, and dynamite in their cars. "Show us where they live," the men offered, "and we'll take care of them"—meaning the big growers. Their "mysterious caravan" then proceeded to the home of W. C. Weis, the union's vice president, got him out of bed, and pronounced: "We are the firing squad and are going to take over the strike." At a union meeting the next day, Okey Odell, the union leader, declared: "We don't need these people here. . . . We don't want any violence. We can't keep them from coming here, but we have no use for them."[55]

Guns nonetheless begat more guns. In the nearby town of Mc-Guffey, a fire started by nitroglycerin burned the home of the mayor, who was supporting the growers. When police, without evidence, then arrested Okey Odell, two hundred vigilantes removed him from the jail, took him out of town, beat him, and dumped him beside a road, while hundreds of other armed vigilantes took over the town. Odell hitchhiked back and marched with his brother right through the center of town, unarmed, daring the mob to kill him. Later, a huge armed mob swarmed his house, which "was turned into a miniature fortress by friends who appeared ready to back up Odell in his threat to 'kill the first man who tries to get me.'"⁵⁶ A photo in the Marion, Ohio, *Star* showed four white women of varying ages wearing filmy summer dresses, described as part of Odell's "defense" team, lined up in a row on a couch, each holding a gun pointed grimly at the camera.⁵⁷

In Lima and its hinterland alike, the Black Legion both thrived on gun culture and fed it further. For every gun that actually went off, every roadhouse that was actually burned down, the threat of further violence magnified the Legion's power and ability to terrorize. By 1935 the Black Legion was armed and dangerous and armed with dangerous ideas, with an unstable fanatic at its helm and thousands of men at his command, in paramilitary formation.

"GOOD CITIZENS": THE LEAGUE'S MEMBERSHIP

Who were those thousands of members in Lima, then? What were they looking for when they joined the Black Legion? It's easy to focus on Effinger, the leader. But identifying and understanding the members, and unpacking their beliefs and motivations, is far more challenging and, for today, pressing.

Lima, its population 42,267 in 1930, lay between Toledo and Columbus in northwestern Ohio. It was a classic Upper Midwest industrial city, in which an estimated eight thousand residents, mostly men, worked at a Standard Oil refinery, a steel foundry, or other factories making electrical instruments, neon signs, school buses, funeral coaches, women's aprons, and soles and heels for footwear. The jewel in Lima's economic crown was its locomotive plant, one of the three biggest in the country, with over 1,200 workers. People also found work at commercial establishments catering to both the town and its agricultural hinterland. Men got jobs in construction; women got jobs as domestic servants.⁵⁸

A 1936 guide to Lima produced by the WPA's Federal Writers' Project, sponsored by the Better Business Bureau, described "poorly constructed frame houses and somewhat squalid living conditions" near the factories, in contrast to an "older residential section in the northwestern part of the city . . . distinguished by large, beautifully kept homes"—paid for in many cases, we can assume, by the labor of the factory workers living in the "squalid" homes. "Between these economic extremes are the homes of those who form the majority of

Lima's population—typical middle-class Americans."[59] That formulation was more than a bit mythical: if eight thousand Lima residents worked in factories, and each had a family of, say, four, then it's more accurate to say that thirty-two thousand of forty-two thousand Lima residents were working-class. If we add to them the city's domestic servants, elevator operators, janitors, the casually employed, and others who didn't work in factories, plus their children, then the vast majority of people living in Lima were not in fact "typical middle-class" at all. They would have led lives of routine insecurity, although many may have achieved a small home with a front porch, like Effinger's house on a corner lot at 1114 Harrison Avenue. Lima's true middle class, of professionals, managers, and local business owners, would have been quite tiny.

Over 96 percent of Lima's residents in 1930 were white, according to the US census.[60] If we zero in closer, one out of every four or five white men in Lima was a member of the Black Legion in the mid-1930s, an estimated five thousand people in total. Of those, the names of sixty-one reported members can be found in the historical record. The occupations of thirty-eight men out of those members are, in turn, identifiable. Sixteen worked in the skilled trades: plumbers and pipefitters, electricians, floor sanders, painters, printers, a crane operator, a hydraulic pressman. Eight worked in industry in unskilled or semiskilled jobs or in jobs whose skill level was unclear: blacksmith's helper, baker, watchman, two janitors, and three laborers. One worked as a gas station attendant, another as a "garage worker." These men were the Legion's core membership, neither the poorest of the poor, nor the elite. Some middle-class people did belong, too: an elementary school principal, a lawyer, a "manager." The chief of detectives also belonged, and two other policemen.[61]

In trying to understand why these men were attracted to the Black Legion, we can begin with its elaborate oaths, its passwords, its secrecy, the way it made its members feel like special insiders. Many, perhaps most, Legion members would have been familiar with such rituals because they already belonged to fraternal organizations in Lima such as the Masons, the Elks, the Eagles, or the Order of United American Mechanics, in whose hall the Black Legion met.[62]

The Black Legion, like the fraternal societies, also offered its members an opportunity for male bonding, much like going fishing or hunting together—a night out away from their wives. To that, the Legion added a frisson of militarism. Those who were veterans got to relive their time in the military when they'd bonded with other men. Others, who hadn't served, got to have the quasi-military experience they might have felt they had missed out on. Members also, as adults, got to play dress-up, in long silly robes. With pirate hats! They got to drive around in cars late at night with friends—circling the houses of defectors, leaving hate mail. They got to tromp around in the woods carrying flashlights—in a terrorist version of saying "boo!" They got all the fun of robes and secrecy and outrageous oaths designed to curdle one's blood but for real now, as the toy guns of childhood crossed over into actual .45s loaded and shoved into the backs of actual people, and boyhood pranks became burning down roadhouses.

The second powerful attraction was the bigotry. It offered both an explanation for the nature of the problems facing white people during the Great Depression, and a path forward to act on their racism, antisemitism, and anti-Catholicism in concrete ways.

White people in Lima had a long history of racist hate stretching back well before the 1930s. On election day in 1888, for example, a riot broke out after a group of African American men entered a bar and were accosted by a group of drunken white men, many of them Irish immigrants, who expanded into a mob that tried to lynch the Black men. In 1909, another white mob tried to lynch an African American man accused of killing a white woman. In the summer of 1916, yet another mob tried to lynch an African American man accused of assaulting a white woman. When the white sheriff spirited the accused man out of town to a different jail, the furious mob hung the sheriff himself with a noose until he confessed to the accused's whereabouts. For days the mob, sometimes numbering as many as two thousand people, rioted in the streets of Lima searching for African Americans to attack. One in five Black people in Lima fled town after the first day of rioting.[63] This was only thirteen years before the Great Depression.

The 1920s Ku Klux Klan, in particular, provided Lima's white people with a bedrock of hate with which to address the Depression when it arrived. "Many men, I mean hundreds of men, I would say all of the churches of Lima . . . were secretly part of this. . . . They joined in great numbers," recalled the Reverend E. J. Penhorwood, the white pastor of South Side Church of Christ.[64] This Second Ku Klux Klan had counted five hundred thousand members in Ohio in the 1920s. In Lima, it had its own meeting hall. A photo has survived of a Klan rally in Lima on August 4, 1923, captioned "Public Demonstration—Knights of the Ku-Klux-Klan—Lima, O, Class of 3000," in which thousands of unrobed men can be seen kneeling, their heads down, evidently in the process of being sworn into the Klan. They're surrounded by other men wearing white Klan robes, masks off. Behind a podium hangs a forty-foot American flag between giant burning crosses.[65] George Scheid Jr. recalled that his father "was a member of the Ku Klux Klan earlier and the Ku Klux Klan was very active in Lima. I can remember klansmen [sic] marching in the streets and completely filling this 80-foot rightaway [right-of-way] here for eight or ten blocks marching in their white robes and all."[66] Jim Christoff, a Lima grocery store owner originally from Macedonia, told an interviewer in 1979: "They burnt crosses right here, across the street," on Findlay Road.[67]

Joseph Emmons, a former Black Legion member in Lima, recounted that the Black Legion "was the aftermath of the Ku Klux Klan, you may say, managed, controlled by members and former officials of the Ku Klux Klan."[68] When Amann, the historian, asked Scheid Jr. if the Black Legion "was a sort of successor organization to the Klan," Scheid replied, "Oh yes, there was no question about it. . . . It's an outgrowth of the Klan. My dad told me that." Was it "the same people, more or less"? asked Amann. "Yes, that's right," answered Scheid. "Yeah, they just changed their rob[es]."[69] Although Dr. Shepard, the Black Legion's founder, told reporters that the Black Legion had been kicked out of the KKK in 1924, the two organizations appear to have had harmonious relations in Lima throughout the 1930s. The Black Legion held meetings in the Klan's hall, for example.[70]

A white attorney in Lima named Harry Meredith, though, insisted that there was no continuity between Klan members and Legion members. "I've always felt that the Klan had nothing whatsoever to do with that," he told Amann. Meredith volunteered that "they were very active in this area" and that he himself had "attended meetings, here . . . in Lima," but, he insisted, "the Klan was composed in my judgement of a fair class and a more substantial class of people" than the Black Legion. When Amann asked him if the Legion's leadership was "primarily a lower class," Meredith agreed.[71]

These observations underscore that both the KKK in the 1920s and the Black Legion in the '30s were considered by many white people in Lima, perhaps most, to be mainstream—that is, normal in their vicious, exclusionary hate. Rev. Penhorwood, who said that he and Bert Effinger were "the best of friends," recalled that "my feelings were not quite in line with all this," but "many of the men of the community were active in that organization thinking nothing about it." Penhorwood said that another minister "whose name I won't mention . . . was quite active in it." In his own church, "a large group of men . . . they let you know that they were very active in it."[72]

Many commentators depicted the Black Legion as nonthreatening. In May 1935, C. William Ramseyer, a former Republican congressmember from Lima, wrote to a former Lima prosecuting attorney attaching a news clip about the Black Legion. The recipient replied to Ramseyer that he had always denounced the Klan and never had the support of the Legion. "As a rule I found them to be a misguided and 'harmless bunch.' . . . I never dreamed that they wore their hoods for any other purpose than to frighten and intimidate 'women and children' and those of the male sex who lacked courage." Notice how this former Lima prosecutor is saying he found those latter activities "harmless."[73] Scheid Jr., who made clear he disapproved of both the Klan and Black Legion, in which his father had been involved, commented that the Lima Klan had "burned a few crosses as they usually do, but they were a relatively harmless organization."[74]

Residents in Bellaire, Ohio, similarly used the word "harmless," over and over, when queried in 1935 about Dr. Shepard, the Black Legion's founder. "Bellaire's 8,000 residents know 'Doctor Billy' as a joiner, a jovial drug store orator and a man who likes to be a bit mysterious at times, but, withal, a harmless fellow who can absorb a lot of kidding," a *Detroit News* reporter found. The FBI interviewee noted above, who recounted Shepard's threats against the bank and against Catholics, said that "he knew Dr. Shepard was a boastful talker and he knew he didn't mean what he said."[75]

What's going on here? In these statements, white men in both towns, who were not—apparently—members of the Legion themselves, were consistently dismissing the terror it deployed. They cast racist fascism as both innocent and normal.

If we listen closely to the stories told by those who resisted initiation, defected, or informed on the Black Legion, we can learn even more. Some men clearly were forced to join against their will and were horrified or terrified when suddenly confronted with an armed initiation ritual—such as William Smith, the farmer, and the dozens of recruits beside him with their teeth chattering. But other than Smith, we don't know that much about the non-joiners' exact criticisms of the Legion. Rev. Penhorwood said that Effinger wanted him to join but he declined because in a previous town, Tiffin, where he'd been a minister, divisions over the Black Legion had torn apart the congregation. Note how he didn't say he refused to join because he objected to the Legion's politics.[76]

Scheid Sr., the plumber who had been a member for three years and ascended to the rank of major, told his son that he informed to the FBI "because he said the concept of the Black Legion had changed. . . . . The Black Legion was originally America for Americans, it was [an] anti-semetic [sic] anti-black organization. And it changed that to a revolutionary type of organization." That was where Scheid Sr. drew the line: "He said that they got a little carried [away] and they were talking about raiding government arsinals [sic] and taking away arms and ammunitions and starting a revolution against the government, and at that point he separated from them."[77] In other words, Scheid found bigotry, fascism, and terror acceptable, indeed appealing, but just didn't want to be part of an armed revolution.

Others drew the line at committing felonies. Two former members questioned by the FBI in May 1936 "stated that they had joined the Legion about two years ago, when it was held up as a patriotic organization that had been formed to combat the various isms that were then gaining a foothold in the country, but had been forced to withdraw when they had been ordered to commit several felonious acts"—including being ordered by Effinger to burn down the Peacock Inn.[78]

The former apartment manager who Effinger talked to all night told the FBI that he had been "an organizer of things, of the Ku Klux Klan and other organizations of a like nature," but after his visit with Effinger, had concluded that rank-and-file members of the Legion were "being led into what I believe serious personal trouble by being led on by men like . . . Effinger," who would protect himself but "cause other men that would be good citizens otherwise to get into serious personal trouble." The informant made clear that otherwise, he shared Effinger's politics; he only eschewed the Legion because he didn't want to get caught by law enforcement. Legion members, in his view, were "good citizens."[79]

At least five women joined the Black Legion in Lima, but their motivations and activities are almost entirely opaque. One, Amy McGinniss, worked for the Federal Emergency Relief Administration (FERA) as a nurse. A second, listed as "Mrs. Schafer," worked for the FERA as a telephone operator. Along with a "Mrs. Joe Louis," they were members of a Ladies' Auxiliary to the Black Legion.[80] A fourth, Mrs. George Scheid, joined her husband in informing to the FBI, and was also presumably a member of the Ladies' Auxiliary, given that she knew that Mrs. Louis had been a member of it, and that her husband had been in the Legion for three years and risen to the rank of major.[81]

The fifth was Mary Effinger, Virgil's wife. She appears to have been a willing partner in her husband's project, not by any means deferring to him, and in some cases speaking on his behalf or controlling his replies to queries.[82] Rev. Penhorwood recalled that she "was a lovely person, but [in] very poor health for many years. And she never objected to what he was doing. Seemingly kind of backed him as I would sense it. But never publicly able to be active like Bert was."[83] An FBI agent who visited their home in April 1936 reported that "Mrs. Effinger . . . stated that they were members of the Ku Klux [K]lan but not of the Black Legion." He reported that "Mrs. Effinger appeared to be of refined and quiet manners while Mr. Effinger was of the loud and braggart type of material. They live in a bungalow in a good section of town, together with their married daughter and grandchild. On the whole the home was of a refined atmosphere."[84] In 1936, when Effinger faced criminal charges in Detroit, a *Lima News* reporter seeking to contact Virgil wrote that Mrs. Effinger had intimated "that she and her husband had talked about the accusation and indicated the Lima man [i.e., Virgil] would disclaim any knowledge of the society."[85]

Many, perhaps most women in the Black Legion, would have had their own histories in the Ku Klux Klan, as Mary Effinger did. In her pathbreaking study of women in the Ku Klux Klan in 1920s Indiana, Kathleen Blee has shown that hundreds of thousands nationwide joined a Women's Ku Klux Klan of "100% American Women," in which they donned robes; boycotted stores owned by Catholics, Jews, and African Americans; organized singing quartets, picnics, and Klan funerals; and dressed their babies and toddlers in little KKK outfits. They looked to the Klan as a source of female empowerment. Male Klan members, though, had a different view of women's proper role; they cast their own activities as chivalry, riding violently to the rescue of weak white women who were at risk from African American men, priests, and at times their husbands' physical abuse. "Behind the mask of chivalry," to quote historian Nancy MacLean, lay Klan members' domination of white women, as well as African Americans, Jews, and Catholics.[86]

Chivalry did at times rear its head in the Lima Black Legion, although not often, it appears. Cordrey, the Lima postal inspector, reported to a state relief investigator that a "Mr. Cain" had "revealed secrets of the 'Black Knights' to his wife who, in turn broadcasted them." Cain, he said, "beat up on his wife for this"; so members of the Black Legion then "beat up on Cain unmercifully." Cordrey (who himself may have been a Legion member) "said he thought Cain deserved it for beating up on his wife."[87] Again, violence begat more violence. The Black Legion also evoked great fear among women married to defectors. Cordrey reported that "wives are placed in mortal fear because of inquiries by strange men, in the absence of husbands."[88]

Somebody, presumably female, sewed all those shining black robes. "I remember his robes," George Scheid Jr. said of his father going off to night meetings of the Legion. "He used to carry 'em in a suitcase, a little traveling bag." Once, Junior peeked into the bag. "They were kind of a satin robe, black, very black, and they were lined with red. Very handsome."[89] In May 1936, the *New York Times*, speaking of the Legion in Michigan, reported that "the new member is obliged to buy a cheap black robe at the earliest possible moment from a 'brigade commander.' The price is $7; it can be made up for $1.25. The mask is cut crudely from black cloth."[90] Was there some secret robe factory in someone's basement? At five thousand members in Lima alone, that's a lot of robes. It seems supremely unlikely that men did the sewing. Did the Ladies' Auxiliary take responsibility for making the robes and hats—buying the fabric and the thread, cutting the cloth using a shared pattern, sitting at their sewing machines for hours, then finishing the robes with meticulous hand sewing, night after night, year after year, as the membership grew?

An original Black Legion robe, cape, and pirate hat have survived today in a Michigan archive.[91] Viewing them in person at first diminishes their deliberately constructed mysterious power, and hence that of the Legion itself. But a closer look shows how impeccably constructed the outfit was, raising new, disturbing questions. Someone did all that careful work: reinforced the pirate hat with stiff fabric to keep it from flopping too much, cut the skull and crossbones carefully out of white felt, added the red satin interior to the cape, and even opened up a little eight-inch slit in the back at the robe's bottom to give the wearer a bit more leg room, its edges skillfully stitched under on either side. We can only reflect on what the robe's maker was thinking as she did all that work. It seems unlikely that she was coerced, although perhaps she was—these were violent men. More probably, she felt committed to the same white-supremacist, antisemitic, anti-Catholic, and even, yes, armed revolutionary goals as the husband or father or brother who would wear those robes. She could have believed that she was supporting a noble, patriotic cause. While the men bonded by driving around and waving flashlights in the woods together, she and her daughters, mother, cousins, and friends may have been enjoying nice gossipy evenings together, sewing robes, sowing terror. Hate flowed into those careful stitches, in the name of patriotism.

STATE POWER

White people joined the Black Legion, lastly, because it could provide them with jobs. Unpacking how that worked takes us deep into a final layer of the Legion's power and appeal—into local politics, into complex intersections of race and class, and into law enforcement and its sobering failures.

The Great Depression hit Lima like a sledgehammer. The steel plant cut back. The all-important locomotive plant shut down. Scheid Jr., the plumber's son, recalled: "My dad was bankrupt, the builders went bankrupt, . . . all the associated contracting firms, mechanical contractors they went bankrupt. Bankruptcy was more the rule." A downward spiral rippled through the whole town. "It was very, very bad in this area, this was a tremendously depressed area. As the coal trains went through here, the tracks were lined with people who would go out and gather the coal that rolled off the trains to keep their houses warm." Scheid estimated that unemployment in Lima hit 25–30 percent.[92] Meredith, the attorney, estimated it was 50 percent.[93]

Whether they had worked in the steel, electrical, or locomotive plants, with contractors in town, or on their own, the skilled and semiskilled white male craft workers who filled the ranks of the Black Legion experienced great economic trauma. "The ones that were hardest hit by the Depression were . . . not the people who were classed as a kind of a privileged class," Scheid Jr. recalled. "We used to look with envy at the school teacher because they had a steady job. And the doctors and attorneys were in a class way up high by themselves." He stressed that "it was the ordinary working man who was the shop worker who was economically depressed. . . . The people I knew that belonged to [the Black Legion] were all in this class."[94] Meredith, the attorney who disparaged the inferior class status of Legion members as opposed to those of the Klan, said that those who joined the Black Legion "had been oppressed down the ladder quite a ways and the Depression had hurt, and they were looking, grasping for something to help. Anything to help."

Peter Amann, his interviewer, followed up: "And here came Effinger who said, 'Follow me Men.'"

"That's right," Meredith confirmed.[95]

It was all about that ladder—staying on it, and not slipping down. Neither Meredith nor Scheid Sr. ever acknowledged the existence of, or expressed concern over, anyone in Lima whose class position was below those of Legion members, such as the city's janitors, unskilled factory workers, domestic servants, casual laborers, and long-term unemployed. The white Protestant men who joined the Legion, for the most part, were used to being above all those people. Now they themselves were unemployed, impoverished, scared. To that fear they brought a deep sense of entitlement to staying in their proper place on the ladder. Their sense of entitlement, in turn, bred resentment against potential competitors. And resentment, in the nativist, racist, antisemitic sea in which they swam, led to blaming those below them on the ladder. And hence attacking them. They believed deeply that they had earned and were owed what W. E. B. Du Bois and David Roediger have called "the wages of whiteness": not just the economic privileges associated with being white, but the psychological wage of believing they were superior.[96] The Black Legion was designed to make sure all those wages kept coming in. Its members didn't want to do away with the ladder by making everyone equal. They accepted it, albeit with some grumbling about the rich.

The Black Legion also, it turns out, helped hundreds of its members get actual wages. By 1933–35, as New Deal funds poured in, at least 1,200 people in Lima got work through the Federal Emergency Relief Administration, perhaps hundreds more.[97] An estimated 83–90 percent of those jobs in Lima went to members of the Black Legion.[98] The Legion also filled almost all the staff positions at the FERA office itself. J. C. Timberlake, the director of relief for Allen County, told investigators that "in July, 1934, . . . I learned that every male employee of my office, number 48, with the exception of myself, [the] chief engineer, his assistant, and my secretary were members."[99] Glenn E. Webb, the master timekeeper at the FERA office in charge of keeping employees' work records, for example, was a member, as was William Zimmerman, a paymaster. Effinger's son Guy worked in the office too.[100] At least one source suggested that director Timberlake was himself a member.[101]

Historians know that the distribution of government relief during the 1930s was deeply racist. We know that people of color were regularly denied relief. We know that at a deep, institutional level, the larger New Deal relief system was designed to shore up the white patriarchal family, by selectively hiring male heads of households and discriminating against women, especially married women.[102] But this is a startling new discovery: in Lima, an organized group of self-conscious white-supremacist fascists themselves controlled the distribution of relief. "The Legion controlled all relief jobs in Allen County through Burt Effinger, head of the local Legion," George Armstrong, a former Legion member, told investigators from the Ohio legislature. "Discrimination was shown in the manner in which relief jobs were issued, especially [against] Catholics and colored workers."[103] He said that the Black Legion "maneuvered so that its members became foremen on various relief projects."[104] In Lima, in other words, Legion members did not just discriminate against African Americans, Catholics, and Jews; they proactively *served* white, native-born Protestant men. That's who got the jobs instead of those denied relief.[105] Their efforts echo those of Southern white racists who sought to control New Deal relief programs at the state and local level, then used those programs to support white supremacy by denying aid to African Americans and added to their own profits by forcing them into fieldwork.[106]

In January 1935, an agent for the Ohio State Relief Commission, identified only as "No. 34," submitted an extensive investigation he had conducted into the Black Legion's infiltration of the Allen County FERA office in Lima. He found Black Legion members all over the place. Two Legion members, he reported, held responsibility for dispatching relief recipients to jobs, which they assigned to fellow members, some of whom did not even qualify for relief. They supervised a crew of electricians that regularly took time out of official jobs to work on the private homes of other FERA staff members. The FERA office's payroll books, No. 34 reported, were thoroughly cooked and often unintelligible. He uncovered complex scams involving extensive overtime pay for work that was never performed, for example.[107]

Fear was palpable at the Allen County FERA, No. 34 reported. Every time he talked to an alleged Legion member, "the person addressed seems to turn white and get very nervous. None will admit that they belong." Two men told No. 34 they were terrified of losing their jobs if they displeased the Legion; one feared "bodily harm." A third said that after he'd defected from it, he was no longer assigned FERA work. Agent No. 34 also reported "an 'undercurrent' and compassionate friendliness of alleged members within the Allen County Administrative Office [of the FERA] that is hard to get around."[108]

The Black Legion's control over Lima's FERA apparently grew out of an earlier relationship between Legion members and the local Unemployed League. During the early 1930s, unemployed men and women in Lima, as elsewhere in the United States, successfully organized to pressure authorities to provide more relief, in the form of food and gasoline and by creating jobs. In 1932, a hundred unemployed people and their family members crowded into a meeting of the City Commissioners to demand a food commissary and denounce the current relief system, including its favoritism, inefficient distribution, "wormy rolled oats, and mouldy bread."[109] In 1933, fifty unemployed people demanded that the commissioners increase supplies of fuel and food.[110] At least two men active in the Lima Unemployed League were in the

Black Legion: George Armstrong, who testified to the Ohio legislature about the Legion's control of the FERA office; and the Unemployed League's president, C. H. Cain, the Legion member who was beaten up for beating his wife.[111] Harry Meredith, the attorney, remembered seeing multiple protests by a "dangerous crowd" of the unemployed in front of the post office during the 1930s; he said they were threatening to burn it down.[112] As noted, multiple sources reported that the Black Legion planned to burn down the post office.[113]

The New Deal thus delivered brilliantly for Legion members in Lima at an even higher level of institutionalized racism than we have heretofore known. Its constituency was precisely the idealized white, downtrodden "working man" that the New Deal was designed to serve. As former wage workers who worked in industry or construction, they were eligible for the new protections that would be provided by unemployment insurance, the Social Security Act, the National Labor Relations Act, and the Fair Labor Standards Act—but weren't provided to farmworkers, domestic servants, government employees, or housewives. On top of that, in Lima, we now know, they got almost all the New Deal's relief jobs, by imposing white supremacist fascism. After work, they could drive around in black robes, terrorizing the people whom they'd denied those jobs.

At least two women who were members of the Ladies' Auxiliary of the Black Legion also got jobs through the FERA office—one of them as a nurse, the other as a switchboard operator.[114] In Lima, as nationwide, women had been publicly active in the early 1930s movement demanding relief. They show up repeatedly in accounts of demonstrations by the Lima Unemployed League. But when the federal government, in response to their movement, did create jobs, women were hired in much fewer numbers than men were, and only in occupations deemed appropriate to their gender: clerical, sales, or light manufacturing work, with much lower pay than men received. Like the Black Legion, the New Deal relief office had a place for women, but that place was under men, in a patriarchal family in which economic dependency was presumed and enforced.

The class politics of the Black Legion, then, could meld seamlessly with white male Protestant supremacy: skilled white men wanted jobs, for themselves. They used racism, nativism, and antisemitism to slice off others from eligibility as "workers," making it possible for white Protestant men to stay on the ladder. An inclusionary politics of class was not on the table.

Yet, in 1911, Lima had elected a Socialist mayor and city council members, as did hundreds of US towns and cities in the second decade of the twentieth century. The Lima mayor's platform was mild, merely promising clean government and managerial efficiency; once in office he swiftly moved rightward, betraying the Socialists. But a socialist possibility would have still lingered in the memories of working-class white men and women of Lima in the 1930s. As the Depression advanced, they also had the example of thousands of increasingly visible white Socialist and Communist activists throughout other Midwestern cities, who were in the forefront of an often interracial mass movement of the unemployed.[115]

Many, perhaps most, of the skilled white men who formed the backbone of the Black Legion in Lima would also have had experiences with racist, exclusionary "class" politics through their unions. Effinger, for example, had been a member of the International Brotherhood of Electrical Workers, and run for office in 1921 on a "Labor Ticket."[116] Plumbers, printers, painters, electricians, carpenters, mechanics, machinists—they would all have belonged to, or been closely acquainted with, craft unions affiliated with the American Federation of Labor that since their founding in the nineteenth century had served as exclusionary clubs, keeping out Black men, all women, and immigrants from Southern and Eastern Europe. The craft unions carefully controlled access to skills, then used their monopolies on skills to strengthen their members' power in relation to employers.[117] In the early years of the Great Depression, though, AFL craft unions were like deer in the headlamps in the face of mass layoffs. Meanwhile, in 1933–34, more inclusionary organizations known as "industrial unions" organized mass strikes among Southern textile workers, Minneapolis teamsters, San Francisco dock workers, and right next door to Lima, at the Toledo Auto-Lite factory, where four thousand workers walked out in 1934.[118] The WPA's guide to Lima, sponsored by the Better Business Bureau, reported approvingly in 1936: "The city has been especially fortunate in avoiding labor disputes and violence. Strike waves sweeping other communities have been only of news interest to local residents."[119]

LAW AND ORDER

There was one final, essential piece of the puzzle of the Black Legion's power in Lima, and that was the vote. Effinger was clear that he wanted to use his fascist armed organization to take over the US government. Members swore to "forget your party and vote for the best man if ordered to do so by your superior officer."[120] As the former apartment manager pointed out to his interlocutor, voting as the Legion mandated could mean voting for a different party than a member was used to; the informant himself was a Southern Democrat, for example, but the Legion preferred local Republicans.[121]

In Lima, the Black Legion functioned as a highly developed get-out-the-vote machine for Republicans. "Unlike the old Klan group," the Troy, Ohio, *State Indicator* reported from Lima in June 1936, "this new group are [sic] said to have been building a machine of members for the last six years until at the present time they have a machine of tremendous voting power."[122] At election time, members handed out cards with the Legion's slate, dropped off marked ballots at members' houses, and posted armed guards at voting booths to terrorize members—and others—into voting the Legion's slate.[123] At the FERA office, a supervisor passed out the Legion's voting cards to relief recipients.[124] One Lima informant who spoke to the FBI in early 1936 "stated that he feels quite certain that the Legion is primarily a political organization and that by using the method that it does in its initiation and organization it is better able to control absolutely the votes of its members."[125]

In 1934 the Legion's all-Republican slate won every race in Allen County.[126] It was a long way from Lima's Socialist mayor of 1911, elected by the same pool of white men from the working class, and a long way from the Democrats who were delivering the New Deal at that very moment.

One of those Republicans was Robert F. Jones, a Lima-born attorney who was elected to be Allen County prosecutor for the first time in 1934, when he was twenty-seven. Glenn E. Webb, a FERA paymaster, later testified to the US Senate that he had personally initiated Jones into the Black Legion at Tapscott's farm on a "chilly spring evening" in 1934, and that he had "actively supported" Jones's election as prosecutor in 1934 and 1936 and then to the US Congress in 1938, where Jones remained for four terms. Frank Barber, a proud member of both the KKK and Black Legion throughout the 1930s (and beyond), swore in a 1947 affidavit for the US Senate that "I definitely remember" that the initiation "was before Robert Jones became county attorney, because it was the [Black Legion] which helped put him in office." Virgil Effinger himself confirmed: "We supported Bob Jones not only morally and spiritually, but vocationally we supported Bob Jones both times he ran for Congress. We then got out and spent our time, effort, and energy to get him elected."[127]

Overall, it was a vicious cycle, in which the Legion elected officials who in turn protected Legion members' crimes and countenanced its control of FERA jobs. Multiple sources reported that Lima's mayor, Allen L. Metheany, was a member of the Black Legion, although he reportedly "received a private initiation."[128] Asked in May 1936 by the *Columbus Dispatch* about the Legion's reported control of the FERA office, Metheany "'laughed off' the suggestion that perhaps the Legion was active but the activities were unknown to his office." He insisted: "We have made repeated investigations of reports but nothing was ever found." Metheany admitted that in 1935 authorities had investigated rumors that the Legion was going to blow up city hall, and that he had heard of the Bullet Club, but he concluded "there was never any activity on their part."[129]

Chief of Police Ward Taylor was a member too. One informant told the FBI that he had "personally disarmed" Taylor in the spring of 1934 during the chief's initiation.[130] William Murphy, a Catholic who ran unsuccessfully for mayor in 1934, told an agent that in June 1935 he had run into the police chief on the street and "asked Taylor point blank during a conversation if he was a Black Legionnaire," and Taylor had admitted he was.[131] Other informants named the chief of detectives, additional detectives and patrol officers, the city solicitor, and a local representative to the state legislature.[132]

Add all this up, and it's clear that in the mid-1930s, law enforcement in Lima lay pretty much entirely in the hands of the Black Legion. And the law was not enforced. Mayor Metheany declared in May 1936: "Information had come to [m]e that the group still holds meetings but they have never done anything that requires the attention of the police."[133] When prosecutors in Detroit wanted to raid Effinger's home in 1936, Harry Colburn, their chief investigator, told the FBI that "they could get no cooperation from law enforcing agencies in Ohio because they were all members of the Black Legion."[134] William Smith, the farmer who refused initiation, told the press that he'd recounted his story to the sheriff that same day. But no one was ever arrested.[135] An informant recounted to Postal Inspector Cordrey that "on one occasion the Lima police had received a broadcast relative to a holdup and had picked up several men in a machine [i.e., a vehicle] answering the description of the holdup getaway car." Then the suspects were let off: "Subsequent investigation had revealed that the men were Blacks [i.e., members of the Black Legion] just returning from a meeting and despite the fact that they were all armed they had been released without being charged."[136] The informant, a former member himself, said that "it was impossible to get the local police to do anything regarding the terrorist methods of the Black Legion" since the chief of police and head of detectives were members.[137]

It wasn't just that the police protected the Black Legion. The police and the Black Legion were, more accurately, two arms of the same policing project working hand in black leather glove, one the official institutions of law enforcement (with their own terrors), the other paramilitary terrorists. Together, Legionnaires, cops, and Legionnaire cops policed the daily lives of African American, Catholic, and Jewish members of "their" town. They policed white Protestants they didn't like, too, and, increasingly, each other. They had a lot of weaponry, and a lot of votes, which they deployed through democratic processes to install and instill terror.

"YOU TAKE CARE OF YOURSELVES, WE'LL TAKE CARE OF OURSELVES"

Lima's policed—its African Americans, Italians, Poles, Russians, Irish, Greeks, Catholics, Jews—had to survive both the Great Depression and the Black Legion in the 1930s. We have no record, unfortunately, of what, exactly, they thought of the Legion. Overt resistance would have been spectacularly dangerous. But survival was itself resistance, and people in all these communities survived and found ways to thrive in beautiful comradeship. Their stories take us away from the world of the Black Legion's membership, and into other Limas, other daily lives, and remind us that the Legion's imagined enemies had their own points of view.

The Black Legion's ascendance would not have been startling news to Black people in Lima, who had lived with vicious racism their whole lives and had a long history of strategies of how to deal with it. Lima's 1,422 African American residents could only get a very few jobs: women as domestic servants or cleaners, men as janitors, chauffeurs, porters in hotels, or, at times, in casual labor on construction sites or in the rail yards. Overwhelmingly, African Americans in Lima worked long, long hours in direct subservience to and under the direct surveillance of white employers, often inside white homes. They had almost no other choices: whites would not hire them as store clerks, bank employees, nurses, attorneys, waiters or waitresses, nor in the big industrial plants. The city refused to hire a Black teacher until 1953.[138] For Lima's African Americans, the Great Depression meant even fewer jobs, even lower wages. "I had worked as a night porter and I started out working at $60 a month, during the Depression," one man recalled, "and then we started falling off and everything like that." His pay plummeted to $15 a month. "I was broke," he said. "It was a really rough time for everybody."[139]

Whites forced African Americans into two neighborhoods: the West End, home to older generations, some of who'd been in Lima since the nineteenth century; and the South End, where poorer, more recent residents who'd come from the South during the Great Migration began to settle. The Lima city schools weren't segregated, but pretty much everything else was. Black people weren't allowed to patronize its restaurants, hotels, YMCA, or the city's three most prominent movie theaters. The streetcars had signs announcing that whites came first and Black people could only sit down in seats that whites didn't want. African Americans could only picnic in one of the city's parks, Hover Park. In 1940 the city opened up a big new community pool but didn't allow African Americans.[140] "There were no signs, but you knew where not to go," James Williamson, a longtime community leader and historian of Lima's Black community, recounted.[141]

Lima's new whites-only pool and its glistening whites-only bathhouses, the big new whites-only public park in which they were located, and the park's whites-only new observatory were all donated by Thomas R. Schoonover, a white man after whom they were all named. Schoonover, a classic "philanthropist," was president of Lima's City Savings and Loan. He had accumulated his wealth lending money to farmers in the Lima hinterland and then throughout Ohio. His granddaughter recalled him "standing on the street, in his banker's dress of immaculate cashmere coat and white silk scarf, . . . discussing the crops or quality of farmland with a farmer in overalls." He rode out into the country in a chauffeured Cadillac. At family dinners over which he presided, Schoonover "enjoyed telling humorous stories in various accents such as Irish, Jewish, Asian and Black." He also targeted Italians and Catholics. She remembered that her grandmother's African American servant, Albert Bobson, "was always in a way her slave."[142]

The Schoonovers and their peers were members of the whites-only Shawnee Country Club. Founded in 1904, it was the home of the city's true elites, along with the Lima Club, where they congregated in winter. Club members like Schoonover—wrapped in their cashmere coats and claiming a status far above the constituency of the Black Legion and a big notch above the police chief, the mayor, and small businessmen—held the ultimate power in Lima to institutionalize racism and to countenance the latent terrorism that enforced it, arranged over drinks at the club. James Williamson's mother and grandmother, Summie and Salena Williamson, worked in the Shawnee Club's kitchen prepping salads. But they weren't allowed to work out front, as waitresses or receptionists.[143]

In an interview, James reflected: "Segregation was a way of life. Black people said: 'What are we here going to do for ourselves? We don't need you.' It was like 'You take care of yourselves. We'll take care of ourselves.'" That meant a rich world of community activism, independent institutions, and carefully sustained cultural resources, much of it invisible to white people. Black men and women in Lima belonged to their own mutual aid associations dating back to the nineteenth century, including the Free and Associated Masons, the Grand United Order of Odd Fellows, and the Sisters of the Mysterious Ten. They worshiped at two established churches, St. Paul's African Methodist Episcopal and Second Baptist, or at the smaller Fourth Street Baptist Church or the Old Time Methodist Church ("small in number but strong in the faith," one longtime resident observed).[144] Black women ran their own social clubs including the Needlework Club, the Pleasant Hour Pinochle Club, the Aeolian Club, and the Morning Glory Club, which, on the birthday of Mrs. Marian Pearle in 1933, presented her with a "beautifully decorated and well-filled basket"; later in the evening, the ladies "presented the hostess with a purse."[145]

As the city was beginning to build its new segregated pool, Lima's Black residents responded by forming a new community association, the Lima League for Cooperation and Improvement, led by Dr. J. C. Bradfield. During the deepest depths of the Great Depression, the League was able to raise the funds to open its own new pool and community center in 1938, named the Bradfield Community Center. To help pay for it, women made chicken dinners and sold them door-to-door in their neighborhoods.[146] During the 1930s, Lima's Black people could eat and drink and dance and have their hair done at their own restaurants, nightclubs, saloons, pool halls, beauty parlors, and barbershops. When they passed away, they were attended to by Black morticians who, like the barbers and beauticians, had a guaranteed market because white people wouldn't touch Black bodies. When they got married, they could get their portrait taken by the city's one Black photographer.[147] They had one Black doctor to treat them—Dr. Bradfield, and then, after he died in 1936, Dr. Arkley A. Dalton, whose office was burned down right after he arrived. When Dalton discovered one of his Black patients at St. Rita's Hospital parked in a bed in the hall because the hospital wouldn't allow her to share a room with a white woman, he protested and successfully integrated St. Rita's.[148]

Lima's African Americans in fact held a measure of electoral power in the city through their eight to nine hundred votes. Historically, most African Americans voted Republican well into the twentieth century, staying loyal since Emancipation to "the Party of Lincoln." But in response to the New Deal, Black people nationwide were switching their loyalty to the Democrats. In Lima, the Republican Party's chief Black operative in the 1930s was a bookkeeper and insurance salesman named Rolland Moxley. Moxley was on the board of the city's Republican Party, on the original board of Bradfield Community Center, and a member of St. Paul's AME Church. "He has been a faithful precinct worker since the 1920s," reported a 1971 history of African Americans in Lima.[149] Moxley's work suggests an effective patronage system that delivered Republican votes in exchange for a few jobs. He himself got a job at the post office in 1927, and another as a bookkeeper for the state highway construction office during the 1930s (where Effinger also worked for a time).[150] However Lima's African Americans chose to cast their ballots, though, they would likely have known that the

Republican Party, in mid-1930s Lima, was interlaced with the Black Legion and its collaborators.[151]

Lima's six hundred Italians—if we count both immigrants and their native-born children—had their own tight-knit community, which overlapped residentially with African Americans and with other Southern and Eastern Europeans in the South End. Italian men had been recruited to Lima to work as section hands on the railroads. It was terrible work, cleaning the tracks in the blazing sun in the summer, chipping off ice in the snow at night in the winter. Italian women, including married women with children, worked in cigar and candy factories, on top of cooking and raising the kids and boiling laundry to clean their menfolk's clothes when they came home blackened with coal dust. A few families ran grocery stores or other small businesses.[152]

However despised by the Black Legion, Catholicism provided Lima's Italians with community, faith, sacred rituals, and beloved institutions. In the 1930s the city had three Catholic churches, St. Rose, St. John's, and St. Gerard, with their own elementary schools and two high schools, taught by nuns. The Knights of Columbus, a Catholic mutual benefit society, ran a recreation center, organized parties, and, on Columbus Day, put on a big parade and a picnic.[153] More informally, Italian men hung out in cigar stores and grocery stores owned by fellow countrymen, where they'd buy stogies and tobacco and spaghetti and cash their paychecks.[154] Fondi DeFinis, who grew up in South Lima during the 1930s going to mass every morning at 7 a.m., remembered the women of her mother's generation as "straight laced" and "ornery" but also capable of great fun. "A lot of times when we would go down to Union Street and these women would get together and they would have their cup of coffee and they would start talking and one of them would loosen up and they would all start loosing [sic] up." The kids would sneak up and try to listen through a door or window. "[The women] would tell jokes and talk about their husbands and would talk about their sex life."[155]

The Italians and Black people who lived side by side in DeFinis's neighborhood, she said, got along well; her father had Black friends. At her father's work, though, "there was a lot of bigotry and I think there was a lot of name calling." Her dad, who hated it, had to keep his mouth shut or he'd lose his job; and he hated having to keep his mouth shut. During an oral history interview, DeFinis pointed to a large, imposing white man in a group photo on display in her home. "This man here . . . he disliked the blacks and he was afraid of them." He was "vicious with his mouth," she said, and mean, and always carried a gun. He would randomly show up at their house to drink the family's homemade wine and eat their food; so would other foremen and supervisors from her father's rail yard. They'd come over once a week, or once a month. "We always knew that on Christmas Eve one of the Supervisors was going to come over and ruin our Christmas," she said. Her parents fought ferociously over the issue. But if they said no, her father would get fired. As the family understood well, the visitations were a deliberately humiliating show of power—and in the case of at least one of the perpetrators, with a gun for emphasis. Another gun at a Lima dinner table in the 1930s.[156]

An additional thousand European immigrants lived in Lima in the 1930s, often residing amicably in the South End alongside the African Americans and Italians, including small numbers of Poles, Lithuanians, Greeks, Macedonians, and Russians. Many of them would have been part of the same Catholic congregations as the Italians, along with some of the city's thousand or so Germans and Austrians and their descendants. Northern European immigrants such as the Germans, though, were interspersed in multiple white Lima neighborhoods and considered largely acceptable to the Black Legion's constituency, who themselves in some cases had descended from earlier generations of Northern European immigrants.[157]

Lima's 1,200 Irish immigrants and their native-born children, by contrast, kept to themselves. Irish Catholics caught the ire of the Black Legion, but their position in the community was distinct from that of the Italians. Many were native born, the product of continuous generations of immigrants since the 1840s and long before. Residents of the North End, they spoke English and were accepted in Lima as "white." Irish men could find good jobs in the factories. Mrs. DeFinis recalled that the mean foreman with the gun was probably Irish, for example. Since the mid-nineteenth century, when native-born white Protestants had equated the Irish with Africans in vicious stereotypes, Irish immigrants had responded to their own class and ethnic oppression by turning on Black people, often violently, as in Lima's 1888 race riot. Relations between Irish and African Americans remained tense into the 1930s.[158]

Less is known about the final targets of the Black Legion's ire, the city's Jews. The community's three to four hundred members, many of whom had roots in late nineteenth-century Lima, owned a few small factories and businesses in town, and sustained two synagogues—one Reformed, Beth Israel, and one Orthodox, Shaare Zedek.[159] They had their own community center, their own charities. In 1921 a white Protestant historian of Allen County reported "occasional outbreaks of anti-Semitism," which he diminished as "the merest propaganda." "Rich as a Jew" was "a common expression," he reported, used by people in Lima who believed that "the Jews are winning control of the finances of the world."[160]

We can only speculate what people in all these targeted groups knew or didn't know about the Black Legion. They had their own gossip networks, their own codes for signaling to each other who was known to be particularly dangerous.[161] Most importantly, they had their own rich strategies for survival and for seizing life with their families and communities. While white ladies in the Black Legion were enjoying their sewing circles, Black women on the South Side were frying up their chicken dinners to sell door-to-door for the new pool, and Mrs. DeFinis and her friends were gossiping away over their coffee on Union Street.

BREAKOUTS: THE BLACK LEGION IN MICHIGAN

Suddenly, in May 1936, Detroit authorities launched charges against the Black Legion. Overnight, its dangers became national news, its nationwide spread was revealed, and the arc finally bent toward justice.

Very, very carefully, and very bravely, during 1935 and early '36, law enforcement authorities in Michigan, surrounded by colleagues who were themselves Legion members, began investigating the Legion's activities in Detroit and nearby towns. In late May, three police investigators broke the murder case of a white former autoworker named Charles Poole. The night of May 12, 1936, four carloads of men had invited Poole, a Protestant with a Catholic wife, to a party. They took him out in the country, shot him five times, killing him, and left his body in a ditch. Police solved the case in ten days and immediately arrested several of the perpetrators. One of them, Dayton Dean, a disgruntled mid-level activist in the Legion, who'd been flogged by fellow members for allegedly molesting his daughter, agreed to talk. On June 16 he pled guilty to the murder of Poole, of another man, and of the attempted murders of four others. Dean's confessions quickly led the authorities to the Black Legion itself, including a stash of knives, clubs, guns, snake whips, and even hats and robes, which two policemen modeled awkwardly for the media.[162]

The September trial of twelve members of the Black Legion, including Dean, for Poole's murder was spread across the national news. Handsome, cocky, with a square forehead, light brown hair, and a charming, sheepish grin, Dayton Dean was the star witness, meticulously exposing the Legion's activities and beliefs.[163] In newsreel footage that screened in movie theaters across the country, the twelve defendants can be seen in close-up, slumped on benches at the back of the courtroom, some holding up a hand or their hat to try to block the camera, others looking downward or straight ahead with glassy eyes.[164] Within days, nine of the men were convicted of murder. Duncan McCrea, the prosecutor, emerged seemingly heroic. Dean and multiple other sources, though, swore under oath that McCrea himself had been a member of the Black Legion.[165]

As the dam broke, evidence quickly emerged of the enormous extent of Black Legion activity in Detroit and elsewhere in Michigan.[166] Two vicious and quickly infamous figures led the state's Legion: Arthur F. Lupp, brigadier-general for Detroit, and Isaac "Peg-Leg" White, a former milk inspector whom Effinger had authorized to recruit throughout the Upper Midwest. Both were under Effinger's command, as he traveled regularly back and forth to Michigan.[167] By 1936, the Legion had enlisted 6,500 members in Detroit and 1,600–2,000 members each in the neighboring cities of Flint, Highland Park, and Royal Oak, plus thousands more, totaling 20,000–30,000 members statewide.[168]

Michigan members' reasons for joining and staying in the Black Legion matched those in Lima. Arthur Lupp, the Legion's Detroit general, testified that during the Depression "many men were depressed. They had no purpose in life. They were floundering around. This organization gave them a purpose in life."[169] Legionnaires in Detroit signed on to the same program of racist, anti-Catholic, antisemitic hate as did their Lima brothers and sisters. In a filmed interview during the Poole trial, Lupp proclaimed that African Americans, Jews, and Catholics "are known in this country as a foreign body. . . . It's been the policy of myself and all loyal Americans to propound the doctrine of pure Americanism at all times. America for Americans."[170] One source reported that Lupp had developed a complex plot to distribute typhoid in entire Jewish neighborhoods.[171] Michigan women, for their part, contributed potluck dinners to the Legion and belonged to a women's group assigned to spy on conversations overheard while playing cards or at the local store.[172]

The Legion was much more successfully violent in Detroit than in Lima, however (although, again, we don't really know the true extent of what it did or didn't do in Lima). Ira Holloway Marmon, chief investigator for the Michigan State Police, stated publicly in September 1936 that he believed the Black Legion was responsible for at least fifty killings in the state. In 1933 and 1934, Legion members killed two white men, George Marchuk, a high-ranking official in the United Auto Workers, and John Bielak, an organizer for the American Federation of Labor.[173] In another case, Dayton Dean, the star witness in the Poole trial, confessed that he and other members had decided to kill a Black man "just for the hell of it," he said. The night of May 25, 1935, they lured a randomly chosen African American man named Silas Coleman by promising him $18 in back pay, then shot him up and left his body in a sinkhole pond, aware that law enforcement would show no interest in the killing of a Black man.[174] In Lansing, Michigan, Malcolm X's father, Earl Little, left the house one evening in 1931 and was found later that night near-dead in a white part of town, ostensibly run over by a streetcar. He died several hours later. Little's family members and the African American community of Lansing heard, and believed, that the Black Legion had attacked him, then left him on the tracks to be run over in order to disguise the killing.[175]

Vivid accounts also emerged of the Legion whipping members who balked, defected, or resisted commands. One informant reported that Legion leaders deliberately staged vicious whippings in front of audiences of their own members, who watched as their fellow members each took a turn taking a lash to the offender's body.[176]

In contrast to Lima, though, the Michigan Legion was hostile to the labor movement, which in these years was beginning to emerge as a powerful force in the state's auto industry. Multiple sources alleged that Legion members were working closely with anti-union goon squads managed by the big auto companies, especially Ford.[177] The Michigan

Black Legion was also aggressively anti-Communist. In April 1933 and again in March 1935, its members burned down a Communist educational camp northeast of Detroit; in 1934 they burned the farmhouse of an alleged Communist music professor at Michigan State.[178] Dayton Dean, the star squealer, reported that members repeatedly threatened and tried to kill Maurice Sugar, a prominent Communist-affiliated labor lawyer who ran unsuccessfully for judge in 1934.[179]

As in Lima, Michigan's Black Legion was thoroughly interlaced with public officials and law enforcement. Kenneth Dvorak, who has studied the Black Legion in Michigan, found that its members included not only Prosecutor McCrea himself, and Heinrich Pickert, the Detroit police commissioner, but also the mayor of Highland Park, a former governor, and much of Detroit's top inner political circle. A study at the time of Oakland County, to Detroit's northwest, found sixty-four officials at the city, county, and state levels, Democrats and Republicans alike, who had been or were currently members of the Black Legion.[180]

As Detroit area prosecutors expanded their investigations in the Black Legion, eventually convicting dozens of its members in multiple cases, and as media alarm exploded, all roads led to Lima and Virgil Effinger.[181] On August 21, 1936, McCrea and the Michigan authorities who were prosecuting the Poole murders indicted Effinger, along with twenty-one others, on criminal syndicalism charges and, in Effinger's case, additionally for possession of grenades, which a defendant swore he'd seen in Effinger's suitcase.[182] Reporters rushed to interview Effinger. Cigar in hand, leaning back in the swing on his front porch, he held forth about how innocent and all-American he was, how wholesome the Black Legion.[183] He turned himself in, but Chief of Police Ward Taylor, a Legion member, declared that he wouldn't arrest him since Michigan's arrest warrant wasn't valid in Ohio.[184] Michigan authorities then sought an extradition order from the State of Ohio. On August 25, in Columbus, Ohio, Governor Martin Davey—whose daughter the Black Legion had reportedly threatened—presided over a hearing to consider extradition. Effinger sat in the courtroom fanning himself with his straw hat, then, during a break in the proceedings, slipped outside and disappeared for the next fifteen months.[185] Governor Davey signed the extradition order, but it didn't matter.[186]

State authorities immediately launched a four-state manhunt, covered closely by the national media, with government agents reportedly watching trains and highways.[187] Was Effinger in Columbus, as rumored, or, later, New York City?[188] In Lima, meanwhile, authorities practiced impressive foot-dragging. "While maintaining they had evidence Effinger was being sheltered in Lima or the immediate territory," the *Lima News* reported six days after his disappearance, "officers said they are content to move slowly and give the Harrison [Avenue] man every opportunity to surrender rather than to 'put on the heat' in a hunt for him."[189] In early September, the chief investigator for the Michigan attorney general's office visited an FBI agent and told him that both the sheriff's department and police in Lima "had refused to cooperate" in Effinger's extradition. If "an attempt were made to remove Effinger it would result in bloodshed" by the Black Legion, he reported. "Armed resistance would be given to any attempt to remove this man."[190] Officially, at least, Effinger was nowhere to be seen all those fifteen months. "I don't know where he is," sighed Mary Effinger to a local reporter, a month after her husband disappeared, "but I sure do miss him."[191]

Finally, in early December 1937, Chief Taylor drove up in front of Effinger's house, honked the horn, and Effinger and his daughter came out. Together they all rode down to police headquarters. In five minutes Effinger was booked and out of there and remained free on bail.[192] His lawyers did everything they could to delay his Michigan trial. In March 1939, Michigan authorities dropped the grenade charges when the only witness, a Black Legion member who'd been convicted in the Poole killings, escaped from an Indiana prison farm. In May they dropped the remaining charges. Effinger never spent a day in jail.[193] "They're scared he'll expose too many big shots," a Detroit informant told the FBI.[194]

Through all this, Robert F. Jones, the Allen County prosecutor who'd traded membership in the Legion for his 1934 and 1936 elections, and who was responsible in part for eventually delivering Effinger, squirmed and squirmed. He didn't, apparently, cooperate in enforcing Michigan's extradition request or in capturing Effinger. Nor did he himself prosecute Effinger for dozens of local crimes of which Jones would have been well aware. In January 1937, after Effinger had been at large for almost six months, but before he turned himself in in December of that year, Jones wrote to FBI director J. Edgar Hoover pleading for help: "There is a great amount of rumor in this vicinity that members of the police department and high city officials are members of the Black Legion. For this reason rumors prevail that Effinger is hid [sic] in the city of Lima and reports come to this office from reputable sources that he has been seen on the city streets." As a result, Jones told Hoover, respect for the Lima police had plummeted. "I sincerely request that you help locate Virgil E. Effinger because of the widespread effect upon law enforcement in this community failure to locate him has. This is a situation which you can readily see county officials cannot cope with," he wrote.[195]

There's a lot going on here. It's plausible Jones was feeling sincerely trapped, in a tight squeeze between, on one side, Legion members, including the mayor and police, and on the other side powerful figures in town who might or might not have opposed the Legion, but were aware of the national publicity besmirching Lima and wanted Effinger dispatched. It seems just as likely, though, that Jones was worried that his personal reputation was plummeting because he wouldn't capture Effinger—or because he might. He was, after all, an elected official, with high ambitions, who would run for Congress the next year. Word would have been circulating that he himself was, or had been, a Legion member. If the FBI captured Effinger, Jones would be off the hook.[196]

When Effinger finally surrendered in early December of that year, Jones was in charge of delivering him to the Michigan authorities, and this time he did. According to the *Lima News*, "The spirit of cooperation was evidenced through telephonic conversation with Michigan authorities by Prosecutor Robert F. Jones after Chief of Police Ward Taylor became embroiled in a verbal battle over the telephone with Wayne [County, Michigan] Prosecutor Duncan McCrea." That phone call must have been quite thick, given that all three men had been members of the Black Legion themselves, and perhaps still were.[197]

FASCISM, U.S.A.

Once the Detroit killings hit national headlines in May 1936, reporters fanned out to cover the Black Legion in their home communities, where local authorities in some cases launched their own investigations. The national extent and power of the Black Legion became increasingly evident and terrifying. Now, journalists, politicians, ordinary people, even Hollywood grappled with the very real possibility of a fascist takeover of the United States.

In Toledo, to give just one brief example, Democrats on the city council launched an investigation of the Black Legion that revealed a membership of three thousand men, including two judges and at least three policemen, and three thousand women, who organized clubs for young children and teenagers. The *Toledo Blade* discovered a boys' order called the "Red Circle of the Black Legion," which counted at least eighty members and had allegedly kidnapped and beaten up a thirteen-year-old boy. The Legion was reported to have a "gas machine" that it was already using to emit poison into Italian neighborhoods, sickening many.[198] Later that fall, Legion members lobbed tear gas into a Communist rally, then into a meeting of sixty women of the Ladies' Auxiliary of the South Side Workers Alliance and onto the front porch of two reportedly "left-wing" activists who had been involved in relief and unemployed protests.[199]

As more and more revelations of Black Legion activities emerged, pulp magazines quickly picked up the story, mixing fascination with subtle affection. *True Detective Mysteries* offered "Black Legion Secrets . . . An Appalling and Fearless Exposé," featuring a hooded, armed Legionnaire on the cover. *Official Detective Stories* presented a robed Legionnaire's face behind a smoking gun, promising "The Inside Story of Michigan's Black Legion Murder By the Detectives Who Cracked The Case." In subsequent issues both magazines crossed over into soft porn, such as an *Official Detective* cover entitled "Secrets of the Black Legion—Revealed by Triggerman Dayton Dean," which showed a tied-up white woman, her minuscule red dress slipping down to mid-nipple level, while behind her loomed the dark shadow of a man about to inject her with drugs. Even Orson Welles picked up the tale (while eschewing the pornography) for his radio show *The Shadow*, in a twenty-nine-minute 1938 episode named "The White Legion."[200]

Hollywood itself quickly cranked out a feature film, *Legion of Terror* (1936), which followed two heroic postal inspectors dispatched from Washington, DC, who investigate a Black Legion–like organization and end up infiltrating it. The film does a great job of depicting the local newspaper editor's role in protecting and supporting the Legion; but the Legion itself is merely presented as a group of "un-American" racketeers who are exploiting people. There's no explicit mention of white supremacy, antisemitism, anti-Catholicism, or fascism, although there are references to the KKK. Warner Brothers' far more power-ful *Black Legion* (1937), in classic film noir style, starred a young, thin-faced Humphrey Bogart as a factory worker in Detroit who enthusiastically joins the Black Legion after he's passed over for a promotion in favor of a Polish man. Bogart's character ends up killing his best friend, confessing to it, and being convicted for life. *Black Legion* does explicitly cast the Black Legion as anti-immigrant and climaxes with a courtroom speech from the judge warning about the perils to democracy of "racism and religious prejudices," but it never specifically mentions antisemitism, anti-Black racism, or fascism.[201]

Black Legion opened in Lima the night of February 7, 1937. The movie columnist for the *Lima News*, in the paper's lineup of the week's films, described *Black Legion* as an "exciting drama of the notorious hooded order." A display advertisement in the *News* showed Bogart and a damsel looking up at a menacing hooded legionnaire. "YOU'LL STAND UP AND CHEER AS A WOMAN'S KISSES EXPOSE THOSE WHOSE LAW WAS 'DEATH TO SQUEALERS!'" the ad promised. We can only imagine which members of the Lima audience did or didn't stand up and cheer, which ones were in fact squealers, and how many pins you could hear drop on the floor.[202]

As the Black Legion story broke in 1936, dozens of individuals wrote directly to FBI director J. Edgar Hoover in Washington, DC, to pass along information about the Legion's activities. Other letters, largely handwritten, arrived as early as 1929 and as late as 1942, reporting activities in Connecticut, Georgia, Idaho, Illinois, Indiana, Kentucky, Michigan, Nebraska, New York, Ohio, Oregon, Pennsylvania, North Carolina, South Carolina, Texas, Virginia, West Virginia, Wisconsin, and Wyoming, as well as in British Columbia. In California, for example, the Legion allegedly had members in Atherton, Menlo Park, and Mountain View, along with a hundred members and a secret downtown office in Los Angeles; in Gardena, it included the chief of police, sheriff's office, and a justice of the peace.[203] A twenty-eight-year-old school janitor in San Luis Obispo, Edward Zyclica, who'd received threats for years, was found "with his head nearly blown off" and a letter signed by the Black Legion that read: "Hope you get this shot. Think you know too much."[204] In Portland, Oregon, a young man recounted to a local woman that after some trouble with his workmates, "one night he was stopped on the street, taken out a country road, and beaten up," by assailants wearing "black robes with a white skull and cross-bones."[205]

Correspondents also forwarded threatening letters. In Cleveland, two officials of the Brotherhood of Locomotive Firemen and Engineers submitted nearly identical letters signed by the Black Legion threatening that if a particular man's allowance was not "restored to him at once," then "we are going to take you for a ride and you may never return." Other letters told the recipient to get out of town, fast.[206]

Most, but not all, of these accounts and their enclosed documents appear reliable, their evidence in keeping with the Black Legion's more well-documented activities in Michigan and Lima—although a few of the correspondents sound well off the deep end, and some of the alleged threats appear to have been sent by freelance vigilantes merely settling personal grievances. Along with the news stories, government investigations, and other available documents, they suggest a broad grassroots dispersion of Black Legion methods and terror throughout the United States during the mid-1930s, including independent spinoffs and the Black Legion itself under a variety of names. The sheriff of Fort Wayne, Indiana, for example, reported in May 1936 that "several" locals had been "flogged . . . by black-hooded terrorists," and "two former township officials were threatened by a hooded organization known as the 'Mystic Order of Black Snakes,'" which reportedly had three thousand to ten thousand members and "might be affiliated with the Black Legion."[207]

For all that evidence, though, we don't really know the Black Legion's full extent in the United States. We do have studies of Detroit and Michigan by Kenneth Dvorak and Tom Stanton, and Peter Amann's one article, but that's it. No one has ever investigated the Legion at the national level, followed up on these FBI missives, or put all the pieces together.[208] If we just count the Legion's estimated 3,500–5,000 members in Lima, 6,000 in Toledo, and 24,000–30,000 members in the Detroit area, that totals around 40,000 just to begin with. Peter Amann, who conducted interviews with former members and amassed hundreds of documents, and focused his own published analysis mostly on Dr. Shepard and Effinger, reached what he called a "fairly conservative" estimate of 60,000–100,000 total members.[209]

In 1936, an investigator in the Wayne County prosecutor's office reported a total of 135,000 members in Michigan alone.[210] Effinger claimed a national total of over three million at times, six million at other times.[211] Whatever the total, that's a lot of robes, and a lot of robe-sewers.

All through the late spring and summer of 1936, as the Black Legion story escalated, newspaper editors and columnists, radio commentators, magazines like *The Nation* and the *New Republic*, and left-affiliated publications raised alarms about fascism coming to the US.[212] The *New York Times* reported that the Midwest "look[s] on the Black Legion not as a revival of the Ku Klux Klan but as a modern forerunner of an American brand of fascism that might have become even more serious a menace to democracy had a 'man on a white horse' appeared with ability to organize on a regional scale."[213]

Indeed, as these writers knew, grassroots fascism and proto-fascism were mushrooming in the United States by 1936. Some of its manifestations explicitly modeled themselves on Adolph Hitler and the Nazis. In Atlanta, a white supremacist Klan spinoff calling itself the "Black Shirts" boomed briefly in late summer and fall of 1930, copying the Nazis' Brownshirts. The Silver Legion of America, known as the "Silver Shirts," founded in North Carolina in 1931, grew to fifteen thousand by 1934, with an especially large contingent in California. It fused Jew-hating and anti-Black racism. Later, in February 1939 the German American Bund, composed of explicitly pro-Nazi German citizens in the United States, staged a rally in New York's Madison Square Garden with twenty thousand cheering participants, shocking many.[214]

But when it came to the "man on the white horse," the true avatars of US fascism were more homegrown, and far more popular. Huey Long, governor of Louisiana and then its US senator, ran the entire state as a dictator and by 1935 had become wildly popular nationwide through his "Share the Wealth" movement, which had millions of adherents. Until he was assassinated by one of his own former followers in September of that year, Long had posed a serious threat to Roosevelt's 1936 reelection. So did Father Coughlin, the "Radio Priest" near Detroit who had his own ten million loyal listeners, hanging on his every word as he denounced the banks and, increasingly, Jews.[215] The Black Legion's Virgil Effinger, with his stuffy awkwardness and minimal charisma, never achieved that kind of cult status. But observers of the Black Legion were aware of the broader context in which he easily might have.

Some scholars have distinguished between "homegrown" US fascism and imported, European-allied formations, but the distinction doesn't hold up. James Q. Whitman has established that the Nazis themselves studied racial law in the United States and brought it back to reinforce their policies in Germany. They looked closely at anti-miscegenation laws, Southern restrictions on African Americans, and legal structures controlling Filipinos, Puerto Ricans, and Native Americans.[216] On the US side, militaristic models of European fascism grafted easily onto the legacy of the Ku Klux Klan and, more broadly, onto the quotidian, deeply institutionalized racism, anti-Catholicism, nativism, and antisemitism that pervaded much of white Protestant culture and politics. In California in the late 1930s, white journalist Carey McWilliams coined the term "farm fascism" to describe the vigilante terrors that elite white farmers and their local minions were unleashing against Mexican and Filipino farmworkers, the labor movement, and the Left.[217]

"What is the meaning of the Black Legion?" *The Nation* magazine asked in 1936. "To dismiss it as a local and passing matter would be fantastic; to call it American fascism would be too easy. Race hatred, religious bigotry, sadism, red-baiting, union-smashing, the vigilante technique—wherever these are found together they point to a festering condition in the social organism."[218]

The Black Legion was not some obscure fringe group. Rather, it emerged out of a swirling nationwide sea of hate, economic anxiety, and repression. Its adherents might not have succeeded in their goal of storming the Capitol, but they nonetheless marched in their own quiet and not-so-quiet ways, from the smallest of small US towns all the way up to the top of the United States government in Washington, DC.

WHO UPHELD THE LAW, WHO DIDN'T

All at once, in mid-1936, as the Detroit news broke, the Black Legion crumbled. The *Chicago Herald and Examiner* reported on May 28 that in Hammond, Indiana, "Black Legion Acts to Disband."[219] The *Toledo Blade* reported the next day: "Black Legion on the Run; Cowed Members Burn Robes."[220] In Indianapolis, notes were found on doorknobs reading: "Comrade: We must reorganize quickly. We suffered a shock that has broke our stride but we will get back to our feet and rush on through the night."[221] The evidence suggests that when individual Legion members heard about the Detroit prosecutions, they simply dropped out one by one, hoping to fade into the woodwork. In Lima, the Black Legion "just seemed to drop dead . . . everybody ran for cover," Rev. Penhorwood recalled.[222] The Black Legion had once been glamorous, implicitly powerful. Now it wasn't. And many who'd been coerced into joining or staying would have cut and run, fast.

The Legion's swift institutional collapse didn't mean, though, that its members suddenly eschewed their beliefs in racism, antisemitism, vigilante terrorism, or even their desire to overthrow the US government. There's no evidence to that effect. It appears they simply didn't want to go to jail—as had always been true of some of its defectors and balkers. Effinger, for his part, even as he was out on bail battling extradition in 1938 and his followers had largely jumped ship, formed a new organization, the Patriotic League of America, Inc., of which he was the commander. Potential members had to attest in an application form that they were "white, Gentile" US citizens who believed in "the maintenance of the white race; pure Christian Americanism" and "a continuance of constitutional government."[223]

Who stopped the Black Legion, then? To answer that, we have to begin with the long list of those who should have and didn't. In Lima, as we've seen, the responsible authorities were themselves members. "We have appealed to County & City officials without any results whatsoever," two factory workers in Lima, Fred Cook and Floyd Sanders, pleaded in a May 28 letter to Hoover.[224] Rev. Penhorwood and the other white Protestant ministers in town didn't speak out; Harry Meredith, the attorney, didn't; the elite Schoonovers and their ilk didn't. The *Lima News* only reported on the Legion gingerly, and never denounced it. Yes, people were afraid. But that's not all that was going on. Silence was complicity. The same pattern largely held in Toledo and Detroit. The big auto companies would have known all about it, for example, and didn't speak out.[225]

To fully understand who didn't try to stop the Legion, though, we have to look closely at the array of state- and federal-level authorities who did vigorously seek to shut it down, and how their superiors, at the very top, actively thwarted them.

In July 1935—a year before the Detroit prosecutions—a joint committee of the Ohio state legislature overseeing relief programs sent three men to Lima to investigate the Black Legion. After interviewing witnesses, the investigators completed an extensive report addressing the threats to kidnap the governor's daughter, the beating of farmer Smith, the arson attack on the Twin Oaks roadhouse, and the takeover of the relief office. But the committee never submitted it to the legislature. Finally, on May 27, 1936, when the Detroit story broke, State Representative H. T. Phillips decided to simply release the report to the public on his own. Another state senator, John R. Davis, introduced a resolution creating a five-member commission "to investigate the blackrobed secret order and frame legislation designed to drive it from the State." Davis said he wanted to investigate "not only this organization but any that have a sinister purpose and whose object is the overthrow of established law and order in the state." The next day his fellow Ohio senators voted down his resolution sixteen to nine.[226]

Federal relief authorities in Ohio, for their part, knew all about the Legion's takeover of their office in Lima, but denied it and refused to act. Agent No. 34 submitted his twelve-page, single-spaced report to his superiors at the Ohio State Relief Commission in January 1935, documenting the Black Legion's extensive control of the FERA in Lima.[227] When in May 1936 the Ohio legislators' own investigation hit national news, reporting that 82 percent of FERA employees in Allen County were Black Legion members, Carl Watson, Ohio director of the Works Progress Administration (the FERA's successor by that point), immediately went into damage-control mode. In a long telegram the next day to Lawrence Westbrook, one of the top administrators of the WPA in Washington, Watson conceded that the Black Legion's membership "may have included some relief officials" but insisted that "it has not been charged and it definitely is not true that the Black Legion has any control over activities of WPA in Allen or any other Ohio county." The WPA would certainly not "permit discrimination against persons employed because of race creed or other condition," Watson insisted. "Since no charge of discrimination for or against members or non members of that group under WPA . . . I do not consider it necessary to make a special investigation in Lima at this time."[228] Squelch.

On May 27, 1936, the day after he announced his charges against the Detroit Legion, prosecutor Duncan McCrea wrote to US attorney general Homer S. Cummings pleading for help investigating it. "I know definitely that the Black Legion is operating in 15 to 18 states. I know that it is very active in the cities of New York and Chicago. I have reason to believe that the activities of the Legion have included the hauling of bodies across boundary lines, which is a federal offense."[229] Cummings replied publicly that he'd known about the Black Legion for "about a year" but that it had not violated any federal laws "either then or now," and therefore lay outside his jurisdiction.[230] In fact, the Department of Justice had known about the Black Legion in Lima since at least October 1934, when an agent had interviewed William Smith, the farmer beaten by the Legion. Smith never heard from him again.[231] In a late 1936 pamphlet, *The Black Legion Rides*, leftist George Morris was scathing about the Justice Department's failure to act despite its knowledge of the Black Legion: "Not a move was made so much as to inform the people of Michigan of the great danger. The murder of Poole, and other murders that have been committed since that time, might have been forestalled."[232]

William Stanley, assistant to the attorney general, had actually solicited a Justice Department investigation into the Lima Black Legion a year before, in April 1935. The resultant memo reported that "Effinger has boasted that approximately 60 or 70 members of the Department of Justice are members of the Black Legion. He is said to have concealed a large yellow map depicting the location of all secret fortifications in the country and has stated that the map was obtained by him through the Department of Justice."[233] The attorney general himself read Postal Inspector Cordrey's 1935 reporting on the Black Legion in Lima, which included similar allegations of Legion membership among Justice Department officers. Assistant Attorney General Joseph B. Keenan forwarded that information to J. Edgar Hoover.[234] Attorney General Cummings, in other words, was deeply aware of the Black Legion, even its potential presence within his department's own ranks, but wouldn't take it on. The Justice Department did poke around a bit, internally, but concluded that none of its employees were implicated.[235]

It was the FBI, though, that knew the most about the Legion, and most aggressively chose not to act. As its internal files—available today through the Freedom of Information Act—thoroughly establish, the FBI received detailed information on the Black Legion nationwide as early as 1929. In 1935 and '36, FBI agents conducted extensive interviews with a wide range of informants in Lima, Detroit, and elsewhere; they clipped newspapers; they forwarded documents—compiling much of the detailed intelligence on the Black Legion in Lima used here. Their meticulous reports made it to Hoover's desk.[236]

To the dozens of correspondents nationwide who wrote in with information, Hoover responded with a standard form letter eschewing any action. "Since there is no existing legislation which gives this Bureau investigative jurisdiction over the matters to which you refer, I regret that the Bureau is unable to give assistance to you in this regard."[237] Once the news broke in Detroit, Hoover explicitly forbade his agents from acting against the Black Legion, or even investigating it. Indianapolis special agent in charge John A. Dowd confirmed to Hoover on May 28 that "it is my understanding that this Bureau Office is not to interest itself in the Black Legion, or its activities, unless its activities are in violation of a Federal Statute over which this Bureau has basic investigative jurisdiction. . . . In other words, no activity is to be engaged in by this office in the absence of Bureau instructions."[238] Hoover wrote to Dowd's superior, Herold Reinecke, the head of the FBI in Detroit, that same day: "It is desired that absolutely no investigation be conducted into the activities of the Black Legion in the absence of specific authorization from the Director of the Bureau." If anyone wanted to share information about the Black Legion, Hoover said, they should be told the FBI wasn't investigating it. "If information is furnished to your office which is believed or alleged to constitute a violation of a Federal Statute within the Bureau's jurisdiction, no action should be taken thereupon by your office, other than to refer the facts immediately to the Bureau for transmittal to the Department for appropriate consideration."[239]

Individuals in the US Congress did take action, but some cut it off at the knees. On May 28, 1936, Representative Samuel Dickstein (D-NY) and Senator Elmer Benson (Farmer-Labor, MN) introduced a joint resolution "to investigate un-American activities of secret orders seeking to establish dictatorship or rule by force and terror in the United States."[240] Congress should act quickly, Benson warned, before "we awake to the day when our cherished American liberty will be a thing of the past."[241] Rep. Dickstein denounced "terrorist" attacks on Jews and Catholics and said that if the Department of Justice and FBI didn't have adequate authority, "I shall call on Congress for further power for our organization to crush this menace."[242] The next week, Dickstein charged on the House floor "that officers of the Michigan National Guard and of the US Army Reserves are members of the 'Black Legion,'" with six million members in eleven states, "and have been planning an armed uprising."[243] Backing up Dickstein, Representative George Sadlowski (D-MI) charged that neither the Michigan State Police nor the governor, who both knew about the Legion, "are going to do much of anything about the matter" because the Michigan Republican Party worked closely with the Black Legion, he said; nor was the US attorney general going to act.[244] The joint resolution passed the Senate Judiciary Committee on June 13, but Congress adjourned without ever taking it up further.[245]

During his interview with Rev. Penhorwood in Lima, Peter Amann, the historian, reflected: "The best I could figure out, was essentially this; Hoover was always very sensitive to national politics and to congressional politics, and he was always worried about his appropriation and usually got what he asked for. Well, there was opposition of any investigation by the southern congressmen who were in control of some of the key committees. The reason being, that the Klan was still active in the South and they didn't want any tie-up or poking around in the South."[246]

"Why doesn't the federal government take action?" asked George Morris in his 1936 pamphlet. "The answer is clear. If the investigation were carried beyond Michigan it would reach into the Southern states where the K.K.K. is strong and where Roosevelt has his main base of support [i.e., Southern Democrats]. Arising during an election year, the issue was simply shelved."[247]

The question of how, legally, the Black Legion could have been stopped by the FBI isn't as simple as it might sound, though. Which, exactly, were its members' punishable federal crimes? Some of the Legion's reported activities were clearly criminal at the state and local level: the kidnapping of farmer Smith outside Lima; the floggings in Fort Wayne; the beating in Portland; the dead janitor in San Luis Obispo; the multiple killings in Michigan. Less violently, staff members at the FERA in Lima illegally discriminated on the basis of race or creed, and illegally provided relief jobs to bedfellows who weren't legally eligible. State, federal, and local authorities chose to look the other way at these and hundreds of other crimes. But the FBI's role is more ambiguous. Hoover was correct: its jurisdiction only included crimes that crossed state lines. Yet Detroit prosecutor Duncan McCrea, for one, believed the Black Legion's alleged crimes fell right into the Bureau's bailiwick: he publicly charged that bodies were carried across state lines. Certainly Hoover and staff at multiple levels had been interested enough in possible crimes within the FBI's jurisdiction that they investigated regularly and deeply for at least two years before he shut down further investigation in mid-1936.

But it wasn't a crime to belong to the Black Legion, or to advocate fascism or white supremacy. The First Amendment protected free speech, and the slope on this front was already slippery. In 1934, Rep. Dickstein had succeeded in creating a new Special Committee on Un-American Activities Authorized to Investigate Nazi Propaganda and Certain Other Propaganda Activities, of which he served as initial vice-chairman. In 1937, Rep. Martin Dies (D-TX) took over the committee and it was soon renamed the House Committee on Un-American Activities, popularly known as the "Dies Committee, or "HUAC," and obsessively hunted down Communists long before McCarthyism.[248] What started out as a ferreting operation hunting fascists, in other words, could soon hunt other prey. (The ferret himself turned out to be a weasel: Dickstein was revealed in 1999 to have been taking money from and providing services to the Soviet spy agency NKVD beginning in 1937.)[249]

I f the foot-draggers, complicit authorities, and silent supporters were formidable in their powers, arrayed on the other side were all the people who did, together, stop the Black Legion, including the individuals who have appeared throughout this story. We need to honor all those people, and feel their power.

Hundreds of government officials did in fact try to uphold the rule of law. In March 1937, prominent progressive senator Robert M. La Follette (Farmer-Labor-WI) announced that his Committee on Violations of Free Speech and Rights of Labor would begin investigating the Black Legion's connections with the auto companies' labor spies.[250] In Kentucky, Florida, Indiana, and Lima, Ohio, postal inspectors raised alarms about the Legion—even though their information, too, was dismissed in Washington.[251] The Toledo City Council launched a wide-spread investigation in 1936. Prosecutors in multiple states took it on.[252]

Then there was all the committed and brave media coverage. The *Toledo Blade*, for example, backed up and publicized the city council's investigations, while raising its own alarms about local Legion atrocities.[253] In Detroit, the big papers carried the trials every day. While they may not have reported every known instance of collusion by police and government officials, they stepped up courageously to expose the assassins by which they were themselves surrounded. At the Associated Press, International News Service, and other big syndication services, reporters chose to cover the Legion, and their editors allowed or encouraged them to. The *New York Times*, *Washington Post*, *Chicago Tribune*, and other prominent papers then ran the syndicated stories and sent their own reporters to Detroit and Lima; by doing so, they legitimated the issue in a way that made it possible, in turn, for papers in mid-sized cities and small towns to reprint those stories and in some cases launch and publish their own local investigations of Legion activities.

We've also seen the hundreds who spoke up individually all over the country, including those who chose to speak privately about the Legion to FBI agents, postal inspectors, local authorities, and investigators from the Ohio legislature and federal relief authorities in Ohio, however fruitlessly. We can mark all those who sent in their carefully crafted observations to J. Edgar Hoover, putting themselves at potential risk from the Legion. Others wrote to Congress. Rep. Dickstein told the press: "I am receiving thousands of appeals daily by letter and telegram to get at the bottom of this thing and save this country from this organization."[254] In Detroit, three thousand people attended a June 12, 1935, rally of the Michigan Civil Rights Congress, demanding that the mayor further investigate the Black Legion.[255] Members and allies of the Communist Party and of other left groups produced pamphlets, books, and other materials raising alarm about the Black Legion.[256]

And finally, there were the people of Lima: dozens of white defectors and informants such as plumber George Scheid Sr., his wife, and the friends who helped guard his house, including Albert Erfer, the veteran. All the white men who refused to join, like farmer Smith, who even after he was brutally beaten by the Legion went to the papers and denounced the organization publicly. White factory workers such as Fred Cook and Floyd Sanders, the ones who begged Hoover to step in. The unnamed Lima official who wrote the FBI about German Lugers stolen from the Allen County Historical Society. Okey Odell, the onion strike leader who refused the Black Legion's offer of help. The Jews, Catholics, and Black people of Lima who didn't leave town, who kept their independent institutions alive, who "took care of themselves." And Mrs. DeFinis, who kept making Christmas dinner for her family year after year even though the supervisor with the gun showed up.

It's useful to reflect, finally, on the impact of the New Deal. By mid-1936, when the Legion collapsed, white Protestant men were beginning to benefit extensively from its programs. Meanwhile, the Roosevelt administration's support for the labor movement—albeit still in its early stages—and the CIO's progressive, inclusionary model of organizing all workers regardless of race and ethnicity were making possible huge union victories in nearby Detroit and throughout the Upper Midwest.[257] Even if Legion members voted Republican, they could begin to grasp that Roosevelt and the Democrats were coming through for them on a grand scale. Their ladder was perhaps not collapsing; their place on its middle rungs was perhaps secure. Meanwhile, the price of vigilante terror had just gotten a lot higher, as powerful legal authorities, the mainstream media, and a whole lot of ordinary people said no to a racist, bigoted fascist takeover of the United States government.

The government did hold, more or less. But we should have no illusions about who it still served. A certain form of organized fascism was defeated, but the normal functioning of a racist criminal justice system hummed along. "The attempted application of force and of private sanctions by unauthorized organizations is entirely contrary to American ideals," pronounced a Detroit judge, Ralph W. Liddy, in a newsreel interview during the Poole trial. "If it appears that such an attempt has been made to usurp governmental functions, the people of America, through their courts, must accept and answer the challenge of such daring defiance of law and order."[258] Judge Liddy was asserting what sociologists and political scientists today refer to as the state's monopoly on violence: the doctrine that only the government and its legitimate authorities can enforce security.[259] In that view, the Black

Legion's paramilitary terror was illegitimate. But marking the Black Legion as "usurpers," as did Liddy, in no way ensured that the government's own laws, its own law enforcement, and its own "legitimate" use of force were always for the common good.

THE BLACK LEGION GOES TO WASHINGTON

The Black Legion had one last act, on a grand stage. In 1938, county prosecutor Robert F. Jones, who had refused to prosecute Black Legion members and evaded extraditing Effinger for over a year, ran for Congress successfully on the Republican ticket. He would go on to serve three more terms. In 1947, he was nominated to serve a seven-year term on the Federal Communications Commission. The day before his Senate confirmation hearing on June 27, 1947, though, someone tipped off Drew Pearson, a prominent muckraking journalist with a syndicated column, a popular radio show, and a nose for scandal, that Representative Jones had been a member of the Black Legion. Hostile to Jones's record as a far-right Republican, Pearson denounced him on the radio that night, then spoke as a witness at Jones's Senate hearing the next day, the first of three.[260]

Pearson testified that sources in Lima told him Jones's father had been a well-known recruiter for the Ku Klux Klan, who had introduced his son at Klan meetings during the early 1920s as "the youngest member of the Klux Klan." Jones not only worked closely with prominent fascist Gerald L. K. Smith, Pearson charged, but "was a member of an equally bigoted organization, anti-Catholic, anti-Jewish, and anti-other racial groups, namely the Black Legion." With such a background, Jones was in no way qualified to have power over who had access to the airwaves, Pearson charged.[261]

Rep. Jones, next on the stand, countered that all Pearson's statements were "unmitigated lies." He had never been a member of either the Ku Klux Klan or the Black Legion. "Nothing in my public or private life shows a scintilla of regard or sympathy for such organizations," he swore to the committee. As a congressmember he had supported Jews and Catholics for appointments to the military academies, he insisted. "Some of my staunchest supporters are Catholic people." And how could he have been in the Black Legion, if he'd heroically "fought for" Effinger's extradition, as he insisted?[262]

Meanwhile, Pearson dispatched his new assistant, Jack Anderson (who would much later inherit Pearson's syndicated column, "Washington Merry-Go-Round"), to Lima. Anderson asked around, interviewed locals at a union hall, and quickly hustled Virgil Effinger and two other former members of the Black Legion onto a train back to Washington, where Pearson put them up in the plush Mayflower Hotel. At Jones's second hearing, on July 3, one of the men, Glenn E. Webb, an inspector at the Westinghouse factory in Lima—who'd been the FERA's timekeeper while a Legion member in 1935—testified that he had personally witnessed Jones being initiated into the Black Legion at Tapscott's farm "on a chilly spring evening" in 1934, beginning around 9 p.m., just as it was getting dark. Jones, he said, had been one of twenty-five or thirty men inducted that night, surrounded by a thousand robed members in a circle holding flashlights. The future congressmember had knelt on one knee and, with one hand on the Bible and a loaded gun pointed at him, had sworn to the oaths of the Legion.[263] Frank Barber, the sheriff of Beaverdam, a village outside Lima, then testified that he personally had sworn Jones to the preliminary oath.[264] Virgil Effinger told the committee that he had sworn Jones to the second oath. Pearson produced an affidavit that Effinger had signed in 1938, two or three weeks before the election in which Jones first ran for Congress, swearing that Jones was a member of the Black Legion. Anderson testified that he had spoken to multiple other individuals in the Lima area who confirmed to him that Jones had been a member but weren't willing to swear to it.[265]

It looked bad for Jones. But as the senators grilled the Lima men, the witnesses' convoluted motives for testifying gradually emerged, and their statements degenerated into a circus of contradictions. None of the three had come because they opposed the Black Legion, it turned out. Webb said that he was only testifying because Jones had denied he was a member.[266] Barber, who said he was still a proud member of both the Black Legion and the KKK, declared that he had "no objections" to Jones's confirmation, and it by no means disqualified Jones to have been a member of the Legion. "He would be one of the finest Presidents in the United States if he lived up to his oaths."[267] Barber said he was testifying, rather, because Jones had turned against those who supported him. "Mr. Jones came to the labor hall before he was elected to Congress. I guess he had an onion in one hand and a handkerchief in the other to wipe away the tears as they came. He was so in sympathy with the laboring man, that if we could just support Mr. Jones, he would do everything he could for the working man. He also went to the old-age pension [sic] with the same story and the same onion." But at "the first vote in Washington," Barber charged, Jones had "voted against both."[268]

A fourth man from Lima, Joseph Emmons, executive secretary for the Lima-area CIO, who'd helped Webb prepare his statements, testified that he'd briefly infiltrated the Black Legion in 1938 to learn about how to combat it. "The Fourth Congressional District is a fertile hotbed of reaction," he denounced. "There we find the stronghold of America Firsters, the Coughlanites, and the rest of these hate organizations, and the stronghold of the Ku Klux Klan, and the aftermath, the Black Legion." Robert Jones fit right in, he said. "That being the disposition of the . . . District, anyone who would play ball, and being the darling of the Fascist organizations, it is only natural that they would be elected." Emmons was ferocious in condemning both the Legion and Jones—for his membership in the Legion, for his connections to more recent US fascist proponents, for his anti-labor record, and for "voting against veterans housing, rural electrification, . . . soldiers vote [sic] and old age pensions" and more.[269] But Emmons's testimony, too, was potentially dubious—had he, in fact, only joined the Legion in order to infiltrate it?

Effinger, on the stand, was a parody of himself. Senator Owen Brewster (R-Maine) produced a second affidavit, signed that same day, July 3, in which Effinger swore that Jones had never, in fact, been a member of the Black Legion—contradicting his 1938 affidavit in which he said he'd sworn Jones in. Confronted with the disparity, Effinger said, well, he hadn't felt like saying Jones *was* a member, and that he had memory problems now. He couldn't even remember if he'd traveled to Washington the day before by bus or by train, he claimed.[270]

Rolland Moxley, Lima's African American operative for the Republican Party, stepped to the stand to support Rep. Jones. He said he'd heard rumors in 1938 that Jones was a Legion member, and that he'd asked him about it personally at the time, and Jones had denied it. "I cannot here today say that he is a member or he is not, but he has proven to my satisfaction and to the satisfaction of 90 percent of the Negroes in the Fourth Congressional District that he was not and is not a member of the Black Legion." Moxley said that up until the last two to four years, "90 to 95 percent" of African Americans in the district had supported Jones. "He has made himself likable." Moxley conceded that "you might say that he was after votes," but he always came through, "and you did not have to ask the second time."[271] Other witnesses from Lima—Catholics, Jews—testified how much Rep. Jones loved the Jews and the Catholics, and how much they loved him. These testimonies suggest the continuing power of Lima's Republican Party, including its patronage system of jobs and favors, its influence over the criminal justice system, and the strategies people might have employed to ensure their safety—although of course the witnesses, along with several other Jews and Catholics who wrote in to support Jones, may have spoken up for many possible reasons.

The night of June 29, two days after the first hearing, J. Edgar Hoover telephoned an FBI agent and asked him for background information on Emmons and Webb, two of the witnesses. The next day, the agent sent Hoover a memo with an array of intelligence that FBI offices had accumulated on them. Both witnesses might be Communist sympathizers, the agent said. No one had ever previously charged that Jones was a Black Legion member; rather, "Congressman Jones . . . was allegedly vigorous in his activity in making Effinger available for extradition."[272] At the second hearing, on July 3, Senator Brewster, the committee's chair, submitted evidence that Glenn Webb, one of the Lima witnesses, had confessed to forging checks from his former employer; that Frank Barber, another witness, had gone to jail for shooting a man, and in 1922 had been committed to the state mental hospital for being homicidal and suicidal, and then escaped; and that Effinger had been convicted of contempt of court in 1940, in addition to having been charged in the Detroit killing—for which Rep. Jones had extradited him, Brewster emphasized. The witnesses' credibility collapsed. The case against Jones fell apart; Drew Pearson was publicly discredited for rushing to present unreliable testimony. The Senate promptly confirmed Jones for a seven-year term.[273]

Of the subcommittee's three members, both of the two Republicans, Chair Brewster from Maine and Homer E. Capehart from Indiana, had been backed by the Ku Klux Klan. The third was a Colorado Democrat, Edwin C. Johnson, who opposed the New Deal.[274]

LEGACIES

Today, Lima is in deep Trump territory. And the economic roots of his appeal are clear.

As the US entered World War II, Lima's industrial economy boomed once again. Westinghouse had even opened a new factory in 1937, followed by an Army tank plant in 1947 and a Ford engine plant in 1957. From the mid-1940s well into the 1960s, thousands of Lima's white working-class men could get stable, well-paying jobs with strong union representation. Beyond that, they had the security of New Deal entitlement programs, which continued to expand into the 1970s.[275]

Then it all fell apart again. By the 1970s, Lima's factories started to shut down or reduce their payrolls. Beginning in 1980, President Ronald Reagan cut the labor movement off at the knees and eviscerated the welfare state; succeeding administrations continued to undermine union power, good jobs, and working people's safety net.[276] By 2016, Trump would feed on the remains. He carried Allen County by 66.4 percent in 2016 and 68.9 percent in 2020.[277] "Trump's helping people. He's helping them get jobs," Trump voter Oscar Clark told the *Lima News* in 2020.[278] In 2019 President Donald Trump himself went to Lima's tank plant to deliver a major speech.[279]

Since 2007, Allen County has also helped elected Jim Jordan to Congress from Ohio's Fourth District—the same district Joseph Emmons described to the Senate in 1947 as "the darling of the Fascist organizations." The Fourth District is so preposterously gerrymandered that it's known as the "duck district," after its convoluted shape. Rep. Jordan still refuses to acknowledge the 2020 presidential election results and remains one of Trump's most fanatical loyalists.[280] He has plenty of compatriots in Lima. Tom Ahl, for example, the owner of multiple car dealerships in town, traveled to Washington, DC, for the January 6 insurrection—although he insisted that he didn't enter the Capitol itself. "All we wanted was justice," he told the *Lima News* proudly the next day.[281] In this Trump heartland, overt racism has mushroomed once again. In June 2020, a white worker at Lima's Ford plant hung a stuffed monkey with a noose around its neck at the workstation of a Black apprentice toolman. Someone also wrote, "Go home n_____" in the restroom.[282]

But Lima's Black population is far larger today than in the 1930s, when it was only 1,400 people. Beginning with World War II, as the booming factories experienced labor shortages, employers started recruiting African Americans from the South. By 1970 a quarter of Lima's total population (53,374 people) was African American, and it remains at 25 percent today.[283] Through long struggle, the Black community was finally able to desegregate Lima's public services, beginning in the early 1940s with Schoonover Pool.

Yet, African American people in Lima continue to struggle with poverty, discrimination, and enforced subservience to white people— especially at the hands of the Lima police. Here the legacy of the Black Legion is clear. On June 6, 1970, for example, after years of incidents, white Lima police shot and killed Christine Ricks, a forty-five-year-old Black woman, as she was trying to stop them from beating a teenage boy who had allegedly failed to move his bicycle. The police said Ricks seized a policeman's gun from his holster and shot at the two officers. The Black community said she took the gun and fired it into the air, to try to stop their attack on the boy. The police never offered Ricks first aid or called an ambulance; they just shot her and drove off.[284]

In contrast to the 1930s, though, in this case Lima's Black community mounted militant protests. The evening after Ricks was killed, two hundred members of the African American community, horrified and incensed, marched in Lima under the leadership of the National Committee to Combat Fascism, an early formation of the Black Panther Party that ran a breakfast program for kids. The march was led by James Williamson, its minister of education—the same man whose mother and grandmother made salads in the kitchen at the Shawnee Country Club and who would later become a key historian of Lima's Black community. Growing up on Lima's South Side, he had been mentored by elders at the Fourth Street Baptist Church and sold *Jet* magazine door-to-door.[285] At 8 p.m., police launched tear gas into the Panthers' march. Looting and small fires broke out; sniper bullets hit patrol cars; the mayor ordered a curfew; police cordoned off twelve square blocks on the South Side and raided the Panthers' headquarters, later claiming to have discovered dynamite inside. Over five hundred members of the National Guard then poured into Lima and took over its Black neighborhoods for five days. There was never an inquest into Ricks's killing.[286]

Thirty-eight years later, on January 4, 2008, a SWAT team of Lima police burst into the home of twenty-six-year-old Tarika Wilson, arrested her partner on drug charges, and then shot and killed Wilson, injuring her one-year-old daughter, who was cradled in her mother's arms while Wilson huddled in a bedroom with her children. Again the Black community of Lima marched, three different nights this time, from the South End to the police station.[287] "The cops in Lima, they is racist like no tomorrow," Junior Cook, a neighbor who watched the raid from his porch, told a reporter. "Why else would you shoot a mother with a baby in her arms?"[288] The *New York Times* reported that "Black people in Lima, from the poorest citizens to religious and business leaders, complain that rogue police officers regularly stop them without cause, point guns in their faces, curse them and physically abuse them." Of seventy-seven police officers in town, only two were Black.[289] C. M. Manley, pastor of New Morning Star Missionary Baptist Church, told a reporter, "There is an evil in this town."[290]

Today, inspired by the Black Lives Matter movement, a new generation of African American activists in Lima, many of them in high school, is speaking out about racial justice. In March and early June 2020, they marched to demand justice for George Floyd and Tarika Wilson and an end to police brutality. "We are the future," proclaimed Alazae Thomas, eighteen, one of the organizers. "Our moms and dads and grandmas and grandads won't always be around to help us fight, so we have to learn how to do that for ourselves so that we aren't being destroyed as a person or a race."[291]

White people are also speaking out in some cases. In response to Lima's Black Lives Matter protests, the white-owned *Lima News* published a sympathetic story with the subhead "Will It Spur Change?" delineating the long history of racial disparity in Lima and implicitly praising efforts to combat racism in town.[292] In October 2021 it featured a column by Dr. Jessica Johnson, a Black professor at Ohio State University, Lima, about a recent forum for adults that had discussed critical race theory. Dr. Johnson recounted a white colleague's presentation about the seemingly invisible race privileges he'd experienced throughout his life that had made his advancements possible.[293] In 2000, 2015, and 2019, the *Lima News* published three long articles about the Black Legion's history in town.[294]

Although Trump carried Allen County with over two-thirds of the vote, he didn't, in fact, carry Lima itself, in either 2016 or 2020.[295] And on November 21, 2021, Lima's majority-white electorate elected the city's first Black mayor, Sharetta Smith, former chief of staff to the white mayor who'd been in office for thirty-two years.[296]

This story is not just about Lima. As in the 1930s, it's about the entire nation, and its precarious future. In May 1936, when news of the Detroit murders originally broke and the Black Legion's power was revealed, the famous journalist Dorothy Thompson concluded her column: "Who is to blame? You and I are to blame. All of us who listen tolerantly to intolerant expressions of racial and religious prejudice, without registering our own indignation. . . . All of us who accept lies which we are able to contradict. All of us who sit snugly by and think that it can't happen here!"[297] Today, as in the 1930s, some of us never have the option of sitting snugly by. But these days, as we speak up together, all of us can learn from the history of the Black Legion and use that knowledge to help stop its descendants today.

EPILOGUE

William Smith, the Lima farmer in his overalls, who talked back to Virgil Effinger even though he was surrounded by hundreds of armed men with flashlights. Ruby Lucas, who sat on the stoop in her squirrel coat with a cup of coffee and announced: "I'm warring on the millionaire bankers whose greed has turned widows and orphans and destitute into slaves." Mary Hart, camped out in a white chair at city hall, who told reporters: "What they been payin ain't enough for carfare." The unnamed elderly man on horseback who, as he crossed the border, threw his hat up in the air and shouted "Viva Mexico!" All of them, along with the inspiring collective actions of which they were part, have seemingly disappeared from history. So, too, the more chilling figures here: The men who held the flashlights. The policemen who threw down their badges and guns when told they could only use sticks, not bullets, against African American relief protesters.

Indeed, a common theme emerges in these chapters: invisibility. Women's domestic labor was invisible to both their menfolk and to the state. The expulsion of a million Mexicans and Mexican Americans was invisible to most non-Mexicans and remains so. And then there was the Black Legion, trying to hide its clandestine work of hate. (The Ku Klux Klan, after all, was known as the "Invisible Empire.") Today, in most mainstream renditions of the Great Depression in the United States, these stories from the grass roots remain largely invisible, largely "forgotten."

We need their stories, though, for our own time, full of its own terrors—resurgent fascism, steel borders, climate change. Neither capitalism nor racism has collapsed; patriarchy hums along. Today, we need our own New Deal, too, an activist state that curbs the rich, defends labor rights, redistributes wealth, and provides a safety net and free health care for everyone. We can join those who advocate for a "Green New Deal" to help stave off climate disaster. Trying to use the state to contain capitalism won't ever be enough, though, because in its very nature the system dedicates itself to slipping out of, and tearing apart, any fetters. We need, like those seeking social justice in the 1930s, to dream of our own new social order, to build social movements that demand it, and to model it in our own collective lives.

During the time I wrote this book, three scary plagues visited my community. The first, of course, was the COVID pandemic. The second was a set of fires in August 2020 that destroyed over seven hundred homes in the Santa Cruz area, including those of people I knew, burned down acres and acres of beloved forests, and crept close enough to my house that the evacuation line was eight blocks away. For another year we prayed for rain, but instead got more drought.

In the last months before I finished this book, drenching rain was finally predicted for the day after Christmas. So I hurriedly planted grass where gophers had torn up the more-or-less lawn covering my backyard and had left bare dirt that turned into gunk that I tracked constantly into the house. I raked the soil, sowed grass seeds, covered them with mulch, then over it all spread burlap coffee sacks to protect the seeds from the birds, anchoring down the corners with bricks.

Then it rained, in biblical proportions, for days and days. Plague Number Three. Sinkholes four blocks from my house appeared on the national news, as did a levee breach in a nearby town that destroyed the homes and livelihoods of hundreds of already-impoverished people. Less disastrously, my own backyard turned into a lake, which inched into my study and garage. It was only one inch deep; no historical research was hurt! But the seeds were underwater. For three weeks I watched the lake drown them. When the lake finally receded, I lifted off the burlap, sadly. The seeds were still there—sparrows, juncos, and towhees arrived every morning to peck away at them. But no grass.

One morning, though, I detected individual, thin, dark blades miraculously scattered across the ex-lake. Then it flooded again, for another entire week. Now I mourned my drowned grasslings, which I imagined waving for help underwater, kelp-like in the murky swamp. Finally, the waters sank for good. With a bit of sun, the grass babies flourished, their roots happy in the rich muck, locking in with each other in spreading horizontal networks that joined other, thicker patches on nearby higher ground. I looked out the window and saw a beautiful sea of green fur.

We are not grass. But we know how to survive fire and flood and beasts that tear up our landscapes. We know how to lay low, then rise up. We know how to survive when we are underwater. We know how to link our roots with others. We know our roots can flourish in deep muck. We know how to thrive.

And we know how to learn from history. William Smith, Ruby Lucas, Mary Hart, and the man on horseback didn't, in fact, disappear. They all appeared in newspapers at the time, which is where I found them, and they are now in this book almost a hundred years later, speaking to us. They aren't invisible. In taking on the terrors of our own time, we can take warning from those who served the powers of darkness during the Great Depression. Most importantly, we can learn from the grassroots activists of the time who sought justice and equality, and carry them in our hearts as we step off our stoops, step over borders, and march into the streets, sinking our toes deep into the rich, messy muck of history.

ACKNOWLEDGMENTS

To begin with, I am more indebted than ever to the archivists and library staff who helped me meet the enormous, complex, and often insurmountable challenges of trying to conduct historical research under COVID restrictions. Dozens of people, most of whom I never met, tracked things down, tipped me off about sources, and through their work made this book possible, while I tore my hair out trying to simply check books out of my university library.

At UC Santa Cruz, my deepest thanks to the circulation and reference staff of the McHenry Library, especially to the staff of Interlibrary Loan—Mallory DeBartolo, María Del Toro, Taylor Gorman, Tyler Green, and Dawson Kelly—and to Teresa Mora and the staff of Special Collections. Thank you to the staff of the National Archives in College Park, Maryland, especially Gene Morris, who helped me map the maze and found a crucial document within it. At Wayne State University, thanks to Kristen Chenery and especially to Elizabeth Clemens for calling my attention to the Black Legion robe in their collection and allowing me access. Thank you to Erica Cooper at the United States Department of Labor Library, who miraculously found the clipping about the wet nurses in an Australian newspaper that contained the Joe Louis, not John L. Lewis, quote. Thanks to Kailee Faber at the Schomburg Center for Research in Black Culture, who made so many documents available to me digitally, and to Ettie Goldwasser at the archives of the American Jewish Historical Society. Thank you, Sarah Dysken at the Chicago Public Library, for sending materials, and Ellen Keith at the Chicago History Museum and Research Center.

In the land of Clark Kerr, thanks to the staff of the Bancroft Library and the University of California, Berkeley, Main Library, especially to

Susan McElrath, for all their help, and to Craig Alderson and Vanessa Tait for helping me navigate it all.

For chapter 2, I am grateful to Clarissa Chavina, Debbie Countess, Sylvia Reina, and Dan Garcia at the San Antonio Public Library for copying news clips; to Rebecca Hankins at the Texas A&M University Library; and to Vianey Zavala at the Houston Public Library. For help in accessing invaluable oral histories, thanks to Natalie Garcia at the California State University, Fullerton, Oral History Collection; Chris Livingston at the California State University, Bakersfield, California Odyssey Oral History Collection; Lisa Weber and Alejandra Zavala at the University of Texas at El Paso Library; and Yolanda Chávez Leyva, director of the Oral History Institute and Borderlands Public History Lab at the University of Texas at El Paso.

At the Library of Congress, my thanks to Amy Reytar and, astonishingly, to Lizzo. On September 26, 2022, I was one of five lucky researchers in the otherwise vacant Main Reading Room when, to my eternal astonishment, Lizzo arrived, climbed atop the circular desk in the middle of the rotunda, and played for us a series of haunting trills on one of the Library of Congress's historic flutes.

At UCSC, my enduring thanks to the Instructional Technology staff who kept it all going—or tried to, under impossible circumstances—especially Kim Hwe, Yuri Cantrell, Alejandra Sicairos, and the ever-amazing Jay Olson. My thanks to the Committee on Research of the Academic Senate for research funds, and to the Senate Committee on Emeriti Relations for the Edward Dickson Emeriti Research Award, for travel funds and faith in my project in its early stages. Thanks to the History Department staff, as always, and to the staff of Humanities Academic Resources, especially Jack Lin.

For chapter 4, I am deeply grateful to the people of Lima who welcomed me into their town, told me their stories, and helped my research. Thank you to the reference staff of the Lima Public Library; to Charles Bates, Brittany Venturella, and especially Anna Selfridge at the Allen County Historical Society; and to Greg Hoersten, formerly of the *Lima News*, whose own research on the Black Legion made this book possible and who gave me a wonderfully generous tour of Lima. My deep thanks to Charlene Smith-Echols and Rev. Ronald Fails of the Lima NAACP for their joyous and sobering conversation and for all the insights and knowledge they so generously shared with me. My greatest thanks to James Williamson, who shared not only decades of research into and knowledge about Lima history, but the history of his own family and his life in struggle.

For encouragement, support, research help, insights, and friendship, my thanks to Eva Bertram, Andrew Cockburn, Leslie Cockburn, Bill Fletcher Jr., Michael Goldfield, Elena Herreda, Bill Ong Hing, Norma Klahn, Paul Ortiz, Wyndee Parker, Tim Rieser, Alex Sadler, Diana Scott, Jane Slaughter, Octavio Solis, and Bill Spencer.

Thanks, as always, to my beloveds Lupita Aguila Arteaga, Craig Alderson, Sandy Brown, Joe Chrastil, Jonathan Fox, Jean Ingebritsen, Ron Pomerantz, Helen Shapiro, Judith Anne Shizuru, Vanessa Tait, and Jane Weed. In Washington, thanks to Annie Bird, Alex Main, and Jean Stokan for years of community and love in struggle. In Honduras, my deepest thanks to Iris Munguía and the whole glorious family for all their astonishing and powerful love and comradeship.

For writing support and ongoing beautiful friendship, my thanks to Cheri Brooks, Andrea Weiss, and Jonathan Blitzer. Thank you, Jennifer Trent Parker and Sarah Fan, for, miraculously, inviting me into *Hammer & Hope*, and for their terrific editing. Thank you to Laura Martin for her wonderful MA thesis and help with its sources; and to Veronica Martínez-Matsuda for her enthusiastic insights and for reminding me about the Karnes City hunger strike. I am indebted to the skilled research of three assistants who rescued me from COVID barriers and made the book possible: Esther Isaac at the University of Chicago, Shelby Sinclair at Princeton, and my beloved "cousin," Karl Neice, in Seattle.

I want to give special thanks to Jacqueline Wolf for her tremendous research on the history of wet nursing, and for generously and with great enthusiasm sharing with me her interviews with the supervising nurses at the Chicago milk station. Special thanks as well to Jim Gregory, whose research underlies so much of this book, both in California and Seattle, who generously shared materials with me, and who remains an exemplar of publicly committed scholarship.

Thank you, Adriana Craciun and John Logan, for writing comradeship, labor lore, and bird love. Thank you, as always, Gerri Dayharsh and Steve McCabe (I promise! This is the last one!) for their enduring friendship and love. Thank you, Becky McCabe and Josh MacCallister and Darcy and Fia, for being my experts on the importance of mutual aid, for their support for chapter 1, and their love.

And then there's Beacon Press. It has been wonderful to return home to it and have the great honor of being part of its extraordinary project of empowerment and social justice. My thanks to Catherine Tung, Joanna Green, Melissa Nasson, and Nicole-Anne Keyton for all their help, advice, and support along the way. As ever, the production staff was impeccable—my thanks to Beth Collins, Susan Lumenello, and especially Brian Baughan for his terrific copyediting. Thanks to the publicity and marketing staff, including Brittany Wallace and my publicist, Perpetua Charles, for all their dedication and all the magic they work. Thanks to Gayatri Patnaik, atop it all now and leading Beacon gloriously into the future, who has been a tremendous support and source of insight since I first pitched the book to her. And thanks most of all to my editor, Amy Caldwell, for her superb editing, great insights on every front, and faith in the book.

For advice on chapters, my deep gratitude to Desma Holcomb and Miriam Frank (no relation, alas) for their enthusiastic help with the wet nurses; to Eric Porter for knowing what needed fixing; and especially to Matt Garcia, who has been such a wonderful colleague for decades now, and whose own work inspires mine. My deep thanks to Rep. Jamie Raskin for reading chapter 4 with such enthusiasm, and for all his amazing and brave work fighting fascism in real time.

My deep gratitude to Jade Brooks for reading the whole manuscript and giving such great advice and support, while being the new mom of a two-month-old baby!

My great thanks to Robin D. G. Kelley for his insights into racial fascism, for his wonderful friendship, for encouraging me to write a book about the 1930s in the first place, and for his endlessly inspiring research and writings, here throughout this book.

Thank you to Alice Yang for her loving friendship and support, and astonishingly positive approach to just about everything. Thank you to Toni Gilpin for splendid comradeship in discussing writing and labor history, and for our enduring friendship. Special thanks to my dear Karin Stallard for her boundless and bounding enthusiasm, her political insights, and for always being there, full of wisdom.

My great thanks to Lisbeth Haas, for her overflowing love, comradeship in writing, and terrific advice on the whole book. My great thanks to Nelson Lichtenstein for his jolly friendship, for his own fabulous scholarship, for cheering on the project, and for reading the manuscript, making it better at every turn.

My deepest thanks to Wendy Mink for her friendship, her comradeship in both my congressional and historian lives, her scholarship on and mastery of the gender and race politics of the New Deal, her superb advice on the whole manuscript, and for saving me from not knowing what I was talking about on multiple fronts.

My deepest thanks to Tera Hunter for her enormous support, her research suggestions, her scholarship shining through the text, the gift of her friendship, and most importantly, her faith in my ability to get this project right.

Thank you from the bottom of my heart to my beloved niece Ramona McCabe, for sustaining me with such love during the lockdown (and always!), for her vast enthusiasm for my writing, and for the great gift of our shared adventures in daily life—and far beyond it.

Lastly, my deepest thanks to Hamsa Heinrich, next door, who greeted my day-to-day whines, obsessions, and enthusiasms about the writing life with endless cheer and support, and filled daily life with great joy.

NOTES

CHAPTER ONE: A NEW SOCIAL ORDER

1. Jesse Jackson, "The Story of Hooverville, in Seattle," manuscript in University of Washington Library (July 1, 1935), 2–3, reprinted in Calvin F. Schmid, *Social Trends in Seattle* (Seattle: Univ. of Washington Press, 1944), 286–93; Donald Frances Roy, "Hooverville: A Study of a Community of Homeless Men in Seattle," master's thesis, Univ. of Washington, 1935; Leslie D. Erb, "Seattle's Hooverville" (Seattle: Seattle Pacific College, 1935); James Gregory, "Hoovervilles and Homelessness," Univ. of Washington Civil Rights and Labor History Consortium, 2009, https://depts.washington.edu/depress/hooverville.shtml; Magic Demirel, "Seattle's 'Hooverville': The Failure of Effective Unemployment Relief in Early 1930s Seattle," Univ. of Washington Civil Rights and Labor History Consortium, n.d., https://depts.washington.edu/depress/hooverville_seattle .shtml; "In 1930s Seattle, Homeless Residents Built Eight Hooverville Settlements," *Seattle Times*, Mar. 16, 2017; Colin Ditz, "Born Out of the Great Depression, Seattle's Hooverville Lasted 10 Years," *Seattle Times*, Mar. 16, 2017, and accompanying photographs.

2. Roy, "Hooverville," 42–44; see also 62–69 for figures for Filipinos, Mexicans, and African Americans. Jackson reported in 1935 that federal authorities had found "every race of the world here, and two dozen nationalities"; 20 percent of the residents, he said, were native born. Jackson, "The Story of Hooverville, in Seattle," 7. For how these demographics compared to those of the city of Seattle at the time, see the extensive information in Schmid, *Social Trends in Seattle.*

3. Jackson, "The Story of Hooverville, in Seattle," 5.

4. Jackson, "The Story of Hooverville, in Seattle," 5–6; Roy, "Hooverville," 25–32, 35; Erb, "Seattle's Hooverville"; *Unemployed Citizen*, Dec. 2, 1932.

5. Jackson, "The Story of Hooverville, in Seattle," 6; Roy, "Hooverville," 79–86; *Unemployed Citizen*, Dec. 2, 1932.

6. Roy, "Hooverville," 7.

7. Jackson, "The Story of Hooverville, in Seattle," 9.

8. Roy, "Hooverville," 92.

9. Roy, "Hooverville," 92–93. On race relations in Hooverville, see also Joey Smith, "A Tarpaper Carthage: Interpreting Hooverville," Univ. of Washington Civil Rights and Labor History Consortium, n.d., https://depts.washington .edu/depress/hooverville_seattle_tarpaper_carthage.shtml.

10. Roy, "Hooverville," 11–12, 88, 92.

11. Roy, "Hooverville," 12.

12. Jackson, "The Story of Hooverville, in Seattle," 7.

13. Roy, "Hooverville," 14.

14. Jesse Jackson, "The Story of Seattle's Hooverville," reprinted in Schmid, *Social Trends in Seattle*, 202. This document is similar to Jackson, "The Story of Hooverville, in Seattle," but not identical.

15. Jackson, "The Story of Hooverville, in Seattle," 1–2.

16. Jackson, "The Story of Hooverville, in Seattle," 4–5, 10; Roy, "Hooverville," 77–78.

17. Jackson, "The Story of Seattle's Hooverville," 293. For law enforcement, see Jackson, "The Story of Seattle's Hooverville," 8–10; Roy, "Hooverville," 79.

18. Irving Bernstein, *The Lean Years: A History of the American Worker, 1920–1933* (Boston: Houghton Mifflin, 1960), 316–21; T. H. Watkins, *The Great Depression: America in the 1930s* (Boston: Little, Brown, 1993), 52, 55.

19. Studs Terkel, *Hard Times: An Oral History of the Great Depression* (New York: Pantheon, 1970), 92.

20. William A. Sundstrom, "Last Hired, First Fired? Unemployment and Urban Black Workers During the Great Depression," *Journal of Economic History* 52, no. 2 (1992): 417.

21. Sundstrom, "Last Hired, First Fired?" 417.

22. Alice Kessler-Harris, *Out to Work: A History of Wage-Earning Women in the United States* (New York: Oxford Univ. Press, 1992), ch. 9.

23. Lois Rita Helmbold, *Making Choices, Making Do: Survival Strategies of Black and White Working-Class Women During the Great Depression* (Newark, NJ: Rutgers Univ. Press, 2022); Julia Kirk Blackwelder, *Women of the Depression: Caste and Culture in San Antonio, 1929–1939* (College Station: Texas A&M Univ. Press, 1984), e.g., 47; Ruth Milkman, "Women's Work and Economic Crisis: Some Lessons of the Great Depression," *Review of Radical Political Economics* 8, no. 1 (1976): 73–97; Ruth S. Cavan and Katherine H. Ranck, *The Family and the Depression: A Study of One Hundred Chicago Families* (Chicago: Univ. of Chicago Press, 1938); Robert S. Lynd and Helen Merrell Lynd, *Middletown in Transition: A Study in Cultural Conflicts* (New York: Harcourt Brace, 1937); Susan Porter Benson, *Household Accounts: Working-Class Family Economics in the Interwar United States* (Ithaca, NY: Cornell Univ. Press, 2007).

24. Helmbold, *Making Choices, Making Do*; Blackwelder, *Women of the Depression*, e.g., 47; Milkman, "Women's Work and Economic Crisis"; Cavan and Ranck, *The Family and the Depression*; Lynd and Lynd, *Middletown in Transition*; Benson, *Household Accounts*.

25. Quote: Blackwelder, *Women of the Depression*, 47; Milkman, "Women's Work and Economic Crisis"; Benson, *Household Accounts*.

26. Milkman, "Women's Work and Economic Crisis."

27. Ethel Lum, "Chinese During Depression," *Chinese Digest*, Nov. 22, 1935, 10; Lim P. Lee, "The Need for Better Housing in Chinatown," *Chinese Digest*, Dec. 1938, p. 7; Victor G. Nee and Bret de Bary Nee, *Longtime Californ': A Documentary Study of an American Chinatown* (New York: Pantheon,

1972); Judy Yung, *Unbound Feet: A Social History of Chinese Women in San Francisco* (Berkeley: Univ. of California Press, 1995); Nayan Shah, *Contagious Divides: Epidemics and Race in San Francisco's Chinatown* (Berkeley: Univ. of California Press, 2001).

28. Nee and de Bary Nee, *Longtime Californ'*, 100–101.

29. Nee and de Bary Nee, *Longtime Californ'*, 64–65.

30. Gilbert Osofsky, *Harlem, the Making of a Ghetto: Negro New York, 1890–1930* (New York: Harper and Row, 1966); Cheryl Lynn Greenberg, *"Or Does It Explode?" Black Harlem in the Great Depression* (New York: Oxford Univ. Press, 1991); Shannon King, *Whose Harlem Is This, Anyway? Community Politics and Grassroots Activism During the New Negro Era* (New York: New York Univ. Press, 2015).

31. James F. Wilson, *Bulldaggers, Pansies, and Chocolate Babies: Performance, Race, and Sexuality in the Harlem Renaissance* (Ann Arbor: Univ. of Michigan Press), ch. 1; Jervis Anderson, *This Was Harlem: A Cultural Portrait, 1900–1950* (New York: Farrar, Straus, and Giroux, 1981), 152–57; King, *Whose Harlem Is This, Anyway?*, 139–43.

32. For African American women domestic workers who claimed their bodies through dancing, see Tera W. Hunter, *To 'Joy My Freedom: Southern Women's Lives and Labors After the Civil War* (New York: Oxford Univ. Press, 1997), ch. 8.

33. Quoted in Wilson, *Bulldaggers, Pansies, and Chocolate Babies*, 19.

34. Quoted in Anderson, *This Was Harlem*, 156.

35. Quoted in Wilson, *Bulldaggers, Pansies, and Chocolate Babies*, 14. See also Eric Garber, "A Spectacle in Color: The Lesbian and Gay Subculture of Jazz Age Harlem," in *Hidden from History: Reclaiming the Gay and Lesbian Past*, ed. Martin Bauml Duberman, Martha Vicinus, and George Chauncey Jr. (New York: New American Library, 1989), 318–31.

36. Quoted in Robin D. G. Kelley, *Thelonious Monk: The Life and Times of an American Original* (New York: The Free Press, 1999, 35). For musicians and other performers at rent parties, see also Anderson, *This Was Harlem*, 152–57, and a wide range of biographies and autobiographies by musicians who played them.

37. T. H. Watkins, *The Hungry Years: A Narrative History of the Great Depression* (New York: Henry Holt, 1999), 90.

38. David T. Beito, *From Mutual Aid to the Welfare State: Fraternal Societies and Social Services, 1890–1967* (Chapel Hill: Univ. of North Carolina Press, 2000); Alfred H. Katz and Eugene I. Bender, "Self-Help Experiments in the Western Society: History and Progress," *Journal of Applied Behavioral Science* 12, no. 3 (1976); Mary Ann Clawson, *Constructing Brotherhood: Class, Gender, and Fraternalism* (Princeton, NJ: Princeton Univ. Press, 1990), quote: Katz and Bender, "Self-Help Experiments in the Western Society," 276; Lizabeth Cohen, *Making a New Deal: Industrial Workers in Chicago, 1919–1989* (New York: Cambridge Univ. Press, 1990), ch. 2. For the Chinese in the US, see Nee and de Bary Nee, *Longtime Californ'*; Beito, *From Mutual Aid to the Welfare State*, 20. For Puerto Ricans in the US, see Virginia E. Sánchez Korrol, *From Colonia to Community: The History of Puerto Ricans in New York City* (Berkeley: Univ. of California Press, 1983), ch. 5.

39. Virginia Yans-McLaughlin, *Family and Community: Italian Immigrants in Buffalo, 1880–1930* (Ithaca, NY: Cornell Univ. Press, 1971), quote, 131; Robert A. Orsi, *The Madonna of 115th Street* (New Haven, CT: Yale Univ. Press, 1995); Gary R. Mormino and George E. Pozzetta, *The Immigrant World of Ybor City: Italians and Their Latin Neighbors in Tampa, 1885–1985* (Urbana: Univ. of Illinois Press 1987).

40. Jennifer Guglielmo, *Living the Revolution: Italian Women's Resistance and Radicalism in New York City, 1880–1945* (Chapel Hill: Univ. of North Carolina Press, 2010), 221.

41. Emilio Zamora, *The World of the Mexican Worker in Texas* (College Station: Texas A&M Univ. Press, 1993), ch. 4, quote, 93. For a beautifully respectful, community-based study of a mutual benefit society founded in the nineteenth century that arose in part to defend against Anglo land seizures, see José A. Rivera, *La Sociedad: Guardians of Hispanic Culture Along the Río Grande* (Albuquerque: Univ. of New Mexico Press, 2010).

42. Zamora, *The World of the Mexican Worker in Texas*, 99–100. For a summary of mutualistas in the Southwest, see José A. Rivera, "Mutual Aid Societies in the Hispanic Southwest: Alternative Sources of Community Empowerment," Research Report #002, Alternative Financing Project, Office of Assistant Secretary for Planning & Evaluation, US Department of Health and Human Services (Washington, DC: Oct. 1984), including 30–31 for secondary studies.

43. Quoted in Zamora, *The World of the Mexican Worker in Texas*, 106; Zamora, *The World of the Mexican Worker in Texas*, 105–6.

44. Nancy A. Hewitt, *Southern Discomfort: Women's Activism in Tampa, Florida, 1880s–1920s* (Urbana: Univ. of Illinois Press, 2001), 200–204; Beito, *From Mutual Aid to the Welfare State*, 170–71; Mormino and Pozzetta, *The Immigrant World of Ybor City.*

45. Quoted in Mormino and Pozzetta, *The Immigrant World of Ybor City*, 183.

46. Maximilian Hurwitz, *The Workmen's Circle: Its History, Ideals, Organization and Institutions* (New York: The Workmen's Circle, 1936), 105–6.

47. Quoted in Tony Michels, *A Fire in Their Hearts: Yiddish Socialists in New York* (Cambridge, MA: Harvard Univ. Press, 2005), 182.

48. Quoted in Michels, *A Fire in Their Hearts*, 183. For the Workmen's Circle, see Hurwitz, *The Workmen's Circle*; Michels, *A Fire in Their Hearts*, ch. 4; Judah J. Shapiro, *The Friendly Society: A History of the Workmen's Circle* (New York: Media Judaica, 1970); Mary McCune, "Creating a Place for Women in a Socialist Brotherhood: Class and Gender Politics in the Workmen's Circle, 1892–1930," *Feminist Studies* 28, no. 3 (Fall 2002): 585–610.

49. Hurwitz, *The Workmen's Circle*, 105, 109; Michels, *A Fire in Their Hearts*, 208.

50. Shapiro, *The Friendly Society*, 32.

51. Beito, *From Mutual Aid to the Welfare State*, 56.

52. Hurwitz, *The Workmen's Circle*, 109.

53. For activities and goals of the Workmen's Circle, see Hurwitz, *The Workmen's Circle*; Michels, *A Fire in Their Hearts*, ch. 4; Shapiro, *The Friendly Society*; McCune, "Creating a Place for Women in a Socialist Brotherhood."

54. Quoted in Shapiro, *The Friendly Society*, 114.

55. McCune, "Creating a Place for Women in a Socialist Brotherhood," 598–604; Shapiro, *The Friendly Society,* 97–98.

56. McCune, "Creating a Place for Women in a Socialist Brotherhood," 585–610; "herring and potato dinners," 598–99.

57. McCune, "Creating a Place for Women in a Socialist Brotherhood," 598–604.

58. Clawson, *Constructing Brotherhood*; Beito, *From Mutual Aid to the Welfare State,* 104, 222.

59. Beito, *From Mutual Aid to the Welfare State,* 47–48, 222.

60. For shifting racialized perceptions of immigrants in this period, and who was considered "white" and by whom, see Thomas A. Guglielmo, *White on Arrival: Italians, Race, Color, and Power in Chicago, 1890–1945* (New York: Oxford Univ. Press, 2004); Jennifer Guglielmo and Salvatore Salerno, *Are Italians White? How Race Is Made in America* (New York: Routledge, 2003); Noel Ignatiev, *How the Irish Became White* (New York: Routledge, 1995); Karen Sacks, *How the Jews Became White Folks and What That Says About Race in America* (New Brunswick, NJ: Rutgers Univ. Press, 1998).

61. Clawson, *Constructing Brotherhood,* 110.

62. Beito, *From Mutual Aid to the Welfare State,* 32.

63. Joe W. Trotter, "African American Fraternal Societies in American History: An Introduction," *Social Science History* 28, no. 3 (Fall 2004), 355–66; W. E. B. Du Bois, *The Philadelphia Negro* (Philadelphia: Univ. of Pennsylvania Press, 1899); Paul Ortiz, *Emancipation Betrayed: The Hidden History of Black Organizing and White Violence in Florida from Reconstruction to the Bloody Election of 1920* (Berkeley: Univ. of California Press, 2005), ch. 5, quote, 102; Theda Skocpol and Jennifer Lynn Oser, "Organization Despite Adversity: The Origins and Development of African American Fraternal Associations," *Social Science History* 28, no. 3 (Fall 2004): 367–437; Beito, *From Mutual Aid to the Welfare State.*

64. Skocpol and Oser, "Organization Despite Adversity."

65. "Sisters of the Mysterious Ten," Filson Historical Society website, https:// filsonhistorical.omeka.net/exhibits/show/women-at-work/voices-for-reform/smt.

66. Elsa Barkley Brown, "Womanist Consciousness: Maggie Lena Walker and the Independent Order of St. Luke," *Signs* 14, no. 3 (Spring 1989): 610–33, quote, 631. For gender dynamics in the Black mutual aid societies, see also Skocpol and Oser, "Organization Despite Adversity," 211–17.

67. Programs in folder "Branch 151, Meyer London, 1932–1957," and folder "Branches." Workmen's Circle Collection, YIVO Institute for Jewish Research, New York, NY.

68. For the New Deal and the mutual aid societies, see Beito, *From Mutual Aid to the Welfare State,* 228–30.

69. Barbara Ransby, *Ella Baker and the Black Freedom Movement: A Radical Democratic Vision* (Chapel Hill: Univ. of North Carolina Press, 2003), 64–91; Joanne Grant, *Ella Baker: Freedom Bound* (Hoboken, NJ: John Wiley and Sons, 1998), 23–36. For the Young Negroes' Cooperative League, including Baker, see also Jessica Gordon Nembhard, *Collective Courage: A History of African American Cooperative Economic Thought and Practice* (University

Park: Pennsylvania State Univ. Press, 2014), ch. 5. For earlier interest in cooperatives among African Americans, see W. E. B. Du Bois, *Economic Co-operation Among Negro Americans: A Report of a Social Study Made by Atlanta University Under the Patronage of the Carnegie Institution of Washington, D.C., Together with the Proceedings of the 12th Conference for the Study of the Negro Problems, Held at Atlanta University, on Tuesday, May the 28th, 1907* (Atlanta: Atlanta Univ. Press, 1907).

70. Quoted in Ransby, *Ella Baker and the Black Freedom Movement*, 85.

71. Quoted in Ransby, *Ella Baker and the Black Freedom Movement*, 83.

72. George S. Schuyler, "An Appeal to Young Negroes," Box 2, Folder 3, Ella Baker Papers, Schomburg Center for Research in Black Culture, Manuscripts, Archives and Rare Books Division, New York Public Library (hereafter Ella Baker Papers).

73. George S. Schuyler to "My Dear Colleague," Nov. 1930, in Box 2, Folder 2, Ella Baker Papers.

74. Du Bois, *Economic Co-operation Among Negro Americans*.

75. Ransby, *Ella Baker and the Black Freedom Movement*, 82–85; Grant, *Ella Baker*, 32–37; Ella Baker, National Office of the Young Negroes' Cooperative League, New York City, to "My Dear Fellow Cooperator"; Pure Food Co-operative Grocery Stores, Inc., List from Ella Baker "of the shareholders for whom you are responsible," n.d., in Box 2, Folder 3, Ella Baker Papers; Nembhard, *Collective Courage*, ch. 5.

76. Ransby, *Ella Baker and the Black Freedom Movement*, 82–83; Grant, *Ella Baker*, 32–36; for outreach to women's groups, see "Penny-A-Day Plan," 2, Box 2, Folder 3, Ella Baker Papers; "Committees Suggested to Be Formed," n.d., Box 2, Folder 3, Ella Baker Papers; "Program of the First National Conference of the Young Negroes [sic] Co-operative League," Oct. 18, 1931, Box 2, Folder 2, Ella Baker Papers.

77. Schuyler, "An Appeal to Young Negroes," 8.

78. National Office, Young Negroes' Cooperative League, "Report of the First National Conference of the Young Negroes' Co-operative League," Box 2, Folder 2, Ella Baker Papers.

79. "Complete Membership to Date," list in undated document, no first page available, 2, in Box 2, Folder 2, Ella Baker Papers.

80. National Office, Young Negroes' Cooperative League, "Report of the First National Conference of the Young Negroes' Co-operative League."

81. Young Negroes' Cooperative League, New York Local, "Program," n.d., Box 2, Folder 2, Ella Baker Papers.

82. "Red Letter Day: Programme of the Young Negroes [sic] Cooperative League of Columbia, S.C., at Allen University, Sunday, January 3, 1932," Box 2, Folder 2, Ella Baker Papers.

83. George Schuyler to "My Dear Fellow Cooperators," Nov. 1930, Box 2, Ella Baker Papers; Ransby, *Ella Baker and the Black Freedom Movement*, 89.

84. N.A., letterhead of Harlem's Own Cooperative, to the Board of Directors, Box 2, Folder 3, Ella Baker Papers.

85. For financial issues, see, e.g., George Schuyler to the Members of the Y.N.C.L., n.d., Box 2, Folder 2, Ella Baker Papers. For a surviving milk cooperative in New York City in 1939, Harry F. Edward to Dear Director, May 10,

1939, in Box 2, Folder 2, Ella Baker Papers; Ransby, *Ella Baker and the Black Freedom Movement*, 85.

86. Jacob L. Reddix, *A Voice Crying in the Wilderness: The Memoirs of Jacob L. Reddix* (Jackson: Univ. Press of Mississippi, 1974), 117–21, quote, 118; John Hope II, "Rochdale Cooperation Among Negroes," *Phylon* 1, no. 1 (1940): 40–42.

87. Reddix, *A Voice Crying in the Wilderness*, 117–21, quote, 119; Hope II, "Rochdale Cooperation Among Negroes," 40–42.

88. Hope II, "Rochdale Cooperation Among Negroes," 43–46. For other African American cooperatives during the 1930s, see Hope II, and Nembhard, *Collective Courage*, ch. 6.

89. Quoted in Hope II, "Rochdale Cooperation Among Negroes," 44.

90. For the history of the cooperative movement in the US, see Herbert Baxter Adams, *History of Cooperation in the United States*, Johns Hopkins University Studies in Historical and Political Science, Sixth Series (Baltimore: Johns Hopkins Univ. Press, 1888); Albert Sonnichsen, *Consumers' Cooperation* (New York: Macmillan, 1920); Joseph G. Knapp, *The Rise of American Cooperative Enterprise, 1620–1920* (Danville, IL: Interstate Printers and Publishers, 1969); Knapp, *The Advance of American Cooperative Enterprise, 1920–1945* (Danville, IL: Interstate Printers and Publishers, 1973); Du Bois, *Economic Co-operation Among Negro Americans*; John Curl, *For All the People: Uncovering the Hidden History of Cooperation, Cooperative Movements, and Communalism in America* (Oakland, CA: PM Press, 2009).

91. Hope II, "Rochdale Cooperation Among Negroes," 42; Grant, *Ella Baker*, 37.

92. Steve Leiken, *The Practical Utopians: American Workers and the Cooperative Movement in the Gilded Age* (Detroit: Wayne State Univ. Press, 2005); Claire Horner, "Producers' Co-operatives in the United States, 1845–1867," PhD diss., Univ. of Pittsburgh, 1992. For large networks of labor-sponsored cooperatives in Seattle in the 1910s and '20s, see Dana Frank, *Purchasing Power: Consumer Organizing, Gender, and the Seattle Labor Movement, 1919–1929* (New York: Cambridge Univ. Press, 1994), ch. 2.

93. Ellen Furlough, "French Consumer Capitalism, 1885–1930: From the 'Third Pillar' of Socialism to 'A Movement for All Consumers,'" in *Consumers Against Capitalism? Consumer Cooperation in Europe, North America, and Japan, 1840–1990*, ed. Ellen Furlough and Carl Strikwerda (New York: Rowman and Littlefield, 1994), 173–90, and other articles in the collection.

94. Clark Kerr, "Productive Enterprises of the Unemployed, 1931–1938," PhD diss., Univ. of California, Berkeley, 1939, statistics, 289.

95. Curl, *For All the People*, 170–72; Kerr, "Productive Enterprises of the Unemployed," 327–49, 659–99.

96. UXA (Unemployed Exchange Association), "Preliminary Application for Loans Authorized by Federal Emergency Relief Act of 1933," Aug. 14, 1933, in collection, Fieldnotes, etc. Concerning Self-Help and Consumer Cooperatives in the United States, 1930–1938, BANC MSS Z-R-3, Box 2, Folder 20, Bancroft Library, University of California, Berkeley, Berkeley, CA.

97. Clark Kerr and Paul S. Taylor, "The Self-Help Cooperatives in California," in *Essays in Social Economics in Honor of Jessica Blanche Peixotto*

(Berkeley: Univ. of California Press, 1935), 204; Kerr, "Productive Enterprises of the Unemployed," 327–49, 659–99.

98. "Along in February, 1933 . . ." untitled document re UXA in Fieldnotes, etc. Concerning Self-Help and Consumer Cooperatives, BANC MSS Z-R-3, Box 3, Folder 11.

99. UCCA, Document, Apr. 26, 1933, in Fieldnotes, etc. Concerning Self-Help and Consumer Cooperatives, BANC MSS Z-R-3, Box 2, Folder 20.

100. U.X.A. General School, "Lay It on The Table," n.d., in Fieldnotes, etc. Concerning Self-Help and Consumer Cooperatives, BANC MSS Z-R-3, Box 3, Folder 16.

101. George Knox Roth, "The Compton Unemployed Co-operative Relief Association: A Sociological Study," master's thesis, Univ. of Southern California, 1934, 33.

102. Roth, "The Compton Unemployed Co-operative Relief Association," 71.

103. "Self-Help Among the Unemployed in California," *Monthly Labor Review*, Dec. 1935, Serial no. R. 320, 6.

104. Kerr, "Productive Enterprises of the Unemployed," 394–95.

105. UCCA, Document, Apr. 26, 1933.

106. Roth, "The Compton Unemployed Co-operative Relief Association," 72.

107. E. L. Osborn, "An Opinion of the Causes for Cooperative Failures," n.d., in Fieldnotes, etc. Concerning Self-Help and Consumer Cooperatives, BANC MSS Z-R-3, Box 3, Folder 12.

108. Roth, "The Compton Unemployed Co-operative Relief Association," 171–72.

109. For Kansas City, see Hope II, "Rochdale Cooperation Among Negroes," 42–43.

110. Roth, "The Compton Unemployed Co-operative Relief Association," 138.

111. Roth, "The Compton Unemployed Co-operative Relief Association," 187–89.

112. Roth, "The Compton Unemployed Co-operative Relief Association," 138.

113. Roth, "The Compton Unemployed Co-operative Relief Association," 137.

114. Roth, "The Compton Unemployed Co-operative Relief Association," 136.

115. Kerr, "Productive Enterprises of the Unemployed," 680.

116. Kerr, "Productive Enterprises of the Unemployed," 666.

117. Kerr, "Productive Enterprises of the Unemployed," 666.

118. Roth, "The Compton Unemployed Co-operative Relief Association," 102–3.

119. W. Hicks, "Report on Canoga Park, Calif.," May 28, 1935, in Fieldnotes, etc. Concerning Self-Help and Consumer Cooperatives, BANC MSS Z-R-3. Box 3, Folder 4.

120. Hicks, "Report on Canoga Park, Calif."

121. Kerr, "Productive Enterprises of the Unemployed," 1122.

122. Kerr, "Productive Enterprises of the Unemployed," 1121–34.

123. Hicks, "Report on Canoga Park," Calif.; Reddix, *A Voice Crying in the Wilderness*, 118.

124. Constantine Panunzio, *Self-Help Cooperatives in Los Angeles* (Berkeley: Univ. of California Press, 1939); Roth, "The Compton Unemployed Co-operative Relief Association"; Kerr, "Productive Enterprises of the Unemployed," 82–326.

125. Kerr and Taylor, "The Self-Help Cooperatives in California," 199.

126. Kerr, "Productive Enterprises of the Unemployed," 179.

127. Kerr, "Productive Enterprises of the Unemployed," 179.

128. Kerr and Taylor, "The Self-Help Cooperatives in California," 204.

129. Panunzio, *Self-Help Cooperatives in Los Angeles*, 16.

130. "Self-Help Among the Unemployed in California," *Monthly Labor Review*, 6; "Report of E. L. Osborn," July 19, 1935, in Fieldnotes, etc. Concerning Self-Help and Consumer Cooperatives, BANC MSS Z-R-3, Box 3, Folder 17.

131. "Self-Help Among the Unemployed in California," *Monthly Labor Review*, 6.

132. Kerr, "Productive Enterprises of the Unemployed," 179–80.

133. Kerr and Taylor, "The Self-Help Cooperatives in California," 179.

134. Hope II, "Rochdale Cooperation Among Negroes," 42, 45.

135. Kerr and Taylor, "The Self-Help Cooperatives in California," 212.

136. Arthur Hillman, "The Unemployed Citizens' League of Seattle," *University of Washington Publications in the Social Sciences* 5, no. 3 (Feb. 1934), 204.

137. Kerr, "Productive Enterprises of the Unemployed," 114–22.

138. "Report of Halstead, Turning on House Gas & Lights," n.d., in Fieldnotes, etc. Concerning Self-Help and Consumer Cooperatives, BANC MSS Z-R-3, Box 3, Folder 5.

139. "Report of Halstead, Conscious Left Wing in Action in Co-ops," n.d., in Fieldnotes, etc. Concerning Self-Help and Consumer Cooperatives, BANC MSS Z-R-3, Box 3, Folder 17.

140. Laura Renata Martin, "'California's Unemployed Feed Themselves': Conservative Intervention in the Los Angeles Cooperative Movement, 1931–1934," *Pacific Historical Review* 82, no. 1 (2012): 33–62. See also Walter Furth, "Report," Jan. 13, 1934, pp. 12–13, in Fieldnotes, etc. Concerning Self-Help and Consumer Cooperatives, BANC MSS Z-R-3, Box 3, Folder 4 and Box 1, Folder 5; Kerr, "Productive Enterprises of the Unemployed," 125, 151.

141. Martin, "'California's Unemployed Feed Themselves,'" 52.

142. Martin, "'California's Unemployed Feed Themselves,'" 47–48.

143. Quoted in Martin, "'California's Unemployed Feed Themselves,'" 49–51.

144. Martin, "'California's Unemployed Feed Themselves,'" 50–51.

145. Quoted in Martin, "'California's Unemployed Feed Themselves,'" 53–54; Dana Frank, *Buy American: The Untold Story of Economic Nationalism* (Boston: Beacon Press, 1999), 60. Donald Trump, in his inaugural speech, copied one of Hearst's slogans exactly: "We will follow two simple rules: Buy American and hire American." Frank, "Our History Shows There's a Dark Side to 'Buy American,'" *Washington Post*, Jan. 20, 2017.

146. Quoted in Martin, "'California's Unemployed Feed Themselves,'" 54.

147. Quoted in Martin, "'California's Unemployed Feed Themselves,'" 55–56.

148. Quoted in Martin, "'California's Unemployed Feed Themselves,'" 55.

149. Martin, "'California's Unemployed Feed Themselves,'" 37, 55–57.

150. Kerr and Taylor, "The Self-Help Cooperatives in California," 4. In a one-page prefatory summary he phrased his conclusions even more bluntly: "Influence on social attitude[:] Activism and organizing energies of participants were directed toward efficient production rather than protest." "Dissertation: Productive Enterprises of the Unemployed, 1931–38," frontispiece to Kerr, "Productive Enterprises of the Unemployed."

151. Paul S. Taylor and Clark Kerr, "Whither Self-Help?" *Survey Graphic* 23, no. 7 (July 1934): 348.

152. Paul S. Taylor and Clark Kerr, "Putting the Unemployed at Productive Labor," *Annals of the American Association of Political and Social Science* 176, no. 1 (1934): 3. For another example of their anti-left attitudes, see Taylor and Kerr, "Whither Self-Help?" *Survey Graphic*.

153. Kerr and Taylor, "The Self-Help Cooperatives in California," 207; Taylor and Kerr, "Putting the Unemployed at Productive Labor," biographies of authors, 110.

154. Reddix, *A Voice in the Wilderness*, 122–23, 128–29.

155. Linda Gordon, *Dorothea Lange: A Life Beyond Limits* (New York: Norton, 2009), 156–59; Taylor and Kerr, "Putting the Unemployed at Productive Labor," biographies of authors, 110.

156. Clark Kerr and Arthur Harris, "Self-Help Cooperatives in California," Bureau of Public Administration, Univ. of California, Berkeley, *Legislative Problems*, no. 9, May 8, 1939, 16. For an overview of California cooperatives and the impact of the New Deal, see also Taylor and Kerr, "Whither Self-Help?"

157. Kerr and Taylor, "The Self-Help Cooperatives in California," 208. For the availability of funding, see 210–11.

158. Hope II, "Rochdale Cooperation Among Negroes," 44.

159. Upton Sinclair, *Co-op: A Novel of Living Together* (Pasadena, CA: Upton Sinclair, 1936), quoted in Curl, *For All the People*, 182.

160. Taylor and Kerr, "Putting the Unemployed at Productive Labor."

161. Curl, *For All the People*, 181–82.

162. Panunzio, *Self-Help Cooperatives in Los Angeles*, 117.

163. Kerr and Harris, "Self-Help Cooperatives in California," 4.

164. Kerr and Harris, "Self-Help Cooperatives in California," 3.

165. *Wilkes-Barre Times Leader*, Sept. 29, 1936; *Knoxville Journal*, Sept. 29, 1936.

166. Roy Rosenzweig, "Organizing the Unemployed: The Early Years of the Great Depression," *Radical America* 10, no. 4 (July–Aug. 1976), 37–60; Daniel J. Leab, "'United We Eat . . .': The Out-of-Work, the Unemployed Councils, and the Communists, 1930–1933," master's thesis, Columbia University, 1934; James J. Lorence, *Organizing the Unemployed: Community and Union Activists in the Industrial Heartland* (Albany: State Univ. of New York Press, 1996); Lorence, *The Unemployed People's Movement: Leftists, Liberals, and Labor in Georgia, 1929–1941* (Athens: Univ. of Georgia Press, 2009); Randi Storch, *Red Chicago: American Communism at Its Grassroots, 1928–35* (Urbana: Univ. of

Illinois Press, 2007); Mark Naison, "From Eviction Resistance to Rent Control: Tenant Activism in the Great Depression," in Ronald Lawson, ed., *The Tenant Movement in New York City, 1904–1984* (New Brunswick, NJ: Rutgers Univ. Press, 1986), 94–133; Naison, *Communists in Harlem During the Great Depression* (Urbana: Univ. of Illinois Press, 1983); Mark Wild, *Street Meetings: Multiethnic Neighborhoods in Early Twentieth-Century Los Angeles* (Berkeley: Univ. of California Press, 2005), ch. 7; Chris Wright, *Popular Radicalism and the Unemployed in Chicago During the Great Depression* (New York: Anthem Press, 2022).

167. "Program on Unemployed Work," Oct. 3, 1932, Box 3, Folder 20, Clara Michelson Papers, TAM.240, Tamiment Library and Robert F. Wagner Archive, New York University.

168. "How to Form Block Committees," n.d., Box 3, Folder 20, Clara Michelson Papers, TAM.240, Tamiment Library and Robert F. Wagner Archive, New York University.

169. Terkel, *Hard Times*, 119; Gilpin's interview was published under a pseudonym, "Larry Van Deusen," that Terkel invented for him. Interview by the author with Toni Gilpin, Dec. 28, 2022.

170. Zaragosa Vargas, *Labor Rights Are Civil Rights: Mexican American Workers in Twentieth-Century America* (Princeton, NJ: Princeton Univ. Press, 2005), 1229–30; Justin Akers Chacón, *Radicals in the Barrio: Magonistas, Socialists, Wobblies, and Communists in the Mexican American Working Class* (Chicago: Haymarket Books, 2018), 456. For multiethnic unemployed organizing in Los Angeles, see Wild, *Street Meetings*, ch. 7.

171. *Washington Post*, Mar. 6, 7, 1930; Diane Bernard, "In 1930 Blacks and Whites Protested Unemployment Together. Police Attacked Them," *Washington Post*, Mar. 6, 2021.

172. *Washington Post*, Mar. 6, 1930.

173. For the video, see Bernard, "In 1930 Blacks and Whites Protested Unemployment Together."

174. *Washington Post*, Mar. 7, 1930; Los Angeles quote from Christina Heatherton, *Arise! Global Radicalism in the Era of the Mexican Revolution* (Berkeley: Univ. of California Press, 2022), 139; for the Los Angeles protest, see also Wild, *Street Meetings*, 187–88.

175. *New York Times*, Mar. 7, 1930.

176. *New York Times*, Mar. 7, 1930; *New York Daily News*, Mar. 7, 1930; Harvey Klehr, *The Heyday of American Communism: The Depression Decade* (New York: Basic Books, 1984), 33–34.

177. *New York Times*, Mar. 7, 1930.

178. The classic study of the Communist Party in the US remains Theodore Draper, *The Roots of American Communism* (New York: Viking, 1957). For the 1930s, another useful overview is Klehr, *The Heyday of American Communism*. Membership estimates: Klehr, 91.

179. Draper, *The Roots of American Communism*; for the appeal of the Party, see Vivian Gornick, *The Romance of American Communism* (New York: Basic Books, 1978); and Nell Irvin Painter, *The Narrative of Hosea Hudson: His Life as a Negro Communist in the South* (Cambridge, MA: Harvard Univ. Press, 1979). For the Communist Party in Birmingham, see Robin D. G. Kelley,

Hammer and Hoe: Alabama Communists During the Great Depression (Chapel Hill: Univ. of North Carolina Press, 1990), ch. 6.

180. Painter, "Nell Painter's Introduction," in *The Narrative of Hosea Hudson*, 1–44; Kelley, *Hammer and Hoe*, ch. 6; James Goodman, *Stories of Scottsboro* (New York: Pantheon Books, 1994); Dan T. Carter, *Scottsboro: A Tragedy of the American South* (Baton Rouge: Louisiana State Univ. Press, 1969).

181. Painter, "Nell Painter's Introduction"; Kelley, *Hammer and Hoe*, ch. 6; Goodman, *Stories of Scottsboro*; Carter, *Scottsboro*.

182. Kelley, *Hammer and Hoe*, 20.

183. Josephine Fowler, *Japanese and Chinese Immigrant Activists: Organizing in American and International Communist Movements, 1919–1933* (New Brunswick, NJ: Rutgers Univ. Press, 2007); Scott Kurashige, *The Shifting Grounds of Race: Black and Japanese Americans in the Making of Multiethnic Los Angeles* (Princeton, NJ: Princeton Univ. Press, 2008), 77–84, 138–39; Wild, *Street Meetings*; Vargas, *Labor Rights Are Civil Rights*; Chacón, *Radicals in the Barrio*.

184. Fowler, *Japanese and Chinese Immigrant Activists*, 161–62, 194, and throughout. For Japanese in the Communist Party, see also Karl G. Yoneda, *Ganbatte: Sixty-Year Struggle of a Kibei Worker* (Los Angeles: Resource Development and Publications, Asian American Studies Center, Univ. of California, Los Angeles, 1983); Vivian McGuckin Raineri, *The Red Angel: The Life and Times of Elaine Black Yoneda, 1906–1988* (New York: International Publishers, 1991).

185. Wild, *Street Meetings*, 191.

186. Membership estimate: Klehr, *The Heyday of American Communism*, 9.

187. For African American points of view on the Communist Party, see Painter, *The Narrative of Hosea Hudson*; Harry Haywood, *Black Bolshevik: Autobiography of an Afro-American Communist* (Chicago: Liberator Press, 1978); Angelo Herndon, *Let Me Live* (New York: Random House, 1937); Kelley, *Hammer and Hoe*; LaShawn Harris, "Running with the Reds: African American Women and the Communist Party During the Great Depression, *Journal of African American History* 94, no. 1 (2009): 21–43; Erik S. McDuffie, *Sojourning for Freedom: Black Women, American Communism, and the Making of Black Left Feminism* (Durham, NC: Duke Univ. Press, 2011).

188. Painter, *The Narrative of Hosea Hudson*, 21.

189. Painter, *The Narrative of Hosea Hudson*, 22.

190. Klehr, *The Heyday of American Communism*, 161–65.

191. Yet, as Annelise Orleck has underscored, during the 1930s female Party members worked with non-Communist, grassroots housewives' organizations. Working-class housewives who were not themselves in the Party joined its housing, relief, and other protests. Orleck, "'We Are That Mythical Thing Called the Public': Militant Housewives During the Great Depression," *Feminist Studies* 19, no. 1 (Spring 1993): 147–72. For more on housewives' activism during the 1930s, see Emily E. LaBarbera-Twarog, *Politics of the Pantry: Housewives, Food, and Consumer Protest in Twentieth-Century America* (New York: Oxford Univ. Press, 2017).

192. For women in the Communist Party, see Harris, "Running with the Reds"; Elsa Dixler, "'The Woman Question': Women and the American

Communist Party, 1929–1940," PhD diss., Yale University, 1974; Ella Kay Trimberger, "Women in the Old and New Left: The Evolution of a Politics of Personal Life," *Feminist Studies* 5, no. 3 (Autumn 1979): 431–50: Kelley, *Hammer and Hoe*; McDuffie, *Sojourning for Freedom*; Gornick, *The Romance of American Communism*; Charisse Burden-Stelly and Jodi Dean, *Organize, Fight, Win: Black Communist Women's Political Writing* (New York: Verso Books, 2022). For biographies and autobiographies, see Kim Chernin, *In My Mother's House* (New Haven, CT: Ticknor and Fields, 1983); Peggy Dennis, *The Autobiography of an American Communist: A Personal View of a Political Life, 1925–1975* (Westport, CT: L. Hill, 1977); Carol Boyce Davies, *Left of Karl Marx: The Political Life of Black Communist Claudia Jones* (Durham, NC: Duke Univ. Press, 2008); Ella Reeve Bloor, *We Are Many: An Autobiography* (New York, International Publishers, 1940); Dorothy Healey and Maurice Isserman, *Dorothy Healey Remembers: A Life in the American Communist Party* (New York: Oxford Univ. Press, 1990).

193. Naison, in "From Eviction Resistance to Rent Control," estimates there were "hundreds, perhaps thousands" of eviction protests in New York City alone. For a map of over seven hundred unemployed protests reported in the Communist Party's paper, the *Daily Worker*, see University of Washington Mapping American Social Movements Project, "Unemployed Protests 1930s," https://depts.washington.edu/moves/unemployed_map.shtml.

194. Edmund Wilson, "Detroit Motors," *New Republic*, no. 66 (Mar. 25, 1931), 145.

195. "1970 Oral History with Katherine Hyndman," conducted by Staughton Lynd, 1970, Libcom, https://libcom.org/article/1970-oral-history-interview -katherine-hyndman; *Union Maids*, directed and produced by Jim Klein, Julia Reichert, and Miles Mogulescu, New Day Films, 1976.

196. "1970 Oral History with Katherine Hyndman."

197. "1970 Oral History with Katherine Hyndman."

198. Painter, *The Narrative of Hosea Hudson*, 142.

199. Terkel, *Hard Times*, 453.

200. Quoted in Mark Naison, "The Communist Party in Harlem: 1928–1936," PhD diss., Columbia University, 1976.

201. Terkel, *Hard Times*, 45.

202. Terkel, *Hard Times*, 45.

203. For the classic exposition of the concept of the moral economy, see E. P. Thompson, "The Moral Economy of the English Crowd in the Eighteenth Century," *Past and Present*, no. 50 (Feb. 1971): 76–136.

204. Frances Fox Piven and Richard Cloward, *Poor People's Movements: Why They Succeed, How They Fail* (New York: Pantheon, 1977), 57.

205. Terkel, *Hard Times*, 119.

206. Wild, *Street Meetings*, 190–91.

207. Storch, *Red Chicago*, 99–100.

208. Storch, *Red Chicago*, 100–101.

209. Hyndman, in *Union Maids*.

210. Chernin, *In My Mother's House*. 94.

211. Chernin, *In My Mother's House*, 94–95.

212. Naison, "From Eviction Resistance to Rent Control."

213. Painter, *The Narrative of Hosea Hudson*, 143–44.

214. Painter, *The Narrative of Hosea Hudson*, 143–44. For Black women's willingness to use violence against relief workers in Birmingham, see Harris, "Running with the Reds," 29.

215. Painter, *The Narrative of Hosea Hudson*, 144–45. For relations between police and Communists in the Birmingham unemployed movement in these years, see Kelley, *Hammer and Hoe*, 31–33.

216. LaShawn Harris, "Running with the Reds," 29; Melissa Ford, *A Brick and a Bible: Black Women's Activism in the Midwest During the Great Depression* (Carbondale: Southern Illinois Univ. Press, 2022), 140–60, quote, 148.

217. Terkel, *Hard Times*, 466.

218. Terkel, *Hard Times*, 454.

219. James Weinstein, *The Decline of Socialism in America, 1912–1925* (New York: Vintage, 1969), 116–18.

220. Roy Rosenzweig, "'Socialism in Our Time': The Socialist Party and the Unemployed, 1929–1936," *Labor History* 20, no. 4 (1979): 485–509; Storch, *Red Chicago*, 113.

221. Roy Rosenzweig, "Radicals and the Jobless: The Musteites and the Unemployed Leagues, 1932–1936," *Labor History* 16 (Winter 1975): 52–77.

222. Rosenzweig, "Radicals and the Jobless," 60.

223. Hillman, "The Unemployed Citizens' League of Seattle," 181–270; Terry R. Willis, "Unemployed Citizens of Seattle, 1900–1939: Hulet Wells, Seattle Labor, and the Struggle for Economy Security," PhD diss., Univ. of Washington, 1997; *Unemployed Citizen*, 1932–33; James Gregory, "Unemployed Citizens League and Poverty Activism," Univ. of Washington Civil Rights and Labor History Consortium, 2020, https://depts.washington.edu/depress/Unemployed_Citizens_League.shtmlLINK; *The Vanguard*, Sept. 1931; Rosenzweig, "Radicals and the Jobless."

224. *Vanguard*, Feb. 1932.

225. E.g., Hillman, "The Unemployed Citizens' League of Seattle," 191.

226. Gregory, "Unemployed Citizens League and Poverty Activism"; *Vanguard*, Sept. 1931.

227. A 1932 article in the *Unemployed Citizen*, the successor to the *The Vanguard*, asserted "Children Should Have American Standard," and referred to the concept of the "American standard of living," popular at the time, as contrasted to a purported "Asiatic standard of living," in which Chinese people were allegedly happy to "live on a bowl of rice"—which white Americans, in this cliché, wouldn't accept. *Unemployed Citizen*, Dec. 16, 1932.

228. Willis, "Unemployed Citizens of Seattle," 202.

229. On another occasion, the *The Vanguard* did explicitly denounce an attack against Filipino workers in the White River Valley for accepting lower wages than white men had been offered, and it emphasized "the need for more intensive organization of all groups of workers." The paper blamed farmers, landowners, and profit-seeking steamship companies for the situation. It nonetheless referred to Filipino workers as "the gullible brown boys," and singled out "Japanese farmers" for criticism. *The Vanguard*, May–June 1930. For the Scandinavians, Frank, *Purchasing Power*, 42.

230. Hillman, "The Unemployed Citizens' League of Seattle," 209–10, 216–43; Willis, "Unemployed Citizens of Seattle," 228–58.

231. Rosenzweig, "Organizing the Unemployed," 46–47; Klehr, *Heyday of American Communism*, ch. 15.

232. Claudia Goldin, *Understanding the Gender Gap: An Economic History of American Women* (New York: Oxford Univ. Press, 1990), 17.

233. For a reformulation, see Michael Denning, "Wageless Life," *New Left Review*, Second Series, no. 66 (Nov.–Dec. 2010): 81.

234. Piven and Cloward, *Poor People's Movements*, 63–64.

235. Piven and Cloward, *Poor People's Movements*, 62; Bernstein, *The Lean Years*, ch. 7.

236. David A. Shannon, *The Great Depression* (Englewood Cliffs, NJ: Prentice-Hall, 1960), 48.

237. Bernstein, *The Lean Years*, 468–74, quote, 287.

238. Piven and Cloward, *Poor People's Movements*, 42.

239. Frances Fox Piven and Richard Cloward, *Regulating the Poor: The Functions of Public Welfare* (New York: Pantheon, 1971), 43.

240. Molly Ladd-Taylor, *Mother-Work: Women, Child Welfare, and the State, 1890–1930* (Urbana: Univ. of Illinois Press, 1994); Gwendolyn Mink, *The Wages of Motherhood: Inequality in the Welfare State, 1917–1942* (Ithaca, NY: Cornell Univ. Press, 1993), ch. 2.

241. Alice Walker, "The Revenge of Hannah Kemhuff," *Ms.*, July 1973, repr. in Walker, *In Love & Trouble: Stories of Black Women* (New York: Harcourt Brace Jovanovich, 1974), 60–80. Walker recounts her mother's real-life experience that inspired the story in "Zora Neale Hurston's *Their Eyes Were Watching God*," C-SPAN, video, Mar. 28, 2012, https://www.c-span.org/video/?305212-1/zora-neale-hurstons-their-eyes-watching-god.

242. Piven and Cloward, *Regulating the Poor*, 62.

243. Piven and Cloward, *Regulating the Poor*, 61–68; Piven and Cloward, *Poor People's Movements*, 60.

244. Paul Dickson and Thomas B. Allen, *The Bonus Army: An American Epic* (New York: Walker and Company, 2004); Bernstein, *The Lean Years*, ch. 13; W. W. Waters as told to William C. White, *B.E.F: The Whole Story of the Bonus Army* (New York: Arno Press and New York Times, 1969); Felix Morrow, *The Bonus March* (New York: International Publishers, 1932).

245. Dickson and Allen, *The Bonus Army*, 127–30.

246. Bernstein, *The Lean Years*, 453–54; Dickson and Allen, *The Bonus Army*, 162–77.

247. Dickson and Allen, *The Bonus Army*, 177–83; Bernstein, *The Lean Years*, 454.

248. Dickson and Allen, *The Bonus Army*, 184–92; Bernstein, *The Lean Years*, 454.

249. The literature on the New Deal is too vast to summarize here. A good basic starting point remains William E. Leuchtenberg, *Franklin D. Roosevelt and the New Deal, 1932–1940* (New York: Harper and Row, 1963). For the First New Deal, see Anthony J. Badger, *FDR: The First Hundred Days* (New York: Hill and Wang, 2008).

250. For an accessible overview, see Nancy E. Rose, *Put to Work: Relief Programs in the Great Depression* (New York: Cornerstone Books, 1994).

251. Piven and Cloward, *Regulating the Poor*, 20–84.

252. Robert C. Lieberman, *Shifting the Color Line: Race and the American Welfare State* (Cambridge, MA: Harvard Univ. Press, 1998); Ira Katznelson, *When Affirmative Action Was White: An Untold History of Racial Inequality in Twentieth-Century America* (New York: W. W. Norton, 2005), 35–52; Cybelle Fox, *Three Worlds of Relief: Race, Immigration, and the American Welfare State from the Progressive Era to the New Deal* (Princeton, NJ: Princeton Univ. Press, 2012), 191–95; for individual stories of the denial of relief to African Americans, see Stephanie J. Shaw, "Using the WPA Ex-Slave Narratives to Study the Impact of the Great Depression," *Journal of Southern History* 69, no. 3 (Aug. 2003): 623–58. For the deep origins of race, gender, and the welfare state, see Gwendolyn Mink, "The Lady and the Tramp: Gender, Race, and the Origins of American Welfare State," in Linda Gordon, ed., *Women, the State, and Welfare* (Madison: Univ. of Wisconsin Press, 1990), 92–122.

253. For an extensive analysis of Mexicans and the relief system in the 1930s, see Fox, *Three Worlds of Relief*. For denial of relief, see also John Weber, *From South Texas to the Nation: The Exploitation of Mexican Labor in the Twentieth Century* (Chapel Hill: Univ. of North Carolina Press, 2015), ch. 5; for repatriation, see Abraham Hoffman, *Unwanted Mexican Americans in the Great Depression: Repatriation Pressures, 1929–1939* (Tucson: Univ. of Arizona Press, 1974); Francisco E. Balderrama and Raymond Rodríguez, *Decade of Betrayal: Mexican Repatriation in the 1930s* (Albuquerque: Univ. of New Mexico Press, 2006); R. Reynolds McKay, "Texas Mexican Repatriation During the Great Depression," PhD diss., Univ. of Oklahoma, 1982; Camille Guerin-Gonzales, *Mexican Workers and American Dreams: Immigration, Repatriation, and California Farm Labor, 1900–1930* (New Brunswick, NJ: Rutgers Univ. Press, 1994).

254. Gordon, *Women, the State, and Welfare*; Gordon, *Pitied but Not Entitled: Single Mothers and the History of Welfare, 1890–1935* (New York: Free Press, 1994).

255. Lois Scharf, *To Work and to Wed: Female Employment, Feminism, and the Great Depression* (Westport, CT: Greenwood Press, 1980); Kessler-Harris, *Out to Work*, ch. 9.

256. "Employment Covered Under the Social Security Program, 1935–84," *Social Security Bulletin* 48, no. 4 (Apr. 1985): 35–38; Katznelson, *When Affirmative Action Was White*, ch. 3.

257. Mink, *The Wages of Motherhood*, ch. 6; Gordon, *Pitied But Not Entitled*; Mink, "The Lady and the Tramp"; Barbara J. Nelson, "The Origins of the Two-Channel Welfare State: Workmen's Compensation and Mother's Aid," in Gordon, *Women, the State, and Welfare*, 123–52; Dorothy Roberts, *Killing the Black Body: Race, Reproduction, and the Meaning of Liberty* (New York: Vintage, 1997), 203–8; Robert C. Lieberman, *Shifting the Color Line: Race and the American Welfare State* (Cambridge, MA: Harvard Univ. Press, 1998), ch. 4. For federal unemployment insurance, see Lieberman, *Shifting the Color Line*, ch. 5.

258. "Employment Covered Under the Social Security Program, 1985," *Social Security Bulletin* 51, no. 10 (Oct. 1988): 52; Lieberman, *Shifting the Color Line*, ch. 3.

259. For the expansion of Social Security's old-age pensions, see Jill Quadagno, *The Expansion of Old-Age Security: Class and Politics in the American Welfare State* (Chicago: Univ. of Chicago Press, 1988). The National Labor Relations Act's broad exclusions, however, almost all still remain. See "Jurisdictional Standards," National Labor Relations Board, n.d., https://www.nlrb.gov/about-nlrb/rights-we-protect/the-law/jurisdictional-standards. For a list of expanded, but still limited, coverage under the Fair Labor Standards Act, see "Fact Sheet #14: Coverage Under the Fair Labor Standards Act (FSLA)," Wages and Hour Division, US Department of Labor, July 2009, https://www.dol.gov/agencies/whd/fact-sheets/14-flsa-coverage.

260. Jia Tolentino, "What Mutual Aid Can Do During a Pandemic," *New Yorker*, May 11, 2020; Dean Spade, *Mutual Aid: Building Solidarity During This Crisis (and the Next)* (London: Verso, 2020).

261. Maira Khwaja et al., "Our Year of Mutual Aid," *New York Times*, Mar. 11, 2021.

262. For mutual aid, COVID, and crises, see Spade, *Mutual Aid*; Tolentino, "What Mutual Aid Can Do During a Pandemic."

263. Rebecca Solnit, *A Paradise Built in Hell: The Extraordinary Communities That Arise in Disaster* (New York: Viking, 2009).

264. Robin D. G. Kelley, "Looking Backward: The Limits of Self-Help Ideology," in *Yo' Mama's DisFUNKtional: Fighting the Culture Wars in Urban America* (Boston: Beacon Press, 1997), 81; Kelley, "Twenty Years of Freedom Dreams," *Boston Review*, Aug. 1, 2022; Kelley, "Looking Forward, Looking Back . . . Ten Years Later," introduction to the Tenth Anniversary Edition, in *Yo' Mama's DisFUNKtional: Fighting the Culture Wars in Urban America* (Boston: Beacon Press, 2007), xii–xiii.

265. Antonio Machado, "Caminante, No Hay Camino," in *Campos de Castilla* (Madrid: Renacimiento, 1912), repr. in Biblioteca Nacional Miguel de Cervantes, https://www.cervantesvirtual.com/obra-visor/campos-de-castilla-983795/html/53182a83-438f-4e63-8093-1a1e1ffb0861_2.html. Paulo Freire and Myles Horton paid homage to the poem in the title of an extended conversation with each other, published as Myles Horton, Paulo Freire, Brenda Bell, John Gaventa, and John Marshall Peters, *We Make the Road By Walking: Conversations on Education and Social Change* (Philadelphia: Temple Univ. Press, 1990).

266. Dodai Stewart, "A Secret Society Tied to Underground Railroad Fights to Save Its Home," *New York Times*, Dec. 20, 2022.

267. Stewart, "A Secret Society Tied to Underground Railroad"; "Help Preserve Historic Black Women's Aid Group," https://www.gofundme.com/f/f9fzn-help-preserve-historic-black-womens-aid-group.

CHAPTER TWO: A TALE OF TWO CARAVANS

1. Francisco E. Balderrama and Raymond Rodríguez, *Decade of Betrayal: Mexican Repatriation in the 1930s* (Albuquerque: Univ. of New Mexico Press, 2006); Abraham Hoffman, *Unwanted Mexican Americans in the Great*

Depression: Repatriation Pressures, 1929–1939 (Tucson: Univ. of Arizona Press, 1974); R. Reynolds McKay, "Texas Mexican Repatriation During the Great Depression," PhD diss., Univ. of Oklahoma, 1982; Camille Guerin-Gonzales, *Mexican Workers and American Dreams: Immigration, Repatriation, and California Farm Labor, 1900–1930* (New Brunswick, NJ: Rutgers Univ. Press, 1994); Mercedes Carreras de Velasco, *Los Mexicanos que devolvió la crisis, 1929–1932* (Tlatelolco, Mexico, DF: Secretaría de Relaciones Exteriores, 1974); Dennis Nodín Valdés, "Mexican Revolutionary Nationalism and Repatriation During the Great Depression," *Mexican Studies/Estudios Mexicanos* 4, no. 4 (Winter 1988): 1–23; Marilyn D. Rhinehart and Thomas H. Kreneck, "'In the Shadow of Uncertainty': Texas Mexicans and Repatriation in Houston During the Great Depression," *Houston Review* (1988): 21–33; George J. Sánchez, *Becoming Mexican American: Ethnicity, Culture and Identity in Chicano Los Angeles, 1900–1945* (New York: Oxford Univ. Press, 1993), ch. 10; Zaragosa Vargas, *Labor Rights Are Civil Rights: Mexican American Workers in Twentieth-Century America* (Princeton, NJ: Princeton Univ. Press, 2005), 46–61; Gilbert G. Gonzáles, *Mexican Consuls and Labor Organizing: Imperial Politics in the American Southwest* (Austin: Univ. of Texas Press, 1999), 31–36; Gabriela F. Arredondo, *Mexican Chicago: Race, Ethnicity, and Nation, 1916–39* (Urbana: Univ. of Illinois Press, 2008), 96–100; Christine Marin, "Always a Struggle: Mexican Americans in Miami, Arizona, 1909–1951," PhD diss., Arizona State Univ., 2005, ch. 3. For estimates of total numbers repatriated, see Balderrama and Rodríguez, *Decade of Betrayal*, 149, 265–66. For a fictionalized story of repatriation based on the author's family, see Santos C. Vega, *The Worm in My Tomato: A Novel Inspired by a True Story About the Repatriation of a Mexican American Family by the United States Government* (Tempe, AZ: Community Documentation Press, 2018).

2. Photograph no. 3744-B and text on back side of photograph, Box 33, W. D. Smithers Collection of Photographs, Harry Ransom Center, University of Texas at Austin.

3. Quotes, *La Prensa* (San Antonio, TX), Oct. 10 and 20, 1931. Translations by the author. For the Karnes City caravan, McKay, "Texas Mexican Repatriation During the Great Depression," 365–86; *La Prensa*, Sept. 27, 29, 30; Oct. 2, 3, 4, 7, 8, 9, 10, 11, 12, 13, 14, 15, 16, 17, 18, 19, 20, 21, 22, 23, 28, 1931; Hoffman, *Unwanted Mexican Americans in the Great Depression*, photograph of caravan, 131.

4. *San Antonio Express*, Oct. 18, 1931.

5. *San Antonio Express*, Oct. 19, 1931.

6. *San Antonio Express*, Oct. 19, 1931; *Laredo Times*, Oct. 19, 1931, cited in McKay, "Texas Mexican Repatriation During the Great Depression," 454.

7. *San Antonio Express*, Oct. 19, 1931.

8. *La Prensa*, Oct. 20, 1931.

9. *Laredo Times*, Oct. 19, 1931, cited in McKay, "Texas Mexican Repatriation During the Great Depression," 456.

10. *La Prensa*, Oct. 21, 1931.

11. "INS Records for 1930s Mexican Repatriations," US Citizenship and Immigration Services, https://www.uscis.gov/about-us/our-history/history-office -and-library/featured-stories-from-the-uscis-history-office-and-library/ins -records-for-1930s-mexican-repatriations.

12. James N. Gregory, *American Exodus: The Dust Bowl Migration and Okie Culture in California* (New York: Oxford Univ. Press, 1989); Walter J. Stein, *California and the Dust Bowl Migration* (Westport, CT: Greenwood Press, 1973).

13. Interview with Boyd Monford Morgan by Stacey Jagels, May 2, 1981, Interview #131, 1, 13–14, Oral History Program, California Odyssey: The 1930s Migration to the Southern San Joaquin Valley, Historical Research Center, California State University, Bakersfield (hereafter California Odyssey Oral History project).

14. Dorothea Lange, Paul S. Taylor, Howard M. Levin, and Katherine Northrup, *Dorothea Lange: Farm Security Administration Photographs, 1935–1939: From the Library of Congress* (Glencoe, IL: Text-Fiche Press, 1980).

15. John Steinbeck, *The Grapes of Wrath* (New York: Viking Press, 1939).

16. *The Grapes of Wrath*, dir. John Ford, Twentieth Century-Fox, 1940.

17. Use of "exodus": *La Prensa*, Oct. 18, 1931; Dorothea Lange and Paul Schuster Taylor, *American Exodus: A Record of Human Erosion* (New York: Reynal & Hitchcock, 1939); Gregory, *American Exodus*.

18. US Census Bureau, Population of the Minor Races by Nativity, for the United States: 1900 to 1930, *Fifteenth Census of the United States: 1930*, vol. 2, *Population*, General Report, Statistics by Subjects (Washington, DC: US Government Printing Office, 1933), 34, https://www.census.gov/library/publications /1933/dec/1930a-vol-02-population.html.

19. Paul S. Taylor, *Mexican Labor in the United States*, vol. 1 (Berkeley: Univ. of California Press, 1930); Rodolfo Acuña, *Occupied America: A History of Chicanos*, 2nd ed. (New York: Harper & Row, 1981); Manuel Gamio, *Mexican Immigration to the United States: A Study of Human Migration and Adjustment* (Chicago: Univ. of Chicago Press, 1930); Carey McWilliams, *North from Mexico: The Spanish-Speaking People of the United States* (Philadelphia: J. P. Lippincott, 1949); McWilliams, *Factories in the Field: The Story of Migratory Farm Labor in California* (Boston: Little, Brown, 1939); Sánchez, *Becoming Mexican American*; David Montejano, *Anglos and Mexicans in the Making of Texas, 1836–1986* (Austin: Univ. of Texas Press, 1987); David G. Gutiérrez, *Walls and Mirrors: Mexican Americans, Mexican Immigrants, and the Politics of Ethnicity* (Berkeley: Univ. of California Press, 1995); Emilio Zamora, *The World of the Mexican Worker in Texas* (College Station: Texas A&M Univ. Press, 1993); Dennis Noldín Valdés, *Al Norte: Agricultural Workers in the Great Lakes Region, 1917–1970* (Austin: Univ. of Texas Press, 1991); Arredondo, *Mexican Chicago*; Guerin-Gonzales, *Mexican Workers and American Dreams*; Vargas, *Labor Rights Are Civil Rights*; Cletus E. Daniel, *Bitter Harvest: A History of California Farmworkers, 1870–1941* (Berkeley: Univ. of California Press, 1981).

20. Quoted in *La Prensa*, Oct. 17, 1931.

21. "A Caravan of Sorrows," *El Universal*, Mar. 29, 1927, translated and reprinted in *Living Age* 333 (July–Dec. 1927): 870–71.

22. Sánchez, *Becoming Mexican American*, 18.

23. Taylor, *Mexican Labor in the United States*, vol. 1; Valdés, *Al Norte*; McWilliams, *Factories in the Field*; McWilliams, *North from Mexico*; Arredondo, *Mexican Chicago*, 97; Sánchez, *Becoming Mexican American*, 45, 314n3; Gutiérrez, *Walls and Mirrors*, 45.

24. Sánchez, *Becoming Mexican American*, 133; Balderrama and Rodríguez, *Decade of Betrayal*, 119; Kelly Lytle-Hernández, *Migra! A History of the US Border Patrol* (Berkeley: Univ. of California Press, 2010), chs. 1–4; Mae M. Ngai, *Impossible Subjects: Illegal Aliens and the Making of Modern America* (Princeton, NJ: Princeton Univ. Press, 2004), chs. 1–2; Erika Lee, *America for Americans: A History of Xenophobia in the United States* (New York: Basic Books, 2019), ch. 5; Alexandra Minna Stern, *Eugenic Nation: Faults and Frontiers of Better Breeding in America* (Berkeley: Univ. of California Press, 2005), 57–81.

25. Zamora, *The World of the Mexican Worker in Texas*, ch. 4; Gutiérrez, *Walls and Mirrors*, 95–99; Arredondo, *Mexican Chicago*, 92–93, 170. For another society of the same name, in Indiana, see Eva Mendieta, "Celebrating Mexican Culture and Lending a Helping Hand: Indiana Harbor's *Sociedad Mutualista Benito Juárez*, 1924–1957," *Indiana Magazine of History*, no. 108 (Dec. 2012): 311–44.

26. Zamora, *The World of the Mexican Worker in Texas*, 86–87.

27. Emilia Castañeda de Valenciana, interview by Christine Valenciana, Sept. 8, 1971, Oral History No. 700, California State University, Fullerton, Oral History Program, Mexican American Project, Repatriation of the 1930s, 16. Courtesy of Lawrence DeGraaf Center for Oral and Public History, California State University, Fullerton.

28. Arredondo, *Mexican Chicago*, 90–93, 100, 157; Sánchez, *Becoming Mexican American*, 4, 222, 248, 251, 261, 275–76.

29. Vargas, *Labor Rights Are Civil Rights*, 35–43; McKay, "Texas Mexican Repatriation During the Great Depression," 162–219.

30. *La Prensa*, Sept. 27, 1931.

31. McKay, "Texas Mexican Repatriation During the Great Depression," 201.

32. Sánchez, *Becoming Mexican American*, 210. Railroad work, which also employed many Mexicans, was hard hit. "With the cessation of the railroads' activities in constructing new lines, many Mexicans have been thrown out of employment," reported the US vice consul in Ciudad Juárez, Mexico, in Feb. 1933. Records of the Department of State, RG 59, 1930–1939, 311.1215–1221, Box 1909. For railroad workers, see Jeffrey Marcos Garcílazo, *Traqueros: Mexican Railroad Workers in the United States, 1870–1930* (Denton: Univ. of North Texas Press, 2012).

33. Castañeda interview, 1–3, 6–7, 9–13.

34. Balderrama and Rodríguez, *Decade of Betrayal*, 89–112.

35. McKay, "Texas Mexican Repatriation During the Great Depression," 225 (relief payment amounts), 220–56; John Weber, *From South Texas to the Nation: The Exploitation of Mexican Labor in the Twentieth Century* (Chapel Hill: Univ. of North Carolina Press, 2015), 143–47.

36. Rex Thomson to Alejandro V. Martinez, Mexican Consulate, Jan. 19, 1934, Records of the Department of State, RG 59, 1930–1939, 311.1215–1221, Box 1909.

37. Castañeda interview, 12–14.

38. Valdés, "Mexican Revolutionary Nationalism and Repatriation During the Great Depression," 7–9.

39. Montejano, *Anglos and Mexicans in the Making of Texas*, 220–28; Lee, *America for Americans*, 155–59; Natalia Molina, *How Race Is Made in America: Immigration, Citizenship, and the Historical Power of Racial Scripts* (Berkeley: Univ. of California Press, 2014); Ngai, *Impossible Subjects*.

40. Lee, *America for Americans*, 148.

41. Severo Márquez, interview by Oscar J. Martínez, Apr. 15, 1974, University of Texas, El Paso Institute of Oral History, Interview #175. Quote, 48.

42. Quoted in Sánchez, *Becoming Mexican American*, 111.

43. Sánchez, *Becoming Mexican American*, 211.

44. Quoted in McKay, "Texas Mexican Repatriation During the Great Depression," 344. For hostility in Denver, for example, to Mexicans and Mexican Americans receiving relief, see Gertrude H. Milner and multiple authors to Cordell Hull, Secretary of State, May 13, 1935, Records of the Department of State, RG 59, 1930–1939, 311.1215–1221, Box 1909.

45. Weber, *From South Texas to the Nation*, 135.

46. Lee, *America for Americans*, 65.

47. Hoffman, *Unwanted Mexican Americans During the Great Depression*, 43.

48. Hoffman, *Unwanted Mexican Americans During the Great Depression*, 38–66; Balderrama and Rodríguez, *Decade of Betrayal*, 71–75.

49. Hoffman, *Unwanted Mexican Americans During the Great Depression*, 50–63; Balderrama and Rodríguez, *Decade of Betrayal*, 70–80.

50. Quoted in Balderrama and Rodríguez, *Decade of Betrayal*, 71–72.

51. "INS Records for 1930s Mexican Repatriations."

52. Rhinehart and Kreneck, "'In the Shadow of Uncertainty,'" 25–26. For deportations from Texas, see McKay, "Texas Mexican Repatriation During the Great Depression," 107–48.

53. Lee, *America for Americans*, 160–61; Cybelle Fox, *Three Worlds of Relief: Race, Immigration, and the American Welfare State from the Progressive Era to the New Deal* (Princeton, NJ: Princeton Univ. Press, 2012), 213–49.

54. Vargas, *Labor Rights Are Civil Rights*, 69–75; McKay, "Texas Mexican Repatriation During the Great Depression," 220–56; Balderrama and Rodríguez, *Decade of Betrayal*, 103–12; Valdés, "Mexican Revolutionary Nationalism and Repatriation During the Great Depression," 7–9; Fox, *Three Worlds of Relief*, 193–99, 213–49.

55. Quoted in Balderrama and Rodríguez, *Decade of Betrayal*, 102.

56. Valdés, "Mexican Revolutionary Nationalism and Repatriation During the Great Depression," 7–9.

57. Balderrama and Rodríguez, *Decade of Betrayal*, 132.

58. McWilliams, *North from Mexico*, 193. Daniel Morales found that 24,313 Mexicans were on relief in San Antonio in 1933; but the city only paid 15 cents for each recipient, and after anti-Mexican sentiment increased, "they were often denied despite their citizenship." Morales, "*Tejas, Afuera de México*: Newspapers, the Mexican Government, *Mutualistas*, and Migrants in San Antonio, 1910–1940," *Journal of American Ethnic History* 40, no. 2 (Winter 2021): 73–75.

59. McWilliams, *Factories in the Field*, 125. For the complex position of growers in the Southern California citrus industry, see Matt Garcia, *A World*

of Its Own: Race, Labor, and Citrus in the Making of Greater Los Angeles, 1900–1970 (Chapel Hill: Univ. of North Carolina Press, 2001), 106–20. For growers in Texas, Weber, *From South Texas to the Nation*, 140–41.

60. Daniel, *Bitter Harvest*, 105–40; McWilliams, *Factories in the Field*, 213–19; Acuña, *Occupied America*, 218–20; Ronald W. López, "The El Monte Berry Strike of 1933," *Aztlán* 1, no. 1 (Spring 1970): 101–14.

61. Daniel, *Bitter Harvest*, 141–221; Devra Weber, *Dark Sweat, White Gold: California Farm Workers, Cotton, and the New Deal* (Berkeley: Univ. of California Press, 1994), 79–111; Gonzáles, *Mexican Consuls and Labor Organizing*, chs. 3–4.

62. McWilliams, *Factories in the Field*, ch. 14 title.

63. McWilliams, *Factories in the Field*, 230–63; Don Mitchell, *The Lie of the Land: Migrant Workers and the California Landscape* (Minneapolis: Univ. of Minnesota Press, 1996), 156–75; D. H. Dinwiddie, "Deportation: The Immigration Service and the Chicano Labor Movement in the 1930s," *New Mexico Historical Review* 52, no. 3 (July 1977): 193–206. For beet growers' manipulation of Mexican immigrant labor in order to repress the labor movement, see George Kaplan to Cordell Hull and Governor Johnson, May 11, 1935, Records of the Department of State, RG 59, 1930–1939, 311.1215–1221, Box 1909.

64. Daniel, *Bitter Harvest*, 222–57; Gonzáles, *Mexican Consuls and Labor Organizing*, ch. 5.

65. McWilliams, *Factories in the Field*, 133.

66. Ngai, *Impossible Subjects*, 96–126; Dorothy B. Fujita Rony, *American Workers, Colonial Power: Philippine Seattle and the Transpacific West, 1919–1941* (Berkeley: Univ. of California Press, 2003).

67. Balderrama and Rodríguez, *Decade of Betrayal*, 166–67.

68. McKay, "Texas Mexican Repatriation During the Great Depression," 302–4, 320–25, 347–48, 368–86, 400–410; Balderrama and Rodríguez, *Decade of Betrayal*, 166–85; Carreras de Velasco, *Los Mexicanos que devolvió la crisis, 1929–1932*; Guerin-Gonzales, *Mexican Workers and American Dreams*, 86–94; Valdés, "Mexican Revolutionary Nationalism and Repatriation During the Great Depression"; Hoffman, *Unwanted Mexican Americans During the Great Depression*, 133–39. For the consuls, Gilbert G. Gonzáles, *Mexican Consuls and Labor Organizing: Imperial Politics in the American Southwest* (Austin: Univ. of Texas Press, 1999). Quotes: *La Prensa*, Oct. 17, 1931. For *La Prensa* and its relationship with the Mexican government, the *mutualistas*, and the Mexican community, see Morales, "*Tejas, Afuera de México*."

69. Morales, "*Tejas, Afuera de México*," quote, 53.

70. *La Prensa*, Oct. 16, 1931.

71. Quote: *La Prensa*, Oct. 22, 1931. McKay, "Texas Mexican Repatriation During the Great Depression," 365–86; *La Prensa*, Sept. 27, 29, and 30, and Oct. 2, 3, 4, 7, 8, 9, 10, 11, 12, 13, 14, 15, 16, 17, 18, 19, 20, 21, 22, 23, and 28, 1931.

72. *La Prensa*, Oct. 11, 13, 1931.

73. Márquez interview, 46.

74. Castañeda interview, 10–17, quote, 16.

75. Rachel Tamayo, interviewed by Tom Krinick and Marilyn Reinhart, Apr. 6, 1933, Oral History Interview HPL OH 305_01, 5–6, Houston Public Library, Houston History Research Center.

76. Photograph No. 3744-B, and text on back side of photograph, Box 33, W. D. Smithers Collection of Photographs.

77. *La Prensa*, Oct. 17, 1931.

78. Balderrama and Rodríguez, *Decade of Betrayal*, 127.

79. *Houston Chronicle*, May 3, 1932.

80. Arredondo, *Mexican Chicago*, 97.

81. Richard F. Boyce, American Consul to the Secretary of State, Jan. 8, 1931, Records of the Department of State, RG 59, 1930–1939, 311.1215–1221, Box 1909.

82. Sánchez, *Becoming Mexican American*, 213.

83. Balderrama and Rodríguez, *Decade of Betrayal*, 127.

84. Márquez interview, 51.

85. Balderrama and Rodríguez, *Decade of Betrayal*, 121–24; Guerin-Gonzales, *Mexican Workers and American Dreams*, 89; Hoffman, *Unwanted Mexican Americans During the Great Depression*, 87–90, 93–94.

86. Tamayo interview, 7.

87. Castañeda interview, 19.

88. McWilliams, *North from Mexico*, 193.

89. Interview with Reverend Allan A. Hunter by Christine Valenciana, Aug. 22, 1971, 3–4, Oral History No. 744, California State University, Fullerton, Oral History Program, Mexican American Project, Repatriation of the 1930s. Courtesy of Lawrence DeGraaf Center for Oral and Public History, California State University, Fullerton. "If they weren't coerced to leave, I would like to know what coercion is" (15). But Hunter, when asked, also recalled that the white-led ACLU was disorganized in response to repatriation and didn't do much.

90. Márquez interview, 51.

91. Robert N. McLean, "Goodbye, Vicente!," *Survey*, no. 66 (May 1, 1931): 182.

92. Balderrama and Rodríguez, *Decade of Betrayal*, 142–43n96.

93. *La Prensa*, Oct. 10, 1931.

94. *La Prensa*, Oct. 19, 1931.

95. *La Prensa*, Oct. 21, 1931.

96. *Houston Chronicle*, May 3, 1932.

97. Francisco E. Balderrama, *In Defense of La Raza: The Los Angeles Mexican Consulate and the Mexican Community, 1929 to 1936* (Tucson: Univ. of Arizona Press, 1982), 22–23.

98. Valdés, "Mexican Revolutionary Nationalism and Repatriation During the Great Depression," 15.

99. Benjamin Márquez, *LULAC: The Evolution of a Mexican American Political Organization* (Austin: Univ. of Texas Press, 1993); Cynthia Orozco, *No Mexicans, Women, or Dogs Allowed: The Rise of the Mexican American Civil Rights Movement* (Austin: Univ. of Texas Press, 2009).

100. Vargas, *Labor Rights Are Civil Rights*, 134–43.

101. Vargas, *Labor Rights Are Civil Rights*, 134–43; Acuña, *Occupied America*, 234–35; Justin Akers Chacón, *Radicals in the Barrio: Magonistas, Socialists, Wobblies, and Communists in the Mexican American Working Class* (Chicago: Haymarket Books, 2018), chs. 25–28.

102. Gregory, *American Exodus*; Stein, *California and the Dust Bowl Migration*. Some were neither white nor Black, including Native Americans; see discussion below of Dorothea Lange's *Migrant Mother*.

103. Gregory, *American Exodus*, 10.

104. Morgan interview, 9.

105. Juanita Everly Price, interview by Stacey Jagels, Jan. 26 and 29, 1981, interview #105, p. 4, California Odyssey Oral History project.

106. Robert Lewis Kessler Jr., interviewed by Michael Neely, Mar. 26 and 28, Interview #138, pp. 1, 4, 11, California Odyssey Oral History project.

107. Gregory, *American Exodus*, 10.

108. David Eugene Conrad, *The Forgotten Farmers: The Story of Sharecroppers in the New Deal* (Urbana: Univ. of Illinois Press, 1965); Donald Grubb, *Cry from the Cotton: The Southern Tenant Farmers' Union and the New Deal* (Chapel Hill: Univ. of North Carolina Press, 1971); Neil Foley, *The White Scourge: Mexicans, Blacks, and Poor Whites in Texas Cotton Culture* (Berkeley: Univ. of California Press, 1997), 163–82; McKay, "Texas Mexican Repatriation During the Great Depression," 176–86.

109. Gregory, *American Exodus*, 15.

110. Morgan interview, 13. Lois Smith Barnes, interview by Michael Neely, June 15 and 18, 1981, Interview #143, California Odyssey Oral History project, 6–7.

111. Barnes interview, 15.

112. Barnes interview, 15.

113. Earl Butler, interview by Judith Gannon, Feb. 3 and Mar. 7, 1981, Interview #108, p. 18; Reverend Billie H. Pate, interview by Michael Neely, Mar. 5 and 12, 1981, Interview #117, p. 11, California Odyssey Oral History project.

114. Hattye Shields, interview by Judith Gannon, May 24, 1981, Interview #209, pp. 1, 13–14, California Odyssey Oral History project.

115. Shields interview, 8.

116. Stein, *California and the Dust Bowl Migration*, 73–75; Gordon, *Dorothea Lange*, 256–57; Edwards v. People of State of California, 1941, 314 US 160, Supreme Court of the United States.

117. Morgan interview, 21.

118. Gregory, *American Exodus*, 25, 62–70.

119. Pate interview, 17.

120. Pate interview, 25.

121. Morgan interview, 20–21.

122. Shields interview, 11.

123. Gordon, *Dorothea Lange*, 225–26; Gregory, *American Exodus*, 58.

124. Pate interview, 7, 17.

125. Morgan interview, 4–5, 18.

126. Gregory, *American Exodus*, 15, 39.

127. Kessler interview, 5, 11, 16.

128. Gregory, *American Exodus*, 61.

129. Gregory, *American Exodus*, 49–51.

130. Gregory, *American Exodus*, 69–70.

131. Gregory, *American Exodus*, 25, 69–71, 85–86; Stein, *California and the Dust Bowl Migration*, 109–30; Weber, *Dark Sweat, White Gold*, 167–73.

132. Christina Heatherton, *Arise! Global Radicalism in the Era of the Mexican Revolution* (Berkeley: Univ. of California Press, 2022), 135–36.

133. Christina Veola Williams McClanahan, interview by Judith Gannon, June 20, 1981, Interview #133, p. 11, California Odyssey Oral History project.

134. Price interview, 9.

135. Gordon, *Dorothea Lange*, 226; Stein, *California and the Dust Bowl Migration*, 63.

136. Morgan interview, 22–23.

137. Pate interview, 13–14.

138. Kessler interview, 7–8.

139. Pate interview, 12.

140. Quoted in Weber, *Dark Sweat, White Gold*, 149. (De La Cruz interviewed by Weber.)

141. McClanahan interview, 1–3.

142. Price interview, 1.

143. Price interview, 6.

144. Price interview, 9.

145. Price interview, 9, 12.

146. Weber, *Dark Sweat, White Gold*, 138.

147. Weber, *Dark Sweat, White Gold*, 206 (quote); see also Gregory, *American Exodus*, 158–64.

148. Weber, *Dark Sweat, White Gold*, 150.

149. Daniel, *Bitter Harvest*, 223.

150. Gordon, *Dorothea Lange*, 158–69.

151. Gordon, *Dorothea Lange*, 221.

152. Gordon, *Dorothea Lange*, 220.

153. Gordon, *Dorothea Lange*, 235–39.

154. Gordon, *Dorothea Lange*, 222–23.

155. Gordon, *Dorothea Lange*, 225.

156. Lawrence W. Levine, "The Historian and the Icon: Photography and the History of the American People in the 1930s and 1940s," in *The Unpredictable Past: Explorations in American Cultural History* (New York: Oxford Univ. Press, 1993), 258.

157. For Lange's class background, see Gordon, *Dorothea Lange*, 6–8, 15–16, 56–57, and chapters 1–2 in general.

158. Geoffrey Dunn, "Photographic License," *New Times* (San Luis Obispo, CA), Dec. 3, 2003; Errol Morris, "The Case of the Inappropriate Alarm Clock (Part 7)," *New York Times*, Oct. 24, 2009; Lennard J. Davis, "Migrant Mother and the Truth of Photography," *Los Angeles Review of Books*, Mar. 4, 2020; Gordon, *Dorothea Lange*, 240–43; Douglas Cazaux Sackman, *Orange Empire: California and the Fruits of Eden* (Berkeley: Univ. of California Press, 2005), 239–48.

159. *Los Angeles Times*, Nov. 18, 1978, quoted in Davis, "Migrant Mother and the Truth of Photography."

160. Dunn, "Photographic License."

161. Dunn, "Photographic License."

162. Morgan interview, 1.

163. Kessler interview, 2.

164. Price interview, 3.

165. Theda Perdue and Michael D. Green, *The Cherokee Nation and the Trail of Tears* (New York: Viking, 2007).

166. Barnes interview, 1–2.

167. Jackson J. Benson, *The True Adventures of John Steinbeck, Writer* (New York: Penguin, 1984), ch. 21; Jay Parini, *John Steinbeck: A Biography* (London: William Heinmann, 1994), 289, 533–34; Rebecca Sutton, "10 Things You Might Not Know About the Grapes of Wrath," Dec. 8, 2020, National Endowment for the Arts, https://www.arts.gov/stories/blog/2020/ten-things-you-might-not-know-about-grapes-wrath.

168. Steinbeck, *The Grapes of Wrath*, 256.

169. Benson, *The True Adventures of John Steinbeck, Writer*, 336–46; Parini, *John Steinbeck*, 222–26.

170. Parini, *John Steinbeck*, 248–53.

171. *The Grapes of Wrath*, dir. John Ford.

172. John Steinbeck, *Tortilla Flat* (New York: Covici-Friede, 1935), 22.

173. John Steinbeck, *In Dubious Battle* (New York: Covici-Friede, 1936). For an analysis of the relationship between the novel and the strikes on which it was based, see Jackson J. Benson and Anne Loftis, "John Steinbeck and Farm Labor Unionization: The Background of 'In Dubious Battle,'" *American Literature* 52, no. 2 (May 1980): 194–223.

174. Steinbeck to George Albee, Jan. 15, 1935, in Elaine Steinbeck and Robert Wallsten, eds., *John Steinbeck: A Life in Letters* (New York: Viking Press, 1975), 98. He did, though, fervently convey his commitment to farmworkers later in a statement in advance of the 1936 essays he wrote for the *San Francisco News*: "I am completely partisan. Every effort I can bring to bear is and has been at the call of the common working people to the end that they may eat what they raise, wear what they weave, use what they produce, and in every way and in completeness share in the works of their hands and their heads." Quoted in Sackman, *Orange Empire*, 183.

175. John Steinbeck, *Their Blood Is Strong* (San Francisco: Simon J. Lubin Society, 1938), reprinted as *Harvest Gypsies: On the Road to the Grapes of Wrath* (Berkeley: Heyday Books, 1988), 55. Lange did not herself control the usage of her photographs. But we can certainly ask whether the unnamed woman in the cover photo wanted to have her breast exposed to the twenty-five thousand people who bought the 25-cent pamphlet, or even knew she'd been used on it. And the photo underscores Lange's class politics: she presumably would not have photographed a middle- or upper-class white woman with her breast and nipple exposed. The Simon J. Lubin Society, which published the pamphlet, presumably chose the image; it's not clear if Steinbeck himself had any role.

176. Steinbeck, *Harvest Gypsies*, 55.

177. Steinbeck, *Harvest Gypsies*, 21.

178. Steinbeck, *Harvest Gypsies*, 21–22. Walter Stein repeated these myths whole hog in his 1973 study, *California and the Dust Bowl Migration*, 44.

For displaced Filipino farmers, see Fujita Rony, *American Workers, Colonial Power*, 25–50.

179. Steinbeck, *Harvest Gypsies*, 52–56.

180. Steinbeck, *Harvest Gypsies*, 22.

181. Steinbeck, *Harvest Gypsies*, 56–57. "The same pride and self-respect that deters white migrant labor from accepting charity and relief . . . will also cause the white American labor to refuse to accept the role of field peon, with its attendant terrorism, squalor and starvation."

182. For a different interpretation, see Sackman, *Orange Empire*, 244.

183. Steinbeck, *The Grapes of Wrath*, 315.

184. Morgan interview, 13.

185. Barnes interview, 13.

186. Price interview, 26–27.

187. Hunter interview, 3–4.

188. Valdés, "Mexican Revolutionary Nationalism and Repatriation During the Great Depression," 15–16.

189. McWilliams, *Factories in the Field*; Frank Bardacke, *Trampling Out the Vintage: Cesar Chavez and the Two Souls of the United Farm Workers* (London: Verso, 2011), 47.

190. Américo Paredes, *George Washington Gómez: A Mexicotexan Novel* (Houston: Arte Publico Press, 1990), and introduction by Rolando Hinojosa.

191. Carlos Bulosan, *America Is in the Heart* (New York: Harcourt Brace, 1946).

192. Price interview, 10.

193. Gordon, *Dorothea Lange*, 230; Verónica Martínez-Matsuda, *Migrant Citizenship: Race, Rights, and Reform in the U.S. Farm Labor Camp Program* (Philadelphia: Univ. of Pennsylvania Press, 2020), 85.

194. Robert C. Lieberman, *Shifting the Color Line: Race and the American Welfare State* (Cambridge, MA: Harvard Univ. Press, 1998); Ira Katznelson, *When Affirmative Action Was White: An Untold History of Racial Inequality in Twentieth-Century America* (New York: W. W. Norton, 2005), 25–79; Daniel, *Bitter Harvest*, 258–85; Weber, *Dark Sweat, White Gold*, 167–73.

195. Lytle-Hernández, *Migra!*, 122.

196. Sánchez, *Becoming Mexican American*, 220–26; Hoffman, *Unwanted Mexican Americans During the Great Depression*, 112–14.

197. Samuel Sokobin, American Consul, to the Honorable Secretary of State, Nov. 5, 1921, Records of the Department of State, RG 59, 1930–1939, 311.1215–1221, Box 1909.

198. Edward I. Nathan, American Consul, to the Secretary of State, Nov. 12, 1931, Records of the Department of State, RG 59, 1930–1939, 311.1215–1221, Box 1909.

199. McKay, "Texas Mexican Repatriation During the Great Depression," 491–539; Valdés, "Mexican Revolutionary Nationalism and Repatriation During the Great Depression"; Hoffman, *Unwanted Mexican Americans During the Great Depression*, 133–51; Balderrama and Rodríguez, *Decade of Betrayal*, 195–226.

200. Hoffman, *Unwanted Mexican Americans During the Great Depression*, 146. For further evidence, see Stewart E. McMillin, American Consul, to

Elmer C. Sandmeyer, June 1, 1934, Records of the Department of State, RG 59, 1930–1939, 311.1215–1221, Box 1909. For returnees, see Carreras de Velasco, *Los Mexicanos que devolvió la crisis, 1929–1932*; McKay, "Texas Mexican Repatriation During the Great Depression," 469–88.

201. Márquez interview, 59–60.

202. Castañeda interview, 20–46, quote, 36.

203. Castañeda interview, 25, 47–48.

204. Balderrama and Rodríguez, *Decade of Betrayal*, 248.

205. Tamayo interview, 1, 5–7, 18.

206. Márquez interview, 61; Balderrama and Rodríguez, *Decade of Betrayal*, 237–59.

207. Balderrama and Rodríguez, *Decade of Betrayal*, 237–59.

208. Castañeda interview, 41.

209. Balderrama and Rodríguez, *Decade of Betrayal*, 274–76; for barriers to returning, see, e.g., Bartley F. Yost, American Consul, to the Secretary of State, Nov. 12, 1931, Records of the Department of State, RG 59, 1930–1939, 311.1215–1221, Box 1909.

210. Tamayo interview, 20.

211. Castañeda interview, 34–35, 40, 54.

212. Richard Polenberg, *War and Society: The United States, 1941–1945* (Philadelphia: W. W. Lippincott, 1972); Joel Seidman, *American Labor from Defense to Reconversion* (Chicago: Univ. of Chicago Press, 1978); David Lucander, *Winning the War for Democracy: The March on Washington Movement, 1941–1946* (Urbana: Univ. of Illinois Press, 2014).

213. Martínez-Matsuda, *Migrant Citizenship*, quote, 5; Stein, *California and the Dust Bowl Migration*, 166–86.

214. Ngai, *Impossible Subjects*, 138. For the Bracero Program, see Ernesto Galarza, *Merchants of Labor: The Mexican Bracero Story: An Account of the Managed Migration of Mexican Farm Workers to California, 1942–1960* (Charlotte, NC: McNally & Loftin, 1964); Deborah Cohen, *Braceros: Migrant Citizens and Transnational Subjects in the Postwar United States and Mexico* (Chapel Hill: Univ. of North Carolina Press, 2011); Kitty Calavita, *Inside the State: The Bracero Program, Immigration, and the I.N.S.* (New York: Routledge, 1992); Anna Elizabeth Rosas, *Abrazando el Espíritu: Bracero Families Confront the US-Mexican Border* (Oakland: Univ. of California Press, 1978).

215. Jesus Rivera L., for example, recounted in his oral history that his father was forced to leave the US in 1932, but came back as a bracero in 1942. Jesús Rivera L., interview by Perla Guerrero, May 13, 2006, Institute of Oral History, University of Texas, El Paso, Interview #1178.

216. Martínez-Matsuda, *Migrant Citizenship*, 221–51.

217. Mario Jimenez Sifuentez, *Of Forests and Fields: Mexican Labor in the Pacific Northwest* (New Brunswick, NJ: Rutgers Univ. Press, 2016), 23–35.

218. Mireya Loza, *Defiant Braceros: How Migrant Workers Fought for Racial, Sexual, and Political Freedom* (Chapel Hill: Univ. of North Carolina Press, 2016), ch. 3.

219. Ngai, *Impossible Subjects*, 139.

220. Balderrama and Rodríguez, *Decade of Betrayal*, 170.

221. Balderrama and Rodríguez, *Decade of Betrayal*, 300.

222. Quoted in Balderrama and Rodríguez, *Decade of Betrayal*, 267.

223. Balderrama and Rodríguez, *Decade of Betrayal*, 299–318.

224. Larry Hosford, "Salinas," Warner Brothers Records, 1977.

225. Octavio Solis, *Mother Road*, Oregon Shakespeare Festival, 2019.

226. "Migrant Mother, 1936 Dorothea Lange 5 Shower Curtain," Fine Art America, https://fineartamerica.com/featured/migrant-mother-1936-by-dorothea-lange-5-celestial-images.html?product=shower-curtain.

227. Julia Jacobo and Anne Laurent, "Migrant Mother Seen Fleeing Tear Gas with Children: 'I Felt I Was Going to Die,'" ABC News, Nov. 28, 2018, https://abcnews.go.com/International/felt-die-migrant-mother-fleeing-tear-gas-children/story?id=59456810. For an example of the use of Lange's photo to depict Honduran immigrant women as pure suffering victims, without any opinions of their own or agency as political activists, see, e.g., "We Found Miriam," *Contra Corriente*, July 13, 2018, https://contracorriente.red/en/2018/07/13/we-found-miriam. For the photograph and the aftermath of the 2009 Honduran coup, see Robin Anderson, "The Photography Seen 'Around the World': The Media, the Migrant Mother from Honduras, and the U.S.-Backed Military Coup of 2009," in *Media, Central American Refugees, and the U.S. Border Crisis*, ed. Robin Anderson and Adrian Bergmann (New York: Routledge, 2020), ch. 3.

228. *Houston Chronicle*, Apr. 14, 2015; Aura Bogado, "Why Mothers Are on Strike at Karnes Immigrant Detention Center," *ColorLines*, Mar. 31, 2015; Roque Planas, "Mothers Launch a Second Hunger Strike at Karnes City Family Detention Center," *HuffPost*, Apr. 14, 2015; Will S. Hylton, "A Federal Judge and a Hunger Strike Take on the Government's Immigrant Detention Facilities," *New York Times Magazine*, Apr. 10, 2015; Sara Rathod, "These Migrant Moms Are on Hunger Strike to Protest Being Locked Up Indefinitely," *Mother Jones*, Aug. 19, 2016.

CHAPTER THREE: WHOSE LABOR MOVEMENT?

1. *Chicago Tribune*, Mar. 16, 1937; *Chicago Defender*, Mar. 20, 1937; *Life*, Apr. 5, 1937, 21.

2. *Life*, Apr. 5, 1937, 21; *Chicago Tribune*, Mar. 16, 1937; *Chicago Defender*, Mar. 20, 1937. The photo shows six women, but almost all the news stories, from very diverse outlets, report seven strikers, and one of the news stories lists seven names, so I am assuming seven strikers. For the full seven names, see *Chicago Defender*, Mar. 20, 1937.

3. Sidney Fine, *Sit-Down: The General Motors Strike of 1936–37* (Ann Arbor: Univ. of Michigan Press, 1969), statistic, 331.

4. For pioneering debates, see Lise Vogel, *Marxism and the Oppression of Women: Toward a Unitary Theory* (Rutgers, NJ: Rutgers Univ. Press, 1983); Heidi Hartmann, "The Unhappy Marriage of Marxism and Feminism: Towards a More Progressive Union," *Capital and Class* 3, no. 2 (June 1979): 1–33; Mariarosa Dalla Costa and Selma James, *The Power of Women and the Subversion of the Community* (Bristol, UK: Falling Wall Press, 1972). For women of color performing reproductive labor, see Evelyn Nakano Glenn, "From Servitude to Service Work: Historical Continuities in the Racial Division of Paid Reproductive Labor," *Signs* 18, no. 1 (Fall 1992): 1–43; Rhacel Parreñas, *Servants*

of *Globalization: Migration and Domestic Work* (Stanford, CA: Stanford Univ. Press, 2015); Evelyn Nakano Glenn, *Forced to Care: Coercion and Caregiving in America* (Cambridge, MA: Harvard Univ. Press, 2010). For wet nursing as reproductive labor, see Lara Vapnek, "The Labor of Infant Feeding: Wet-Nursing at the Nursery and Children's Hospital, 1854–1910," *Journal of American History* 109, no. 1 (June 2022): 90–115.

5. Valerie A. Fildes, *Wet Nursing: A History from Antiquity to the Present* (Oxford: Basil Blackwell, 1988).

6. Janet Golden, *A Social History of Wet Nursing in America: From Breast to Bottle* (Cambridge: Cambridge Univ. Press, 1996).

7. For wet nursing under slavery, see Stephanie E. Jones-Rogers, *They Were Her Property: White Women as Slaveholders in the American South* (New Haven, CT: Yale Univ. Press, 2019), ch. 5; Emily West with R. J. Knight, "Mothers' Milk: Slavery, Wet-Nursing, and Black and White Women in the Antebellum South," *Journal of Southern History* 83, no. 1 (Feb. 2017). For the "mammy" stereotype and wet nurses, see Kimberly Wallace-Sanders, *Mammy: A Century of Race, Gender, and Southern Memory* (Ann Arbor: Univ. of Michigan Press, 2007); on the mammy stereotype, see Deborah Gray White, *Ar'n't I a Woman: Female Slaves in the Plantation South* (New York: W. W. Norton, 1985), 46–61. For the racialized concepts of African-descent women that underlay wet nursing under slavery, see Jennifer L. Morgan, *Laboring Women: Reproduction and Gender in New World Slavery* (Philadelphia: Univ. of Pennsylvania Press, 2004), ch. 1.

8. Jones-Rogers, *They Were Her Property*, 112.

9. Quoted in Jones-Rogers, *They Were Her Property*, 113.

10. Quoted in West and Knight, "Mothers' Milk," 53.

11. Sally McMillen, "Mothers' Sacred Duty: Breast-Feeding Patterns among Middle- and Upper-Class Women in the Antebellum South," *Journal of Southern History* 51 (Aug. 1985): 336.

12. Jones-Rogers, *They Were Her Property*, 105; West and Knight, "Mothers' Milk."

13. Marcus Wood, *Black Milk: Imagining Slavery in the Visual Cultures of Brazil and America* (Oxford: Oxford Univ. Press, 2013), 2.

14. Quoted in West and Knight, "Mothers' Milk," 52. In cases in which the wet nurse's own baby had died, a woman would be forced to sit there, hour after hour, day and night, week after week, sharing her breast with someone else's baby. West and Knight, "Mothers' Milk," 51–53, 62; Jones-Rogers, *They Were Her Property*, 120.

15. West and Knight, "Mothers' Milk," 63–64.

16. Harriet A. Jacobs, *Incidents in the Life of a Slave Girl, Written by Herself*, ed. Jean Fagan Yellin (1861; repr., Cambridge, MA: Harvard Univ. Press, 1987), 12.

17. Jones-Rogers, *They Were Her Property*, 118 and ch. 5; West and Knight, "Mothers' Milk," 64–65.

18. West and Knight, "Mothers' Milk," 50. They note: "That white women rarely complained about their slaves wet nurses suggests that opportunities for enslaved women to resist were limited" (50). Yet constant vigilance was

required, suggesting that if the mistress turned her back, the wet nurse resisted in some form.

19. White, *Ar'n't I a Woman*, 63, 70–90; Stephanie M. H. Camp, *Closer to Freedom: Enslaved Women and Everyday Resistance in the Plantation South* (Chapel Hill: Univ. of North Carolina Press, 2004); Thavolia Glymph, *Out of the House of Bondage: The Transformation of the Plantation Household* (Cambridge, UK: Cambridge Univ. Press, 2008), 91–96; Brenda E. Stevenson, *Life in Black and White: Family and Community in the Slave South* (Bloomington: Indiana Univ. Press, 1996).

20. As Lara Vapnek has put it, poor immigrant women "became cash cows." Vapnek, "The Labor of Infant Feeding," 100.

21. Golden, *A Social History of Wet Nursing in America*, ch. 7; Jaqueline H. Wolf, *Don't Kill Your Baby: Public Health and the Decline of Breastfeeding in the 19th and 20th Centuries* (Columbus: Ohio State Univ. Press, 2001).

22. Golden, *A Social History of Wet Nursing in America*, ch. 6; Wolf, *Don't Kill Your Baby*, 137–43.

23. Golden, *A Social History of Wet Nursing in America*; Wolf, *Don't Kill Your Baby*, ch. 5. Love quote: Golden, 154. Tera W. Hunter, *To 'Joy My Freedom: Southern Black Women's Lives and Labors After the Civil War* (Cambridge, MA: Harvard Univ. Press, 1997), ch. 9.

24. Golden, *A Social History of Wet Nursing in America*, 72–74, 152–54; West and Knight, "Mothers' Milk," 50; Wolf, *Don't Kill Your Baby*, 129.

25. Golden, *A Social History of Wet Nursing in America*, 145.

26. Sherri Broder, "Child Care or Child Neglect? Baby Farming in Late-Nineteenth-Century Philadelphia," *Gender and Society* 2, no. 2 (June 1988): 128–48.

27. Fritz B. Talbot, "The Wet-Nurse Problem," *National Conference on Infant Mortality, Report of the Proceedings* (1913): 324, cited in Jacqueline H. Wolf, "'Mercenary Hirelings' or 'A Great Blessing'? Doctors' and Mothers' Conflicted Perceptions of Wet Nurses and the Ramifications for Infant Feeding in Chicago, 1871–1961," *Journal of Social History* 33, no. 1 (Fall 1999): 103.

28. Golden, *A Social History of Wet Nursing in America*, 97.

29. Wolf, *Don't Kill Your Baby*, 138.

30. Wolf, *Don't Kill Your Baby*, 138, and 137–43; Golden, *A Social History of Wet Nursing in America*, ch. 6; Hunter, *To 'Joy My Freedom*, 60.

31. Golden, *A Social History of Wet Nursing in America*, chs. 5 and 7; Wolf, *Don't Kill Your Baby*, ch. 3, 149–57.

32. Wolf, *Don't Kill Your Baby*, ch. 2; Kara W. Swanson, *Banking on the Body: The Market in Blood, Milk, and Sperm in Modern America* (Cambridge, MA: Harvard Univ. Press, 2014).

33. Wolf, *Don't Kill Your Baby*, 152–56; Swanson, *Banking on the Body*, 30–38.

34. Golden, *A Social History of Wet Nursing in America*, 198. Historian Kara Swanson places the invention of "milk banks" in the context of evolving blood and sperm banks—what she calls "body banks." "A body bank takes a private, intimate piece of a body," she observes, "and makes it publicly accessible to strangers, as a commodity." Kara W. Swanson, "Body Banks: A

History of Milk Banks, Blood Banks, and Sperm Banks in the United States,"
Enterprise and Society 12, no. 4 (Dec. 2011): 756; Swanson, *Banking on the
Body*. For later practices of "milk sharing," see Shannon K. Carter and Beatriz
M. Reyes-Foster, *Sharing Milk: Intimacy, Materiality, and Bio-Communities of
Practice* (Bristol, UK: Bristol Univ. Press, 2020).

35. Wolf, *Don't Kill Your Baby*, 149–57; Julian H. Hess, "Chicago Plan for
Care of Premature Infants," *Journal of the American Medical Association* 146,
no. 10 (July 1951): 891–93; Jacqueline H. Wolf, "Evelyn Lundeen, 1900–1963,"
in *American Nursing: A Biographical Dictionary*, vol. 3, ed. Vern L. Bullough
and Lilli Sentz (New York: Springer, 2004), 183–87; Jacqueline H. Wolf,
"Gertrude Plotzke, 1906–1997," in Bullough and Sentz, *American Nursing*,
3: 234–36; City of Chicago Department of Public Health, "Healthy Chicago:
Historical Highlights of Public Health in Chicago, 1834–2012 (Chicago: City of
Chicago Department of Public Health, 2012), 6; *Chicago's Report to the People, 1933–1946* (Chicago: City of Chicago, 1947), 136–39; Julius H. Hess and
Evelyn C. Lundeen, *The Premature Infant: Its Medical and Nursing Care* (Philadelphia: J. B. Lippincott, 1941), in Julius Hays Hess Papers, 1843–1958, Box
8, Folder 5, University of Chicago Library; Evelyn C. Lundeen, "History of the
Hortense Joseph Premature Station," n.d., p. 1, Hess Papers, Box 4, Folder 9.

36. "Sarah Morris Hospital Premature Station," placard, Box 52, Hess
Papers.

37. Quote: Hess and Lundeen, *The Premature Infant*, 58. Wolf, "Evelyn
Lundeen"; Wolf, "Gertrude Plotzke"; Hess, "Chicago Plan for Care of Premature Infants"; Hess and Lundeen, *The Premature Infant*, 58; *Chicago's Report
to the People*, 136–39; Jacqueline H. Wolf, interview with Gertrude Rosenberger [Plotzke], Chicago, Dec. 10, 1996, in possession of the author. My great
thanks to Jacqueline Wolf for sharing the interview with me. In her interview,
Plotzke says her milk station opened in 1937. The City of Chicago reported
in 1947 that the "breast-milk program" was inaugurated in 1935—but the
program may have distributed milk from hospitals before the South Side milk
station opened. *Chicago's Report to the People* also noted that "Stations are
located at 54 West Hubbard Street, 2401 South Kedzie Avenue, and 3704 Vincennes Avenue" (139).

38. Wolf, "Gertrude Plotzke," "Evelyn Lundeen"; Jacqueline H. Wolf, interview with Josephine Zuzak Sobolewski, Chicago, Apr. 28, 1997, in possession
of the author. My great thanks to Jacqueline Wolf for sharing the interview
with me.

39. Wolf, "Evelyn Lundeen," 184; Hess, "Chicago Plan for Care of Premature Infants"; "A Hospital Staffed Only by Women for 100 Years," *Journal of
the American Medical Association* 193, no. 6 (Aug. 1965): 30–38.

40. Sobolewski interview.

41. Wolf, "Evelyn Lundeen," 1.

42. Sobolewski interview; Hess, "Chicago Plan for Care of Premature
Infants." The 1947 report from the City of Chicago stated, "Today this benefaction is available regardless of race, creed, or color." City of Chicago, *Chicago's Report to the People*, 139. For Mexicans in Chicago, see Gabriela F.

Arrendondo, *Mexican Chicago: Race, Identity, and Nation, 1916–39* (Urbana: Univ. of Illinois, 2008).

43. Plotzke interview.

44. The *Arizona Gleam*, Mar. 26, 1937, reported that of sixteen total, six were white. "The white women, it was said, refused to join the strike." The *Pittsburgh Courier* said two white women "did not join the strike" (Mar. 17, 1937).

45. Plotzke interview. Josephine Sobolewski, who took over supervision of the milk station in 1944, told Wolf in her 1997 interview that the wet nurses were all African American.

46. *Chicago's Report to the People*, 139.

47. Sobolewski interview.

48. Plotzke interview.

49. Sobolewski interview. By refusing pumps, the wet nurses may have been pushing back against not only Plotzke but Dr. Julius Hess, her supervisor, who had himself invented a pump, which he called an "improved breast-milk collector," and published a 1916 article about it for the *Journal of the American Medical Association*. Julius H. Hess, "An Improved Breast-Milk Collector," *Journal of the American Medical Association* 66, no. 4 (Jan. 1916): 272. An undated partial article discussing the milk station at Sarah Morris lists "electric breast pump" among the equipment recommended for milk stations. "Nursing Staff: Equipment of the Station," p. 11, Box 5, Folder 6, Hess Papers.

50. *Chicago's Report to the People*, 137.

51. Lundeen, "History of the Hortense Joseph Premature Station," 4; Wolf, Plotzke and Sobolewski interviews; *Chicago's Report to the People*, 136–39.

52. Plotzke and Sobolewski interviews.

53. Plotzke interview.

54. Plotzke interview.

55. Plotzke interview.

56. Sobolewski interview.

57. Plotzke interview.

58. Plotzke interview; *La Crosse* (WI) *Tribune and Leader-Press*, Mar. 15, 1937.

59. *La Crosse Tribune and Leader-Press*, Mar. 15, 1937; *Kokomo* (IN) *Tribune*, Mar. 15, 1937.

60. *Kokomo Tribune*, Mar. 15, 1937.

61. *Chicago Tribune*, Mar. 16, 1937.

62. *Chicago Tribune*, Mar. 16, 1937; *New York Amsterdam News*, Mar. 27, 1937.

63. *Kokomo Tribune*, Mar. 15, 1937.

64. *Chicago Tribune*, Mar. 16, 1937.

65. *Chicago Defender*, Mar. 20, 1937.

66. *Pittsburgh Courier*, Mar. 17, 1937.

67. *Chicago Tribune*, Mar. 16, 1937; *Arizona Gleam*, Mar. 26, 1937.

68. Lundeen, "History of the Hortense Joseph Premature Station," 4.

69. Plotzke interview.

70. Jones-Rogers, *They Were Her Property*, 114–15.

71. Plotzke interview.

72. Sobolewski interview.

73. Morgan, *Laboring Women*, ch. 1.

74. B. Raymond Hoobler, "Human Milk: Its Commercial Production and Distribution," *Journal of the American Medical Association* 84, no. 3 (Jan. 1925): 165–66.

75. Henry Dwight Chapin, "The Production and Handling of Human Milk," *Journal of the American Medical Association* 87, no. 17 (Oct. 23, 1926): 1364–66.

76. Plotzke interview.

77. Plotzke and Sobolewski interviews.

78. Plotzke and Sobolewski interviews.

79. *Chicago Tribune*, Mar. 16, 1937.

80. *Chicago Tribune*, Mar. 16, 1937; *Chicago Defender*, Mar. 20, 1937; *New York Amsterdam News*, Mar. 27, 1937.

81. *Chicago Tribune*, Mar. 16, 1937.

82. *Chicago Herald and Examiner*, Mar. 17, 1937.

83. *Chicago Tribune*, Mar. 16, 1937.

84. *New York Amsterdam News*, Mar. 27, 1937.

85. *Chicago Defender*, Mar. 20, 1937.

86. *Chicago Herald and Examiner*, Mar. 16, 1937.

87. *Los Angeles Times*, Mar. 16, 1937. First quote is Bundesen speaking; second is the *Times*.

88. *Los Angeles Times*, Mar. 16, 1937.

89. *Los Angeles Times*, Mar. 16, 1937.

90. *Chicago Tribune*, Mar. 16, 1937.

91. *Chicago Herald and Examiner*, Mar. 16, 17, 1937.

92. *Chicago Herald and Examiner*, Mar. 17, 1937.

93. *Los Angeles Times*, Mar. 16, 1937.

94. *New York Amsterdam News*, Mar. 27, 1937.

95. *Arizona Gleam*, Mar. 26, 1937.

96. *Philadelphia Tribune*, Mar. 18, 1937.

97. *Kokomo Tribune*, Mar. 15, 1937.

98. *Chicago Tribune*, Mar. 16, 1937.

99. *Daily News*, Mar. 16, 1937; *Pharos-Tribune* (Logansport, IN), Mar. 16, 1937.

100. Moorhead (MN) *Daily News*, Mar. 16, 1937; *Pharos-Tribune* (Logansport, IN), Mar. 16, 1937.

101. *El Paso Herald-Post*, Mar. 16, 1937.

102. *Life*, Apr. 5, 1937, 21.

103. William Vandivert, "Wet Nurse Strike," 1937, *Life*, https://artsandculture.google.com/asset/wet-nurse-strike/FgGMvAd8HnBplw.

104. The woman in the back is not Evelyn Lundeen or Gertrude Plotzke; they would have been younger.

105. *Chicago Tribune*, Mar. 16, 1937; *Chicago Defender*, Mar. 20, 1937.

106. *Chicago Tribune*, Mar. 16, 1937; *Chicago Defender*, Mar. 20, 1937; *Kokomo Tribune*, Mar. 15, 1937.

107. *Chicago Defender*, Mar. 20, 1937.

108. *Chicago Defender*, Mar. 20, 1937.

109. *Kokomo Tribune*, Mar. 15, 1937.

110. *Chicago Defender*, Mar. 20, 1937.

111. Sixteenth Census of the United States, 1940, Cook County, Illinois, Roll: m-t0627–00924, Page 1A, Enumeration District 103–113, NARA microfilm roll 924, Line number 14, Sheet A, Sheet number 1.

112. *Chicago Tribune*, Mar. 16, 1937; *Chicago Defender*, Mar. 20, 1937.

113. Sixteenth Census of the United States, 1940, Cook County, Illinois, Ward 3 (Tract 184), Enumeration District 103–1253, Sheet Letter B, Sheet Number 6, Household ID 130, Line number 49.

114. Horace R. Cayton and St. Clair Drake, *Black Metropolis: A Study of Negro Life in a Northern City* (New York: Harcourt Brace, 1945), 8.

115. Cayton and Drake, *Black Metropolis*, 8, 58–64; James R. Grossman, *Land of Hope: Chicago, Black Southerners, and the Great Migration* (Chicago: Univ. of Chicago Press, 1991).

116. Cayton and Drake, *Black Metropolis*, 576.

117. Cayton and Drake, *Black Metropolis*, 577.

118. Cayton and Drake, *Black Metropolis*, 575.

119. Cayton and Drake, *Black Metropolis*, 572. For girls' lives, see Marcia Chatelain, *South Side Girls: Growing Up in the Great Migration* (Durham, NC: Duke Univ. Press, 2015).

120. *Chicago Defender*, Mar. 20, 1937.

121. Cayton and Drake, *Black Metropolis*, ch. 20, quote, 592.

122. Estelle Hill Scott, *Occupational Changes Among Negroes in Chicago* (Chicago: Work Projects Administration, 1939); Cayton and Drake, *Black Metropolis*, ch. 9.

123. Scott, *Occupational Changes Among Negroes in Chicago*; Cayton and Drake, *Black Metropolis*, ch. 9; Rick Halpern, *Down on the Killing Floor: Black and White Workers in Chicago's Packinghouses, 1904–54* (Urbana: Univ. of Illinois Press, 1997); Roger Horowitz, *"Negro and White, Unite and Fight!": A Social History of Industrial Unionism in Meatpacking, 1930–90* (Urbana: Univ. of Illinois Press, 1997); quote, Halpern, 83.

124. Lois Rita Helmbold, "Downward Occupational Mobility During the Great Depression: Urban Black and White Working Class Women," *Labor History* 29, no. 2 (Spring 1988): 135–72; Helmbold, "Beyond the Family Economy: Black and White Working-Class Women During the Great Depression," *Feminist Studies* 13, no. 3 (Autumn 1987): 629–53; Mary Anderson, "The Plight of Negro Domestic Labor," *Journal of Negro Education* 5, no. 1 (Jan. 1936): 66–72 Cayton and Drake, *Black Metropolis*, 221, 223.

125. Cayton and Drake, *Black Metropolis*, 598.

126. Cynthia M. Blair, *I've Got to Make My Livin': Black Women's Sex Work in Turn-of-the-Century Chicago* (Chicago: Univ. of Chicago Press, 2010), 233.

127. Cayton and Drake, *Black Metropolis*, 597.

128. Cayton and Drake, *Black Metropolis*, 598. LaShawn Harris, in her study of Black women who worked as prostitutes, psychics, and numbers runners in New York City during the early twentieth century, writes that work in

the informal economy allowed them to create "employment opportunities, occupational identities, and survival strategies that provided financial stability and a sense of labor autonomy and mobility." LaShawn Harris, *Sex Workers, Psychics, and Numbers Runners: Black Women in New York City's Underground Economy* (Urbana: Univ. of Illinois Press, 2016). 2.

129. Harris, *Sex Workers, Psychics, and Numbers Runners*, 2; Sharon Harley, "'Working for Nothing but for a Living': Black Women in the Underground Economy," in *Sister Circle: Black Women and Work*, ed. Sharon Harley and the Black Women and Work Collective (New Brunswick, NJ: Rutgers Univ. Press, 2002), 48–56; Elizabeth Schroeder Schlabach, *Dream Books and Gamblers: Black Women's Work in Chicago's Policy Game* (Urbana: Univ. of Illinois Press, 2022).

130. Cayton and Drake, *Black Metropolis*, 387.

131. Cayton and Drake, *Black Metropolis*, 387.

132. Hunter, *To 'Joy My Freedom*, 182–83.

133. Shane White and Graham White, *Stylin': African American Expressive Culture from Its Beginnings to the Zoot Suit* (Ithaca, NY: Cornell Univ. Press, 1998).

134. Saidiya Hartman, *Wayward Lives, Beautiful Experiments: Intimate Histories of Riotous Black Girls, Troublesome Women, and Queer Radicals* (New York: W. W. Norton, 2019), 3.

135. Cayton and Drake, *Black Metropolis*, 470–94, 500; Schlabach, *Dream Books and Gamblers*.

136. Cayton and Drake, *Black Metropolis*, 609–10.

137. Hunter, *To 'Joy My Freedom*, 178–79, 181, 183.

138. Wallace D. Best, *Passionately Human, No Less Divine: Religion and Culture in Black Chicago, 1915–1952* (Princeton, NJ: Princeton Univ. Press, 2005), quote, 2.

139. Cayton and Drake, *Black Metropolis*, 412–29, 611–57, quote, 611.

140. Cayton and Drake, *Black Metropolis*, 112.

141. *New York Amsterdam News*, Mar. 27, 1937.

142. Judith Stein, *The World of Marcus Garvey: Race and Class in Modern Society* (Baton Rouge: Louisiana State Univ. Press, 1996); Richard Brent Turner, *Islam in the African American Experience* (Bloomington: Indiana Univ. Press, 1997); Beth Tompkins Bates, *Pullman Porters and the Rise of Protest Politics in Black America, 1925–1945* (Chapel Hill: Univ. of North Carolina Press, 2001), 112–13, 118–22; Arvah E. Strickland, *History of the Chicago Urban League* (Urbana: Univ. of Illinois Press, 1966), ch. 5; Christopher Robert Reed, *The Depression Comes to the South Side: Protest and Politics in the Black Metropolis, 1930–1933* (Bloomington: Univ. of Indiana Press, 2011); A'Lelia Bundles, *On Her Own Ground: The Life and Times of Madame C. J. Walker* (New York: Scribner's, 2001); Ida B. Wells-Barnett, *Crusade for Justice: The Autobiography of Ida B. Wells*, ed. Alfreda M. Duster (Chicago: Univ. of Chicago Press, 1970); Mia Bay, *To Tell the Truth Freely: The Life of Ida B. Wells* (New York: Hill and Wang, 2009).

143. Ethan Michaeli, *The Defender: How the Legendary Black Newspaper Changed America* (New York: Houghton Mifflin, 2016); for *Defender*-sponsored parades, see also Cayton and Drake, *Black Metropolis*, 237.

144. *Chicago Defender*, Mar. 13, 20, 1937.

145. Richard Wright, "Joe Louis Uncovers Dynamite," *New Masses* 17, no. 2 (Oct. 8, 1935): 18–19.

146. *The Mail* (Adelaide, South Australia), Apr. 13, 1937; *Philadelphia Tribune*, Mar. 18, 1937.

147. William H. Harris, *Keeping the Faith: A. Philip Randolph, Milton Webster, and the Brotherhood of Sleeping Car Porters, 1925–1937* (Urbana: Univ. of Illinois Press, 1977); Bates, *Pullman Porters and the Rise of Protest Politics in Black America*; Melinda Chateauvert, *Marching Together: Women of the Brotherhood of Sleeping Car Porters* (Urbana: Univ. of Illinois Press, 1998); Reed, *The Depression Comes to the South Side*.

148. Bates, *Pullman Porters and the Rise of Protest Politics in Black America*; Chateauvert, *Marching Together*.

149. Bates, *Pullman Porters and the Rise of Protest Politics in Black America*, 113–16, quote, 115. For the YWCA, see also Anne Meis Knupfer, *The Chicago Black Renaissance and Women's Activism* (Urbana: Univ. of Illinois Press, 2006), ch. 2.

150. Bates, *Pullman Porters and the Rise of Protest Politics in Black America*, 116; George Schuyler, "Negro Workers Lead in Great Lakes Steel Drive," *Pittsburgh Courier*, July 31, 1937.

151. Bates, *Pullman Porters and the Rise of Protest Politics in Black America*, 116, 141; Cayton and Drake, *Black Metropolis*, 247; Schuyler, "Negro Workers Lead in Great Lakes Steel Drive"; Louise Thompson, "Toward a Brighter Dawn," *Woman Today* 1, no. 14 (Apr. 1936), reprinted in *Organize, Fight, Win: Black Communist Women's Political Writings*, ed. Charisse Burden-Stelly and Jodi Dean (New York: Verso, 2022), 72; Esther V. Cooper, "The Negro Woman Domestic Worker in Relation to Trade Unionism," excerpted in Burden-Stelly and Dean, *Organize, Fight, Win*, 120–21.

152. Randi Storch, *Red Chicago: American Communism at Its Grassroots, 1928–35* (Urbana: Univ. of Illinois Press, 2007), quote, 221; Bates, *Pullman Porters and the Rise of Protest Politics in Black America*, 110–13, 121–25; Schuyler, "Negro Workers Lead in Great Lakes Steel Drive." Like Thelma Wheaton, some of the women associated with the Communist Party were highly educated. Thyra J. Edwards, for example, was trained as a social worker. In 1932–33, she attended Brookwood Labor College in New York State, studied Black and white miners in Southern Illinois, then returned to Chicago and was honored by the women of the Sleeping Car Porters. After that, she traveled to Denmark to a folk school to learn about the cooperative movement, studied at the Lenin School in the Soviet Union, and through it all wrote regularly for the Black press. Edwards finally returned to Chicago to build interracial coalitions committed to fighting segregation. Gregg Andrews, *Thyra J. Edwards: Black Activist in the Global Freedom Struggle* (Columbia: Univ. of Missouri Press, 2011); Bates, *Pullman Porters and the Rise of Protest Politics in Black America*, 116–18; Thompson, "Toward a Brighter Dawn," 72.

153. Schuyler, "Negro Workers Lead in Great Lakes Steel Drive"; Bates, *Pullman Porters and the Rise of Protest Politics in Black America*, 138–41; Andrews, *Thyra J. Edwards*, 84–86.

154. Schuyler, "Negro Workers Lead in Great Lakes Steel Drive"; Bates, *Pullman Porters and the Rise of Protest Politics in Black America*, 102, 138; Storch, *Red Chicago*, 74–75. For laundry workers' extensive and militant union activism in New York City in this period, see Jenny Carson and Nell Geiser, "'The Democratic Initiative': The Promises and Limitations of Industrial Unionism for New York City's Laundry Workers, 1930–1950," *Labor: Studies in Working-Class History of the Americas* 8, no. 4 (2011): 65–87.

155. Melissa Ford, "Suppose They Are Communists! The Unemployed Councils and the 1933 Chicago Sopkins Dressmakers' Strike," *American Communist History* 16, nos. 1–2 (2017): 46–64; Storch, *Red Chicago*, 165, 167–68; Bates, *Pullman Porters and the Rise of Protest Politics in Black America*, 121, quote, 121; "Wage-Starved Girls Beaten by Police in Shop Strike," *Chicago Defender*, July 1, 1933.

156. Robert H. Zieger, *The CIO, 1935–1955* (Chapel Hill: Univ. of North Carolina Press, 1995); Fine, *Sit-Down*; Nelson Lichtenstein, *The Most Dangerous Man in Detroit: Walter Reuther and the Fate of American Labor* (New York: Basic Books, 1995); Melvyn Dubofsky and Warren Van Tine, *John L. Lewis: A Biography* (New York: Quadrangle, 1977), 279.

157. Halpern, *Down on the Killing Floor*; Horowitz, "*Negro and White, Unite and Fight!*"; Ahmed White, *The Last Great Strike: Little Steel, the CIO, and the Struggle for Labor Rights in New Deal America* (Berkeley: Univ. of California Press, 2016); Bates, *Pullman Porters and the Rise of Protest Politics in Black America*, 139–40; Zieger, *The CIO, 1935–1955*, 83; Arrendondo, *Mexican Chicago*, 60, 161; Paul Street, "The 'Best Union Members': Class, Race, Culture, and Black Worker Militancy in Chicago's Stockyards During the 1930s," *Journal of American Ethnic History* 20, no. 1 (2000): 18.

158. Cayton and Drake, *Black Metropolis*, 248; Schuyler, "Negro Workers Lead in Great Lakes Steel Drive"; Barbara Warne Newell, *Chicago and the Labor Movement: Metropolitan Unionism in the 1930s* (Urbana: Univ. of Illinois Press, 1961), 240; Dorothy Sue Cobble, *Dishing It Out: Waitresses and Their Unions in the Twentieth Century* (Urbana: Univ. of Illinois Press, 1991), 26, 77–79, 88.

159. Cayton and Drake, *Black Metropolis*, 251.

160. Dana Frank, "Women Strikers Occupy Chain Store, Win Big," in Howard Zinn, Dana Frank, and Robin D. G. Kelley, *Three Strikes: Miners, Musicians, Salesgirls, and the Fighting Spirit of Labor's Last Century* (Boston: Beacon Press, 2001), 75–118; Carlos A. Schwantes, "'We've Got 'Em on the Run, Brothers': The 1937 Non-Automotive Sit-Down Strikes in Detroit," *Michigan History* (Fall 1992): 179–99.

161. *Chicago Tribune*, Mar. 14, 1937.

162. *Chicago Tribune*, Mar. 2, 6, and 7, 1937.

163. *Chicago Tribune*, Mar. 13, 1937.

164. *Chicago Tribune*, Mar. 15, 1937.

165. Frank, "Women Strikers Occupy Chain Store, Win Big."

166. *Indianapolis Star*, Mar. 17, 1937; Wilfred Carsel, *A History of the Chicago Ladies' Garment Workers' Union* (Chicago: Normandie House, 1940),

235; Schuyler, "Negro Workers Lead in Great Lakes Steel Drive"; "Orders Arrest of Women Pickets in Garment Strike," *Pittsburgh Courier*, Apr. 10, 1937; "Chicago Walkout Called Skirmish," *Boston Globe*, Mar. 15, 1937.

167. *Chicago Tribune*, Mar. 16, 1937.

168. See, for example, Ford, "Suppose They Are Communists!," 55.

169. Joseph A. McCartin, "An Embattled New Deal Legacy: Public Sector Unionism and the Struggle for a Progressive Order," in *Beyond the New Deal Order: U.S. Politics from the Great Depression to the Great Recession*, ed. Gary Gerstle, Nelson Lichtenstein, and Alice O'Connor (Philadelphia: Univ. of Pennsylvania Press, 2019), 213–32; William P. Jones, "The Other Operation Dixie: Public Employees and the Resilience of Urban Liberalism," in *Capitalism Contested: The New Deal and Its Legacies*, ed. Romain Huret, Nelson Lichtenstein, and Jean-Christian Vin (Philadelphia: Univ. of Pennsylvania Press, 2020), 224–39.

170. *Kokomo Tribune*, Mar. 15, 1937.

171. Staughton Lynd, ed., *"We Are All Leaders": The Alternative Unionism of the Early 1930s* (Chicago: Univ. of Illinois Press, 1996).

172. *Chicago Tribune*, Mar. 13, 1937; Cayton and Drake, *Black Metropolis*, 250–51.

173. Bates, *Pullman Porters and the Rise of Protest Politics in Black America*, 114.

174. *Chicago Tribune*, Mar. 17, 1937.

175. *Los Angeles Times*, Mar. 16, 1937.

176. *Philadelphia Tribune*, Mar. 18, 1937; *Pittsburgh Courier*, Mar. 17, 1937; *Chicago Herald and Examiner*, Mar. 17, 1937; *New York Amsterdam News*, Mar. 17, 1937.

177. *Chicago Herald and Examiner*, Mar. 16, 1937.

178. Ford, "Suppose They Are Communists!"

179. White, *The Last Great Strike*.

180. *Life*, Apr. 5, 1937, 21.

181. *Kokomo Tribune*, Mar. 15, 1937.

182. Plotzke interview.

183. In 1939, the window of opportunity for sit-down strikes closed when the US Supreme Court ruled them illegal in *NLRB v. Fansteel*, a case based on yet another Chicago strike-down strike, this one undertaken by three hundred men on February 17, 1937, in a steel plant. National Labor Relations Board v. Fansteel Metallurgical Corporation, 306 U.S. 240 (1939), https://caselaw.findlaw.com/us-supreme-court/306/240.html.

184. Ira Katznelson, *When Affirmative Action Was White: An Untold History of Racial Inequality in Twentieth-Century America* (New York: W. W. Norton, 2006); Teresa L. Amott and Julie A. Matthaei, *Race, Gender and Work: A Multicultural Economic History of Women in the United States* (Boston: South End Press, 1991), 158.

185. Katznelson, *When Affirmative Action Was White*; for the minimum wage, see Ellen Mutari, Marilyn Power, and Deborah M. Figart, "Neither Mothers nor Breadwinners: African-American Women's Exclusion from US Minimum

Wage Policies, 1912–1938," *Feminist Economics* 8, no. 2 (2002): 37–61. For government employees, see McCartin, "An Embattled New Deal Legacy"; Jones, "The Other Operation Dixie: Public Employees and the Resilience of Urban Liberalism."

186. For an overview of the NIRA and the NRA strikes, see Irving Bernstein, *The Turbulent Years: A History of the American Worker, 1933–1941* (Boston: Houghton Mifflin, 1971).

187. A good place to start on the CIO is Zieger, *The CIO, 1935–1955.* Membership totals: Priscilla Murolo and A. B. Chitty, *From the Folks Who Brought You the Weekend: A Short, Illustrated History of Labor in the United States* (New York: The New Press, 2001), 213.

188. Vicki L. Ruiz, *Cannery Women, Cannery Lives: Mexican Women, Unionization, and the California Food Processing Industry* (Albuquerque: Univ. of New Mexico Press, 1987); Zaragosa Vargas, *Labor Rights Are Civil Rights: Mexican American Workers in Twentieth-Century America* (Princeton, NJ: Princeton Univ. Press, 2005), 134–43; Murolo and Chitty, *From the Folks Who Brought You the Weekend*, 213; Ruth Milkman, *Gender at Work: The Dynamics of Job Segregation by Sex During World War II* (Urbana: Univ. of Illinois Press, 1987); Nancy F. Gabin, *Feminism in the Labor Movement: Women and the United Auto Workers, 1935–1975* (Ithaca, NY: Cornell Univ. Press, 1990); Halpern, *Down on the Killing Floor*; Horowitz, *"Negro and White, United and Fight!"*

189. Jenny Carson, *A Matter of Moral Justice: Black Women Laundry Workers and the Fight for Justice* (Urbana: Univ. of Illinois Press, 2021).

190. Cobble, *Dishing It Out*, 86–107.

191. Amott and Matthei, *Race, Gender, and Work*, 334–35.

192. Vanessa H. May, *Unprotected Labor: Household Workers, Politics, and Middle-Class Reformers in New York, 1870–1940* (Chapel Hill: Univ. of North Carolina Press, 2011), 155–65; Cooper, "The Negro Woman Domestic Worker in Relation to Trade Unionism," 111–22; Premilla Nadasen, *Household Workers Unite: The Untold Story of African American Women Who Built a Union* (Boston: Beacon Press, 2015), 13–17; Christina Heatherton, *Arise! Global Radicalism in the Era of the Mexican Revolution* (Berkeley: Univ. of California Press, 2022), 166–67.

193. Amott and Matthei, *Race, Gender, and Work*, 179; Kate Bronfenbrenner and Dorian T. Warren, "Race, Gender, and the Rebirth of Trade Unionism," *New Labor Forum* 16, nos. 3/4 (Fall 2007): 142–48.

CHAPTER FOUR: A NEST OF FASCISTS

1. J. F. Cordrey, to Inspector in Charge, Feb. 23, 1935, Federal Bureau of Investigation; C. E. Smith, FBI Memo, May 24, 1935, both in Section 1A, Federal Bureau of Investigation Records, Internet Archive (hereafter FBI), available at https://archive.org/details/BlackLegion/black11a/:BlackL.1.A. Other accounts of the Black Legion's initiation include: George T. Scheid Jr., interview by Peter Amann, Lima, Ohio, June 19, 1979, in Peter Amann Papers, Box 15, Folder 13, Archives of Labor and Urban Affairs, Walter Reuther Library, Wayne State University (hereafter Peter Amann Papers); *Pittsburgh Press*, May 27, 1936; *New*

York Times, May 27, 1936; *Lima News*, May 27, 1936; *Toledo Blade*, May 27, 1936; Hearings Before a Subcommittee of the Committee on Interstate and Foreign Commerce, United States Senate, Eightieth Congress, First Session, on Nomination of Robert Franklin Jones, of Ohio, to Be a Member of the Federal Communications Commission for a Term of 7 Years from July 1, 1947, June 27, July 3 and 7, 1947 (Washington, DC: US Government Printing Office, 1947) (hereafter Jones Hearing), 45–46.

2. For the Black Legion in general, especially its leaders, see Peter H. Amann, "Vigilante Fascism: The Black Legion as an American Hybrid," *Comparative Studies in Society and History* 25, no. 3 (July 1983): 490–524. Amann's extensive research collection is available at the Archives of Labor and Urban Affairs, Walter Reuther Library, Wayne State University. I am especially grateful to Amann for the oral histories he conducted in Lima in 1979. For other works on the Black Legion, see George Morris, *The Black Legion Rides* (New York: Workers' Library, 1936); Kenneth R. Dvorak, "Terror in Detroit: The Rise and Fall of Michigan's Black Legion," PhD diss., Bowling Green State Univ., 2000; Tom Stanton, *Terror in the City of Champions: Murder, Baseball, and the Secret Society That Shocked Depression-Era Detroit* (Guilford, CT: Lyons Press, 2016); Mark S. English, "Under the Star of the Guard: The Story of the Black Legion," MLS thesis, University of Michigan, 1993.

3. Manning Marable, *Malcolm X: A Life of Reinvention* (New York: Viking, 2011), 30–31.

4. A. B. Magil and Henry Stevens, *The Peril of Fascism: The Crisis of American Democracy* (New York: International Publishers, 1938), 197. In the late 1950s, a Lima historian named Frank M. Hackman entitled a two-part pamphlet about the mainstream history of the town, *It Happened Here*. He makes no mention of the Black Legion, so it appears the title was chosen unwittingly. Frank M. Hackman, *It Happened Here: Lima—Seat of Justice* (Lima, OH: Shawnee Historical Publications, 1958); *It Happened Here: Portraits of the Great Black Swamp* (Lima, OH: Shawnee Historical Publications, 1959).

5. "Caliban in America," unsigned editorial, *The Nation*, June 10, 1936, 728.

6. "Founder of Black Legion Is Just Plain 'Doctor Billy' to Bellaire Home Foks," *Detroit News*, n.d. [May or June 1935], FBI 1C; W. L. Buchanan, FBI report, Cincinnati, OH, July 8, 1935, FBI 1A.

7. "Founder of Black Legion Is Just Plain 'Doctor Billy' to Bellaire Home Folks"; W. L. Buchanan, FBI report, July 8, 1935.

8. Amann, "Vigilante Fascism," 493–95.

9. For the Second Klan, see David M. Chalmers, *Hooded Americanism: The First Century of the Ku Klux Klan, 1865–1965* (Garden City, NY: Doubleday, 1965); Kathleen M. Blee, *Women of the Klan: Racism and Gender in the 1920s* (Berkeley: Univ. of California Press, 1991); Leonard J. Moore: *Citizen Klansmen: The Ku Klux Klan in Indiana, 1921–1928* (Chapel Hill: Univ. of North Carolina Press, 1991); Nancy MacLean, *Behind the Mask of Chivalry: The Making of the Second Ku Klux Klan* (New York: Oxford Univ. Press, 1994); Linda Gordon, *The Second Coming of the KKK: The Ku Klux Klan of the 1920s and the American Political Tradition* (New York: Liveright, 2017).

10. Blee, *Women of the Klan*, 87–91.

11. Blee, *Women of the Klan*, 77–78.

12. Chalmers, *Hooded Americanism*; Blee, *Women of the Klan*; Moore, *Citizen Klansmen*; MacLean, *Behind the Mask of Chivalry*; Gordon, *The Second Coming of the KKK*.

13. Amann, "Vigilante Fascism"; "Founder of Black Legion Is Just Plain 'Doctor Billy' to Bellaire Home Folks"; W. L. Buchanan, FBI report, July 8, 1935.

14. Amann, "Vigilante Fascism," 501–8.

15. Harry Meredith, interview with Peter Amann, June 19, 1979, Lima, OH, p. 6, Box 15, Folder 8, Peter Amann Papers.

16. James N. Bissell to Edgar J. Hoover [sic], Oct. 21, 1936, FBI 2B; *Lima News*, Aug. 21, 1936, Jan. 30, 1927, June 12, 1934; N. E. Manson, FBI Memo, Cleveland, OH, Apr. 14, 1936, p. 3, FBI 1B.

17. Scheid interview, 9. Dues were recorded on a card that read "Accident Insurance Prospect Card." Cordey to Inspector in Charge, Feb. 23, 1935, p. 5.

18. *Lima News*, Feb. 13, 1929; "Dry Crusader Roney Arrested on Pen Charge," *Lima News*., n.d. in Effinger file, Allen County Historical Museum; Manson FBI Memo, Apr. 14, 1936.

19. *Lima News*, July 5, 1925.

20. *Lima News*, Aug. 8, 1921.

21. *Lima News*, June 12, 1934.

22. *Lima News*, Aug. 12, 1934.

23. *New York Times*, May 25, 1936; Smith FBI Memo, May 24, 1935, p. 11.

24. *Lima News*, May 26, 1936. For a summary of Effinger's views based on an Apr. 8, 1936, interview with an FBI agent, see Manson FBI Memo, Apr. 14, 1936.

25. E. J. Penhorwood interview with Peter Amann, June 20, 1979, Lima, OH, pp. 2–3, 11, Box 15, Folder 11, Peter Amann Papers.

26. "Statement of, taken in the office of the Prosecuting Attorney by Chief Investigator, Harry Colburn August 6, 1936, at 10:46 a.m. in the presence of Charley Spare [sic] August 6, 1935," attached to John Edgar Hoover to Special Agent in Charge, Detroit, Michigan, Aug. 12, 1936, FBI 2A. "ISMs" also appears in Manson FBI Memo, Apr. 14, 1936, p. 4.

27. Statement taken by Harry Colburn, Aug. 6, 1936, 5–6.

28. Smith FBI Memo, May 24, 1935, p. 6.

29. Smith FBI Memo, May 24, 1935, p. 5. Effinger told an FBI agent in 1936, "It is sometimes right and necessary . . . for the patriotic citizens of this country to take the law into their own hands and to cope with situations that the local law enforcers have failed to handle." Manson FBI Memo, Apr. 14, 1936, p. 3. In 1932, Effinger reportedly told "a large crowd" in Lima that "we are going to take over the government," and that "we are prepared to use the horsewhip and pistol if we have to." *Lima News*, Aug. 21, 1936.

30. No. 34, "Investigation Re: Bullet Club, Black Knights, Night Riders, Etc., Lima, Ohio," Jan. 23, 1935, attached to Bates Raney, State Relief Commission of Ohio, to Major H. M. Pool, G.S.C, Jan. 28, 1935, p. 4; Smith FBI Memo, May 24, 1935, pp. 3, 14, and throughout.

31. Smith FBI Memo, May 24, 1935.

32. Scheid interview, 12.

33. Smith FBI Memo, May 24, 1935, 7–8. Much earlier, in August 1932, Effinger wrote to the county sheriff offering the services of five hundred vigilantes "who mean business" to help "rid Lima and Allen [County] of the 'curses' of all 'questionable joints, slot machines, gangsters, and so-called big-time booze handlers.'" *Lima News*, Aug. 16, 1932.

34. Smith FBI Memo, May 24, 1935, p. 4. The informant was presumably George Scheid Sr., whose son, George Jr., told the *Lima News* in 2000 that his father left the Legion "after Effinger ordered him to bomb the Sigma Theater on Lima's Public Square in retaliation for showing a film that Effinger regarded as 'Catholic propaganda.'" *Lima News*, Apr. 9, 2000.

35. *Lima News*, Jan. 29, 1934.

36. "Violent Crimes in Ohio Laid to Black Legion; Threat to Kidnap Davey's Daughter Is Cited," *New York Times*, May 28, 1936; Smith FBI Memo, May 24, 1935, pp. 3–4.

37. *Evening Review* (East Liverpool, OH), May 28, 1936; *Evening Independent* (Massillon, OH), May 28, 1926; *Daily Times* (Portsmouth, OH), May 28, 1936. The interviews were conducted and the report was written in 1935, but it wasn't released until 1936.

38. *Pittsburgh Press*, May 27, 1936; *New York Times*, May 27, 1936; *Lima News*, May 27, 1936; *Toledo Blade*, May 27, 1936.

39. "Memorandum," n.d. [1935?], p. 3, FBI; Corres. . . . , Apr–June, 1935," Box 1, Folder 5, Peter Amann Papers.

40. Smith FBI Memo, May 24, 1935, p. 11.

41. Smith FBI Memo, May 24, 1935, p. 10.

42. Smith FBI Memo, May 24, 1935, p. 7.

43. Smith FBI Memo, May 24, 1935, p. 4.

44. Scheid interview, 2–3, 12.

45. *Lima News*, Apr. 9, 2000.

46. Cordrey report, Feb. 23, 1935, p. 2.

47. Smith FBI Memo, May 24, 1935, p. 7.

48. Memo, "On August 10, 1935 Special Agent in Charge J. P. MacFarland received a letter from XXXX which is as follows," Lima, OH, Aug. 9, 1935, FBI 1A.

49. Scheid interview, 15.

50. Scheid interview, 2.

51. Smith FBI Memo, May 24, 1935, 6.

52. *Los Angeles Times*, Aug. 15, 1936.

53. Smith FBI Memo, May 24, 1935, 6.

54. John Edgar Hoover, "Memorandum for the Attorney General," Aug. 12, 1936, and attached statement taken by Harry Colburn, Aug. 6, 1936, FBI 2A.

55. *Lima News*, July 13, 1934.

56. Quoted in *Tribune* (Coshocton, OH), Aug. 27, 1934.

57. *Marion Star*, Aug. 27, 1924. For the onion workers' strike, see *Sandusky Register*, July 10, 1934; *Marysville Journal-Tribune*, July 10, 1934; *Tribune* (Coshocton, OH), Aug. 27, 1934; *Lima News*, July 13, 1934; "'Black League' in

Onion Region Is Terrorism Threat," July 13, 1934, news story manuscript copy, Box 10, Peter Amann Papers; "Violent Crimes in Ohio Laid to Black Legion," *New York Times*, May 28, 1936; Bernard Sternsher, "Scioto Marsh Onion Workers Strike, Hardin, Ohio, 1934," *Northwest Ohio Quarterly* 58, nos. 2–3 (Spring/Summer 1986): 39–92; Tom Rumer, *Unearthing the Land: The Story of Ohio's Scioto Marsh* (Akron: Univ. of Ohio Press, 1999).

58. US Bureau of the Census, *Fifteenth Census of the United States: 1930*, vol. 1, *Population* (Washington, DC: US Government Printing Office, 1931), 493; Federal Writers' Project, Workers Progress Administration, Ohio, *A Guide to Lima and Allen County Ohio* (Federal Writers' Project, 1938), 11, 23, 25–29, 35; Eric Hirsimaki, *Lima: The History* (Edmonds, WA: Hundman Publishing, 1986); Marilyn R. Stark, *A Pictorial History of Lima/Allen County, Ohio* (Virginia Beach, VA: Donning Co., 1993), 75–109; Perry Bush, *Rust Belt Resistance: How A Small Community Took On Big Oil And Won* (Kent, OH: Kent State Univ. Press, 2012), 11–48.

59. Federal Writers' Project, *A Guide to Lima and Allen County Ohio*, 11, 14.

60. US Bureau of the Census, *Fifteenth Census of the United States: 1930*, vol. 1, *Population*, 493.

61. This list is compiled from names given in dozens of documents and news stories, almost all of which are cited here. The most extensive list is in Smith FBI Memo, May 24, 1935, pp. 12–13. Occupations are also drawn from *Polk's Lima City Directory, 1930–40* (Southfield, MI: R. L. Polk & Co., 1929–39).

62. For the history of fraternal organizations in Lima, see Harry D. Poulston, "Service Clubs and Fraternal Organizations in Lima," in Allen County Historical Society, *The 1976 History of Allen County, Ohio* (Evansville, IN: Unigraphic, 1976), 683–92.

63. Perry Bush, "'We Have Them Whipped Here': Lynching and the Rule of Law in Lima, Ohio," *Ohio History* 128, no. 2 (2021): 7–41; David Meyers and Elise Meyers Walker, *Lynching and Mob Violence in Ohio, 1772–1938* (Jefferson, NC: McFarland, 2019); Michael E. Brooks and Bob Fitrakis, *A History of Hate in Ohio: Then and Now* (Columbus: Ohio State Univ. Press, 2021).

64. Penhorwood interview, 10. For more on Penhorwood, see "11 Years of Service in Easter Sunday Program," *Lima News*, Apr. 7, 1939.

65. "Ku Klux Klan Demonstration Photograph," Ku Klux Klan Collection, Ohio History Connection, https://ohiomemory.org/digital/collection/p267401coll32/id/10473.

66. Scheid interview, 1.

67. Jim Christoff, Oral History, Feb. 9, 1987, p. 14, in Allen County Historical Museum. For the KKK in Ohio, see Michael E. Brooks, *The Klux Klan in Wood County, Ohio* (Charleston, SC: History Press, 2014); William D. Jenkins, *Steel Valley Klan: The Ku Klux Klan In Ohio's Mahoning Valley* (Kent, OH: Kent State Univ. Press, 1990); see also Craig Fox, *Everyday Klansfolk: White Protestant Life and the KKK in 1920s Michigan* (East Lansing: Michigan State Univ. Press, 2011).

68. Jones Hearing, 93.

69. Scheid interview, 6.

70. Smith FBI Memo, May 24, 1935, p. 13.

71. Meredith interview, 7–8.

72. Penhorwood interview, 1–2, 4.

73. N.A. to C. Wm. Ramseyer, May 28, 1935. "U.S. Department of Justice: Corres., May 25–31, 1936," Box 3, Folders 5–7, Peter Amann Papers.

74. Scheid interview, 1.

75. W. L. Buchanan report, July 9, 1935.

76. Penhorwood interview, 4, 9–10.

77. Scheid interview, 2.

78. Smith FBI Memo, May 24, 1935, p. 5.

79. Statement taken by Harry Colburn, Aug. 6, 1936, p. 6.

80. Smith FBI Memo, May 24, 1935, p. 13; E. H. Williams, FBI Memo, Dec. 12, 1935, p. 2., FBI 1B.

81. Williams FBI Memo, Dec. 12, 1935, p. 2.

82. Williams FBI Memo, Dec. 12, 1935, p. 2.

83. Penhorwood interview, 7–8.

84. Manson FBI Memo, Apr. 14, 1936, p. 5.

85. *Lima News*, May 25, 1936. For Virgil consulting with, and deferring to, Mary, see also Jones Hearing, 30.

86. Blee, *Women of the Klan*; MacLean, *Behind the Mask of Chivalry*; Gordon, *The Second Coming of the KKK*, chs. 6–7.

87. Agent No. 34, "Investigation Re: Bullet Club . . . ," p. 2. For Cordrey's possible membership, see Agent No. 34, "Investigation Re: Bullet Club . . . ," 2–3.

88. Cordrey to Inspector in Charge, Feb. 23, 1935, p. 3.

89. Scheid interview, 1.

90. *New York Times*, May 25, 1936.

91. Textiles Collection, Archives of Labor and Urban Affairs, Walter Reuther Library, Wayne State University, Detroit, Michigan. My thanks to Elizabeth Clements for her help in accessing the robes.

92. Scheid interview, 7.

93. Meredith interview, 7.

94. Scheid interview, 8–9.

95. Meredith interview, 9.

96. W. E. B. Du Bois, *Black Reconstruction in America: An Essay Toward a History of the Part Which Black Folk Played in the Attempt to Reconstruct Democracy in America, 1860–1880* (New York: Harcourt Brace, 1935), 700–701; David R. Roediger, *The Wages of Whiteness: Race and the Making of the American Working Class* (London: Verso Books, 1991).

97. *Lima News*, Apr. 11, 1934.

98. Cordrey to Inspector in Charge, Feb. 23, 1935, p. 2; "Memorandum," p. 2; Smith FBI Memo, May 24, 1935, p. 4; *New York Times*, May 25, 1936. See also C. E. Smith, FBI Memo, Sept. 6, 1935, FBI 1A.

99. *Columbus Dispatch*, May 27, 1936.

100. Smith FBI Memo, May 24, 1935, p. 2; Agent No. 34, "Investigation Re: Bullet Club . . . ," p. 1; *Lima News*, July 24, 1935.

101. N.A. to C. William Ramseyer, May 28, 1935, p. 1. "Since Mr. Timberlake was a Republican, I apprehend that he too was very friendly because here in Lima, we considered the Ku Klux Klan as an adjunct of the Republican Party, and I know I found fault with Timberlake and his organization because all of the appointees were Republicans."

102. Linda Gordon, *Pitied but Not Entitled: Single Mothers and the History of Welfare, 1890–1935* (New York: Free Press, 1994); Nancy E. Rose, *Workfare or Fair Work: Women, Welfare, and Government Work Programs from the 1930s to the 1990s* (New Brunswick, NJ: Rutgers Univ. Press, 1995).

103. Smith FBI Memo, Sept. 6, 1935, p. 1. The *Lima News* reported that Armstrong "asserted that discrimination was used in this manner against the colored workers and members of the Catholic faith." July 14, 1935. For Effinger saying he controlled FERA jobs, see also *New York Times*, May 27, 1936.

104. *Lima News*, July 14, 1935.

105. The Black Legion also apparently helped its members get jobs other than those at the FERA. The *New York Times* reported about the Michigan Black Legion: "One purpose of the Black Legion was to get jobs for its members. Not one of those who have been in custody or questioned is unemployed. Several attributed their jobs to the aid of other members." *New York Times*, May 25, 1936.

106. Ira Katznelson, *When Affirmative Action Was White: An Untold History of Racial Inequality in Twentieth-Century America* (New York: W. W. Norton, 2005), 37–52.

107. Agent No. 34, "Investigation Re: Bullet Club . . . "; Agent No. 34, "Investigation of Irregularities in Allen County Works Division, complaint of Mr. Fred Cook, 729 Elm St., Lima Ohio and F. D. Sanders, 424 E. North St., Lima, Ohio," n.d., attached to Agent No. 34, "Investigation Re: Bullet Club . . . ," Box 3, Folder 2, Peter Amann Papers.

108. Agent No. 34, "Investigation Re: Bullet Club . . . ," 5; Agent No. 34, "Investigation of Irregularities . . . ," 1–4.

109. *Lima News*, Mar. 16, 1932.

110. For the unemployed movement in Lima, see *Lima News*, Mar. 16, Aug. 20, 1932; Feb. 2, 1933; May 14, Aug. 16, Nov. 23, 1934. For the Unemployed Leagues, see Roy Rosenzweig, "Radicals and the Jobless: Museteites and the Unemployed Leagues, 1932–36," *Labor History* 16, no. 1 (Winter 1975): 52–77; see also Rosenzweig, "Organizing the Unemployed: The Early Years of the Great Depression, 1929–1933," *Radical America* 10, no. 4 (July–Aug. 1976): 37–60; Rosenzweig, "'Socialism in Our Time': The Socialist Party and the Unemployed, 1932–1936," *Labor History* 20, no. 4 (Fall 1979): 475–509; James J. Lorence, *Organizing the Unemployed: Community and Union Activists in the Industrial Heartland* (Albany: State Univ. of New York Press, 1996).

111. *Lima News*, Aug. 16, 1934.

112. Meredith interview, 5–6.

113. E.g., "Violent Crimes in Ohio Laid to Black Legion," *New York Times*, May 28, 1936.

114. Smith FBI Memo, May 24, 1935, p. 13.

115. Richard W. Judd, *Socialist Cities: Municipal Politics and the Grass Roots of American Socialism* (Albany: State Univ. of New York Press, 1989),

ch. 6; James Weinstein, *The Decline of Socialism in America, 1912–1925* (New York: Vintage Books, 1967); Rosenzweig, "Radicals and the Jobless"; Rosenzweig, "Organizing the Unemployed"; Rosenzweig, "'Socialism in Our Time'"; Lorence, *Organizing the Unemployed.*

116. *Lima News,* Aug. 8, 1921.

117. Priscilla Murolo and A. B. Chitty, *From the Folks Who Brought You the Weekend: A Short, Illustrated History of Labor in the United States* (New York: The New Press, 2001), 130, 146–47; Herman D. Bloch, "Craft Unions and the Negro in Historical Perspective," *Journal of Negro History* 43, no. 1 (Jan. 1958): 10–33.

118. Irving Bernstein, *The Turbulent Years: A History of the American Worker, 1933–41* (Boston: Houghton Mifflin, 1971); Farrell Dobbs, *Teamster Rebellion* (New York: Monad Press, 1972); Mike Quinn, *The Big Strike* (Olema, CA: Olema Publishing, 1949).

119. Federal Writers' Project, *A Guide to Lima and Allen County Ohio,* 30. For the labor movement in Lima in these years, see Thomas A. Thompson and Furl Williams, "Labor," in Allen County Historical Society, *The 1976 History of Allen County, Ohio,* 299–301.

120. Smith FBI Memo, May 24, 1935, p. 10.

121. Statement taken by Harry Colburn, Aug. 6, 1936, p. 9.

122. *State Indicator* (Troy, OH), June 4, 1936, FBI 3B.

123. Agent No. 34, "Investigation Re: Bullet Club . . . ," p. 3; Agent No. 34, "Investigation of Irregularities . . . ," p. 1; "On August 10, 1935, Special Agent in Charge J. P. MacFarland," Aug. 9, 1935.

124. Agent No. 34, "Investigation Re: Bullet Club . . . ," p. 3.

125. B. M. Hirsch, FBI Memo, Mar. 7, 1936, p. 2, FBI 1B.

126. Agent No. 34, "Investigation Re: Bullet Club . . . ," p. 3. In a letter to former congressman Christian William Ramseyer (a Republican), the former publisher of the *Lima News* wrote that Timberlake, the head of the FERA in town, must be in the Black Legion because "here in Lima, we considered the Ku Klux Klan as an adjunct of the Republican Party." N.A. to C. William Ramseyer, May 28, 1935.

127. Jones Hearing, 38, 49, 51, 53, 59–60. See also p. 33.

128. Quote: Hirsch FBI Memo, Mar. 7, 1936; Scheid interview, 5.

129. *Columbus Dispatch,* May 27, 1936.

130. Smith FBI Memo, May 24, 1935, p. 7; "Memorandum," n.a. [FBI], n.d. [1935], p. 4, "FBI; Corres., Apr–Jun. 1935," Box 1, Folder 5, Peter Amann Papers.

131. Williams FBI Memo, Dec. 12, 1935, p. 2; Hirsch FBI Memo, Mar. 7, 1936.

132. Hirsch FBI memo, Mar. 7, 1936, p. 2; Williams FBI Memo, Dec. 12, 1935, p. 2; "Memorandum," n.a. [FBI], n.d. [1935]; Smith FBI Memo, May 24, 1935.

133. *Columbus Dispatch,* May 27, 1936.

134. H. H. Reinecke to FBI Director, Aug. 7, 1936, p. 2, FBI 1G.

135. *Pittsburgh Press,* May 27, 1936; *New York Times,* May 27, 1936; *Lima News,* May 27, 1936; *Toledo Blade,* May 27, 1936.

136. Smith FBI Memo, May 24, 1935, p. 7.

137. Smith FBI Memo, May 24, 1935, p. 7.

138. US Census Bureau, *Fifteenth Census of the United States: 1930*, vol. 1, *Population*, 493; Jill Rowe-Adjibogoun, "The Impact of Structural Constraints on the Quality of Life for African American Males in Lima, Ohio: A Community History," PhD diss., Michigan State Univ., 2004, 8; "The Black History of Lima: A Preliminary Study," Spring Quarter History 260 Class, Ohio State, Lima, June 1971, in Allen County Historical Museum, 26 29. For background on Black women's work as domestic servants in Ohio in these years, see Alexander D. Gaither, "Negro Women Employed in Domestic Service in Columbus, Ohio," master's thesis, Ohio State Univ., 1938; Rolland Moxley, "Negroes in Allen County," in Allen County Historical Society, *The 1976 History of Allen County, Ohio*, 754–62.

139. Interview quoted in Rowe-Adjibogoun, "The Impact of Structural Constraints on the Quality of Life for African American Males," 54.

140. Rowe-Adjibogoun, "The Impact of Structural Constraints on the Quality of Life for African American Males," 49; History 260 Class, "The Black History of Lima," 12–13, 25; "Reminiscences with Rolland Moxley," in Allen County Historical Society, *The 1976 History of Allen County, Ohio*, 754–55; James Williamson, telephone interviews with the author, May 12, 2022, July 5, 2022; Greg Hoersten, "Reminiscence: Recalling Schoonover Pool," *Lima News*, May 30, 2023. For the earlier period, see David A. Gerber, *Black Ohio and the Color Line, 1860–1915* (Urbana: Univ. of Illinois Press, 1976); William W. Giffin, *African Americans and the Color Line in Ohio, 1915–1930* (Columbus: Ohio State Univ. Press, 2005).

141. Williamson interview, May 12, 2022. Williamson recounted that when a new skating rink opened in the 1950s, African Americans were only allowed in on Monday night, which was known as "N. . . . Night."

142. N.A. [Christine Zachary], "Racism, Segregation and Intolerance: Lima, in Ohio in the 1950s," Mar. 15, 2015, https://thomasschoonover.blogspot.com /2015/03/racism-segregation-and-intolerance-lima.html; Christine Zachary, "Thomas R. Schoonover's Travelogue of 1952 Africa," https://www.caronia2 .info/trsindx.php.

143. N.A., *Shawnee: The First Seventy-Five Years* (Lima, OH, n.p., 1979).

144. *Lima News*, Sept. 26, 2020; Moxley, "Negroes in Allen County," 750–51; Anne Beehler, "Religion," in Allen County Historical Society, *The 1976 History of Allen County, Ohio*; Stark, *A Pictorial History of Lima/Allen County*, 72. Quote: Moxley, "Negroes in Allen County," 751.

145. For women's clubs, see "News in Colored Circles," regular feature in the *Lima News*; presentation of purse, Jan. 22, 1933.

146. Rowe-Adjibogoun, "The Impact of Structural Constraints on the Quality of Life for African American Males," 41; History 260 Class, "The Black History of Lima," 11, 16–20; Williamson interviews, May 12, July 5, 2022; *Lima News*, Sept. 26, 2020, Feb. 1, 2022. For chicken dinners and fundraising in the African American community, see Adrian Miller, *Soul Food: The Surprising Story of an American Cuisine, One Plate at a Time* (Chapel Hill: Univ. of North Carolina Press, 2013), ch. 4.

147. Williamson interviews, May 12, July 5, 2022.

148. Moxley, "Negroes in Allen County," 755, 757–62; Rowe-Adjibogoun, "The Impact of Structural Constraints on the Quality of Life for African American Males," 45–46; Stark, *A Pictorial History of Lima/Allen County*, 87, 100–101; History 260 Class, "The Black History of Lima," 27. For Dalton, see *Lima News*, Feb. 1, 2022; Williamson interview, May 12, 2022; Moxley, "Negroes in Allen County," 754.

149. History 260 Class, "The Black History of Lima," quote, 146; Rolland Moxley biography, Allen County Historical Society, *The 1976 History of Allen County, Ohio*, 748; Jones Hearing, 99–100.

150. Moxley, "Negroes in Allen County," 748. For Moxley and patronage system, see also Jones Hearing, 99–100.

151. The Ohio State, Lima, students who researched Lima's African American history reported that "several local Blacks were appointed to local government jobs in 1936 and 1938." History 260 Class, "The Black History of Lima," 12–13.

152. US Census Bureau, *Fifteenth Census of the United States: 1930*, vol. 1, *Population*, 503, 507; Stark, *A Pictorial History of Lima/Allen County*, 93.

153. Virginia L. Moore, "Catholicism" in Allen County Historical Society, *The 1976 History of Allen County, Ohio*, 442–51; Lima Central Catholic High School, "Catholic Schools in the Lima Community," https://www.lcchs.edu/page/history; Fondi DeFinis, interview with M. F. Weis, Feb. 28, 1989, Allen County Historical Society, 11; Stark, *A Pictorial History of Lima/Allen County*, 60, 69.

154. DeFinis interview, 15–16.

155. DeFinis interview, 10. William Rusler, *A Standard History of Allen County, Ohio: An Authentic Narrative of the Past, with Particular Attention to the Modern Era in the Commercial, Industrial, Educational, Civic and Social Development* (New York: American Historical Society, 1921), 280; Rowe-Adjibogoun, "The Impact of Structural Constraints on the Quality of Life for African American Males," 40–41.

156. DeFinis interview, 2–5, 13, and throughout; Williamson interview, May 12, 2022. For the racial/ethnic positioning of Italian immigrants, see Thomas A. Guglielmo, *White on Arrival: Italians, Race, Color and Power in Chicago, 1890–1945* (New York: Oxford Univ. Press, 2004); Jennifer Guglielmo and Salvatore Salerno, *Are Italians White? How Race Is Made in America* (New York: Routledge, 2003).

157. US Census Bureau, *Fifteenth Census of the United States: 1930*, vol. 1, *Population*, 503–7.

158. US Census Bureau, *Fifteenth Census of the United States: 1930*, vol. 1, *Population*, 502, 506; Williams interviews, May 12, July 5, 2022; Bush, "'We Have Them Whipped Here'"; DeFinis interview, 5; Rusler, *A Standard History of Allen County, Ohio*, 278; Noel Ignatiev, *How the Irish Became White* (New York: Routledge, 1995).

159. Zerlene S. Blattner, "Judaism," in Allen County Historical Society, *The 1976 History of Allen County, Ohio*, 452–55; *Lima News*, Sept. 26, 2020; Stark, *A Pictorial History of Lima/Allen County*, 72; Rusler, *A Standard History of Allen County, Ohio*, 279–80. According to the US Census, there were fifty-three people in Lima in 1930 whose mother tongue was Yiddish. US

Census Bureau, *Fifteenth Census of the United States: 1930*, vol. 1, *Population*, 390.

160. Rusler, *A Standard History of Allen County, Ohio*, 279–80.

161. I am grateful to Charlene Smith-Echols, secretary-treasurer, Lima NAACP, for pointing out that members of the African American community would have shared codes in order to deal with Black Legion members. Interview by the author with Charlene Smith-Echols, Lima, Ohio, Apr. 26, 2022.

162. Dvorak, "Terror in Detroit," 160–62, 164; Stanton, *Terror in the City of Champions*, 123, 230–34, 237–40.

163. Dvorak, "Terror in Detroit," 164; Stanton, *Terror in the City of Champions*, 244, 273.

164. "New Hate Cult Exposed! Nation Shocked as Arrests Reveal Black Legion's Campaign of Terror," Hearst production footage, HCOc654r1, HCOc654r2, X11273, HNRv7n272, UCLA Film and Television Archive, Santa Clarita, CA. My thanks to Kara Molitor for sharing these clippings.

165. Stanton, *Terror in the City of Champions*, 245, 272; Dvorak, "Terror in Detroit," 165–66; Ervin Lee, deposition, State of Michigan, County of Wayne, Oct. 19, 1936, "People v. Virgil Effinger, 1939," Box 3, Folder 10, Peter Amann Papers; Elvis Black, deposition, State of Michigan, County of Wayne, Oct. 19, 1936, "People v. Virgil Effinger, 1939," Box 3, Folder 10, Peter Amann Papers; Morris, *The Black Legion Rides*, 26. McCrea was presumably using the Poole trial to try to clean up his own reputation.

166. For the Black Legion in Detroit, see Dvorak, "Terror in Detroit," and Stanton, *Terror in the City of Champions*; see also Amann, "Vigilante Terrorism."

167. Amann, "Vigilante Terrorism," 505–6; Dvorak, "Terror in Detroit," 127–30, 134–37.

168. See Amann, "Vigilante Terrorism," 507, for a discussion of his estimates.

169. *New York Times*, May 30, 1036, cited in Dvorak, "Terror in Detroit," 26–27.

170. "New Hate Cult Exposed!"

171. Dvorak, "Terror in Detroit," 159.

172. Stanton, *Terror in the City of Champions*, 55–56; see Blee, *Women of the Klan*, for similar activities in the 1920s Indiana Ku Klux Klan.

173. Dvorak, "Terror in Detroit," 144–47.

174. Stanton, *Terror in the City of Champions*, 128–29, 132–34, 258; Dvorak, "Terror in Detroit," 158.

175. Marable, *Malcolm X*, 30–32; *The Autobiography of Malcolm X* (1965; repr., New York: Grove Press, 1966), 9–10.

176. Dvorak, "Terror in Detroit," 140–42, 162. When Dayton Dean's wife went to the Legion and charged him with molesting their daughter, he was taken out of town, handcuffed, and whipped by fifteen different members. Stanton, *Terror in the City of Champions*, 94.

177. Dvorak, "Terror in Detroit," 146–48.

178. Dvorak, "Terror in Detroit," 149–51.

179. Stanton, *Terror in the City of Champions*, 87–89, 101, 106–7, 110–12, 182. For Sugar's extensive research, writing, and comments on the Black Legion, see Maurice Sugar Papers, Archives of Labor and Urban Affairs, Walter

Reuther Library, Wayne State University, Detroit, Michigan, Boxes 18–23. For Sugar, see Christopher H. Johnson, *Maurice Sugar: Law, Labor, and the Left in Detroit, 1912–1950* (Detroit: Wayne State Univ. Press, 1988).

180. Dvorak, "Terror in Detroit," 153–57, 170. For Oakland County document, see "COPY—WCNS 39," n.a., n.d., p. 1, FBI 3B; *New York Times*, June 1, 1936; Morris, *The Black Legion Rides*, 23–28.

181. "Major Wayne County Black Legion Cases," n.a., n.d., Box 6, Folder 21, Peter Amann Papers; George Morris, in late 1936, reported that "at this writing . . . more than 60 members of the terror organization have been arrested, charged with a part in the crimes." Morris, *The Black Legion Rides*, 4. Stanton reports multiple successful prosecutions in the Detroit region. Stanton, *Terror in the City of Champions*, 273.

182. *Lima News*, Aug. 21, 1936.

183. *Lima News*, Aug. 16, 1936.

184. *Lima News*, Aug. 16, 26, 1936; *Washington Post*, Aug. 23, 1936; *New York Times*, Aug. 23, 1936, Dec. 4, 1937. For Taylor's refusal to cooperate, see also *Los Angeles Times*, Aug. 23, 1936.

185. *Cleveland Plain Dealer*, Aug. 26, 1936.

186. *Toledo Blade*, Aug. 28, 1936.

187. E.g., *Lima News*, Aug. 26, 30, 31, 1936; *New York Post*, Aug. 26, 1936; *Washington Post*, Aug. 26, 1936.

188. *Lima News*, July 27, 1936.

189. *Lima News*, Aug. 31, 1936.

190. Herold H. Reinecke to J. Edgar Hoover, Sept. 5, 1936, FBI 2A.

191. *Lima News*, Aug. 13, 1936. For Effinger's presence in Lima, see also *Lima News*, Oct. 7, 1937. On December 20, 1936—when Effinger had already been underground in Lima for four months—Herb Coates, a staff writer for the *Lima News*, asked the town's top law enforcement officials what they wanted for Christmas. Sheriff R. S. Marshall replied that "his idea of a really 'Merry Christmas' would be to see Effinger 'behind the bars of the Allen [County] jail. . . . I'd like to get that bird for a Christmas present.'" Police Chief Ward Taylor answered, "Oh I don't know of a thing I want." But, Coates added, "from the gleam of his eye, however, we gathered the chief would greatly appreciate reporters who refrain from asking so many questions." Prosecutor Robert Jones said he looked forward to playing with the toy electric train his son was getting. Readers would have understood the evasive subtext of the officials' words. *Lima News*, Dec. 20, 1936.

192. *New York Times*, Dec. 4, 1937.

193. *Lima News*, May 18, 1939.

194. Quoted in Stanton, *Terror in the City of Champions*, 274.

195. Robert F. Jones to J. Edgar Hoover, Jan. 28, 1937, FBI 2C. The membership of the Black Legion "is reputed to be so large in this section that one cannot hazard a guess as to whom might be depended upon," Jones wrote.

196. Hoover replied that he couldn't help. Hoover to Jones, Feb. 10, 1937, FBI 2C. Four months later, at the trial of a Lima African American man charged with illegally selling whiskey, "fireworks opened" when his lawyer asked a juror if they had been a member of the Black Legion and prosecutor Robert Jones objected to the question. One of the prospective jurors had the last name Effinger

(she subsequently insisted she was unrelated to Virgil). The judge overruled Jones, after the lawyer argued that belonging to the Black Legion would signal hostility to "the colored race." *Lima News*, Apr. 22, 1937.

197. *Lima News*, Dec. 5, 1937.

198. *Toledo Blade*, May 25–28, 30, June 4, 15, 19, 27, July 7, Aug. 13, 26–27, 29, Sept. 4–5, 15, 18, 21, 26, 28, Oct. 1–3, 6, 8–17, 19–21, 23, 26–31, Nov. 1, 1936; clippings in Box 11, Folder 16, Peter Amann Papers; *Lima News*, Oct. 13, 1936. For boys' order, see *Lima News*, Oct. 22, 1936; for boys terrorizing other boys in Michigan, see "Boys, Aping Clan, Try to Hang Companion," *Washington Times*, June 6, 1936, and other clippings, FBI 3B.

199. *Toledo Blade*, July 7, Sept. 29, Oct. 1–3, 6, 8–17, 19–21, 23, 26–31, Nov. 1, 1936.

200. "Black Legion Secrets," *True Detective Mysteries*, Oct. 1936; "The Inside Story of Michigan's Black Legion Murder By The Detectives Who Cracked The Case," *Official Detective Stories*, Sept. 1936; "Secrets of the Black Legion— Revealed by Triggerman Dayton Dean," *Official Detective Stories*, Oct. 1, 1936; Black Legion cover, *Detective Fiction Weekly*, June 12, 1936; Black Legion cover, *True Detective Mysteries*, June 12, 1937; "The White Legion," episode of *The Shadow*, Mar. 20, 1938, RKO.

201. *Legion of Terror*, dir. Charles C. Coleman, Columbia Pictures, 1936; *Black Legion*, dir. Archie Mayo, Warner Brothers, 1937.

202. *Lima News*, Jan. 23, Feb. 7–8, 1937.

203. Mountain View, [Name Redacted] to "Mr. Foster, Agent in Charge," Nov. 1, 1936, FBI 2B; Menlo Park and Atherton: "American" to "U.S. Dept. of Investigation," n.d., received June 10, 1936, FBI 1E; Los Angeles: "A FRIEND" to J. Edgar Hoover, May 26, 1936, FBI 1D; Gardena: Anonymous memo, "Re: Black Legion investigation," received by the FBI, June 24, 1936, FBI 1F.

204. Clipping, "Black Legion Note Found in Slaying," n.d. [1935], FBI 3B. For more on San Luis Obispo, [Name Redacted] to J. Edgar Hoover, n.d., received Sept. 1, 1936, FBI 2A.

205. [Name Redacted] to J. Edgar Hoover, Mar. 30, 1936, FBI 1D.

206. J. P. MacFarland to Director, Federal Bureau of Investigation, Aug. 17, 1936, FBI 2A.

207. *Park City Daily News* (Bowling Green, KY), May 28, 1936.

208. Amann, "Vigilante Terrorism"; Stanton, *Terror in the City of Champions*; Dvorak, "Terror in Detroit"; Morris, *The Black Legion Rides*.

209. Amann, "Vigilante Terrorism," 508.

210. *Washington Post*, May 25, 1936.

211. *Lima News*, May 26, 1936, May 8, 1937.

212. "Caliban in America," *The Nation*, June 10, 1936, 726; John Spivak, "Who Backs the Black Legion?," *New Masses*, June 16, 1936, 9–10, and June 23, 1936, 13–14; Forrest Diamond, "Labor Spies and the Black Legion," *New Republic*, June 17, 1936, 171. For newspaper editorials, e.g., "Battling Against Bigotry," *Washington Times*, May 29, 1936; "Black Legion," *Indianapolis News*, May 29, 1936; "The 'Black Legion' Happened Here," *New York Post*, May 28, 1936; "Uncle Sam's New 'Specimen,'" *New York Daily Mirror*, May 25, 1936; Cartoon, "Wipe Out the Whole Brood!," *Hartford Times*, June 16, 1936.

213. *New York Times*, May 31, 1936.

214. Charles H. Martin, "White Supremacy and Black Workers: Georgia's 'Black Shirts' Combat the Great Depression," *Labor History* 18, no. 3 (1977), 366–81; Susan Canedy, *America's Nazis, a Democratic Dilemma: A History of the German American Bund* (Menlo Park, CA: Markgraf, 1990); Leland V. Bell, *In Hitler's Shadow: The Anatomy of American Nazism* (Port Washington, NY: Kennikat Press, 1973); Sander A. Diamond, *The Nazi Movement in the United States, 1924–1941* (Ithaca, NY: Cornell Univ. Press, 1974); Suzanne G. Ledeboer, "The Man Who Would Be Hitler: William Dudley Pelley and the Silver Legion," *California History* 65, no. 2 (1986): 127–36; Rachel Maddow, *Prequel: An American Fight Against Fascism* (New York: Crown Books, 2023), and preceding podcast, *Rachel Maddow Presents: Ultra*, MSNBC.

215. T. Harry Williams, *Huey Long* (New York: Knopf, 1969); Alan Brinkley, *Voices of Protest: Huey Long, Father Coughlin, and the Great Depression* (New York: Knopf, 1982), 119; Donald I. Warren, *Radio Priest: Charles Coughlin, The Father of Hate Radio* (New York: Free Press, 1996).

216. James Q. Whitman, *Hitler's American Model: The United States and the Making of Nazi Race Law* (Princeton, NJ: Princeton Univ. Press, 2018).

217. Carey McWilliams, *Factories in the Field: The Story of Migratory Farm Labor in California* (New York: Little Brown, 1939), ch. 14. For 1930s fascism, including the Black Legion, in relationship to European fascism, see Peter H. Amann, "A 'Dog in the Nighttime' Problem: American Fascism in the 1930s," in *Fascism*, ed. Michael S. Neiberg (Aldershot, Hampshire, UK: Ashgate, 2006).

218. "Caliban in America," 726.

219. *Chicago Herald and Examiner*, Indiana Section, May 28, 1936 (headline only), FBI 1C.

220. *Toledo Blade*, May 29, 1936.

221. *Indianapolis Times*, May 28, 1936, FBI 1C.

222. Penhorwood interview, 17. Peter Amann argues that the Black Legion was the victim of its own hyper-secrecy, its inadequate dues base, and the coercion underlying its membership. Amann, "Vigilante Terrorism," 513–23.

223. *Lima News*, Mar. 11, 1938.

224. Fred Cook and Floyd Sanders to J. Edgar Hoover, May 25, 1936, FBI 1B. For more on Cook and Sanders, see Agent No. 34, "Investigation of Irregularities . . . ," 5–6.

225. For the role of the auto companies, see Stanton, *Terror in the City of Champions*; Maurice Sugar Papers, Wayne State Univ.

226. *New York Times*, May 28, 29, 1936; "Probe Move Defeated," International News Service, clipping, May 26, 1936; *Evening Review* (East Liverpool, OH), May 28, 1936; *Evening Independent* (Massillon, OH), May 28, 1936; *Portsmouth Daily Times*, May 28, 1936.

227. Agent No. 34, "Investigation Re: Bullet Club . . ."

228. Carl Watson to Col. Lawrence Westbrook, RG 69, Records of the WPA, PC 37, Entry 12–38, Ohio State Series, File 610 Ohio: May–Aug. 1936. My great thanks to Gene Morris at the National Archives and Records Administration for retrieving this document.

229. *Indianapolis News*, May 28, 1936.

230. *Indianapolis News*, June 3, 1936; *Indianapolis Times*, n.d., both in FBI 3C.

231. *Indianapolis News*, May 28, 1936, FBI 1C; *New York Times*, May 27, 1936; *Pittsburgh Press*, May 27, 1936.

232. Morris, *The Black Legion Rides*, 32–37, quote, 37.

233. "Memorandum," n.a. [FBI], n.d. [1935], p. 3.

234. Joseph Keenan to J. Edgar Hoover, Mar. 19, 1935, FBI 1A.

235. J. Edgar Hoover, "Memorandum for Assistant Attorney General Keenan," Apr. 8, 1935, FBI 1A.

236. For evidence of what Hoover knew, see for example, Statement taken by Harry Colburn, Aug. 6, 1936; J. Edgar Hoover, "Memorandum for the Attorney General," Aug. 12, 1936; Morris, *The Black Legion Rides*, 32–24. For Hoover, the definitive work is Beverly Gage, *G-Man: J. Edgar Hoover and the American Century* (New York: Viking, 2022). For an analysis of Hoover and the Black Legion, see Andrew G. Palella, "The Black Legion: J. Edgar Hoover and Fascism in the Depression Era," *Journal of the Study of Radicalism* 12, no. 2 (2018): 81–106.

237. E.g., John Edgar Hoover to Mr. [redacted], General Delivery, Tampa, Florida, Aug. 28, 1936, FBI 2A.

238. John A. Dowd to J. Edgar Hoover, May 28, 1936, FBI 1C.

239. J. Edgar Hoover to H. H. Reinecke, May 29, 1936, FBI 1B. During a 1979 interview with a former law enforcement officer who was a former member of the Black Legion, Alfred Farrell confirmed that the Lima sheriff "and the Police Chief and everybody else" were in the Legion. "The only thing—we were never contacted by the FBI." Peter Amann, "Re-Interview" with Alfred Farrell, Feb. 8, 1979, Box 15, Folders 3–4, Peter Amann Papers.

240. *Congressional Record*, Seventy-Fourth Congress, Second Session, vol. 80, part 8, p. 850, May 28, 1936.

241. *Washington Post*, May 29, 1936.

242. *Detroit News*, May 26, 1936.

243. *Washington Herald*, June 3, 1936, FBI 3C.

244. *Washington Herald*, June 3, 1936.

245. Morris, *The Black Legion Rides*, 34.

246. Penhorwood interview, 16.

247. Morris, *The Black Legion Rides*, 36.

248. Ellen Schrecker, *Many Are the Crimes: McCarthyism in America* (Boston: Little, Brown, 1998).

249. Allen Weinstein and Alexander Vassiliev, *The Haunted Wood: Soviet Espionage in America—the Stalin Era* (New York: Random House, 1999); Peter Duffy, "The Congressman Who Spied for Russia: The Strange Case of Samuel Dickstein," *Politico*, Oct. 6, 2014.

250. *Washington Herald*, May 6, 1937, FBI 3B; *New York Evening Journal*, Apr. 21, 1937, FBI 2C; clipping, "Black Legion Quiz Slated," FBI 3C.

251. "Black Legion Sends Threats," *Washington Times*, Feb. 19, 1938, FBI 3C; Joseph B. Kennan, Assistant Attorney General, to K. P. Aldrich, Chief Inspector, Post Office Department, Washington, DC, Mar. 19, 1935, FBI 3C; Black Legion Committee of Thirteen, Div. No. 7, to Herman Behnke, Feb. 28, 1937, FBI 2C.

252. See *Toledo Blade*, throughout September and October 1936.

253. *Toledo Blade*, July 7, Sept. 29, Oct. 1–3, 6, 8–17, 19–21, 23, 26–31, Nov. 1, 1936.

254. Frank Miller Smith, "The Black Menace," in column "The Greatest Show on Earth," clipping, June 12, 1936, FBI 3A.

255. Dvorak, "Terror in Detroit," 167–68.

256. Michigan Civil Rights Congress Papers, Archives of Labor and Urban Affairs, Walter Reuther Library, Wayne State University, Detroit, Michigan, Box 12; Morris, *The Black Legion Rides*; George Saul, "The Black Legion—Union Busters," pamphlet, Revolutionary Workers League of the U.S., Detroit, Michigan, n.d. For pushback, see also "Black Legion Expose Meeting Announced," June 27, 1036, AP clipping, FBI 3A.

257. Robert H. Zieger, *The CIO: 1935–1955* (Chapel Hill: Univ. of North Carolina Press, 1995).

258. "New Hate Cult Exposed!"

259. The concept of the state's monopoly on violence was first framed by pioneering sociologist Max Weber in his 1918 essay "Politics as Vocation." In *From Max Weber: Essays in Sociology*, trans. and ed. Hans Heinrich Gerth and C. Wright Mills (New York: Free Press, 1946), 77–128.

260. This account is based on the transcript of the Jones Hearing. See also the accounts in Donald A. Ritchie, *The Columnist: Leaks, Lies, and Libel in Drew Pearson's Washington* (New York: Oxford Univ. Press, 2021), 140–44; Jack Anderson with James Boyd, *Confessions of a Muckraker: The Inside Story of Life in Washington During the Truman, Eisenhower, Kennedy and Johnson Years* (New York: Random House, 1979), 32–48; "Says Jones Joined the Black Legion," *New York Times*, July 8, 1947.

261. Jones Hearing, 4–21.

262. Jones Hearing, 21–27.

263. Jones Hearing, 43–51.

264. Jones Hearing, 60–61.

265. Jones Hearing, 125–26.

266. Jones Hearing, 58.

267. Jones Hearing, 61.

268. Jones Hearing, 59–83; onion quote, 75.

269. Jones Hearing, 92–96, 111–25. Fourth District quote, 95; voting record, 115.

270. Jones Hearing, 35–43.

271. Jones Hearing, 99–100.

272. D. L. Ladd to The Director, June 30, 1947; "Joseph B; Emmons, Glenn E. Webb," memo, June 30, 1947, both in FBI 2F; "Undeveloped Leads," n.a., n.d., FBI 1B.

273. Webb, Jones Hearing, 49–57; Barber, Jones Hearing, 68–74; Effinger, Jones Hearing, 41–43; *New York Times*, July 11, 1947. On July 1, Drew Pearson visited J. Edgar Hoover and gave him copies of the affidavits from Effinger, Barber, and Webb in which they had sworn that Jones was a member of the Black Legion. According to Hoover, Pearson "stated that he thought that eventually there [*sic*] might be referred to the Department for Investigation [as] a matter of perjury in that Congressman Jones had testified under oath . . . that

he had never been a member of the Black Legion. I think it might be well to transmit to the Attorney General at once copies of these affidavits, advising him that they have been left with the Bureau by Mr. Pearson." The next day, July 2, Jones wrote to Hoover and the attorney general with the same documents, suggesting in as many words that the three witnesses be investigated for perjury. J. Edgar Hoover, "Memorandum for Mr. Tolson, Mr. Tamm, Mr. Ladd," July 1, 1947, FBI 2F; Robert F. Jones to The Attorney General, Director, FBI, July 2, 1947, in Virgil Effinger file, Allen County Historical Society.

274. For Brewster: John Syrett, "Principle and Expediency: The Ku Klux Klan and Ralph Owen Brewster in 1924," *Maine History* 39, no. 4 (2001): 214–39. For Capehart: Virginia Gardner, "Meet Grand Kleagle Wolfe—Dewey Stalwart," *New Masses*, Nov. 7, 1944, 6. For Johnson: "New Deal in Colorado," Coloradoencyclopida.org, https://coloradoencyclopedia.org/article/new-deal-colorado.

275. Perry Bush, *Rust Belt Resistance: How a Small Community Took On Big Oil and Won* (Kent, OH: Kent State Univ. Press, 2012), 45–53.

276. Bush, *Rust Belt Resistance*; Mark Oprea, "Envisioning a Progressive Future for Lima, Ohio," *Belt Magazine*, Apr. 9, 2021, https://beltmag.com /envisioning-progressive-future-lima-ohio-sharetta-smith; Barry Bluestone and Bennett Harrison, *The Deindustrialization of America* (New York: Basic Books, 1984); Thomas Byrne Edsall, *The New Politics of Inequality* (New York: W. W. Norton, 1984); Gwendolyn Mink, *Welfare's End* (Ithaca, NY: Cornell Univ. Press, 2001); Michael K. Brown, *Race, Money, and the Welfare State* (Ithaca, NY: Cornell Univ. Press, 1999); Marisa Chappell, *The War on Welfare: Family, Poverty, and Politics in Modern America* (Philadelphia: Univ. of Pennsylvania Press, 2010); Felicia Kornbluh and Gwendolyn Mink, *Ensuring Poverty: Welfare Reform in Feminist Perspective* (Pittsburgh: Univ. of Pennsylvania Press, 2018).

277. *Lima News*, Nov. 3, 2020, for both years.

278. *Lima News*, Nov. 3, 2020.

279. "President Trump Remarks at Lima, Army Tank Plant," Mar. 20, 2019, C-SPAN, https://www.c-span.org/video/?458966-1/president-trump-delivers -remarks-lima-army-tank-plant-ohio; "Inside America's Only Army Tank Factory, Which Came Roaring Back to Life Under Trump," *Business Insider*, Mar. 29, 2019.

280. "Rep. Jim Jordan Refuses to Cooperate with Jan. 6 Committee Investigating Capitol Attack," *Washington Post*, Jan. 10, 2022.

281. *Lima News*, Jan. 8, 2021.

282. Jane Slaughter, "Black Workers at Ohio Ford Plant Denounce Racist Taunts," *Labor Notes*, June 30, 2020.

283. Bush, *Rust Belt Resistance*, 45; Williamson interviews, May 12, July 5, 2022; US Census, Quick Facts, Lima, OH, 1970, https://www.census.gov /quickfacts/limacityohio; US Census, Quick Facts, Lima, OH, 2020, https:// www.census.gov/quickfacts/limacityohio.

284. *New York Times*, Aug. 6, 7, 1970; interview by the author with Rev. Ron Fails, Apr. 26, 2022; Williamson interview, May 12, 2022; Bush, *Rust Belt Resistance*, 53–59.

285. *New York Times*, Aug. 6, 7, 1970; Williamson interview, May 12, 2022; photograph of Lima office of National Committee to Combat Fascism, Owen & Eastlake, LTD, https://oweneastlake.com/tag/national-committee-to-combat-fascism; Bush, *Rust Belt Resistance*, 56–59.

286. *New York Times*, Aug. 7, 1970; Williamson interview, May 12, 2022.

287. *Cleveland Plain Dealer*, Jan. 26, 2008; *New York Times*, Jan. 30, 2008.

288. *New York Times*, Jan. 30, 2008.

289. *New York Times*, Jan. 30, 2008.

290. *New York Times*, Jan. 30, 2008; Jag Davies, "Officer Acquitted in Fatal Shooting of Unarmed Woman and Baby," ACLU (blog), Aug. 7, 2008, https://www.aclu.org/blog/smart-justice/mass-incarceration/officer-acquitted-fatal-shooting-unarmed-woman-and-baby.

291. *Lima News*, May 30, June 6, 2020, quote, June 6; Fails interview.

292. Josh Ellebrock, "Racial Protests Create New Sparks in Lima," *Lima News*, June 13, 2020.

293. "Dr. Jessica Johnson: Sharing a Family Story to Explain Critical Race Theory," *Lima News*, Oct. 15, 2021.

294. *Lima News*, July 8, 2000, June 4, 2015, and July 16, 2019. My great thanks to Greg Hoersten for sharing his enormous knowledge of the Black Legion, and of Lima, with me.

295. Allen County Board of Elections, "Official Results—November 8, 2016 General Election," https://www.allen.boe.ohio.gov/?s=results+november+2016; Allen County Board of Elections, "Official Results—Nov 3, 2020 General," https://www.allen.boe.ohio.gov/?s=results+2020. For Democrats in Lima vs. Allen County, Oprea, "Envisioning a Progressive Future for Lima, Ohio."

296. *Lima News*, Nov. 29, 2021; Oprea, "Envisioning a Progressive Future for Lima, Ohio."

297. Dorothy Thompson, "Black Legion Blame Put on Public," *Washington Star*, May 28, 1936, clipping in FBI 3C.

INDEX

Abbott, Robert, 142
ACLU (American Civil Liberties
Union), 87, 261n89
Aeloian Club, 197
Adams, Frank, 148–49
Africa, immigrants from, 10, 141
African American men: in cooperatives, 20; in Brotherhood of
Sleeping Car Porters, 145–46;
employment of, 139, 196; in
eviction protests, 43; gains from
CIO, 163; mutual benefit societies of, 17; New Deal relief and,
44; preachers, 143; relations
with African American women,
139–40; in Seattle's Hooverville,
1–4; in unemployed movement,
46, 47–48
African American press, 133, 154.
See also *Chicago Defender*
African Americans: Black Legion
hostility to 166, 168–69, 171–72,
181–83, 203; and California
border officials, 88; in Chicago,
136–44; Communist Party and,
41–43; cooperatives and, 19–23,
31–32; employment, 139–40,
196; excluded from FSA farm
labor camps, 104; farmworkers, 76–77, 92–93, 108; and
Great Depression, 6, 92–93,
96; Great Migration, 137; KKK
and, 168–69, 186; labor movement and, 145–46, 150, 151,
152, 157, 160; Lange photos
of, 95; in Lima, 181, 195–99,

224–26, 286n141, 287n151;
in Los Angeles, 72; mayor of
Lima, 227; mutual aid projects,
61; mutual benefit societies,
16–17, 26, 63; and New Deal,
35, 57–59; police repression of,
39, 45–46, 47–48, 196, 225–26;
protests against police repression, 224–26; relief and, 54,
90, 104, 189, 190; rent parties,
8–9; Republican Party and, 222
198–99; riots against in Lima,
181; in Seattle's Hooverville,
1–4, 239n2; in Southwest, 91,
94; Southwestern migrants, 67,
84, 87, 88, 92–93; in unemployed movement, 41, 44, 45;
victims of Black Legion, 166,
203; WPA and, 57; WWII employment, 108. *See also* African
American men; African American press; African American
women
African American women: in Chicago, 136–44; churches and,
142–43; Communist Party and,
147–48; cooperatives and, 20;
dancing, 142; domestic workers,
139–40, 179, 197; employment
as prostitutes, psychics, and
numbers runners, 273–74n122;
enslaved, 115–18; in eviction
protests, 43; exclusions from
New Deal, 160–63; labor activism of, 145–51, 163; in Lima,
199–200; mayor of Lima, 227;

police repression of, 157; strikes involving, 148–49, 151, 153–54; in unemployed movement, 47–48; wet nurses, 114–19, 124–25, 129; wet nurses' strike, 113–15, 128, 131–36, 154–59, 163–64; Thelma Wheaton, 275n152

African Legion, 43

Agricultural Adjustment Act, 86, 94

agricultural interests and growers, 73, 77, 88

agriculture, California, 98

Ahl, Tom, 224

Aid to Dependent Children (ADC), 58–60

Aid to Families with Dependent Children (AFDC), 58

Alabama, 148

Albany, New York, 19

Alcaraz, Mauro, 79

Alien Labor Act, 73–74

Allen County (Ohio): Black Legion in 190; Effinger and law enforcement in, 281n33; elections in, 193, 224–26; FERA in, 189–91, 213; government, 189

Allen County Historical Society, 177

Amalgamated Clothing Workers, 160–61

Amann, Peter, 168–69, 182–83, 209, 216, 291n222

America Firsters, 222

America Is in the Heart (Bulosan), 103

American Exodus, 84

American Federation of Labor (AFL), 147–48, 150–51, 154, 159–62, 192, 203

American Friends Service Committee, 26

Americanism, 50, 203

American Medical Association, 118

"Americans," 94, 101, 171–72, 184–85, 207, 212

"American Standard of Living," 252n227

Americans with Disabilities Act, 60

Anacostia, 55–56

anarchism/anarchists, 11, 12, 23

Anderson, Jack, 221

anti-Catholicism. *See* Catholics: hostility to

antisemitism: Black Legion and, 166, 167, 181, 191, 207, 208, 211, 212; Coughlin and, 210; Effinger and, 174–75; films' failure to note, 207–8; KKK and, 50; in Lima, 201; normalcy of, 167, 211; Women's KKK and, 185–96

Appalachia, 13, 97

An Appeal to Young Negroes (Schuyler), 19

Arbeiter Ring. See Workmen's Circle

Argentina, 62

Arizona, 68, 74, 95

Arizona Gleam, 133

Arkansas, 67, 84, 85, 116

"Arkies," 67, 91, 111

Armed Guard, 173

Armstrong, George, 189, 191

arson, 174, 178, 181, 184

Arvin, California, 98, 104, 111

Asia, 10, 115

Asian Americans, 72, 73. *See also specific groups*

Asians, 34, 41, 87, 100, 104, 197. *See also specific groups*

"Asian Standard of Living," 100, 252n227

Associated Farmers, 77

Associated Press, 37, 218

Atascadero, California, 24

Atherton, California, 208

Atlanta, 134, 210

Attorney General, Michigan, 205

Attorney General, US, 214, 216, 293–94n273

Augusta, Georgia, 116

Austrians, 200

auto workers, 150, 152, 160–61

"baby farms," 119

Baer, Max, 144

Baiza, Pablo, 65, 70, 80

Baker, Ella, 4, 22, 26, 29
Bakersfield, 88, 92, 101
Balderrama, Francisco F., 77, 80, 81–83, 107, 110
Baltimore, 19, 53, 119
Bank of America, 77
banks and bankers, 14, 17, 53, 56, 196
Barber, Frank, 193–94, 221–22, 293n273
Barnes, Lois Smith, 85–87, 89, 97, 101–2
barter, 18, 23, 29–30, 33, 36–37, 63
Bates, Beth Thompson, 146, 147
Beard, Uncle John, 47
beauticians, 151, 155
Beaverdam, Ohio, 221
Bellaire, Ohio, 167, 169, 183
Belvedere Gardens, California, 73, 81
Benson, Elmer, 215
Berkeley, California, 49
Bernstein, Irving, 53
Best, Wallace D., 142
Beth Israel Temple, 201
Better Business Bureau, 179, 192
Bielak, John, 203
Birmingham, Alabama, 41, 44, 45, 47, 53
birth rate, 7
Black Cross, 143
Black Guards, 168
Black Knights, 173, 186
Black Legion: and "Americanism," 203; and "Americans," 171–72, 184–85; arrests of members, 289n181; attractions of, 150–52, 187–91, 202–3; and churches, 171, 181, 183–85, 212, 216; decline of, 211–12, 291n222; defectors, 174, 176, 212, 216; and detective magazines, 207; dues, 170, 280n17; electoral politics and politicians, 193–94, 204–5, 221–23; fascism and fascists in, 166–67, 172, 184; and FERA, 185, 189–93, 213, 216, 221, 285n126; history

of, in Lima, 226; Hollywood films about, 166, 206–7; hostility to African Americans, 166, 168–69, 171–72, 181–83, 203; hostility to Catholics, 166, 167, 171–72, 189, 195, 197, 202; hostility to Jews, 171–72, 166; informants, 173, 175, 177, 194–95, 215, 218; initiation rituals, 165–66, 169, 174–76, 184, 193, 194, 221; jobs provided by, 187–91, 284n105; killings by, 201, 203, 208; and KKK, 166, 181–85, 222–23; Ladies Auxiliary, 185–86, 191; law enforcement and, 193–95, 201–6, 292n239; members, 179–87, 202–3; militarism and, 167, 169, 172, 179, 181; national extent of, 206–21; normalcy of, 183; oaths, 165, 171, 221; opposition to, 212–20; origins and founding of, 167–69; potential members as jurors, 289–90n196; robes, 165, 168–69, 175, 181–83, 185–87, 209; Orson Welles and, 207; women in, 185–87, 203; and WPA 213. *See also* Effinger, Virgil "Bert"; Federal Bureau of Investigation (FBI); Jones, Robert F.
Black Lives Matter, 226
Black Metropolis (Cayton and Drake), 137–41, 147, 151
Black Panther Party, 225
Black Shirts, 210
Blair, Cynthia M., 140
Blee, Kathleen, 185–86
Bobson, Albert, 197
"body banks," 269–70n34
Bogart, Humphrey, 208
Bon Dee Golf Ball Company, 152
Bonus Army 55–56
border, California-Arizona, 86–88
border, US-Mexico: Central Americans and, 111–12; in *George Washington Gómez*, 103; increased policing of, 70; novels

about, 103; repatriados and,
65–66, 70, 78–83, 103; slicing
apart families, 68
border patrol, 70, 103
Boston, 39, 121
Botica Central, 79
Boyce, Richard F., 81
braceros, 109, 266n215
Bradfield, J. C. 198
Bradfield Community Center, 198,
199
breast milk, 113, 120–21. *See also*
milk stations; wet nurses
Brewster, Owen, 222–23
Briggs Manufacturing, 152
British Columbia, 208
Bronx, 47
Bronzeville, 137–44. *See also*
Chicago, South Side
Brooklyn, 63, 157
Brotherhood of Sleeping Car
Porters, 20, 145–46, 148
Brown, Elsa Barkley, 17
Brown, Fanny, 148
Brownshirts, 210
Brownsville, Texas, 103
Brownsville Herald, 103
Bryn Mawr Summer School for
Women Workers, 147
Buffalo, New York, 11, 19, 49
Bullet Club, 173, 194
Bulosan, Carlos, 103
"Bum Blockade," 87
Bundesen, Herman, 113, 122, 128,
131–33, 154, 156–59
Burke, Clifford, 6
Burnish, Carrie, 128, 136, 154, 164
Butte, Montana, 49
Buttonwillow, California, 92
"Buy American," 34, 247n145
buying clubs, 22. *See also*
cooperatives

Cain, Mr., 186
California: Black Legion in, 208;
cooperatives in, 23–25, 30–37;
farm fascism in, 211; farm labor
organizing in, 76–77; FSA farm

labor camps in, 103; impact
of Great Depression on, 71;
migrants from Southwest to,
67–68, 84–105, 111; migration
from Mexico to, 69; repatriados
from, 65, 80; Silver Shirts in,
210; Southern, 25; State of, 86,
90, 110; UCAPAWA in, 161;
Unemployed Councils in, 38;
US Conquest of, 68; Workmen's
Circle in, 13
California Highway Patrol, 77
California State University, Bakersfield, 101
Campamento de Hacheros "Vicente
Guerrero," 79
Camp Gray, 147
Canada, 13
cannery and packinghouse workers,
162. *See also* United Cannery,
Agricultural, Packinghouse,
and Allied Workers of America
(UCAPAWA)
Canoga Park, California, 28
Capehart, Homer E., 223
Capetillo, Luisa, 12
capitalism, 5, 11, 38, 61–62, 228–29
Capitol, US, 211, 224
caravans: of Black Legion members,
178; of Central Americans, 105,
111–12; Karnes City, 65–69,
78, 80, 84, 110; of Mexican migrants to US, 69; of repatriados,
65–66, 80–83; Severo Márquez
family, 81
Carter, Mr., 176
Castañeda de Valenciana, Emilia,
71–72, 80, 81, 106–8
Catholicism, 11, 199
Catholics: Black Legion and,
166–67, 189, 195, 197, 202;
charity, 10; Dickstein on attacks
against, 215–16; discrimination
against, 189, 284n103; Effinger
hostility to, 171–72, 281n34;
hostility to, 50, 166–69, 171,
175, 183, 187, 211; Robert
Jones and, 220, 223; KKK and,

185–86; in Lima, 194–95, 200,
219; support for repatriados, 83
Cayton, Horace, 137–41, 143, 147,
151
Central Americans, 105, 111–12
Central Committee of American
Rabbis, 10
Chamber of Commerce, 83
Chambers, Pat, 102
Chapin, Henry Dwight, 130
charity: condescension and hier-
archy of, 4, 10; cooperatives
as conservative alternative to,
33; cooperatives as preferable
to, 27, 30; government, 59;
Hooverville encampment eschewing, 3; private, 5, 53; shame
and stigma of, 5, 51; Steinbeck
on whites and, 265n181
Chateauvert, Melinda, 146
Chávez, Cesar, 11
Cházaro, Eduardo Hernández, 78
Chernin, Kim, 46–47
Cherokee, 96, 97
Chicago: African American cooperatives in, 22; African Americans
and Great Depression in, 6;
anti-immigrant raids in, 75;
Black Legion in, 214; Communists in, 38, 275n152; eviction
protests, 37–38, 43–44, 48–49;
Fansteel case, 277n183; labor
movement in, 145–53; Mexicans in, 69; mutual aid in, 61;
police repression in, 46; Socialists in, 49; unemployed protests
in, 37–38, 43–44, 48–49; wet
nurses' strike in, 113–15, 128,
131–36, 144–45, 154–59,
163–64; wet nursing stations
in, 121–31. *See also* Chicago,
South Side
Chicago, City of, 113, 123, 154,
270n37; city hall, 131, 133;
health department, 124, 134
Chicago, South Side: Communists
in, 148; cultural and political
life, 144–45; eviction protests in,

37, 43–44; hospitals, 121; labor
unions and strikes in, 149–50,
153; living conditions in,
136–38; milk stations, 121–31;
police repression, 46; steel
workers' union, 150
Chicago Board of Health, 113, 122,
125, 133
Chicago Citizens' Committee, 146,
147
Chicago Defender: importance of,
144; and labor movement 146,
146; and Joe Louis, 144; on wet
nurses' strike, 128, 132, 136,
138–39
Chicago Federation of Labor, 148
Chicago Herald and Examiner, 133
157, 211
Chicago Mail Order Company, 152
Chicago's Report to the People,
270n37
Chicago Tribune, 131–33, 136,
152–53, 156, 218
Chicano movement, 110
Chicanos, 92, 110
Chihuahua, Mexico, 72, 81
child separation, 44, 117–18, 119
China, 8, 10
Chinatown (San Francisco), 8, 10
Chinese and Chinese Americans:
arrested in anti–immigrant raid,
91; in Brotherhood of Sleeping
Car Porters, 145; Communists
and, 41, 62; in cooperatives, 31;
exclusion of, by Unemployed
Citizens League, 51; in Los
Angeles, 72; mutual aid, 8–10;
Southwestern migrants and, 91;
Steinbeck and, 99; stereotypes
of, 252n227; in unemployed
movement, 41
Chinese Exclusion Acts, 8
Chinese Unemployed Alliance of
Greater New York, 41
chivalry, 186
Choctaw, 96, 07, 111
Christianity, 96–97, 143, 191.
See also Catholics; churches;

Methodists; Penhorwood, E. J.;
    Protestants
Christoff, Jim, 182
Chrysler Corporation, 161, 163
churches: African American, and
    cooperatives, 21; African Amer-
    ican, as free spaces, 17; African
    American, in Chicago, 142–43;
    African American, in Lima,
    197–98; and Black Legion in
    Lima, 183, 212; Catholic, in
    Lima, 189; and charity, 10, 52;
    and Lima KKK, 180–81, 183;
    support for domestic workers'
    unions, 162
Churchill, Frank Spooner, 120
Church of Jesus Christ of Latter-
    Day Saints (Mormons), 29
Cincinnati, 19–20
Citizens' Committees, 77
citizenship, 51, 71, 73–76, 108
City Commissioners (Lima, Ohio),
    190
City Savings and Loan (Lima,
    Ohio), 196
Civil Rights Act (1964), 163
Civil Rights Movement, 19, 111
Civil Works Administration, 57
Clark, Jean, 137
Clark, Laverne, 137
Clark, Louise, 128, 137, 164
Clark, Margaret, 137
Clark, Oscar, 224
Clark, Randle, 137
class: Black Legion and, 182, 188,
    191–92, 264n174; and *Chicago
    Defender*, 143; CIO and, 150;
    condescension, 139, 182; do-
    mestic worker organizing and,
    147; and Great Depression in
    Lima, 187–88; in Lima, 180;
    and wet nursing, 115, 118, 120
Clawson, Mary Ann, 16
clerical workers, 7, 29, 162–63
Cleveland, 19, 39, 48, 49, 173, 209
clothing, 141
Cloward, Richard, 45, 53–54, 55
Colburn, Harry, 194

Coleman, Silas, 203
Collins, Tom, 98, 104
Colorado, 74, 144, 223
Columbia, South Carolina, 20
Columbus, Ohio, 50, 204, 205
Comintern (Communist Interna-
    tional), 40
Comité Mexicano Pro-Repatriación,
    83
Comités Pro-Repatriación, 78, 83
Comités Pro-Repatriados, 78–79, 83
Committee on Violations of Free
    Speech and Rights of Labor, US
    Senate (LaFollette Committee),
    217
Common Man, 67, 98, 111
Communist Party: and African
    Americans, 41–42; Thyra J.
    Edwards, 275n152; and house-
    wives 42, 250n191; opposition
    to repatriation, 83; politics and
    structure of, 40–42; race and,
    41–43
Communists: African American,
    41–42; African American
    women, 147–49, 275n152;
    anti-Communism, 217; and
    Asians, 42; Black Legion and,
    204, 207, 218; and California
    farmworkers, 102; in Chicago,
    147–50, 154–57; and coop-
    erative movement, 32–33; in
    Harlem, 19; Jewish, 46; in Los
    Angeles, 32–34; Mexican Amer-
    ican, 84; in Midwest, 192; *New
    Masses*, 144; in New York City,
    19, 46–47; opposition to repa-
    triation, 83; and packinghouse
    workers, 150; phrases used
    by, 154; rent strikes, 46–47; in
    Toledo, 207; and unemployed
    movement, 35–39, 46, 51–52.
    See also Communist Party
Compton, California, 25, 27, 30, 31
Confederación de Sociedades Mex-
    icanas, 83
Conference for Progressive Political
    Action, 49–50

Congress, US, 53, 56–58, 77, 215–17, 220–24. *See also* House of Representatives, US; Senate, US

Congress of Industrial Organizations (CIO): and African American women, 162–63; as alternative to Black Legion, 219; and Chicago strikes, 148, 153; in contrast to smaller, less hierarchical unions, 155; formation of, 150–51, 153–55; gains by, 161–62; John L. Lewis, 145; in Lima, 222; and New Deal, 159–62; official killed by Black Legion, 203; women and, 161–62

Constructing Brotherhood (Clawson), 16

construction workers: in Black Legion, 180; layoffs of, 6; in Mormon cooperatives, 29; hostility to Mexicans, 74; Mexican, 70; in Lima, 179–81; and New Deal, 191; Southwestern migrants finding work as, 89

Consumers' Co-operative Societies (Gide), 21

Consumers' Cooperative Trading Company, 24

Cook, Fred, 212, 219

Cook, Junior, 226

Cook, Myrtle, 26

Cook County Hospital, 121–22

Co-op: A Novel of Working Together (Sinclair), 36

Cooper, Esther V., 162

cooperatives, 4–37, 50–52, 248n150, 275n152; producer, 22, 23, 35–36

Cordrey, J. F., 176, 177, 186, 195, 214

cotton economy, 71

cotton workers, 76, 88, 92–93, 99

Coughlin, Charles, 16, 210, 222

Council Hill, Oklahoma, 67

COVID, 61, 220

craft unions, 188, 192

credit unions, 21, 22

Cridersville Town Hall, 172

Cuba, 12, 173

Cubans, 41

Cudahy, 123

Cummings, Homer S., 213–24

Curl, John, 36

Curlett, Betty, 116

Dalton, Arkley A., 197

Davey, Martin, 204

Davis, John R. 213

Dean, Dayton, 201–4, 207

Dearborn, Michigan, 75

Decade of Betrayal (Balderrama and Rodríguez), 77, 107

DeFinis, Fondi, 199–200, 201

De La Cruz, Jessie, 92

DeMet's, 153, 155, 157

Democratic Party, 58, 104, 204

Democrats: Colorado, 223; Detroit, 204; Lima, 175, 193; Roosevelt and, 56, 58, 160, 219; Toledo, 207

Department of Agriculture, US, 95

Department of Homeland Security, US, 112

Department of Justice, US, 214

Department of War, US, 74

deportations, 75–76, 104–5

DePriest, Oscar, 149

detention centers, 112

Detroit: anti-immigrant raids in, 74; Black Legion in, 166, 177, 201–4, 209, 211–13, 215, 219; Charles Coughlin, 210; deportations from, 75; discrimination by relief authorities, 72, 102; eviction protests in, 42–43; Mexicans in, 65, 69, 83, 74–75, 102, 110; newspapers, 218; relief protests in, 53; repatriados from, 65, 83, 110; sit-down strikes in, 161; unemployed march in, 39; wet nursing in, 130

Detroit News, 168, 183

Detroit prosecutors, 177, 194, 201–2, 204

Dickstein, Samuel, 215–18

Dies, Martin, 217
Dies Committee (HUAC), 217
disasters, 61
discrimination: in employment,
     6–7, 139–40, 196; in FERA
     jobs, 189–93; in FSA farm labor
     camps, 104, 108; in housing,
     8–9; 132; in labor movement, 6,
     192; against married women's
     employment, 58; in relief provi-
     sion, 54, 57–58, 72, 75, 90
Division of Self-Help Cooperatives,
     35–37
Doak, William, 74
doctors, 118–21, 198
domestic workers: African American,
     in Chicago, 135–40; African
     American, in Lima, 179, 197;
     and cooperatives, 22; exclusion
     by NLRA, FLSA, and Social Se-
     curity, 163; invisibility of, 229;
     and New Deal, 59; Mexican, 70,
     72; for Pullman Company, 145;
     and reproductive labor, 114;
     union organizing among, 147;
     wet nurses as, 118; 120
Domestic Workers' Union of New
     York, 20
Don Martin (irrigation project), 106
"Don't Buy Where You Can't
     Work," 146
Dorsey, Thomas, 142
Doty, Elizabeth Griffin, 148
Douglass, Frederick, 146
Dowd, John A., 215
Drake, St. Clair, 137–41, 147, 152,
     156
Droguería del Refugio, 66
Du Bois, W. E. B., 19, 188
Dunn, Geoffrey, 96–97
Dust Bowl, 54, 67, 84–86, 92, 98
"Dust Bowl Migrants," 34, 84, 95,
     97. *See* Southwestern migrants
Dvorak, Kenneth, 204, 20

Eagle Lake, 79
Eagles (fraternal order), 180
East, 21, 49

East St. Louis, 153
Ebenezer Baptist Church, 142
*Economic Co-operation Among Ne-
     groes* (Du Bois), 19
Edwards, Thyra J., 175n152
Edwards v. California, 87
Effinger, Guy, 189
Effinger, Mary, 170, 185, 205,
     283n85
Effinger, Virgil "Bert": Amann
     discussion of, 209; biography
     and politics of, 169–72; Black
     Legion leadership and activities
     in Lima, 169–75; in contrast
     to Coughlin and Long, 210;
     Department of Justice memo
     and, 214; extradition, 204–205;
     fascism and, 172, 184; FBI and,
     205, 208, 293n273; hostility to
     African Americans, Catholics,
     and Jews, 171–72; Robert F.
     Jones and, 194, 220–22; later
     activities, 212: law enforce-
     ment, 204–5, 280n29, 281n33,
     289n191; Penhorwood and,
     184–85; and political power,
     193–94; possible family mem-
     ber as juror, 289–90n196; and
     unions, 192
Egypt, 154, 172
El Fenix, 79
Elizondo, Matilde, 65
Elks (fraternal order), 180
Ellington, Duke, 9
Elmira, New York, 19
El Monte, California, 76
El Paso, Texas: discriminatory
     employment law, 74; Mexican
     population in, 69; relief protests,
     72; repatriados in, 65, 65, 74,
     81–82; repression by border au-
     thorities in 70
El Paso Herald-Post, 134
Emeryville, California, 31
Emmons, Joseph, 182, 222–24
encampments, 1–4, 24, 55–56, 239n2
enslavement, 112–19, 268n14,
     268–69n18

entitlement, 59
Equal Employment Opportunity
   Commission (EEOC), 163
Erfer, Albert, 176, 218
Eureka, California, 49
Europe, 10, 15, 56, 108, 115, 211;
   Western Europe, 23
Europeans, 139, 200; Northern, 90,
   96, 101, 118, 200; Southern and
   Eastern, 73, 96, 168, 171, 192,
   199. *See also specific groups*
Evans, Mary G., 143
eviction protests, 5, 32, 37–38,
   42–50, 250n191, 251n193

Factories in the Field (McWilliams),
   81, 102
factory workers: Black Legion and,
   180; Chicago, 148–49; Lima,
   212; Mexican, 84; and unemployment, 6. *See also* auto workers; cannery and packinghouse
   workers; steel workers
Fair Labor Standards Act (FSLA),
   58, 104, 159–60, 191
families: impact of Great Depression
   on, 7–8; Italian, 11–12; Jewish,
   in Workmen's Circle, 13–15;
   Mexican, 70, 72; of repatriados,
   80–82, 106–7; of Southwestern
   migrants, 86–89, 92–93; of wet
   nurses, 136–37
Fannie May Candy Company, 152
farmers: Agricultural Adjustment
   Act and displacement of, 86, 95;
   big, 86; cooperatives of, 21–22;
   Mexican, 65; in Mexico, 105–6;
   poor white, 84; Southwestern
   migrants, 67, 69, 84–86. *See
   also* agricultural interests and
   growers
farm fascism, 77, 211, 219
farm labor camps, 98, 103–4, 108
Farm Security Administration
   (FSA): farm labor camps, 103–4,
   108–9; Lange and, 69, 96; Steinbeck and, 69, 98; Paul Taylor
   works for, 35

farmworkers: African American,
   92–93; Filipino, 76–77; Hawaii
   sugar plantation, 69; Lange
   photos of, 93–97, 99; Mexican,
   65; migrant in California, 104;
   and New Deal, 102, 104, 160;
   Southwestern migrants, 67,
   88–89; Steinbeck and, 96–108,
   264n175; unions and strikes of,
   76–77, 93–94; white, 67, 93–94,
   99–100
Farrell, Alfred, 292n239
fascism, 77, 166–67, 172, 183–84,
   207–8, 210
fascists: congressional concern over,
   217; Charles Coughlin, 210;
   Virgil Effinger, 166–67, 172,
   184; and farmworkers, 103,
   167–67, 193, 206, 210–11, 222;
   Hitler, 166, 172, 210; Robert
   Jones and, 220–22; Huey Long,
   210; Mussolini, 166, 172, 210;
   national alarm over, 166–67,
   206–9; in Ohio Fourth Congressional District, 224; organizations of, during 1930s, 210;
   Drew Pearson investigations
   of, 220–21; Robert Shepard,
   167–69; Gerald L. K. Smith,
   220. *See also* Black Legion
Faygnboym, Benyomen, 14
Federal Bureau of Investigation
   (FBI): and Detroit prosecutors,
   194–95; Effinger extradition
   and, 205–8, 280n29; failure to
   contact Lima law enforcement,
   292; failure to monitor Black
   Legion, 214–15; interviewees
   and informants, 177, 184–85,
   193; investigations of Black Legion, 172, 173, 175; Jones letter
   to Hoover regarding extradition
   of Effinger, 205–6; jurisdiction
   of, 217; letters to Hoover, 212.
   See also Hoover, J. Edgar
Federal Communications Commission, 220–23
Federal Council of Churches, 10

Federal Deposit Insurance Corporation (FDIC), 56
Federal Emergency Relief Administration (FERA): Black Legion and, 189–91, 193, 213, 216, 221; cooperatives and, 35–36; formation of, 57, 185
Federal Reserve Board, 56
Federal Writers' Project, 179
Ferry Morse Seed Company, 152
Filipinos: in Brotherhood of Sleeping Car Porters, 145; Carlos Bulosan, 103; Communists and, 41; exclusion from Unemployed Citizens League, 51; farm labor organizing and strikes, 76–77, 93, 161; FSA farm labor camps and, 108; in Hawaii, 161; hostility to, 34, 252n229; in Lange photos, 99–100; in Los Angeles, 72; mutual aid associations, 18; repression of, 77; in Seattle's Hooverville, 1–3; Steinbeck and, 99–100; in UCAPAWA, 161; in White River Valley, Washington, 252n229
Finns, 1, 41, 162
Firebaugh, California, 88, 89
Firewood, Maryland, 177
First Amendment, 217
First National Bank (Bellaire, Ohio), 168
First National Bank (Laredo, Texas), 79
fish, 1, 3, 9, 15, 31, 63
Flint, Michigan, 114, 150, 152, 202
Florida, 13, 163, 207
Floyd, George, 226
Flynn, Elizabeth Gurley, 12
Fonda, Henry, 98
Foot Legion, 173
Ford, James W., 149
Ford, John, 67, 98, 103
Ford, Melissa, 48
Ford Dance Hall, Old, 172
Fort Wayne, Indiana, 216
Foster, Frank, 136
Foster, Frank (son), 136

Foster, Harold, 136
Foster, Theria, 128, 136–37, 164
Foster, William Z., 39
Fourth Congressional District (Ohio), 222, 224
Fourth Street Baptist Church, 197, 225
France, 23, 152
Francis, Ola Bell, 148
fraternal associations, 12, 15–16, 172, 180
Fresno, 13
fur and leather workers, 148

gambling workers, 141
Gardena, California, 208
garment workers, 7, 27, 140, 149, 153–55, 160–61
Garvey, Marcus, 19, 143
Gary, Indiana, 21–22, 23, 30, 32, 75
Garza, Josefina, 79
gender and gender dynamics: in African American cooperatives, 20; in cooperative movement, 26–30; distinctions between male and female enslaved runaways, 117–18; equality between men and women, 5; in mutual benefit associations, 11–16, 18; in New Deal labor and welfare systems, 58–60
General Motors, 114, 133, 150, 151
George Washington Gómez (Paredes), 103
Georgia, 144, 208
Germans, 200
Germany, 172, 211
Gide, Charles, 21
Gilpin, DeWitt (aka "Larry Van Deusen"), 38, 45, 249n169
Glass-Stegall Banking Act, 5
Gold, Ella, 131, 136, 164
Golden, Janet, 118, 120, 121
Gómez Palacio, Durango, Mexico, 106
Gónzales, Pedro, 75–76
Goodman, Uncle Ned, 47
Goodyear, 150

Gordon, Linda, 95, 96
Grand Junction, Colorado, 49
Grand United Order of Odd Fellows, 197
Grapes of Wrath (Steinbeck), 67, 98–99, 101–4, 110–11
Great Depression: impact on African Americans, 6–7, 196; and farm prices, 85; Mexicans in US and, 71–74; in Mexico, 107; mutual benefit associations and, 11, 17; Southwestern migrants and, 66–68. *See also* unemployed; unemployment
Great Migration, 137, 142, 196
Great Society, 60
Greeks and Greek Americans, 72, 96, 171, 195, 200
Green New Deal, 230
Gregory, James, 84–85, 90
Grey, Abe, 46
Gross, Diana, 46
Guerra de Caso, Arnulfa, 78
gun and weaponry, 176–79, 202, 204, 207, 280n29
Guthrie, Oklahoma, 91, 97
Gutiérrez de Lara, Dr., 79
"gypsies," 168

Hackman, Frank, 27
Half Moon Bay, 76
Hampton, Mabel, 9
Hardaway, Lydia, 129, 131
Harlem, 8–9, 20, 44, 162
Harlem's Own Cooperative, 21
Harris, LaShawn, 48, 141, 273–74n128
Hart, Mary: family of, 136; as leader, 155; in wet nurses' strike, 113, 128, 132–33, 136, 164, 229, 231
Hartman, Saidiya, 141–42
Hartzog, Chas., 177
Harvest Gypsies (Steinbeck), 99
Hawaii, 162
Hawisher Motor Company, 170
Hearst, William Randolph, 34, 134, 247n145

Heatherton, Christina, 90
Hebbronville, Texas, 79
Helmbold, Lois, 7
Herndon, Angelo, 148
Hess, Julius H., 121, 123, 158, 271n49
Hicks, W., 28–29
Highland Park, Michigan, 202, 204
Hitler, Adolph, 166, 172, 210
Hoffman, Abraham, 106
Hollywood, 166, 206, 207
Home Relief Bureau, 44
Hondurans, 111
Hoobler, B. Raymond, 130
Hoover, Herbert, 1, 53, 55–56
Hoover, J. Edgar, 205–6, 208, 212, 214–17, 223, 293–94n273
Hooverville (Seattle), 1–4, 36, 239n2
Hope, John, II, 21
Hosford, Larry, 111
hospitals, 121–23, 126, 128, 198, 270n32
hotel and restaurant workers, 8, 151, 153
Hotel Employees and Restaurant Employees International Union (HERE), 151, 162
House Committee on Un-American Activities (HUAC) (Dies Committee), 217
House of Representatives, US, 55, 217; Special Committee on Un-American Activities Authorized to Investigate Nazi Propaganda and Certain Other Propaganda, 217
housewives, 27, 42, 59, 250n191; housework, 7, 42, 59. *See also* domestic workers
Housewives League, 20
housing, 8–9, 138
Houston, 75, 80, 81, 83, 107, 108
Houston Chronicle, 83
Hover Park, 196
HUAC, 217
Huddleston, George, 53

Hudson, Hosea, 41–42, 44–45, 47–48

Hunter, Allan, 81–82, 102, 261n89

Hunter, Tera W., 119, 141, 142

Huntington, Colonel, 33–34

Huntington, Indiana, 134

Hurston, Marie, 149

Hurwitz, Maximilian, 13–14

Hyndman, Katherine, 43–44, 46

Idaho, 103

Illinois, 144, 166, 208

immigrants: Central American, 111–12; in Chicago: 142; Communist Party and, 41, 83; contrasted with "Americans," 50, 94, 96; exclusion from AFL, 192; exclusion from Unemployed Citizens League, 51; as "foreigners," 171; hostility to, 34, 72–73, 168, 171; mutual benefit societies of, 18, 110–15; in Seattle's Hooverville, 1; Steinbeck on, 100; as wet nurses, 118. *See also* specific groups

immigration, 7–8, 17, 77. *See also* specific groups

Immigration Act of 1924, 73

Immigration and Naturalization Service, 94

immigration officials, 74–75, 111–15

Imperial Roadhouse, 171

Imperial Valley (California), 69, 76, 77

Independent Order of St. Luke, 17

Indiana, 166, 185, 201–6, 217, 223

Indianapolis, 211–12, 215

"Indian Territory" (Oklahoma), 97

individualism, 18

Industrial Committee of the Chicago Council of the National Negro Congress, 148

Industrial Workers of the World (Wobblies), 123

Infants' Aid Society of Chicago, 12, 156

infants and babies, 115–23

insurance, burial, 10, 11, 14, 16, 18

International Brotherhood of Electrical Workers, 192

International Labor Defense, 83

International Ladies' Garment Workers' Union, 153–54, 160–61

International News Service, 133, 218

International Order of Odd Fellows, 16

interracial relationships, 2, 61–62

Ireland, 118

Irish and Irish Americans, 12, 101, 118, 181, 197, 200

Italians and Italian Americans, 11–12, 16, 91, 96, 171, 195, 197, 199–200, 207, 287n156

It Happened Here (Hackman), 279n4

Jackson, Jesse, 3, 239n2

Jackson, Mahalia, 142

Jacobs, Harriet, 116

janitors, 6, 180

Japan, 153

Japanese and Japanese Americans: arrested in anti-immigrant raids, 76; and citizenship, 71; Communist Party and, 41; cooperatives and, 31, 32; exclusion of, by UCL, 51; farm labor organizing in California, 76; hostility to, 34; Lange photos of, 95; in Los Angeles, 72; mutual aid societies, 18; police repression of, 45; Southwestern migrants and, 91; truck gardeners, 30; in UCAPAWA, 16

Japanese Section of the Los Angeles Unemployed Council, 41

Jeffries, Willye, 44–45, 48–49

Jet, 225

Jewish Hospital, 157

Jews: "American" as code for non-Jewish, 50; Black Legion hostility to, 72, 166, 171; Communists and, 41; Charles

Coughlin antisemitism, 210; Dickstein on attacks against, 215–16; discrimination against, in FERA, 188; Effinger hostility to, 171–72; Robert Jones and, 220; Judaism, 14; KKK and, 165, 168–69, 185, 186; and Lange photos, 223; in Lima, 201, 219; in Los Angeles, 72; refugees in Europe, 15; Silver Shirts and, 210; in UCAPAWA, 161. *See also* antisemitism
Johnson, Jack, 144
Johnson, Jeh, 112
Johnson, Jessica, 226
Jones, Robert F.: and Black Legion, 167, 193–94, 205–6, 220–23, 293–94n173; Effinger and, 171, 178; and KKK, 222, 223
Jones-Rogers, Stephanie, 116, 129
Jordan, Jim, 224
Joseph, Hortense Schoen, 122
Journal of the American Medical Association, 130, 271n49

Kansas, 67, 84
Kansas City, Missouri, 19, 26
Karnes City, Texas, 65–66, 78–80, 82, 110, 112, 114
Karnes County, Texas, 71
Keenan, Joseph B., 214
Kelley, Elleza, 62
Kelley, Robin D. G., 41, 62
Kentucky, 166, 208, 217
Kerr, Clark: on cooperatives as counter to the Left, 34–35; on disagreements within cooperatives, 25; dissertation, 23; on gender dynamics within cooperatives, 27–29; as lying lizard, 35n; on race and cooperatives, 31–32, 34–35
Kerrville, Texas, 79
Kessler, Robert, 85, 89, 97
King City, California, 88
Knight, Rosie, 116
Knights of Labor, 23
Knights of Pythias, 17

Kokomo Tribune, 133
Koreans, 91
KPIG, 111
Krueger, Ernie, 34
Ku Klux Klan (KKK): Black Legion and, 166, 168–69, 188, 210; Grand Dragon, 169; in Indiana, 185; Robert Jones and, 222, 223; in Lima, 170, 172, 181–84, 185, 194; Nazis and, 211; in *Reign of Terror*, 208; and Republican Party in Lima, 284n101, 285n12; spinoffs, 210; US Congress and, 216, 223; women in, 185–86
Kuntz, Ma, 44–45, 48, 60

laborers, 6, 180
labor movement, 14, 114, 145–55, 153–55; race relations in, 6, 150 *See also* American Federation of Labor (AFL); Congress of Industrial Organizations (CIO); *individual unions*
Labor Ticket (Lima), 171, 192
La Capilla, Cuahuila, Mexico, 166
Ladies Auxiliary, Black Legion, 185, 186, 191
Ladies of the Maccabees, 16
LaFollette, Robert M., 217
landlords, 6, 8, 137
Lange, Dorothea: and FSA, 98–99; *Migrant Mother*, 95–97, 111–12, 267n257; and New Deal, 98–99; photos of farmworkers, 95–96; photos of Southwestern migrants, 67, 95–96; *Their Blood Is Strong*, 99, 264n175
Lansing, Michigan, 166, 203
Laredo, Texas, 12, 66, 70, 74, 78–79, 81–83
Laredo Times, 66
laundry workers, 8, 139–40, 151, 153, 161
Laundry Workers International Union, 151
League of United Latin American Citizens (LULAC), 84

Lee, Erika, 73
Leech, D. C. W., 177
Legion of Terror (film), 207
Lerdo, Durango, Mexico, 106
Levine, Akosua, 63
Levine, Lawrence, 96
Lewis, Georgia, 164
Lewis, John L., 145, 150, 154
Lewis, Sinclair, 166–67
LGBTQI people, 2–3, 9
Liberty, New York, 14
Liddy, Ralph W., 219–20
Life, 113, 134, 153
Lima, Ohio: African American protests in, 225–26; African Americans in, 195–99, 224–27; Black Legion in, 165–67, 169–201, 281n34; economy and demographics of, 179–80, 224–25; FERA in, 189–91; Great Depression impact on, 187–88; history of racial hate in, 181; Irish in, 181; 200; Italians in, 199–204; Jews in, 201; KKK in, 170, 172, 181–84, 185, 194, 284n101; law enforcement in, 193–95, 201–6, 225–26, 281n33; mayor, 194, 226–27; racist police in, 225–26; silence regarding Black Legion in, 212; South End of, 196, 199, 225–26; West End of, 196
Lima League for Cooperation and Improvement, 198
Lima News: on Black Legion, 226; on *Black Legion* film, 208; on Black Lives Matter, 226; on Virgil Effinger, 170–71, 284n191; on Virgil Effinger surrender, 206; failure to denounce Black Legion, 212; and FERA discrimination, 284n103; interview with Mary Effinger, 185; interview with Scheid Jr., 176, 281n34; on Lima support for Trump and Jan. 6 insurrection, 224; reporting arson, 174
Lincoln, Nebraska, 134

Lithuanians, 10, 200
Little, Earl, 203
Liu, Wei Bat, 8, 10
Logansport, Indiana, 134
Long, Huey, 166, 210
Long Beach, California, 31
longshoremen, 161
Look, 96
López, José, 110
Los Angeles: Black Legion in, 208; City of, 73–74, 75; cooperatives in, 25, 27–28, 30–34, 36–37; County of, 76; East Los Angeles, 73; immigration raids, 74–75; job discrimination, 73–74; Mexicans and Mexican Americans, 69, 65, 73–75, 105; police repression in, 45; relief protests in, 72, 76; repatriados from, 65, 81, 83; unemployed march, 29
Los Angeles Citizens Committee on Coordination of Unemployment Relief, 74
Los Angeles Police Department, 87
Los Angeles Times, 96, 132–33, 136
Los Angeles Unemployed Council, 41
Louis, Joe (boxer), 144–45
Louis, Mrs. Joe (Lima, Ohio), 185
Louisiana, 13, 210
Love, I. N., 118
Loyal Order of Moose, 16
Lucas, Ruby, 37, 45, 60, 229, 231
Lucio, Lucas, 82
Luna, María, 75
Lundeen, Evelyn, 122, 124, 126
Lupp, Arthur F., 202–3
Lynd, Staughton, 43, 155
Lynn Hoag Ranch, 88

Mabley, Jackie "Moms," 9
MacArthur, Douglas, 55–56
Macedonians, 182, 200
Machado, Antonio, 63
MacLean, Nancy, 186
Madison County, Arkansas, 85
Madison Square Garden, 13, 210
Magil, A. B., 167

Maine, 13, 222
Malcolm X, 166, 203
Malone, Annie, 149
"mammy," 116
Manitoba, 13
Manley, C. M., 226
Marchuk, George, 203
Marmo, Bertha, 28–19, 30, 60
Marmon, Ira Holloway, 203
Márquez, Severo, 73, 80, 81, 106, 107
marriage, 7, 58, 138, 160
Marshall, R. S., 289n191. *See also* Sheriff, Allen County, Ohio
Martin, Laura Renata, 32–33
Martínez, Alejandro V., 82
Martínez-Matsuda, Verónica, 108
Mary Thompson Hospital for Women and Children (Women and Children's Hospital), 124, 128
Masons, Free and Associated (African American), 197
Masons (white), 180
Massachusetts, 63
May, Vanessa, 162
Mayflower Hotel, 221
McClanahan, Christina Viola Williams, 90, 92
McCrea, Duncan, 202, 204, 213–14, 217
McCune, Mary, 15
McGinniss, Amy, 185
McGuffey, Ohio, 178
McLean, Robert N., 82
McMillen, Sally, 116
McWilliams, Carey, 76, 77, 81, 102, 211
meatpacking companies, 123
media: African American, 275n152; and Black Legion, 210 218, 226; and sit-down strikes 154; and wet nurses' strike, 131–36, 164. See also *Chicago Defender*
Medicaid, 60
Medicare, 60
Memorial Day Massacre, 157
Memorial Hall, 177

men: as beneficiaries of New Deal, 57–58, 160–61; in mutual benefit associations, 11–17; in Seattle's Hooverville, 1–4; shame of unemployment, 7. *See also* African American men; white men
Menlo Park, California, 208
Meredith, Harry, 182, 188, 212
Mesquita, Miguel, 79
The Messenger, 15
Metheany, Allen L., 194
Methodists, 171, 197
Mexican consulates, 77–78, 82, 83
Mexican government, 77–78, 82, 83, 105–6
Mexican Revolution, 69, 77
Mexicans and Mexican Americans: Agricultural Adjustment Act impact on, 86; arrested in anti-immigrant raids, 75; in Chicago, 124, 150; Communist Party and, 41; discrimination against, by New Deal, 58; farm fascism and 211; FSA farm labor camps and, 104, 108; hostility to, 259n58; job discrimination against, 73–74; labor activism of, 76–77, 93, 150, 161; in Los Angeles, 72; mutualistas, 11–12, 70, 79, 83; racism against, 72–73, 133–34; railroad workers, 252n32; and relief, 58, 72, 75, 90; repatriados and repatriation, 65–68, 75–84, 105–8; repression of, in Los Angeles, 87; in Salinas, 111; in Seattle's Hooverville, 2, 239n2; and Southwestern migrants, 91–95; Steinbeck and, 99–100; in Unemployed Councils, 38; unemployment and, 71–73, 75–76, 90, 252n32
Mexico: braceros, 109; migration from, 68–71, 111; migration to, 86; repatriados in, 105–6; US conquest of, 68, 72; veterans of US war with, 173
Mexico City, 61, 69

México de Afuera, 78
Meza, Maira, 111
Michael Reese Hospital, 121, 128
Michigan: Black Legion in, 166,
    174, 186–87, 201–4, 207–10,
    284n104; Mexican immigrants
    in, 69; prosecutors in, 214–18,
    284n104
Michigan Civil Rights Congress,
    218
Michigan National Guard, 216
Michigan State Police, 203, 216
Midwest, 28, 32, 49–50, 77–78, 85,
    86, 210
Midwest, Upper: Black Legion in,
    113, 169–202; cooperatives
    in, 22; KKK in, 168; Mexican
    mutualistas in, 70; repatriation
    from 65; sit-down strikes in,
    152
Migrant Citizenship
    (Martínez-Matsuda), 108
migrant cycle, 69, 89
Migrant Mother (Lange), 95–97,
    110–12, 267n227
migrants, 65–71, 84–85, 89, 98,
    103, 104. *See also* Mexicans and
    Mexican Americans; Southwest-
    ern migrants
militarism, 167, 169, 172, 179, 181
"milk banks," 269n34
milk stations, 121–31, 270n37,
    271n49
Milwaukee, 49
mine workers, 150, 159
minimum wage. *See* Fair Labor
    Standards Act (FSLA)
Minneapolis, 49, 192
Missouri, 67, 84
Modesto, California, 88
Monk, Thelonious, 9
Monterrey, Nuevo León, Mexico,
    105
Monterrey Chamber of Commerce,
    105
Monthly Labor Review, 25
Moorhead, Minnesota, 134
Morales, Daniel, 78, 259n58

Morales, Delfina, 9
Morgan, Boyd, 67, 85–86, 88–89,
    91, 101
Morgan, Jennifer, 129–30
Mormino, Gary, 13
Mormons (Church of Jesus Christ
    of Latter-Day Saints), 29
Morning Glory Club, 197
Morris, George, 214, 216, 289n181
Morton, Willie, 164
Moscow, 40, 42
Mother Road (Solis), 111
Mountain View, California, 208
Moxley, Rolland, 198, 222–23
Murphy, William, 194
Mussolini, Benito, 166, 172, 210
Muste, A. J., 49, 50
Musteites, 50–52
mutual aid, 5, 10–18, 33, 61–63
mutual assistance societies (*società
    di mutuo soccorso*), 11
mutual benefit associations: African
    American, 16–17, 197; Catho-
    lic, 199; Cuban, 12; decline of,
    17–18; extent and popularity of,
    10–11, 18; Filipino, 18, Finnish,
    162; Japanese, 18; Jewish, in
    Workmen's Circle, 13–15; Ital-
    ian, 11, 12; Mexican, Mexican
    American, and Spanish mutu-
    alistas, 11–12, 70, 79, 83; of
    native-born white men, 15–16;
    New Deal and, 18; Portuguese,
    18; Puerto Rican, 18, Slovak,
    18; of tobacco workers, 12–13
mutualistas, 11–12, 70, 79, 83

NAACP (National Association for
    the Advancement of Colored
    People), 20, 143, 146, 157, 162
Naiman, Max, 58
Naison, Mark, 44, 47, 251
Naranjo de Farías, Julia García, 78
The Nation, 166, 210, 211
National Association of Colored
    Women's Clubs, 20
National Committee for the Repa-
    triated, 105–6

National Committee to Combat Fascism, 225
National Council of Social Welfare, 10
National Development Association, 29–30
National Guard, 161, 172, 216, 225
National Industrial Recovery Act (NIRA), 159–60
nationalism, 19, 34, 70, 77
National Labor Relations Act (NLRA) (Wagner Act): and Black Legion constituency, 191; farmworkers excluded from, 59, 102, 104; formation and content of, 58–59, 159–60, 255n259
National Labor Relations Board v. Fansteel, 277n183
National Negro Congress, 147, 148, 150
National Negro Labor Conference, 146
National Recovery Administration (NRA), 159–60
National Steinbeck Center, 110
Nation of Islam, 143
Native Americans, 3, 84, 86, 97, 115, 211
Native Son (Wright), 144
nativism, 167, 188
Navarro, Adela, 7
Nazis, 210, 211
Nebraska, 208
Nee, Bret de Bary, 8
Nee, Victor G., 8
Needlework Club, 197
Nellie Ann Dress Company, 153
Nevada, 69, 84
Newark, New Jersey, 162
New Deal: agricultural policies, 86, 104; Black Legion and, 191, 219; cooperative movement and, 34–37; farm labor and 95, 104; First, 56–58; impact on unemployed movement, 52, 59–60; labor relations system, 58–60, 114, 159–63; need for today, 229; Second, 58–60; shoring up

white patriarchy, 189; welfare state, 58–60, 159–63. *See also specific agencies, laws*
New Jersey, 103
New Masses, 144
New Mexico, 68–69
New Morning Star Missionary Baptist Church, 226
New Orleans, 61, 81, 116
New Republic, 43, 210
New York (city): Black Legion in, 214; Communists in, 38; domestic workers organizing in, 163; Effinger potentially in, 205; milk stations in, 130; mutual aid, 61; rent parties in, 8; rent strikes, 46–48; sit-down strikes, 153; unemployed march, 39–40; Workmen's Circle in, 13; Young Negroes Cooperative League, 19–21
New York (state), 144
New York Amsterdam News, 133
New York Times, 39–40, 64, 186, 210, 226, 284n105
Night Riders, 173
NKVD, 217
Nogales, Arizona, 74
North Carolina, 208, 210
the Northeast, 38, 142, 152
Norwegians, 1
NRA strikes, 160–61, 192
Nuevo Laredo, Tamaulipas, Mexico, 79
numbers runners, 173n128
nurses, registered, 122–23, 125–31, 136
nurses, wet. *See* wet nurses

Oakland, California, 23–27, 31, 36, 61
Oakland County (Michigan), 204
Odd Fellows, 16, 176, 197
Odell, Elijah, 178
Odell, Okey, 178–79, 219
Official Detective Stories, 207
Ohio: Black Legion in, 166–95, 204–9: CIO in, 150; KKK in,

182; Musteites in, 50; state legislature, 174; State of, 204, 174; Young Negroes Cooperative League in, 20
Ohio State Highway Department, 170, 173, 198
Ohio State Legislature, 174, 189, 213
Ohio State Relief Commission, 190 213
Ohio State University, Lima, 206, 287n151
"Okie Law," 87
"Okies," 67, 85, 90–91, 93, 111
Oklahoma, 67, 84–86, 87, 89, 96, 111
Old Time Methodist Church, 197
Olivet Baptist Church, 142
Olympia, Washington, 51
O'Neil, John, 45
onion workers, 178
Order of Calanthe, 17
Order of United American Mechanics, 172–73, 180
Oregon, 13, 103, 208–9
Oregon Shakespeare Festival, 111
Orleck, Annelise, 250n191
Orozco, Julián, 79
Ortíz, Apolonio, 79
Osborne, C. L. 25–26

Pacific Northwest, 69
packinghouse workers, 140, 150. *See also* United Cannery, Agricultural, Packinghouse, and Allied Workers of America (UCAPAWA)
Packinghouse Workers Organizing Committee, 150
Painter, Nell, 42, 47
Palo Alto, California, 24
Panunzio, Constantine, 31, 37
A Paradise Built in Hell (Solnit), 61
Paredes, Américo, 103
Parsons, Lucy, 149
Pasadena, California, 70
Pate, Billie H., 88, 89, 91–92
patriarchy, 36, 229

Patriotic League of America, 212
patriotism, 184, 187, 280n29
Peacock Inn, 174, 184
Pearle, Marian, 197
Pearson, Drew, 220–23, 293–94n273
pecan shellers, 84, 161
Penhorwood, E. J., 171, 181, 183–85, 212, 216
Pennsylvania, 20
pensions, 58, 60. *See also* Social Security Act
People's Grab-n-Go, 61
Philadelphia, 19–20
Philadelphia Tribune, 133
philanthropists, 123, 196
Philippines, 77, 103, 173
Phillips, H. T., 213
Pittsburgh, 12, 19
Pittsburgh Courier, 19, 148
Piven, Frances Fox, 45, 53–54, 55
Pleasant Hour Pinochle Club, 197
Plotzke, Gertrude, 124–31, 138, 158, 271n49
Poles and Polish Americans, 48, 122, 200
police: Black Legion members, 166, 180, 194–95, 204–6, 221, 292n239; brutality of, 45–48; demands to defund, 61; and Effinger extradition, 204–6; and eviction protests, 32, 43–44; failure to investigate or arrest members of Black Legion, 194, 195, 205; in immigrant raids, 74; investigators of Black Legion, 166, 201, 203; Los Angeles chief of, and cooperatives, 33; Los Angeles police opposing "transients," 225; Mexican consulate protests against repression by, 83; racism of, 45, 46, 48; and relief protests, 45, 48; repression of African Americans, 225–26; repression of farmworkers, 77; repression of Mexicans, 77; and repression of repatriados, 76; in Seattle's

Hooverville, 1, 3–4; and strikes, 148, 149, 152, 157, 178; sympathetic to protesters, 44, 55; and unemployed movement, 39–40, 45, 46, 48, 51–52
Pomona, California, 31
Poole, Charles, 166, 201–4, 214, 219
Poor Peoples' Movements (Piven and Cloward), 53
Porter, John, 33
porters, 145–46, 148, 156
Portland, Oregon, 208–9
postal workers, 22
Pozzetta, George, 13
Prather, California, 24
Price, Juanita Everly: in Bakersfield, 88; family farm in "Indian Territory," 97; on father's work with WPA, 90; on FSA labor camps, 104; on *Grapes of Wrath*, 102; Great Depression and her family's migration to California, 92–93, 97; in Oklahoma, 85–86
prostitutes, 140–41, 173–74n128
Protestants: African American churches, 10, 142; antisemitism, anti-Catholicism, racism, and, 211; as beneficiaries of New Deal, 219; Black Legion and, 165, 188–89, 191–92, 195, 200; charity, 10; vs. "foreigners," 171; KKK and, 169; A. J. Muste, 49; opposition to Irish and African Americans, 200; support for repatriados, 102. *See also* churches; Methodists
Public Law 45, 109
Puerto Ricans, 12, 18, 41, 76, 211
Puig, Baldomeron, 66
Pullman Sleeping Car Company, 145
pumps, breast milk, 125, 271n49

Quebec, 13

R., Mrs., 7
racial law, 211

racism: AFL and 150; in Allen County, 221; "Asiatic Standard of Living," 100, 252n227; Black Legion and African Americans, 166, 168–69, 171–72, 181–83, 203, 212; Communist Party commitment to fighting, 148; and enshrinement of white "Dust Bowl" migrant, 84; toward Filipinos, 252n229; institutionalized, 95, 191, 197, 211; toward Mexicans and Mexican Americans, 72–73, 133–34; and Silver Shirts, 210; among Southwestern migrants, 91–93; Steinbeck, 99–101; toward wet nurses, 130, 133–34. *See also* discrimination; Ku Klux Klan (KKK); segregation; white supremacy
railroad workers, 259n32
Ramírez, Sara Estela, 12
Ramseyer, C. William, 183, 285n126
Randolph, A. Philip, 15, 145
Ransby, Barbara, 19
Reagan, Ronald, 224
Realitos, Texas, 79
reciprocity, 18, 22, 24
Reconstruction Finance Corporation, 52
Red Circle of the Black Legion, 207
Reddix, Jacob L., 21–22, 23, 30, 32, 35
Redmon, Miss, 154
"red riots," 40
Red Squad, 33
Reese, Charles, 174
Reichert, Julia, 43
Reinecke, Herold, 215
relief: African Americans and, 54, 90, 104, 189 190; Black Legion control of, 189–90; California, 90; cities and, 53, 190; Communists and, 32, 39–44; cooperative movement vs., 26, 35–37; farmworkers and, 104; federal, 36, 53, 56–67; Herbert

Hoover and, 53; impact of New Deal government relief on mutual benefit societies, 18; Mexicans and Mexican Americans and, 58, 72, 75–76, 80–81, 90, 259n58; in Monterrey, Mexico, 105; mother's pensions, 54; mutual benefit society payments of, 14; New Deal programs, 36, 52, 56; Republican opposition to, 33; Roosevelt and, 56–57; Seattle's Hooverville system of, 1; Socialists and, 49–51; state- and city-level, 72; states and, 72, 90; stigma of, 53–54; white Southwestern migrants and, 72, 90, 104; women and, 59–60; work relief, 57. *See also* Federal Emergency Relief Administration (FERA); Works Progress Administration (WPA)

relief officials: Black Legion members as, 190–91, 213; concessions by, 45; Mexicans and Mexican American and, 52, 66–67, 75–76, 81, 83; Ohio officials' knowledge of Black Legion, 190–91, 213; and protests, 44–45; repatriados and, 66–67, 75–76, 81; in Seattle's Hooverville, 3–4; shaming by, 53

relief protests, 5, 36, 38–39, 41, 44–45, 47–49, 250n191

Rendón, Fidencio, 79

rent parties, 8–9

repatriados, 65–68, 80–84, 105–10, 266n215

repatriation, 65–68, 75–76, 60–84, 104–5, 109–10, 261n89

reproductive labor, 114

Republicans: African Americans and, 198–99, 223; Black Legion and, 193, 216, 219, 285n126; Effinger and, 171, 175; Robert F. Jones, 167, 193–94, 205–6, 220–23, 293–94n173; in Jones hearing, 220, 223 and KKK in Lima, 284n101, 285n126; Lima,

183, 199; and Los Angeles cooperative movement, 33–34; and New Deal labor system, 160; senators in Jones hearings, 221–23

Reuters, 111

"The Revenge of Hannah Kemhoff" (Walker), 54

Rhodehamel, Carl, 23–24

Richmond, Virginia, 17

Ricks, Christine, 225

Rivera L., Jesus, 266n215

Rochdale Pioneers, 23

Rochdale Principles, 23

Rochester, New York, 15

Rodríguez, Raymond, 77, 80, 81, 107, 110

Roediger, David, 188

Rojas, Jose, Jr., 78, 80

Rolph, James, 34

Roman Empire, 115

Roosevelt, Franklin D.: and Black Legion constituency, 219; elections of, 34, 56, 210; New Deal and, 3, 5, 35, 56, 159–60; and repatriation, 104; Southern Democrats and, 160, 216; support for labor movement, 219

Roosevelt administration, 18, 52

Roosevelt High School, 21

Roth, George Knox, 25–28

Roy, Donald. 2–3

Royal Oak, Michigan, 202

Russell Giffin Ranch, 88

Russian Revolution, 40

Russians, 161, 171, 200

Ryan, Neva, 147

Rydlewski, Norma, 96

Rye, Eleanor, 158

Sacramento Valley, 69

Sadlowski, George, 216

Saldaña, Alberto, 79

Salinas, California (city), 77, 111

"Salinas" (song), 111

Salinas Valley, 99

Saltillo, Coahuila, Mexico, 103

San Agustín Catholic Church, 78

San Antonio, Texas: anti-immigrant raids, 75; bricklayers' complaint about Mexicans in, 74; impact of Great Depression on, 71; Mexican community, 69; Mexican consul, 78, 110; pecan shellers' strike, 84; relief, 72, 259n58; repatriados and, 65–66, 82; Unemployed Councils in, 38; unemployment in, 7
San Antonio Express, 66
Sánchez, George, 104–105
Sánchez de Garza Lozano, Virginia, 78
Sanders, Floyd, 212, 219
San Diego, 65, 74, 81, 162
San Fernando, California, 75
San Fernando Valley, California, 28, 88
San Francisco, 7–8, 61, 62, 74, 161, 192
San Francisco Bay Area, 24, 25, 31
San Francisco News, 98, 99, 264n174
San Joaquin Valley, 76–77, 91, 93, 99
San Jose, California, 24, 94
San Luis Obispo, California, 216
Santa Barbara, California, 191, 96
Santa Clara County, California, 76
Sarah Morris Hospital, 121–22, 124, 125, 271n49
Scandinavians, 51
Schafer, Mrs., 185
Scheid, George, Jr., 176–77, 182–83, 186, 187–88, 281n34
Scheid, George, Sr., 170, 176, 178, 184, 188, 218
Scheid, George, Sr., Mrs., 185
Schenectady, New York, 49
Schoonover, Thomas R., 196–97, 212
Schoonover Pool, 196, 225
Schuyler, George S., 19–21, 148
Schwarzenegger, Arnold, 110
Scioto Marsh, 178
Scottsboro, Alabama, 41
"Scottsboro Boys," 41, 148
Seattle, 1–4, 29, 31, 50–52, 239n2

Second Baptist Church, 197
Secretary of Labor, US, 74
Securities and Exchange Commission (SEC), 56
segregation, 8, 9, 16, 137–38, 196–97
self-government, 3, 5, 36
self-help, 5, 22, 31, 32, 35
Senate, US, 55, 58, 193–94, 216, 217, 220–23
service workers, 61, 160–63
sexuality, 2, 9, 139
sex workers, 61
Shaare Zedek Temple, 201
The Shadow (radio show), 207
Shapiro, Judah, 14
sharecroppers, 41, 69, 85, 86, 92
Share the Wealth Movement, 210
Shawnee Country Club, 193, 225
Shepard, William, 167–69, 182, 183, 209
sheriff, Allen County, Ohio, 171, 175, 181, 195, 205, 209, 281n33, 289n191
sheriffs, 74, 87, 206, 221
Shields, Hattye, 87, 88–89
Sidney, Ohio, 173
Sigma Theater, 174, 281n434
Silver Shirts (Silver Legion of America), 210
Simon J. Lubin Society, 99, 264n175
Sinclair, Upton, 36
Sisters of the Mysterious Ten, 17, 197
sit-down strikes, 113–14, 152–54, 277n183. *See also* wet nurses: strike by
"Six Shooter Bill," 74
skilled trades, 150
slavery, 112–19, 268n14
Sloan, General, 173
Slovaks, 18
small businesses/businesspeople, 6, 32, 69, 79, 105, 197
Smith, Bessie, 9
Smith, Gerald L. K., 220
Smith, Lucy, 143
Smith, Sharetta, 227

Smith, William H., 174–75, 195, 213–14, 216, 218, 229–30
Smith, Willie (The Lion), 9
Sobolewski, Josephine, 122–31
socialism, 11–15, 18, 23, 29
Socialist Party, 14, 49
Socialists, 3, 19, 192, 193, 252n227
Social Security Act, 58–60, 104, 159–60, 191
social workers, 44–45, 54
Sociedad de Damas Profesionalistas en Obstetricia, 79
Sociedad Mexicana Miguel Hidalgo, 70
Sociedad Mutual Protectora Benito Juárez, 70
società di mutuo soccorso, 11
Solis, Octavio, 11
Solnit, Rebecca, 61
Sopkins, Ben, and Sons, 149, 154, 157
South: African American migration from, 8, 137–38, 225; Agricultural Adjustment Act impact on, 86; domestic servants in, 141; KKK in, 168, 216; Unemployed Councils in, 38; wet nursing in, 119
South Carolina, 208
Southeast, 97
South Parkway Branch, YWCA, 146–47
Southside Workers' Alliance, Ladies Auxiliary of, 207
Southwest, 11, 70–71, 75, 78, 85–86
Southwestern migrants, 34, 84–105
Soviet Union, 40, 148, 149, 217, 275n152
Spain, 11, 12
Spanish-American War, 170, 173
Spear, Jane, 47
Springfield, Massachusetts, 10
Standard Oil, 179
State Relief Administration, California, 90
Statue of Liberty, 177
Stanley, William, 214
Star (Marion, Ohio), 179

State Indicator (Troy, Ohio), 193
steel workers, 22, 150, 161, 277n180, 177n183
Steel Workers Organizing Committee (SWOC), 150, 161
Steinbeck, John, 67, 98–102, 104, 111, 264n174, 264n175
Stevens, Henry, 167
St. Gerard Catholic Church, 199
St. John's Catholic Church, 199
St. Louis, 65
St. Luke Penny Savings Bank, 17
St. Paul's African Methodist Episcopal Church, 197, 198
strikes: absence of, in Lima, 152; auto workers', 113–14, 152; by California farmworkers, 76–77, 88, 93; Chicago African American women's, 148–49; Communists and, 102; mutualistas and, 112; NRA, 161; by San Antonio pecan shellers, 84; sit-down, 113–14, 152–54; Steinbeck and, 99
St. Rita's Hospital, 197
St. Rose Catholic Church, 199
Sugar, Maurice, 204
Sullivan, Rachel, 116
Supreme Court, US, 87, 277n183
Survey (journal), 82
Survey Graphic (journal), 35
Swanson, Kara, 269n34
SWAT teams, 225–26
Swedes and Swedish Americans, 1, 18, 122
Swift, 123
synagogues, 201

Tamaulipas, Mexico, 81
Tamayo, Rachel, 80, 81, 107, 108
Tampa, Florida, 12
Tapscott, Henry, 165, 173, 177, 193, 221
Tarín Market, 79
Taylor, Paul Schuster, 231, 34–35, 95
Taylor, Ward, 194, 205–6, 289n191, 292n39

teachers, 53, 13, 32, 53, 140
tenant farmers, 65, 86
Tenayuca, Emma, 38, 84
Tennessee, 97
Terkel, Studs, 6, 38, 44, 45, 48
Texas: Black Legion in, 208; cotton economy, 71; cotton workers, 69; FSA farm labor camps in, 103; Karnes County farmworkers, 65; Mexicans in 70; migrants to California from, 67; migrants from Mexico to, 69; relief payments, 72, repatriados from, 65–66, 80; Southwestern migrants from, 84; support for repatriados in, 65–66, 77–79; UCAPAWA in 161; US conquest of, 68–69; Workmen's Circle in, 13
Their Blood Is Strong (Steinbeck), 99, 101, 264n175
Theroit, Alicia Z. Vda de, 79
Thompson, Dinnie, 17
Thompson, Dorothy, 227
Thompson, Florence Owens, 96–97
Thomsen, Eric, 98
Thurman, Wallace, 9
Tiffin, Ohio, 184
Timberlake, J. C., 189, 184n101, 285n126
tobacco workers, 12
To 'Joy My Freedom (Hunter), 141
Toledo, Ohio, 134, 167, 209, 211–12, 218
Toledo Blade, 207, 211, 218
Toledo City Council, 21
Tortilla Flat (Steinbeck), 99
Trail of Tears, 97
Tresca, Carlo, 13
True Detective Mysteries, 27
Trump, Donald, 224, 226, 247n148
Truth, Sojourner, 146
tuberculosis, 118–19
Tujunga, California, 31
Tulare, California, 67
Turlock, California, 24
Twin Oaks Roadhouse, 174, 213
Tydings-McDuffie Act, 77

Underground Railroad, 63
unemployed: concept of, 52; cultures of assistance among, 5–10; gender and, 52; mutual benefit society support for, 14; Oakland encampment of, 14; and relief in Lima, 190–91; Seattle's Hooverville encampment of, 4–5; self-blame among, 54; work relief and, 57. *See also* unemployed movement; unemployment
Unemployed Citizen, 252n227
Unemployed Citizens League, 29, 50–52
Unemployed Cooperative Relief Association, 31, 32, 33–34, 36
Unemployed Councils, 38, 41–49, 51, 52
Unemployed Exchange Association (UXA), 23–28
Unemployed League, 190–91
unemployed movement, 5, 37–52, 54–55, 190–91
unemployment, 1, 6–7, 21, 2, 71, 85, 188; insurance, 51–52, 159, 191
unions, 6, 61–62, 74, 84, 99. *See also* American Federation of Labor (AFL); Congress of Industrial Organizations (CIO); labor movement; *individual unions*
United Auto Workers (UAW), 114, 150, 152, 161
United Brotherhood of Friendship, 17
United Cannery, Agricultural, Packinghouse, and Allied Workers of America (UCAPAWA), 161
United Farm Workers (UFW), 92, 109
United Mine Workers (UMW), 145, 150, 160
United Order of Tents, 63
United Press International, 133, 134
United States, conquest of Mexico, 68–69

Universal Negro Improvement
Association, 143
University of California, 23
Urban League, 20, 143, 146, 157
US Army, 56; Reserves, 216; tank
plant, Lima, 224
U.S. Camera (journal), 96
US Census, 287n159
US Consul, Saltillo, Mexico, 105
US Steel, 161, 163
Utah, 29–30, 69, 84

Valdés, Dennis Nodín, 75, 83
Vandivert, William, 134–35
The Vanguard, 252n227
Veracruz, Mexico, 81
Vesey, Denmark, 146
veterans, 5, 30–31, 55–56
vigilantes, 168, 178, 208–9, 211–12,
219, 281n33
Villa, Pancho, 69
village associations, 8, 9, 11, 12
Virginia, 208
Visel, Charles P., 74–75
voluntary associations. *See* fraternal
associations; mutual benefit
associations

wages of whiteness, 188
Wagner Act. *See* National Labor
Relations Act (NLRA)
waiters and waitresses, 8, 27, 197
Walker, Alice, 54
Walker, Madam C. J., 143
Walker, Maggie Lena, 17
Waller, Fats, 9
Warner Brothers, 208
Washington, DC: African American
cooperatives in, 19; Black Le-
gion extended to, 211; Bonus
Army, 53–54; domestic workers'
unions in, 162; January 6 in-
surrection, 224; Jones hearing
in, 221; protests and 5; repatri-
ations from, 81; unemployed
march in, 39
Washington Park, 46–47, 143, 147,
149, 154

Washington Post, 39, 218
Washington (state), 103
Watson, Carl, 213
Watsonville, California, 111
Wayne, Michigan, 75
Wayne County (Michigan) prosecu-
tor, 210
*Wayward Lives, Beautiful Experi-
ments*, 141–42
"We Are All Leaders" (Lynd, ed.),
155
Webb, Glenn E., 189, 193, 221, 223,
293–94n273
Weber, Devra, 93
Weis, W. C., 178
welfare. *See* relief
welfare state, 58–60
Welles, Orson, 207
Wells, Ida B. 143
Welsh Americans, 145
West, 6, 70, 78, 89, 168
West, Emily, 116, 117
Westbrook, Lawrence, 213
West Coast, 161
Westinghouse, 221
Westminster, California, 31
West Virginia, 170, 208
wet nurses: African American,
115–18, 124, 129–37; ba-
bies and children of, 119–20,
127, 129, 131, 133, 136–37;
enslaved, 116–18, 168n14,
268n18; families and residences
of, 136–37; inspections and surveillance of, 120–22, 136–37;
Irish, 118; labor movement and,
162; Native American, 115;
and New Deal labor system,
162; resistance by, 118–20,
131, 268n14; strike by 113–15,
128, 131–36, 154–59, 163–64;
strikers and Joe Louis, 144-45;
wet nursing, 113–31; white 115,
124; working conditions, 119,
125–31
Wheaton, Thelma (McWhorter),
146–47, 149, 154, 275n152
White, Graham, 141

White, Isaac "Peg Leg," 202
White, Shane, 141
White Angel (film), 174
white gaze, 136
White House, 55, 56
white men: appeal of Black Legion to, 150–52, 187–91, 202–3; as beneficiaries of New Deal, 58–60; in Black Legion, 165–95, 201–4; as craft workers, 188; employment and unemployment of, in Lima, 180, 187–88; as enslavers, 116–17; as ministers, 171; mutual benefit societies of, 15–17; racial exclusion by fraternal societies of, 197; racism of, in Black Legion, 202–3; refusal to join Black Legion, 218–19; victims of Black Legion, 201–3; working-class, and factory jobs, 224; WWII employment of, 108
whites: attacks on African American men in Lima, 185–87; beneficiaries of whites-only FSA farm labor camps, 104; and California border officials, 88; employment in Lima, 180, 226–27; exclusions and segregation by, in Lima, 196–97; farmers, 84–85; farmworkers, 67, 76–77; housing discrimination by, in Lima, 181–82; and Italians in Lima, 199–200; and Irish in Lima, 200; knowledge of repatriation, 102; Lange and, 95–97; ministers and repatriations, 81–82, 102; and normalcy of Black Legion and KKK, 183; opponents of Black Legion, 203; opposition to repatriation, 102; as percentage of Lima population, 180; relief workers and repatriations, 81–82; Southern white agricultural interests, 160; Southern white racists and New Deal, 190; Southwestern migrants, 67, 84–93; Southwestern migrants'

racism, 91–93; Southwestern migrants' reaction to *Grapes of Wrath*, 101–2; Steinbeck and superiority of whites, 99–101, 265n181; white patriarchal family and New Deal, 189; white Southwestern migrants' race privileges, 89–90
white supremacy, 167, 187, 189, 199–100, 207, 210
white women: as alleged victims of African American men, 185–87; in Black Legion, 166–67; and cooperatives, 20, 153–54; employers of wet nurses, 118–20; as enslavers, 116–17; in KKK, 185–86; and mothers' pensions, 54; and New Deal, 54, 58–60; philanthropists, 123; racial bumping by, 6–7; recipients of African American women's breast milk, 123–25; as registered nurses, 122, 125–27, 156–57; in sit-down strikes, 152; as wet nurses, 115, 118–20, 124, 129
Whitman, James Q., 211
widows, 60, 160
Wild, Mark 45
Williamson, James, 196–97, 225, 286n142
Williamson, Katheryn, 147, 151
Williamson, Salena, 197
Williamson, Summie, 197
Wilson, Edmund, 42–43
Wilson, Tarika, 225–26
Wilson and Bennett (plant), 148
Winn, Marcia, 133–34
Wisconsin, 208
Wizards, Inc., 152
Wolf, Jacqueline H., 118, 124–27, 129
womanist consciousness, 17
women: and Communist Party, 42, 207; discrimination against, in labor movement, 161–62; in mutual benefit associations, 11–17; and New Deal labor system, 160,

162–63; and New Deal welfare state, 54, 58–60; in Seattle's Hooverville, 3–4; in sit-down strikes, 152–53; and unemployment, 6. *See also* African American women; white women
Women and Children's Hospital (Mary Thompson Hospital for Women and Children), 124, 128
Women's Club Branch, Workmen's Circle, 13
Women's Ku Klux Klan, 186–86
Women's Trade Union League, 162
Wood, Marcus, 116
Woolworth's, 153, 157
Workers' Circle. *See* Workmen's Circle
Workmen's Circle, 13–18; Social Service Department, 15
work relief, 57, 188–89. *See also* Federal Emergency Relief Administration (FERA); Works Progress Administration (WPA)
Works Progress Administration (WPA): African Americans and, 57–58, 90; ban on employment of immigrants, 74; and Black Legion, 166, 213; Communist union at, 52; cooperatives

and, 36, 90; discrimination by, 57–58, 213; employment and work relief programs, 57; Federal Writers' Project Guide to Lima, 179–80; formation of 57–58; Southwestern migrants and, 90; women and, 58. *See also* Federal Emergency Relief Administration (FERA)
World War I, 17
World War II, 108, 163, 224–25
Wright, Richard, 144
Wyoming, 208

Yans-McLaughlin, Virginia, 11
Ybor City, Florida, 12
Yiddish, 13, 15, 287n259
Young Men's Christian Association (YMCA), 21–22, 196
Young Negroes' Cooperative League, 4, 19–21, 23, 26
Young Women's Christian Association (YWCA), 146–47, 149, 154

Zacatecas, Mexico, 69, 78
Zamora, Emilio, 11–12, 70
Zanuck, Darryl, 98
Zapatistas, 62
Zimmerman, William, 189